The Rural–Urban Divide

*Economic Disparities and Interactions
in China*

Studies on Contemporary China

The Contemporary China Institute at the School of Oriental and African Studies (University of London) has, since its establishment in 1968, been an international centre for research and publications on twentieth-century China. *Studies on Contemporary China*, which is edited at the Institute, seeks to maintain and extend that tradition by making available the best work of scholars and China specialists throughout the world. It embraces a wide variety of subjects relating to Nationalist and Communist China, including social, political, and economic change, intellectual and cultural developments, foreign relations, and national security.

Series Editor

Dr Frank Dikötter, Director of the Contemporary China Institute

Editorial Advisory Board

The Rural–Urban Divide
Economic Disparities and Interactions in China

JOHN KNIGHT
and
LINA SONG

OXFORD
UNIVERSITY PRESS

OXFORD
UNIVERSITY PRESS

Great Clarendon Street, Oxford OX2 6DP

Oxford University Press is a department of the University of Oxford.
It furthers the University's objective of excellence in research, scholarship,
and education by publishing worldwide in
Oxford New York

Athens Auckland Bangkok Bogotá Buenos Aires Calcutta
Cape Town Chennai Dar es Salaam Delhi Florence Hong Kong Istanbul
Karachi Kuala Lumpur Madrid Melbourne Mexico City Mumbai
Nairobi Paris São Paulo Singapore Taipei Tokyo Toronto Warsaw
with associated companies in Berlin Ibadan

Oxford is a registered trade mark of Oxford University Press
in the UK and in certain other countries

Published in the United States
by Oxford University Press Inc., New York

British Library Cataloguing in Publication Data
Data available

Library of Congress Cataloging in Publication Data
Data available
ISBN 0-19-829330-5

1 3 5 7 9 10 8 6 4 2

Typeset by Best-set Typesetter Ltd., Hong Kong
Printed in Great Britain
on acid-free paper by
Biddles Ltd,
Guildford & Kings Lynn

Preface

Our interest in rural–urban disparities and interactions in China was stimulated by our participation in an earlier research project. This involved the microeconomic analysis of a detailed national household survey, the main results of which were published in 1993 as *The Distribution of Income in China*, edited by Keith Griffin and Zhao Renwei. One of the most remarkable results to emerge from the survey was the extremely high ratio of urban to rural household income per capita. Our recognition that the rural–urban divide therefore deserved study provided the motivation for this book.

Our aim in the book is to describe the rural–urban divide in income and, more generally, in economic welfare, and to explain it. How large is the rural–urban divide? How did it come about? How is it maintained, for instance in the face of equilibrating market forces? What are the implications, both for efficiency and for equity in the Chinese economy?

In the 1950s, when our story begins, development economists, lacking hard information, often wrote on grand issues. Arthur Lewis's *A Theory of Economic Growth*, which appeared in 1955, and Gunnar Myrdal's *The Poverty of Nations*, published in 1968, were outstanding examples. In the 1990s, when our story ends, the conventional approach to development economics is quite different, as a perusal of a recent volume of (say) the *Journal of Development Economics* would illustrate. The normal approach today is to analyse narrow issues rigorously and in depth. Development economists have mostly descended from the high sierra, with its fine views, and now inhabit the jungles and plains, clearing and hoeing a little patch at a time.

When we became aware of the huge rural–urban disparities that exist in China, we looked for a thorough, systemic and rigorous treatment of the subject, but without success. It is a grand issue, and that fact may have deterred others. We decided to accept the challenge. Our approach is generally in line with the detailed, empirical methodology that is conventional today. We decided to write a series of chapters, each chapter on some particular aspect of rural–urban relationships, and sufficiently self-contained to be read on its own. However, the rural–urban divide in China is a systemic phenomenon, requiring the various topics to be integrated so as to bring out the system that they have in common. We have attempted to do this throughout, but particularly in the concluding chapter. We hope, therefore, that the whole adds up to more than the sum of its parts.

Representing 25 per cent of the population of the developing world in 1995, China is of course of great interest in itself. The book could be written solely with China in mind. However, in rural–urban relationships, as in many other respects, China offers fascinating comparisons with other developing countries and other transition countries. Although few explicit comparisons are made with other countries, we approach the Chinese case within a broad theoretical framework of rural–urban relationships. We hope that specialists in the economy of China will find much that is new to them, but we are primarily writing for a broader readership of development economists.

The research was made possible by the financial support of the Leverhulme Trust, which provided a substantial research grant (reference number F. 519L) for this project, and of the Economic and Social Research Council (reference number R000234332), which supported our research on rural–urban migration and, in particular, funded the surveys on which chapter 9 is based. We are grateful to these bodies for the confidence they showed in us. We also benefited from a 'bridging grant' from the University of Oxford.

Our contacts in China played a crucial role in the research. We are overwhelmingly grateful to Tang Roxin, then mayor of Handan, who invited us to conduct rural and urban household surveys in his prefecture. We owe a great deal to our friend and collaborator, Li Shi, who has contributed much to the success of the project by helping to plan and conduct the surveys and in their analysis during more than one visit to Oxford. The Institute of Economics of the Chinese Academy of Social Sciences in Beijing provided support and collaboration, in particular enabling Li Shi to take part in the project. We thank the Institute of Rural Development of the Chinese Academy of Social Sciences for its cooperation, and to Liu Jianjing of that Institute for collaborating in the analysis of rural–urban migration during his visit to Oxford. Finally, we thank the Research Centre for Rural Economy of the Ministry of Agriculture, and in particular its then deputy director-general, Du Ying, for inviting us to three international conferences on related subjects (rural development, rural economic reform, and flows of rural labour), which enabled us to present our ideas and findings to assembled experts and receive feedback.

We are grateful to all the following for helpful discussions or comments in the course of the research: Robert Cassen, Keith Griffin, Stephen Howes, Athar Hussain, Azizur Khan, Stephen Nickell, Martin Ravallion, Carl Riskin, Frances Stewart, Gordon White and Zhao Renwei. At the Institute of Economics and Statistics, which provided wonderful support, we wish to thank Gillian Coates, who administered our grants, Giuseppe Mazzarino, for his computing advice, and Ann Gibson and Caroline Wise, for all their secretarial work.

Contents

List of Figures

List of Tables

PART I

INTRODUCTION

1

Setting the Stage

This book is about the economic relationships between rural and urban China. It derives its motivation from the fact that urban-dwellers have a considerable welfare advantage over rural-dwellers. Accordingly, we examine how the two sectors compare in various dimensions of economic welfare, and we explore the economic policies and sectoral interactions which bring about the urban advantage.

In Section 1.1 of this introductory chapter we discuss the treatment of rural–urban relationships in the literature on economic development. This will help us to assess how far the Chinese experience represents a special case and how far it reflects general tendencies in developing economies. In Section 1.2 we examine the institutional, administrative, and political arrangements which compartmentalize China into rural and urban areas. This will help to explain why China is so sharply divided both socially and economically: dual society, dual economy. Section 1.3 sets out some basic statistics on the rural and urban sectors and evaluates the various definitions and sources of data—an issue more important and contentious than one might suppose. The scope of the book and our methods of analysis are explained in Section 1.4. Finally, Section 1.5 outlines and explains the plan of the book, which is presented analytically rather than chapter by chapter.

1.1 RURAL–URBAN RELATIONSHIPS IN ECONOMIC DEVELOPMENT

The economic relationships between the urban and rural areas of a less developed economy encompass the terms of trade between rural and urban products, the intersectoral transfer of labour, the relative wages of labour in the two sectors, the intersectoral transfer of saving, the relative sectoral returns to investment, the relative sectoral contributions to tax revenue and benefits from public expenditure, and the extent to which government policies favour one sector over the other. There are at least three theoretical frameworks for the analysis of these relationships: the Lewis model of economic growth with surplus rural labour, the 'coercive', or 'price-scissors', model of economic growth financed by extracting a rural surplus, and the notion that economic policy is subject to 'urban bias'. All three have potential relevance to China: we explain each in turn.

According to the Lewis model, the industrial sector expands by drawing on abundant rural labour in perfectly elastic supply and reinvesting industrial profits. With industrial development in a market economy, the supply curve of labour eventually becomes inelastic owing to a rising marginal product of labour in agriculture and a relative improvement in the price of agricultural goods; in a competitive labour market, the urban wage begins to rise. Thus the model implies an eventual improvement in the rural–urban terms of trade, an intersectoral transfer of labour but not of capital, and intersectoral equality in labour income; it is silent on the other issues.

According to the scissors model, it is possible for government to finance the growth of the industrial sector in a socialist economy by reducing the producer prices of agricultural in relation to industrial goods. By coercing rural people and depressing their real consumption, government can effectively transfer rural saving to finance industrial capital accumulation. This is the model that was followed in the Soviet Union. It implies an initial deterioration in the rural–urban terms of trade (from which its name is derived), an intersectoral transfer of both labour and capital, and government policies with regard to pricing, tax and investment that favour industry over agriculture.

According to the theory of urban bias in economic policies, government systematically favours the urban over the rural sector owing to the political power of urban-dwellers. It is argued that, although they normally form a minority of the population of poor countries, urban-dwellers exercise an influence on government policy which is disproportionate to their numbers. This may be because of urban residence *per se*, the proletariat being politically more aware, more vocal, and better organized than the peasantry; or it may be that certain dominant groups, such as the industrialists, the bureaucrats, or the educated, are mainly urban. The forms of urban bias might include credit, trade, exchange rate, tax and public expenditure policies to favour industry or urban areas. The government is seen to encourage or permit the emergence of a wage differential in favour of urban employment. This relative increase in urban private and public consumption in turn induces rural–urban migration in excess of the absorptive capacity of the urban sector, giving rise to urban unemployment and poverty, unless the migration is controlled to protect urban-dwellers. The model implies excessive intersectoral transfer of labour and capital, and relatively high urban wages.

The Lewis and price-scissors models can be depicted simply in Figure 1.1. The horizontal axis, OO', measures the supply of labour in the economy, assumed to be fixed. The curve MPL_a shows the marginal product of labour in the agricultural (here equated with rural) sector. Industrial (urban) employment is measured leftwards from O'. The Chinese economy is characterized by surplus labour: it is a labour surplus economy *par excellence*. This is reflected in the low marginal product of labour in agricul-

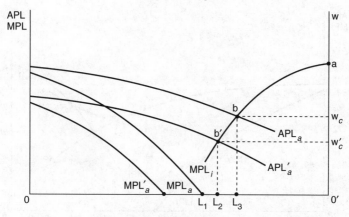

FIG. 1.1 *The Lewis and the price-scissors models*

ture ($MPL_a = 0$ beyond OL_1). In these conditions the rural supply price is dependent on the average product of labour. In a competitive labour market in which the rural supply curve is given by APL_a and the urban demand curve by MPL_i, the competitive wage would be w_c and labour allocation OL_3 in the rural and L_3O' in the urban sector. Profits, shown by the area abw_c, are reinvested, so producing dynamic growth of the industrial sector, a transfer of labour from agriculture to industry, and an eventual increase in the competitive wage, initially held down by the elastic APL_a curve.

The price-scissors model requires only minor modification of the figure. Government intervention to reduce the price of the agricultural product reduces APL_a and MPL_a to APL'_a and MPL$'_a$ respectively. The rural supply price falls, so setting a lower wage, w'_c, in the urban sector. Industrial employment is expanded to L_2O', and the higher industrial profits, $ab'w'_c$, permit faster industrialization.

The urban bias model also requires modification of the basic case (Figure 1.2). Government sets the urban wage higher than the competitive wage, at w_u. In a market economy this would imply urban employment L_5O'. In the framework of probabilistic migration models the 'expected wage'—w_u multiplied by the probability of obtaining it—equals the rural supply price. With the probability equal to the ratio of urban employment to urban labour force, rural–urban migration occurs until this condition is satisfied. Given that the curve xx', passing through the point b, is a rectangular hyperbola, urban open unemployment equal to L_2L_5 is created.

A government pursuing urban bias policies might oppose this outcome. Government can prevent open unemployment by controlling rural–urban migration and by creating surplus jobs, L_3L_5, in the state sector. Thus the labour force is divided into OL_3 (rural employment) and L_3O' (urba

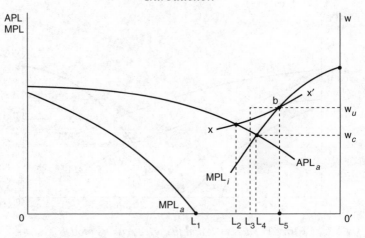

Fig. 1.2 *The urban bias model*

employment). Discontent in the urban sector is reduced by raising the urban wage above the competitive level and by sharing unemployment in disguised form among the urban labour force. Discontent in the rural sector is reduced by sharing out the land equally and so also sharing disguised unemployment among the rural labour force (evidenced by $L_1 L_3$). Urban bias in the form of investment allocation has the dynamic effect of raising MPL_i relative to MPL_a.

These models offer potential frameworks for addressing rural–urban economic relationships in China. Each of them has been the subject of an extensive literature of exposition, criticism, and debate.[1] Rather than present a review at this stage, we prefer to draw on the literature only if and when it becomes relevant to our application of a particular framework to the Chinese economy.

At this stage three general caveats are in order. First, insofar as they rely on market forces, the models should be treated with caution. The Chinese economy has been primarily a centrally planned and controlled economy in which market forces have until recent years been allowed to operate only now and again and in limited respects. Secondly, it is common, in analysing the early stages of economic development, to equate 'rural' and 'agricultural', on the one hand, and 'urban' and 'industrial', on the other. Both the Lewis model and the scissors model make this assumption but the urban bias model is less dependent on it. Again, such a simplification should be examined critically in applying the models to the Chinese economy of recent years. Thirdly, the models are not mutually exclusive: it is probable that each has some relevance to some aspects of rural–urban economic relationships in China at some time during the communist period. A synthesized model 'with Chinese characteristics' is on the cards.

1.2 THE SOURCES OF RURAL–URBAN DIVISION

In this section we explain how the policy of rural–urban division and urban advantage came about. It is shown that the policy followed logically from the situation faced by the new government and from its development priorities, but that the policy was at odds with the ideological objectives of a government brought to power with peasant support and concerned with egalitarianism and social justice. We go on to show how the policy was implemented: how the development of institutions, some for ideological reasons and some for the purpose at hand, gave the Chinese State powers to administer and enforce the policy to a degree that few other countries, if any, could match.

1.2.1 The origins of the policy

When the Chinese Communist Party (CCP) came to power in 1949, it inherited an economy dislocated and damaged by civil war; an agrarian economy, moreover, that was already characterized by land scarcity and labour surplus. The pre-planning years 1949–52 were the period in which new economic policies were formed. Various influences were at work. The CCP was a party that achieved power on the basis of peasant support and that was led mainly by men of peasant origin. It had a strong ideological commitment to egalitarianism and to social justice based on a class analysis. However, these objectives had to be tempered by China's international isolation, the serious economic situation, and the threat of political instability. Rejected by the capitalist world, particularly after involvement in the Korean War, China turned to the USSR as her international ally and model. However, the leadership did so very uneasily and was determined to develop economic self-reliance.

After the civil war the Chinese economy displayed severe shortages of grain and other necessities, high inflation, and urban unemployment. Although grain production improved sharply when peace was restored, the growth of demand kept ahead of supply and generated grain price inflation. Grain became a central concern of the CCP leaders. The hostile international climate and the determination to be self-reliant meant that the traditional solution of grain imports was ruled out. It was decided that the State would have to regulate the supply of and demand for food.

In 1953 a system of state-monopolized purchase and marketing was established to control the food supply. In 1953 and 1954 a rationing system for grain and other necessities was introduced to control the demand by urban-dwellers. The third policy variable was state control over the movement of people. By 1957 a combination of household registration, the formation of the communes, and urban food-rationing had given the State the administrative levers needed to stop migration. This would not only improve the food balance but also ensure that poverty and squalor could be avoided in the cities—in contrast to those countries which were unwilling or unable to control rural–urban migration.

There was a second, equally important, strand to the policy of rural–urban division. This was a belief that land-scarce China could develop rapidly only through industrialization, in particular capital-intensive heavy industrialization in urban centres. Again, international hostility ruled out reliance on foreign capital. Domestic saving would have to be found.

China's economy was then overwhelmingly agrarian: the only potential source of substantial saving was agriculture. The way to transfer saving from agriculture to industry was by means of a price-scissors policy, taking the historical experience of the USSR as a model. The controlled price of food was set low—below what would be the market price—in relation to the price of protected manufactures. In this way urban wages could be kept down in relation to industrial prices, and the resultant high profits would be reinvested in industry. Such a policy was embarked upon with the inception of the first five-year plan in 1952. In allocating investment, the State accorded industry priority over agriculture, and urban areas over rural areas.

Two puzzles stand out in what is otherwise a convincing account of policy formulation. One concerns the degree to which the peasants were expected to bear the burden of industrialization. Bo (1991: 281) provides the most convincing explanation: 'it was necessary and inevitable for China, a backward agricultural economy, to require the peasantry to supply the capital at the start of large-scale industrial construction . . . where could we possibly get capital to industrialize the country if not by asking the peasants to supply it for a certain period?' The sacrifice of peasant interests must nevertheless have been a bitter experience for a party most of whose members were from peasant backgrounds.

The second puzzle concerns the size of the urban–rural income gap that existed even in the mid-1950s. On coming to power, the CCP had to build up urban support. Howe (1973: 55) suggests that political and efficiency wage considerations were important in the period 1949–53: 'rising wages mainly reflected the drive to consolidate political control and recognition of the incentive value of wages rising to stimulate productivity.' The stagnation of real wages thereafter may have reflected growing recognition of the egalitarian concern to cap the urban–rural income differential and of the economic need to accelerate capital accumulation (for instance, Song 1957).

1.2.2 *The enforcement of the policy*

We begin with the institutions of state control. In principle the Chinese State comprises three organs: a political organ (the Communist Party), an

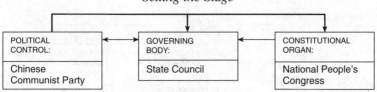

FIG. 1.3 *The structure of the Chinese State*

administrative organ (the State Council), and a constitutional organ (the National People's Congress). Power is shared between the Communist Party and the State Council: the Party provides the ideology and the Council governance. Their relative power has varied over the years but the Party has throughout been the leading force. The Party leadership comprises the Political Bureau (a small core group with ultimate power), the Standing Committee (the second level), and the Central Committee (the third level). However, the Party infiltrates every layer of society. The Congress has been merely a constitutional cloak with little effective power.

The power structure is depicted in Figure 1.3. The arrowed double lines show the political empowerment of the Council and the Congress by the Party. The arrowed single lines show the process of consultation: a two-way feedback in policy-making between the Party and the Council, and suggestions from the Congress to the Council; the Congress lacks access to the political leadership. The ascendancy of the Party was greatest during the Cultural Revolution, when it destroyed the government and ideology dominated everything. During the period of economic reform, however, the power of the Party has weakened and that of the Council and the Congress has strengthened somewhat.

Policy debates between the Communist Party and the State Council take place in secret. Once the State has decided on a policy, it is executed within the structure of control. The structure during the pre-reform period is illustrated in Figure 1.4. It shows the vertical line of command from the policy-makers down to the ordinary people, rural or urban. Both the political and administrative organs are to be found at each layer of control. Almost all managerial staff are members of the Party. Often managerial and ideological considerations have clashed. However, the power structure has guaranteed the Party's leadership: in cases of dispute the Party at all levels has the power to make the final decision.

The dotted line in the figure indicates the rural–urban division of control. Cadres at the county level (having section rank) and commune level (having division rank) are urban residents and are appointed by the State to go and administer the rural areas. Commune (now township) leaders are selected from outside to avoid undue local influence on their governance. Only at brigade (now administrative village) and production team (now natural village) levels are the leadership local residents with rural *hukous*.

Introduction

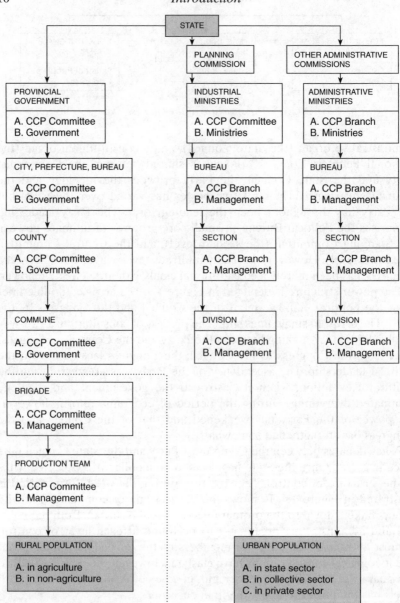

FIG. 1.4 *The structure of control: the power hierarchy and the rural–urban divide*

Note that the Party's power stretches right down to division level (e.g. enterprise, street committee) in the urban areas and to village level in the rural areas. Rural residents, forming the great majority of the Chinese population, have been controlled by the CCP and governed by urban representatives of the State.

Turning to the mechanisms of state control, we examine how the State has controlled the flow of resources—goods, capital, and labour—between the rural and the urban sectors. In the pre-reform period resources could not be transferred directly but only indirectly via the State, according to the state plan and through the state administration.

Consider first the transfer of goods. In 1952 the government set up state purchase stations for grain and other farm products. The channel stretched from ministry level (the State Purchase and Marketing Co-operative) to rural township (commune) level. Its main function was to extract as much of the harvest as possible from the peasants. By the mid-1950s private channels had been taken over and the state purchase stations were the only legal way in which peasants could sell their goods. All prices were set by government: there was no negotiation, no bargaining. When the communes were formed in 1957, the production and sale of each crop by a production team was regulated in accordance with precise criteria, such as the quantity and quality of land. Market forces had become irrelevant.

The other function of the state purchase-supply stations was to sell subsidized inputs to production, such as fertilizer and pesticides, to the peasants. When these were in short supply they would be rationed according to a production team's sales of farm products. Manufactured consumer goods were sold to peasants mainly through local state or collective stores, supplied in turn from the state commerce system. All prices were set by state pricing departments, either strictly or allowing local retailers flexibility within a price range.

Thus goods moved between the urban and rural sectors within the state planning and administrative system, with both quantities and prices being controlled. There was little direct movement of goods between the sectors through the free market, despite the possibilities for mutually beneficial trade. The State generally banned such markets, and the ban was subject to varying degrees of enforcement at different times.

The movement of capital in the pre-reform period was no less state-controlled than the movement of goods. Banking was monopolized by the State and private agents could not borrow from the banks. The allocation of investment was decided by the State through the planning system: banks functioned merely as dependent accounting units of central government. Investment in the rural sector was essentially an intrasector phenomenon. Industry had priority over agriculture: little state investment was directed at the rural sector. The only non-state urban–rural capital flow took the form of money sent by urban households to their rural relatives.

By contrast, the State enforced two forms of rural–urban capital flow. One was through the fiscal system, by means of an agricultural tax. The tax was fixed every five years: on average 15 per cent of the agricultural yield was paid to central government and another 13–15 per cent went to local government. Thus nearly 30 per cent of farm proceeds were paid to the State as taxes. The other flow took place invisibly through the price-scissors policy. The State depressed the terms of trade of the rural sector—reducing the price at which its agents purchased farm products in relation to the price of manufactures produced by state enterprises. Thus the rural sector was required to exchange more farm products for fewer manufactured goods. The manufactures thereby retained by the State were available for investment in the urban sector.

The State was no less efficient in stopping the flow of labour than it was at extracting food and saving from the rural sector. The urban–rural income differential provided a great incentive for peasants to migrate. From 1957 onwards, however, central government acted to prevent all migration that it did not authorize. Job-assignment was carried out by the Ministry of Labour (in charge of 'workers') and the Ministry of Personnel (in charge of 'cadres'). Government planned the labour needs of the growing urban sector and authorized the transfer of peasants only to meet residual needs.

Unauthorized migration was prevented by an array of institutional obstacles. The household registration (*hukou*) system and the commune system, established by 1958, gave the State tight control over the movement of peasants. Rural-dwellers required permission to leave their communes. People without a local urban *hukou* required permission to be in an urban area. They would have to bring their own food or share with urban relatives because the sole source of staple food in the cities after the mid-1950s was through ration coupons issued only to registered residents. Moreover, urban enterprises had no authority to employ labour without permission.

Figure 1.5 shows how intersectoral resource flows were controlled in the pre-reform period. Policies made by the State were implemented by its executive agents. The chain of command is shown by the arrowed heavy line, and the main flows of resources are shown as arrowed light lines. We see that agricultural goods were transferred through the intermediation of the State to the urban sector, and that manufactured goods were transferred in the same way to the rural sector. Rural savings were also gathered by the State's executive agents, to be employed in the urban sector. Direct transfers of resources from one sector to another began to occur on a significant scale only during the period of economic reform, when the State's degree of intermediation and control diminished.

During the commune period the rural sector was expected to be self-reliant. The peasants had to take care of themselves and not be a fiscal burden on the State. The reform period retains a good deal of continuity with the past. Relatively little gross revenue flows down to the rural tiers

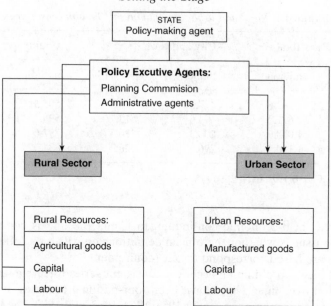

FIG. 1.5 *Control over the flow of resources between the rural and urban sectors*

of government: counties, townships, and villages. Consider their different responsibilities (Wong 1997: 169–74). Counties receive budgetary funds from higher tiers of government which they use mainly for administration and for investment in rural infrastructure and state-owned enterprises. The main expenditure responsibilities of townships relate to social services, law and order, and disaster relief. They receive some funds from the county, and they are active in setting up and running township-owned enterprises for revenue. Villages are not a formal tier of government but they developed a framework of governance during the commune period. The policy stress on self-reliance means that they normally have to raise the residual funds for village social services and infrastructure investment. This provides a rev- enue incentive for investment in village-owned industries.

1.3 RURAL–URBAN DEFINITIONS

We contend that there is in China an institutionally imposed invisible Great Wall which divides rural and urban people and generates a substantial dif- ference in their levels of economic welfare. It is important, therefore, that our statistics on rural and urban areas should correspond as well as possi- ble to that institutional division. In principle this makes our task easier. The usual problem in developing countries is to draw a rural–urban line in what

TABLE 1.1 *Rural and urban population of China in census years*

	Total	City and town		County	
	million	million	%	million	%
1953	582.6	77.3	13.3	505.3	86.7
1964	691.2	94.6	13.7	596.7	86.3
1982	1,003.9	206.3	20.5	797.6	79.5
1990	1,130.5	296.1	26.2	834.4	73.8

Source: PRC, SSB 1993: 68.

is really a socio-economic continuum. In China the line is conceptually clear: the issue is whether the official definitions on which the rural–urban statistics are based correspond to our requirement.

It is difficult to obtain an accurate, consistent series for urban and rural population over time. There have been four national censuses of population during the communist era: in 1953, 1964, 1982, and 1990. The long gap after 1964 spanned the anarchy of the Cultural Revolution and the dissolution of the statistical services during that period. Table 1.1 shows the urban (city and town) and rural (county) populations, in millions and as percentages of the national total, in the census years. Slightly different figures for the census years are to be found in the annual estimates from the same State Statistical Bureau (SSB) source (Table 1.2).

In Table 1.2 'the urban population refers to the population living in areas under the administration of cities and towns. Rural population refers to population of counties but excluding those living in towns of a county' (PRC, SSB 1996: 80). The definition of a town has varied over time. In 1964 a town was defined as consisting of more than 3,000 permanent residents, of whom at least 70 per cent were considered to be 'non-agricultural' (or 2,500 and 85 per cent). In 1984 a town was redefined to include all county seats and areas with at least 2,000 people considered to be non-agricultural (PRC, SSB 1996: 80).

The urban population of China was no more than 62 million (11.2 per cent of the total) in 1950. Urbanization proceeded rapidly during the 1950s, reaching 131 million (19.8 per cent of the total) in 1960. In reaction government introduced rigid controls on movement to the urban areas, being assisted in this policy by the formation of the communes in the late 1950s. For the next twenty years, urban growth was merely in line with natural increase. In 1980 the urban population was 191 million (19.4 per cent of the total). The subsequent acceleration of urban population growth was due partly to an increase in the number of newly designated towns and partly to the loosening of controls over migration after the disbanding of the

TABLE 1.2 *Rural and urban population of China, 1949–95*

	Total	Urban		Rural	
	million	million	%	million	%
1949	541.7	57.7	10.6	484.0	89.4
1950	552.0	61.7	11.2	490.3	88.8
1951	563.0	66.3	11.8	496.7	88.2
1952	574.8	71.6	12.5	503.2	87.5
1953	588.0	78.3	13.3	509.7	86.7
1954	602.7	82.5	13.7	520.2	86.3
1955	614.7	82.9	13.5	531.8	86.5
1956	628.3	91.9	14.6	536.4	85.4
1957	646.5	99.5	15.4	547.0	84.6
1958	659.9	107.2	16.3	552.7	83.8
1959	672.1	123.7	18.4	548.4	81.6
1960	662.1	130.7	19.8	531.3	80.3
1961	658.6	127.1	19.3	531.5	80.7
1962	673.0	116.6	17.3	556.4	82.7
1963	691.7	116.5	16.8	575.3	83.2
1964	705.0	129.5	18.4	575.5	81.6
1965	725.4	130.5	18.0	594.9	82.0
1966	745.4	133.1	17.9	612.3	82.1
1967	763.7	135.5	17.7	628.2	82.3
1968	785.3	138.4	17.6	647.0	82.4
1969	806.7	141.2	17.5	665.5	82.5
1970	829.9	144.2	17.4	685.7	82.6
1971	852.3	147.1	17.3	705.2	82.7
1972	871.8	149.4	17.1	722.4	82.9
1973	892.1	153.5	17.2	738.7	82.8
1974	908.6	156.0	17.2	752.6	82.7
1975	924.2	160.3	17.3	763.9	82.6
1976	937.2	163.4	17.4	773.8	82.6
1977	949.7	166.7	17.6	783.1	82.5
1978	962.6	172.4	17.9	790.1	82.1
1979	975.4	185.0	19.0	790.5	81.0
1980	981.1	191.4	19.4	795.7	80.6
1981	1,000.7	201.7	20.2	799.0	79.8
1982	1,016.5	214.8	21.1	801.7	78.9
1983	1,030.1	222.7	21.6	807.3	78.4
1984	1,043.6	240.2	23.0	803.4	77.0
1985	1,058.5	250.9	23.7	807.6	76.3
1986	1,075.1	263.7	24.5	811.4	75.5
1987	1,093.0	276.7	25.3	816.3	74.7
1988	1,110.3	286.6	25.8	823.7	74.2
1989	1,127.0	295.4	26.2	831.6	73.8
1990	1,143.3	301.9	26.4	841.4	73.6

TABLE 1.2 *Continued*

	Total	Urban		Rural	
	million	million	%	million	%
1991	1,158.2	305.4	26.4	852.8	73.6
1992	1,171.7	332.7	27.6	848.0	72.4
1993	1,185.2	333.5	28.1	851.7	71.9
1994	1,198.5	343.0	28.6	855.5	71.4
1995	1,211.2	351.7	29.0	859.5	71.0

Sources: PRC, SSB 1993: 65; 1996: 69.

communes. In 1995 the urban population stood at 352 million, or 29.0 per cent of the total population.

The same SSB source also provides a larger estimate of rural population in particular years, using a different definition (PRC, SSB 1996: 353). The rural areas are defined according to the 1964 town classification, and thus the rural estimates for subsequent years include people in localities that were by then reclassified as towns. On that basis the 1985 rural population (844 million) is 37 million more, and the 1995 population (917 million) is 58 million more, than on the conventional definition.

Another distinction made is one between the 'agricultural' and 'non-agricultural' populations. The non-agricultural population comprises persons entitled to food grain rations. In 1991 the agricultural population was estimated to be 901 million, the non-agricultural population 241 million, and the total population 1,142 million (PRC, EBCAY 1992: 181). This estimate of the agricultural population is very close to that based on the broad (1964) definition of rural population (905 million in 1991), although the concepts are different. Whereas the latter includes urban residents of formerly rural localities, the former includes urban residents who are not entitled to food rations, for instance because they are allocated farm land.

Using the narrow (1984) definition of rural, the agricultural population exceeded the rural population by 48 million, or by 4.1 per cent of the national population, in 1991. The differences between the 'agricultural' and the narrow, and the broad and the narrow, definitions of rural population represent an intermediate grey area blurring the rural–urban divide. In terms of facilities, these people were better off than rural and worse off than urban people. Some had access to land and some had access to subsidized food and housing. Table 1.2 uses the 1984 definition of rural areas, that is it excludes the residents of newly established towns from the rural population.

Finally, a distinction is made between the population of the 2,371 (rural) counties and the population resident outside the counties. The county population includes people in county towns and therefore yields a rather high estimate. For instance, in 1985 the county population was 829 million whereas the rural population, broadly defined, was 844 million, a difference of 15 million (PRC, SSB 1989; PRC, SSB 1993: 295).

The fact that the various estimates of the rural and urban populations are generally ill-defined and have been revised in succeeding issues of the SSB's *Statistical Yearbook* has given rise to academic debate (see, for instance, Chan and Xu 1985; Chan 1987; Scharping 1987; and Martin 1992). One example will suffice. The *Statistical Yearbooks* of the late 1980s showed urban population rising implausibly, from 191 million (19.4 per cent of the total) in 1980, to 385 million (36.6 per cent) in 1985, and to 575 million (51.7 per cent) in 1989 (PRC, SSB 1990: 89), but in the 1991 and subsequent issues the estimates were revised sharply downwards to the figures in Table 1.2. The explosion had been due to administrative redefinition of rural places as towns and of towns and their surrounding rural areas as cities (89 million people being thus reclassified between 1983 and 1984 alone). These were clearly not sensible estimates of urban population and its growth.

A final point should be noted. Whichever definition of rural and urban areas is used, until 1990 the official statistics counted people in their place of normal residence, defined by their *hukou* registration, and not according to where they happened to be. Thus temporary migrants were recorded in their place of origin. This means that the official statistics were likely to understate the number of people present in the urban areas, particularly during the period of economic reform. The 1990 census of population extended residence beyond *hukou* registration to include persons who were resident in a place and whose registration was unsettled or who had been away from their *hukou* place for over a year. However, this would still understate the number of people present in the urban areas.

1.4 THE SCOPE AND METHODS OF ANALYSIS

In preparing this book we have had to face up to certain challenges inherent in the history of rural–urban relationships over the period of Communist Party rule, and in the documentation of those relationships. Our approach and methods need to be understood in the light of the following considerations.

First, the same issues require analysis under distinctly different economic systems. These can be divided loosely into the phase of the communes and centralized planning and the phase of economic reform, marketization, and privatization. Both are needed. The latter is important for policy-making whereas the former is important for understanding. Institutions established under central planning continued to mould rural–urban relationships under economic reform.

Secondly, the two phases require different methodologies. Under central planning all rural–urban relationships were the result of state institutions, interventions, and policies. Standard economic analysis was largely irrelevant. Statistical information was limited, particularly during the Cultural Revolution. In his book *China's Political Economy*, Riskin (1987) reflects the limitations of data and economic analysis and the importance of institutions and government in understanding the Chinese economy up to the mid-1980s. With the marketization of the economy, the tools of Western economists became increasingly helpful. With economic reform and greater openness, accurate statistical information became more plentiful and more available. We have at our disposal a number of recent datasets that are of high quality and amenable to econometric analysis. We intend to use conventional economic analysis and econometric methods to answer our questions. However, we recognize the need also to analyse state institutions and government interventions in order to understand. This is true particularly of the pre-reform period but also of the reform period right up to the present.

Thirdly, the most important data source for the study of rural–urban disparities is available for only one year, 1988. This was the first nationally representative household survey, covering both rural and urban China, to be available at the disaggregated (household and individual) level. It formed the basis of an international research project involving economists from the Institute of Economics, Chinese Academy of Social Sciences (CASS), and foreign scholars, including the authors. We are confident that the data are of extremely high quality. The main results of the research were published in *The Distribution of Income in China*, edited by Griffin and Zhao (1993). One of the most remarkable statistics to emerge from the survey was the size of the ratio of urban to rural household income per capita (2.42). This was higher than the ratio derived from the State Statistical Bureau's household survey for 1988 (2.19), mainly because the CASS survey incorporated more of the benefits-in-kind received by urban people. It was apparent that the rural–urban divide therefore deserved study, and that the survey could be copiously exploited for that purpose.

Fourthly, the Chinese economy is growing at a remarkable pace (by almost 10 per cent per annum over the period 1978–95), and growth is accompanied by structural transformation. Moreover, economic reforms have advanced in stages and are continuing apace. Another complication is that the extent and speed of reforms vary widely across the regions of this vast country. Although the gradualist reform strategy in China has been described as 'crossing a river by feeling for the stones', the river we cross today is not the river we waded in last year. This raises two problems. First, although the text is peppered with qualifying dates, there is no doubt still too much unqualified use of the past or present tense. Secondly, the rural–urban relationships we seek to analyse are evolving rapidly, and the relevant literature is growing exponentially as more data become available and more scholars become engaged. This has required the revision of chapters—a process which could go on indefinitely. It was necessary to impose a—somewhat ragged—end-date, and to ignore subsequent events and information.

Fifthly, the rural–urban disparities and contrasts that we might examine are many and various. We analyse those which appeared most interesting to us, or most amenable to our methods. Others, while being worthy of study, are neglected or merely touched upon. These include social security and social welfare (other than housing and health), nutrition, fertility and family planning. Our approach is not an all-embracing one, although it is probably broader than that of most economists.

1.5 THE PLAN OF THE STUDY

1.5.1 Comparing rural and urban well-being

Ultimately we are concerned with describing, comparing, and then explaining 'well-being' in rural and urban China. We use the term 'well-being' to connote the broadest concept of economic welfare. Amartya Sen, in his many writings (for instance, Sen 1985, 1988, and 1990) has developed the concept of a person's capabilities to achieve various 'functionings', i.e. doings and beings, such as being well-nourished, well-sheltered, healthy and long-lived, and having self-respect. Sen considers the normal concept of economic welfare to be too narrow because it ignores various freedoms and is concerned with subjective and not objective deprivation. He argues that a person's functionings are important in themselves and not just because they yield utility, and that the metric of desire and satisfaction can be misleading if seriously deprived people accept their fate. Equality of income may conceal inequality of well-being because of the limited lives that some people are forced to live. The argument for a comprehensive concept of welfare is persuasive, especially in a country where an interventionist government replaces the market in many spheres.

How can these notions be applied in a comparison of rural and urban China? Table 1.3 shows the different components of well-being that might be relevant to the rural–urban comparison. Economists are most at home in measuring income (§1 and §2). These are the subjects of Chapters 2 and 3, which compare dimensions of rural and urban incomes. In China various forms of government provision and subsidy (§3) are important components of well-being, although their value is difficult to measure. We attempt to examine these in Chapters 4, 5, and 6.

The need for security (§4) is especially important in a poor society. There are risks of losing one's house, land, job, or income—risks which

TABLE 1.3 *The components of well-being*

§	Component
1	Cash income
2	Income-in-kind
3	Government direct subsidies minus direct taxes
3a	food
3b	education
3c	housing
3d	social welfare
3e	health
4	Security
4a	housing
4b	land
4c	jobs
4d	income variability
4e	social security
5	Freedoms
5a	spatial mobility
5b	socio-economic mobility
5c	social control
6	Status
6a	income distribution
6b	community participation

government, by its laws, conduct, and social insurance, can reduce. These issues are discussed, albeit only qualitatively, in Chapters 2 and 3 and elsewhere. The relative freedoms of rural and urban people (§5) are examined in various places, for instance as they relate to freedom to pursue economic self-interests (Chapter 2), socio-economic mobility (Chapter 4), and spatial mobility (Chapters 8 and 9). Finally, status or self-respect depends partly on economic factors such as the distribution of income (§6), and this is discussed in Chapters 2 and 3.

Our general hypotheses are twofold. First, urban and rural people have different ways of life, which are not adequately reflected in an income measure. Secondly, in almost all dimensions of well-being, with the possible exception of housing, urban-dwellers enjoy an advantage over rural-dwellers.

1.5.2 *Explaining the urban advantage*

We adopt various approaches to explaining the urban advantage, each involving some aspect of rural–urban economic relationships. One approach is to examine the rural–urban income gap over time and to explain the reasons for the movements in the gap (Chapter 2). Another is to analyse the spatial variation in the rural–urban income gap and to consider whether it can help to explain the gap itself (Chapter 3). Similarly, the determinants of non-marketed services such as education (Chapter 4), health (Chapter 5), and housing (Chapter 6) are analysed to help explain the urban advantage in the provision of subsidized public services.

These three chapters (4–6) are particularly helpful in evaluating the urban bias model of rural–urban relationships. The price-scissors model, used to explain discrimination against rural-dwellers, receives specific attention in Chapter 7. The Lewis model comes under scrutiny in Chapters 2 and 3, which raise the question: how has China's rural surplus labour been absorbed? The main prediction of the model is the transfer of rural labour to the urban, industrial sector: in Chapters 8 and 9 we examine the extent and causes of, and impediments to, rural–urban migration.

Finally, in Chapter 10 we attempt to draw conclusions and to consider the lessons both for China and more generally. Our general conclusions are that the land shortage and labour surplus inherited by the communist government, the institutions which it established, and its objective of rapid capital accumulation and industrialization made possible, logical, and acceptable the subordination of the peasants to State interests. The government implicitly accepted the Lewis model of economic development with surplus labour and intervened by means of price-scissors to promote the process. However, the institutional divide that was erected and the latent power of workers relative to peasants produced an outcome which greatly favoured urban-dwellers. The policy bias in favour of urban people is deep-seated and has survived even the rural economic reforms and the marketization of the economy.

NOTE

1. Including Lewis (1954), Ranis and Fei (1961), and Lewis (1979) on the Lewis model; Sah and Stiglitz (1984) and Knight (1995) on the price-scissors model; and Lipton (1977), Harris and Todaro (1970), Bates (1983), and Gelb, Knight, and Sabot (1990), and *Journal of Development Studies* (1993), especially Oi, on the urban bias model.

REFERENCES

Bates, Robert H. (1983). *Essays on the Political Economy of Rural Africa*, Cambridge: Cambridge University Press.

Bo Yibo (1991). *Review of Some Important Policies and Events*, Beijing: Zhong Gong Zhong Yong Dang Xiao Publication House.

Chan Kam Wing (1987). 'Urbanization in China since 1949: reply', *China Quarterly*, 109 (Mar.): 104–9.

Chan Kam Wing, and Xu Xueqiang (1985). 'Urban population and urbanization in China since 1949: constructing a baseline', *China Quarterly*, 104 (Dec.): 583–613.

Gelb, A., Knight, J. B., and Sabot, R. H. (1991). 'Public sector employment, rent seeking and economic growth', *Economic Journal*, 101 (408): 1186–99.

Griffin, Keith, and Zhao Renwei (1993). *The Distribution of Income in China*, London: Macmillan.

Harris, John, and Todaro, Michael (1970). 'Migration, unemployment and development: a two-sector analysis', *American Economic Review*, 60 (Mar.): 126–41.

Howe, Christopher (1973). *Wage Patterns and Wage Policy in Modern China 1919–1972*, Cambridge: Cambridge University Press.

Journal of Development Studies (1993). Special Issue 'Beyond Urban Bias', 29 (4).

Knight, John (1995). 'Price scissors and intersectoral resource transfers: who paid for industrialization in China?', *Oxford Economic Papers*, 47 (1): 117–35.

Lewis, W. Arthur (1954). 'Economic development with unlimited supplies of labour', *The Manchester School*, 22 (May): 139–92.

——(1979). 'The dual economy revisited', *The Manchester School*, 47 (3): 211–29.

Lipton, Michael (1977). *Why Poor People Stay Poor: Urban Bias in World Development*, Cambridge, Mass.: Harvard University Press.

Martin, Michael F. (1992). 'Defining China's rural population', *China Quarterly*, 130 (June): 392–401.

Oi, Jean C. (1993). 'Reform and urban bias in China', *Journal of Development Studies*, 29 (4).

Peoples' Republic of China, Editorial Board of the China Agricultural Yearbook (PRC, EBCAY) (1993). *China Agricultural Yearbook 1992*, Beijing: Agricultural Publishing House.

——State Statistical Bureau (PRC, SSB) (1989). *Chinese Rural Economic Statistics. Summary by Counties 1980–87*, Beijing (in Chinese).

———(PRC, SSB) (1990). *China Statistical Yearbook 1990*, Beijing (in Chinese).

———(PRC, SSB) (1993). *China Statistical Yearbook 1993*, Beijing.

———(PRC, SSB) (1996). *China Statistical Yearbook 1996*, Beijing.

Ranis, Gustav, and Fei, John C. H. (1961). 'A theory of economic development', *American Economic Review*, 51 (4): 533–65.

Riskin, Carl (1987). *China's Political Economy. The Quest for Development Since 1949*, Oxford: Oxford University Press.

Sah, R. K., and Stiglitz, J. E. (1984). 'The economics of price scissors', *American Economic Review*, 74 (1): 125–38.

Scharping, Thomas (1987). 'Urbanization in China since 1949: comment', *China Quarterly*, 109 (Mar.): 101–4.

Sen, Amartya (1985). *Commodities and Capabilities*, Amsterdam: North-Holland.

——(1988). 'The concept of development', in Hollis Chenery and T. N. Srinivasan (eds.), *Handbook of Development Economics, 1*, Amsterdam: North-Holland.

——(1990). 'Development as capability expansion', in Keith Griffin and John Knight (eds.), *Human Development and the International Development Strategy for the 1990s*, London: Macmillan.

Song Ping (1957). 'Why we must implement a rational low-wage system', *Xuexi (Study)*, 23, repr. in Christopher Howe and Kenneth R. Walker (eds.) (1989), *The*

Foundations of the Chinese Planned Economy. A Documentary Survey 1953–65, London: Macmillan.

Wong, Christine P. W. (1997). 'Rural public finance', in Christine P. W. Wong (ed.), *Financing Local Government in the Peoples' Republic of China*, Hong Kong: Asian Development Bank and Oxford University Press.

PART II

RURAL–URBAN COMPARISONS OF INCOME

2

The Rural–Urban Income Divide:
Macroeconomics

The strategy of the Chinese government after 1949 was to promote rapid urban industrialization. Rural poverty would be alleviated through the transfer of peasants into the urban industrial economy. The industrialization strategy was successful but its benefits were offset by population growth. Table 2.1 presents a summary view of the labour force in rural and urban China over more than forty years. The labour force grew on average by 2.6 per cent per annum: 2.1 per cent in rural areas and 4.6 per cent in urban areas. In 1952 rural workers represented 88 per cent of the total, and in 1995 72 per cent. Urban employees, known as 'staff and workers', increased in number by 5.5 per cent per annum, from 8 per cent of the labour force in 1952 to 25 per cent in 1995. Despite the rapid industrialization and urbanization, rural labour increased one-and-a-half-fold over the period, whereas land was already fully occupied in 1952 and its use could not be expanded significantly. By 1995 there were 450 million workers in rural areas and 173 million in urban areas, of which 113 million were staff and workers in the state-owned sector.

It is an important fact, needing to be explained, that the ratio of urban to rural income, and consumption, per capita was substantial throughout the period of Communist Party rule as Table 2.2 and Figure 2.1 illustrate. The ratio of income per capita exceeded 3.0 in the mid-1950s, and was as high as 2.4 in 1978. It fell to 1.9 in 1984 but subsequently rose to 2.7 in 1995. The ratio of consumption per capita peaked at above 3.0 during the disastrous Great Leap Forward, was as high as 2.9 in 1978, fell to 2.3 in 1984, and rose again to no less than 3.4 in 1995.

How is the income gap, and its movement over time, to be explained? To what extent is it the result of what has come to be known as 'urban bias' in government policies? Since the Communist Party came to power on the basis of what was essentially a peasant revolution, was led by people with peasant backgrounds, and claimed to represent 'poor and lower-middle' peasants, state policies might well have shown 'rural bias'. A third possibility is that the State, primarily concerned to maintain power and control, displayed 'state bias', i.e. pursued whatever policies were necessary to secure its own objectives.

These three options were set out in Nolan and White (1984). Our intention is to evaluate the rival interpretations. Our approach goes beyond the

Rural–Urban Comparisons of Income

TABLE 2.1 *The rural and urban labour force, 1952–95*

	Labour force			Urban employees	
	Total	Rural	Urban	Total	State sector
Million					
1952	207	182	25	16	16
1962	259	214	45	43	33
1975	382	299	82	82	64
1985	499	371	128	124	90
1995	624	450	173	158	113
Percentage of total					
1952	100	88	12	8	8
1962	100	82	18	17	13
1975	100	78	22	21	17
1985	100	74	26	25	18
1995	100	72	28	25	18
Rate of growth (% p.a.)					
1952–95	2.6	2.1	4.6	5.5	4.7

Source: PRC, SSB 1996: 90.

TABLE 2.2 *Urban and rural income and consumption per capita, and their ratio,*
1952–95

	Net income per capita			Consumption per capita		
	Urban	Rural	Urban (rural = 100)	Urban	Rural	Urban (rural = 100)
1952		57		149	62	2.40
1953				181	69	2.62
1954		64		183	70	2.61
1955				188	76	2.47
1956	243	73	3.33	197	78	2.53
1957	254	73	3.48	205	79	2.59
1958				195	83	2.35
1959				206	65	3.17
1960				214	68	3.15
1961				225	82	2.74
1962		99		226	88	2.57
1963	232	101	2.30	222	89	2.49
1964	243	102	2.38	234	95	2.46
1965		107		237	100	2.37
1966				244	106	2.30

TABLE 2.2 *Continued*

	Net income per capita			Consumption per capita		
	Urban	Rural	Urban (rural = 100)	Urban	Rural	Urban (rural = 100)
1967				251	110	2.28
1968				250	106	2.36
1969				255	108	2.36
1970				260	114	2.28
1971				267	116	2.30
1972				295	116	2.54
1973				306	123	2.49
1974				313	123	2.54
1975				324	124	2.61
1976		113		340	125	2.72
1977		117		360	124	2.90
1978	316	134	2.36	383	132	2.90
1979	377	160	2.36	406	152	2.67
1980	439	191	2.30	468	173	2.71
1981	500	223	2.24	520	192	2.71
1982	535	270	1.98	526	210	2.50
1983	573	310	1.85	547	232	2.36
1984	660	355	1.86	598	265	2.26
1985	749	398	1.88	802	347	2.31
1986	910	424	2.15	920	376	2.45
1987	1,012	463	2.19	1,089	417	2.61
1988	1,192	545	2.19	1,431	508	2.82
1989	1,388	602	2.31	1,568	553	2.84
1990	1,523	686	2.22	1,686	571	2.95
1991	1,713	709	2.42	1,925	621	3.10
1992	2,032	784	2.59	2,356	718	3.28
1993	2,583	922	2.80	3,027	855	3.54
1994	3,502	1,221	2.87	3,979	1,138	3.50
1995	4,288	1,578	2.72	5,044	1,479	3.41

Notes: 1. The figures have been subject to considerable revision from one issue of the *Statistical Yearbook* to another. The latest among the available figures is used.

      2. In the case of consumption per capita, the distinction made is between 'agricultural' and 'non-agricultural residents'.

Sources: PRC, SSB, 1986; 1991; 1995; 1996.

conventional boundaries of economics into the realm of politics. In doing so we generally make use of secondary sources and rely on the evidence and interpretation of political scientists and political economists. In particular we draw on Nolan and White (1984), Riskin (1987), Nolan (1988),

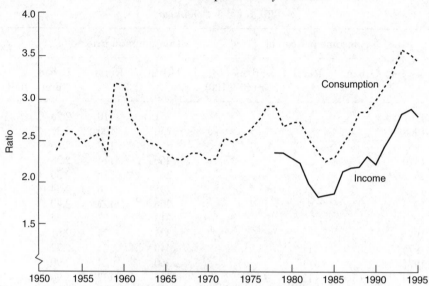

Fig. 2.1 *Ratio of average urban/rural income, and consumption, per capita*

Oi (1989), Kelliher (1992), Korzec (1992), Takahara (1992), Ash (1993), Hua, Zhang, and Luo (1993), Selden (1988), Lin (1994), and White (1993). We follow White (1993: 14) in our presumption that 'institutions and groups in Chinese society possess political resources which enable them to exert pressures (implicit or explicit, passive or active) which CCP leaders ignore at their cost'. We divide the period into two eras, corresponding to Mao and to Deng: 1949–77 and 1978–95.

2.1 THE RURAL SECTOR

2.1.1 The Maoist era, 1949–77

Figure 2.2 shows the movement in rural household annual mean real income per capita (in the years for which it is available) and consumption per capita over the period 1952–95. The data are expressed in 1978 prices, being deflated by the general consumer price index up to 1985 and thereafter by the separate rural consumer price index (available from 1985). The figure illustrates the important features that require explanation: the fall in income and consumption in the period 1959–61, the stagnation throughout the period 1962–78, the sharp increase in the years 1978–84, and the subsequent standstill until the early 1990s, when progress was again visible.

The new government confiscated land from landlords and rich peasants without compensation, and redistributed it to poor and landless households.

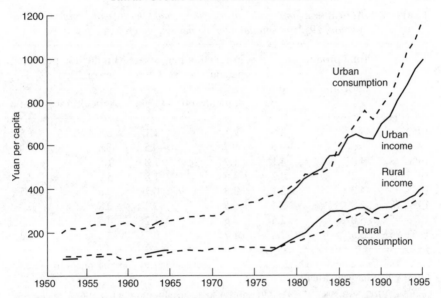

FIG. 2.2 *Urban and rural annual real income, and consumption, per capita*

In 1950 officially defined 'poor peasants' (accounting for 52 per cent of the rural population) held 14 per cent of the land, whereas 'rich peasants' and 'landlords' (9 per cent of the rural population) held 52 per cent of the land. In 1954 these groups held 47 and 9 per cent of the land respectively (Lin 1994: 33, citing official figures). The average land area cultivated by poor peasants increased from 8.9 to 12.5 mu (Riskin 1987: table 3.2).

The land reform of 1950–3 was enormously popular among Chinese peasants. It gave the State legitimacy and forged bonds of support for and commitment to the new government. The gradual collectivization of agriculture therefore encountered no serious resistance from the majority of peasants. First, 'mutual aid' teams were formed, sharing implements and exchanging labour. This led on to elementary cooperatives, which pooled resources and unified management. Thirdly, advanced cooperatives were created, in which all factors of production, including land, were collectively owned, and people were remunerated according to the amount of work they contributed. Each change was accompanied by an expansion in the number of households forming the collective. Agricultural production grew in real terms by 25 per cent, and grain production by 19 per cent, between 1952 and 1957 (Table 2.3).

The apparent success of collectivization and the need to extract more agricultural surplus for industrialization emboldened the leadership to establish people's communes. Within a mere three months, in late 1958 the 750,000 collective farms were forcibly transformed into 24,000 communes,

TABLE 2.3 *Agricultural and grain production, total, per person, and per rural person, 1952–95, annual average percentage growth rates*

	Total production		Production per person		Production per rural person	
	Agricultural	Grain	Agricultural	Grain	Agricultural	Grain
1952–7	4.6	3.5	2.1	1.1	2.8	1.8
1958–61	−9.8	−9.6	−9.7	−9.5	−8.6	−8.4
1962–78	4.0	4.1	1.7	1.8	1.8	1.9
1978–85	6.2	3.2	4.8	1.8	5.9	2.8
1985–95	4.2	2.1	2.8	0.7	3.6	1.5
1952–78	2.5	2.4	0.5	0.4	0.8	0.7
1978–95	5.0	2.5	3.6	1.2	4.5	2.0
1952–95	3.5	2.4	1.7	0.7	2.2	1.2

Note: The agricultural production series is of gross output at constant prices; it excludes forestry, hunting, and fishing.

Sources: PRC, SSB 1986: 25, 143; 1991: table 9.30; 1996: tables 11-6, 11-18; 1996*a*: table 5-23.

averaging some 5,000 households each. Private plots were abolished and households were remunerated less according to their work and more according to their need. Simultaneously the leadership abandoned the Second Five-Year Plan and embarked on a Great Leap Forward. Poor management of the communes, the leadership's exhortation to produce 'backyard' iron and steel, the loss of individual incentives to work the land, and three successive years of bad weather resulted in a rural crisis. Both agricultural and grain production collapsed by 26 per cent between 1958 and 1961 (Table 2.3).

It has been estimated that 30 million peasants (5.5 per cent of the rural population) died as a result of the ensuing famine (Aston *et al.* 1984). The famine raged on for three years without public admission that it was occurring. Even the leadership, being fed exaggerated reports of commune production, were initially ignorant of the calamity. Moreover, personal and ideological in-fighting among the leadership delayed remedial action and contributed to the scale of the famine (Hua, Zhang, and Luo 1993: 16). Comparing the role of government in this and in Indian famines, Drèze and Sen (1989: 210–5) attribute some of the blame to the Chinese system of political monopoly and press control.

The brunt of the famine was borne by the peasants. The absolute annual net procurement of foodgrains for the urban population averaged 35 million tonnes in the period 1955–8, 35 million tonnes during the Great Leap Forward of 1959–61, and 30 million tonnes in the period of recovery, 1962–5. The corresponding proportions of foodgrains procured were 18, 22, and 17 per cent respectively (Riskin 1987: table 6.5). It is unclear how far this protection of urban-dwellers was deliberate policy and how far it was due to exaggerated harvest reports at a time of ideological fervour.

The leadership responded to the 1959–61 tragedy by trying to improve incentives. It delegated management tasks in each commune to the production team, and made it the accounting unit. Private plots were again permitted and workpoints were reintroduced as the basis for remuneration. The remaining fifteen years of the Maoist era were characterized by the social upheaval of the Cultural Revolution, 1966–76, and by an emphasis on 'self-reliance' for the communes. The high mandatory targets for grain production and the stress on local self-reliance in grain meant that the benefits of producing higher-valued crops and of local specialization in farming activities were lost. Nevertheless, various technological improvements were made in agriculture: the irrigated area rose from 30 per cent of cultivated land in 1962 to 45 per cent in 1978, there was increased use of electricity and chemical fertilizers, and high-yielding seed varieties spread rapidly (Lin 1994: 36–8).

Despite these advances, agriculture performed badly during the period of the communes. The State failed to solve the problems of incentives, monitoring, and supervision posed by even the reformed commune system of production (Lin 1990). According to Wen (1989) (cited in Lin 1994: 52), total factor productivity in agriculture (with 1952 = 100) fell from 106 in 1958 to 78 in 1961, then kept below 90 and was only 79 in 1977, rising rapidly thereafter with decollectivization. Table 2.3 shows the growth of farm production, not only in total but also per person (as an indicator of the capacity to feed the expanding population) and per rural person (as an indicator of the capacity of the peasants to feed themselves). We see that during the Maoist period farm output barely kept up with the growth of population. For instance, the availability of grain per person rose by only 0.4 per cent per annum over the period 1952–78.

It is possible to provide an economic interpretation of the thrust of rural economic policy in the Maoist period. The leadership gave priority to rapid urban industrialization, and saw the rural sector as the source of marketed and investible surplus for that industrialization. The State relied on coercion rather than incentives to secure the harvest. It introduced compulsory procurement of peasant output at low prices, and it imposed collectivization to acquire greater control over the surplus. The price-scissors policy kept down agricultural prices in relation to industrial prices, so permitting lower industrial wages and higher surpluses in the state-owned industrial sector. We pursue these ideas in the analysis of rural–urban capital flows in Chapter 7.

This economic interpretation of government policy is narrow and incomplete. Politics, not economics, was in command. Mao Zedong was hostile to both bureaucratic and market solutions: he favoured decentralization subject to general directives from above. The communes could be seen as institutions of local government sufficiently large in size for effective local resource-mobilizing efforts, and sufficiently few in number for effective communication from the leadership to the peasants. There was extreme politicization of economic decision-making, with extensive use of simple directives and slogans, and the replacement of economic criteria by ideological values. The formation of the communes provided social and political control as well as economic control, and enabled the leadership to pursue political objectives, such as egalitarianism and collective rather than individual behaviour and way of life.

Collectivization was initially voluntary but eventually became coercive. Probably with the creation of the communes in 1958, and certainly with the disastrous Great Leap Forward that ensued, the partnership between the State and the peasants dissolved. The ideological assault on the peasants intensified. 'Despite Mao's lifelong dedication to peasant interests, the government eventually became all but deaf to peasant complaints of deprivation' (Kelliher 1992: 9). The peasants had very little capacity to control their own lives or to alter government policies. Peasant dissatisfaction swelled during the Cultural Revolution without serious consequences for the State. Resistance could merely take the forms of passivity, evasion, and tension with the procurement agencies. The Chinese State was unusually strong and rural society was unusually weak: organizations that might compete with the State—such as clans, private companies, and religious organizations—did not exist. State dominance over the peasants had been firmly established.

2.1.2 The rural reforms, 1978–95

In the Third Plenum, December 1978, the reformers Deng Xiaoping and Chen Yun seized control; so began a remarkable process of rural reform. The basic reason for the initial policy-switch was a reordering of priorities from the political to the economic. The reforming coalition interpreted the State's predicament in the following way. It was now necessary to promote development and welfare in order to provide a new form of legitimacy for the regime: failure to reform would mean economic stagnation, social tension, and political decline.

The sector most urgently requiring reform was the farm sector, which had stagnated for many years. Owing to population growth a falling proportion of the harvest was being procured. Agriculture had become the bottleneck. The ambitious target for economic growth could not be achieved without an acceleration of agricultural growth. Agriculture was crucial to exports and thus to foreign exchange and access to foreign technology. Continued coercion of peasants was rejected. It was perceived both to have failed economically and to be politically dangerous: 'the peasants bear in mind those who show real concern for them and serve them; but whoever forgets about the peasants and does not serve them, the peasants will cast aside' (Deng Liqun, quoted in Kelliher 1992: 52). Discontent was now widespread in the countryside (Zhang and Yi 1994). The State's reform initiative could thus be interpreted as reflecting state interests foremost and peasant interests incidentally.

We follow Kelliher (1992) in examining three aspects of the rural reforms: the restoration of household production, the reform of marketing to create price incentives for production, and the development of enterprise and markets. The initial reforms, announced in 1978, involved a shift from heavy to light industry in order to provide incentive goods, the raising of farm prices to provide production incentives, and a lowering of the level of the accounting unit, again to improve incentives.

The rural reforms rapidly outstripped these measures. The peasants interpreted them as a signal that change was possible, and the reform initiative passed from the State to the peasants. They manipulated the reforms and pushed them further than they were meant to go. They were able to do this because their interests coincided with those of the State. If peasants were not to be coerced to produce more, they had to be given incentives to do so, and they could not be alienated. The new goal of economic growth effectively increased peasant power.

This was not organized power; the peasants were not a pressure group. Peasants took the initiative through individual, atomized behaviour. Because state policy had been uniformly and rigidly imposed, they responded in identical ways in overwhelming numbers but as unorganized individuals. Both poor peasants (who were hungry) and rich peasants (whose consumption was capped) wanted to take advantage of the new political climate. They acted in concert. The rural reforms were that rare economic event, a Pareto improvement, benefiting almost all rural people. The national leadership lost control of the pace and nature of reform.

(a) The household as production unit

In many, but not all, areas of China the peasants led the State in the creation of family farms. Spontaneous experiments were permitted in the initiating provinces (Anhui and Sichuan); in some other provinces (such as Hubei) the experiments involved secrecy and conflict. Peasants throughout much of China felt a positive attraction for family farming, because it seemed to offer higher incomes, security, and independence. Village cadres sensed a new confidence in peasants, and experienced peasant hostility if they failed to uphold peasant interests. They often colluded with the peasants. The Third Plenum of 1978 had banned family farming. On this matter, as in others, the central leadership, having opened the way for reform, lost control over much of the creative process. The move to the household production unit proceeded very rapidly because it proved to be economically successful. The practice, first banned and then tolerated, became official policy, to be followed uniformly throughout China.

Why were the reform leaders timid and indecisive? It was partly to gauge the economic success of the experimentation. It was partly that there were cracks in the reform coalition—factional and bureaucratic rivalries. The reformers could not mobilize constituencies within the state apparatus strong enough to launch bold agricultural policy changes (Kelliher 1992: 71–5). At the same time the State dared not risk the uncooperative hostility of the peasants. Eventually the State took over the policy and imposed it uniformly without sensitivity to local conditions. Its imposition against the will of some peasants indicates the limits to peasant power.

Lin (1992) conducted an econometric analysis of agricultural output over the years 1970–87. Using a production function approach, he found that half of the growth of crop production over the period 1978–84 was attributable to total factor productivity growth. Almost all of this productivity growth was in turn due to the institutional change from the collective system to the household responsibility system. Similarly, Wen (1989) showed that total factor productivity rose from 79 in 1977 (with 1952 = 100) to 124 in 1984. Decollectivization thus had a dramatic, albeit a once-for-all, effect on farm production and income. Agricultural production grew by more than 6 per cent per annum over the period 1978–85 (Table 2.3).

(b) Pricing policy

In pricing the State introduced two major reforms: higher procurement prices from 1979 to 1981 and the easing of mandatory procurement in 1985. Peasants responded to the price incentives by increasing production and switching away from grain to the more profitable crops. They also manipulated the system in order to raise their proceeds. There were three prices, the quota price, the extra-quota price, and the floating price. Peasants could gain not only by increasing production but also by specialization, swapping, and varying stocks. The 1983 and 1984 harvests were record harvests, with the result that the free market prices actually fell short of the state prices; but normally free market prices exceeded procurement prices. Document No. 1 of 1985 introduced 'contract purchasing', by which government would negotiate purchase prices before each planting season. It established a dual system, in which some sales were governed by the market and others by the State. However, peasants lacked incentives to grow the staple crops at prevailing prices. Subsidized agricultural inputs were accordingly tied to the fulfilment of quotas under contract. Although the decree appeared to abolish compulsory procurement, mandatory quotas were effectively continued for the three main crops, grain, cotton, and edible oil: peasants had to sign procurement contracts.

Urban ration prices were well below procurement prices. As the average price paid to peasants rose, so the cost of the food subsidies given to urban workers also rose. Between 1978 and 1985 the producer price of grain rose by 133 per cent, and urban food subsidies escalated to equal 10.6 per cent of government budget revenue (PRC, SSB 1993: 183, 199, 234). The phasing out of mandatory procurement would require further increases either in the prices or in the subsidies of urban food. The government was caught in a cleft stick: on the one hand, urban consumer subsidies would impose a serious financial burden, and on the other hand, urban real incomes had to be protected. Government was dependent on the urban state-owned and collective enterprises for much of its revenue, and therefore needed to keep those workers contented (Lin 1994: 62). The State accorded priority to urban people because 'any display of discontent on their part is far more dangerous to the regime than localized peasant uprisings, easily dispersed by the authorities' (Aubert 1990: 28). Accordingly, in 1985 the decision was taken to avoid further increases in agricultural purchasing prices (Ash 1993: 32), a decision that was adhered to until 1988 and, more loosely, until 1991. Moreover, as budgetary problems mounted, increasingly peasants were not paid on time. For instance, a survey in the 1988 summer procurement season showed that only eight of sixteen provinces had the funds to pay peasants for their deliveries; many peasants received promissory notes ('white slips') instead.

Reflecting the relative prices of food and manufactures, farm production suffered by another route. The decentralization of economic powers from central to local governments gave local governments incentives to raise revenues by owning, encouraging, and taxing local economic activities. The profitable opportunities were to be found in industry rather than agriculture. In 1985 Chen Yun complained that 'No industry, then no money' had overwhelmed 'No grain, then no stability' (Hua, Zhang, and Luo 1993: 180).

With the urban population subdued after the massacre of civilians in 1989, it was safer to raise the urban selling price of grain. In 1992, the State Council ended the subsidy on grain, although apparently leaving the other subsidies in place. The dual system continued but grain procurement shrank rapidly and state purchasing prices approached market prices. Nevertheless, urban consumer subsidies on agricultural goods, including subsidies to compensate for price increases, were still 3.6 per cent of government budget revenue in 1995 (PRC 1996: 221, 243). The gradual withdrawal of government from the market for food was facilitated by the rapid increase in urban real wages in the 1990s (see Figure 2.4 and Table 2.6).

(c) Privatization and marketization

The privatization and marketization of rural China was a process of cumulative causation which government could not control. When one aspect of economic life was privatized or marketized, gains in efficiency were impeded unless other aspects of economic life were allowed to follow. Consider four aspects: land tenure, credit, labour, and entrepreneurship.

Land was allocated on a leasehold basis to households within each village according to the number of household members. The initial short-term contracts were replaced in 1984 by leasehold contracts of fifteen years or more. This was a necessary consequence of the need to provide incentives for long-term farm investments. Gradually peasants came to treat their land as private property: the need for farm credit and off-farm employment opportunities caused peasants to lease it, rent it, hire labour to work it, and to use it as security for loans. Local communities were allowed to work out their own solutions to the need to transfer land among households; in many cases such transfers involved payment of rents.

Once the household became the production unit it was inevitable that capital and labour markets would follow. Inadequacy of the official credit system in providing credit to farmers caused a private credit market to spring up. The State tacitly accepted this development, despite the high rates of interest associated with unsecured loans. Similarly, a market for hired labour emerged, in response to the needs of private businesses for labour and of poor, underemployed peasant households for employment.

When the restraints on non-agricultural activities were relaxed a new entrepreneurial class began to form. Many of the new entrepreneurs were former cadres. They were in a good position to take over the former collective enterprises, and through connections they had access to credit, information, and telephones. Other new businessmen were young and relatively well educated. The State aligned itself with this entrepreneurial class partly to promote rural development and partly to maintain its power. A new social basis for power was needed because of the widespread peasant indifference to the Communist Party. The State targeted the economic leaders—entrepreneurs and successful farmers—who had the greatest stake in the reform policies. The Party welcomed them into official positions, so that the economic leaders tended also to be the political leaders. Their influence over the villagers was strengthened through patron–client relationships (Oi 1989: ch. 9).

2.1.3 The underlying determinants of rural development

China is a country characterized by heavy population pressure on the land. It is a surplus labour economy *par excellence*. The level of rural income depends heavily on the supply of land and capital in relation to labour, and its distribution on their distribution among households. The growth of population in rural China reduces the marginal product of labour and poses a threat to rural living standards. It can be ameliorated in various ways.

First, there can be migration of labour from rural to urban areas.

However, the government has attempted to enforce tight controls on such movement. Migration will be explored in Chapters 8 and 9. Secondly, the agricultural terms of trade can be improved, as indeed happened to some extent in the period of economic reform. The terms of trade will be explored in Chapter 7. Thirdly, resources can be used more efficiently, as occurred in the period 1978–85 when the communes were abandoned and individual incentives were restored. Fourthly, rural labour can be transferred from agriculture into rural industry and other non-agricultural enterprises. This was a remarkable phenomenon of the 1980s, when rural industry became the most dynamic sector of the Chinese economy. We examine that process in this section and, more analytically, in Chapter 3.

China reached the limits of its land availability decades ago. The total land area sown in 1995 was no more than 6 per cent higher than it had been in 1952, having peaked in 1978. Yet population continued to grow. Over the same period the rural labour force increased by one-and-a-half-fold. By implication, the sown area of land fell from 11.6 to 5.0 mu per rural worker. These figures are all derived from Table 2.4. Population growth fell dramatically in the 1980s, as a result of the introduction of the one-child family policy in 1980. However, the high rural birth rates of the 1960s (no less than 4.3 per cent per annum at the peak in 1963), continuing into the 1970s, ensured that the growth of the labour force was no less than 2.9 per cent per annum during the period of decollectivization and 2.0 per cent during the subsequent decade. This is reflected in the sharply falling dependency ratio after 1978 (Table 2.4).

Surplus labour was present in the communes but camouflaged by the workpoint system. It became more evident under the household responsibility system. There have been numerous attempts to measure the extent of surplus labour in rural China. These have produced a range of estimates but the majority suggest that surplus labour represented about 30 per cent of the labour force (surveyed in Taylor 1988). The absorption of the growing labour force into productive activities was thus a central problem facing the Chinese government.

Over the reform period 1978–95 the rural labour force increased by 147 million. Of this increase, 24 million were assigned to urban jobs and 123 million remained registered in the rural areas. There was a remarkable growth of employment in township, village, and private (TVP) enterprises: from 28 million in 1978 to 129 million in 1995, when it represented 29 per cent of the rural labour force. Thus 101 million were absorbed into (at least part-time) non-agricultural activities, leaving only the residual increment of 22 million to become farmers. We see in Table 2.4 that sown area per non-enterprise rural worker fell little, from 8.3 mu in 1978 to 7.0 mu in 1995. Thus the growth of non-agricultural enterprises served as a safety valve to ease the growing population pressure on the land. The remarkable dynamism of this sector may reflect an initial market disequilibrium and TVPs'

Table 2.4 *Population, labour force, enterprise employment, and land, in rural China, 1952–95*

	1952	1962	1978	1985	1995	Average annual rate of change (%)			
						1952–62	1962–78	1978–85	1985–95
Rural population (million)	503.1	556.4	790.1	807.6	859.5	1.0	2.2	0.3	0.6
Rural labour force (million)	182.4	213.7	303.4	370.7	450.4	1.6	2.2	2.9	2.0
Rate of natural increase, rural population (% p.a.)	—	2.70	1.25	—	1.11				
Rural labour force as proportion of rural population (%)	36.3	38.4	38.4	45.9	52.4				
TVP enterprise employees (million)	—	—	28.3	79.4	128.6			15.9	4.9
TVP enterprise employees as proportion of rural labour force (%)	—	—	9.3	21.4	28.6				
Sown area of land (million mu)	2,119	2,103	2,252	2,154	2,248	−0.1	0.4	−0.6	0.4
Sown area of land per rural worker (mu)	11.6	9.8	7.4	5.8	5.0	−1.7	−1.7	−3.4	−1.1
Sown area of land per rural non-enterprise worker (mu)	11.6	9.8	8.3	7.4	7.0	−1.7	−1.0	−1.6	−0.6

Note: The number of township, village, and private (TVP) enterprise employees in 1978 excludes employees in private enterprises.

Sources: PRC, SSB 1986: 92, 137; 1996: 69, 87, 368, 388.

TABLE 2.5 *Economic performance in rural China, 1985–95*

	1985 = 100			Average annual rate of change (%)		
	1985	1991	1995	1985–91	1991–5	1985–95
Rural						
Household real income per capita	100.0	105.5	136.1	1.0	6.6	3.1
County real net output per capita	100.0	145.2		6.4		
Agricultural real production	100.0	123.9	169.7	3.6	8.2	5.4
Farm producer price: food	100.0	160.9	316.5	8.2	18.4	12.2
grain	100.0	150.9	350.9	7.1	29.2	13.4
Rural consumer price	100.0	168.9	291.4	9.1	14.6	11.3
Farm input price	100.0	162.3	297.5	8.4	16.4	11.5
Urban						
Urban retail price: food	100.0	179.1	372.1	10.2	20.0	14.0
grain	100.0	166.5	612.5	8.9	38.5	19.9

Note: The county statistical series has been discontinued.

Sources: Howes and Hussain 1994: table 3; PRC, SSB 1995, 1996.

competitive advantages over (urban) state enterprises: lower labour costs and superior labour motivation and effort.

The period of decollectivization saw rapid rural economic progress of a once-for-all nature. The subsequent decade, 1985–95, provides a better guide to long-run rural economic performance and prospects. In the mid-1980s the State transferred its preoccupation from rural to urban economic reform, and became concerned about rising food prices. We see in Table 2.5 that farm producer prices grew less rapidly than rural consumer prices and farm input prices over the years 1985–91. According to the national house-hold surveys conducted by the State Statistical Bureau (SSB), rural real income per capita rose very little—by 1 per cent per annum—between 1985 and 1991 (Table 2.5). However, it is possible that these household surveys understate the growth of rural incomes at a time of rapid rural industrialization. Howes and Hussain (1994) calculated net rural output over the period 1985–91, using the annual statistical yearbooks on the 2,400 counties of China. They showed that real output per capita grew more than 6 per cent per annum over the six years (Table 2.5).

The authors have three main explanations for this discrepancy: rapid growth of non-household incomes, different output and consumption deflators, and the use of a broader definition of 'rural' in the output estimates. This last explanation appears to be important. Matsuda (1990), in his account and critique of the SSB's national household surveys, stated that the rural household survey was still restricted in scope to farm households and excluded households that did not farm. In 1981 this group was only 1 per cent of the rural population but in 1987 it represented 12 per cent (Matsuda 1990: 342). Howes and Hussain (1994: tables 4, 6) noted that, whereas the proportion of agricultural income in production income fell from 75 to 71 per cent between 1985 and 1991, the share of agriculture in total rural net output fell from 73 to 56 per cent over the same period. The output data were said to relate to 5 per cent more of the population, i.e. using the 1964 rather than the 1984 definition of 'rural'.

The household income data faithfully reflect the stagnation of agriculture in the late 1980s but probably fail fully to reflect the boom in rural industry. The spatially selective nature of this boom meant, however, that most rural households benefited little from it. The Gini coefficient of rural output per capita among counties rose from 0.24 in 1985 to 0.33 in 1991. Moreover, real output per capita in the poorest 5 per cent of counties fell (Howes and Hussain 1994: tables 3, 5). Thus the real incomes of many rural households stagnated over that period.

There was a groundswell of discontent among Chinese peasants in the late 1980s and early 1990s, reflecting a growing perception that they had to shoulder an unfair burden. Much of this had to do with the issue of promissory notes instead of cash by state purchasing agencies, and a plethora of informal, random levies and charges by local governments, for instance for construction projects, and administrative expenses. There are journalistic reports of peasant complaints, protests, and riots (for instance, Kristoff and Wudunn 1994: 161, 173–4, 180–1, 183) and an official acknowledgement that 'massive boycotts' had taken place (PRC, MOA 1993: 43). The introduction of more local democracy and participation might be part of the solution. In the words of a Ministry of Agriculture report: 'the aggravated burden on farmers, disordered village accounting, tensions between cadres and villagers, as well as deteriorating public security, etc. are all related to the long-term delay in the construction of a rural democratic system, in comparison with the more advanced rural economic reform' (ibid. 44).

In 1991 producer prices for food began to rise rapidly, reflecting the government decision to increase the prices that urban residents would have to pay for subsidized staples. Between 1991 and 1995 the urban retail price of grain rose annually by 39 per cent and that of food generally by 20 per cent. Similarly, the average producer prices of grain and of food increased annually by 29 and 18 per cent respectively. By contrast, the annual inflation rate for farm inputs was 16 per cent and for rural consumer prices 15 per cent. This is all shown in Table 2.5. The new pricing policy elicited a supply response: farm production grew annually by 8 per cent. Both price and quantity effects raised the growth rate of real income per capita of rural households—to more than 6 per cent per annum over the four years (Table 2.5). The experience of the last decade shows the importance of government farm pricing policies for rural development.

The underlying problem of the late 1990s remained the need to find productive employment for the growing rural labour force. The issue that was then of greatest political concern—the reform of the urban state-owned enterprises—had important implications. It would govern the growth not only of TVP employment but also of rural–urban migration. The increased efficiency of state-owned enterprises and associated labour redundancies could be predicted to retard both these sources of non-farm employment for rural people—the former through increased competition and the latter through the preferential treatment of redundant urban workers. Again, the interests of the State appeared to require that the interests of the rural majority be subordinated to the interests of the urban minority.

2.2 THE URBAN SECTOR

The movement in urban household mean income and consumption per capita, deflated by the urban consumer price index to reflect 1978 prices, is illustrated in Figure 2.2. The consumption series shows slow but steady growth from 1962 to 1978, whereas the income series (in the years for which it is available) shows stagnation until 1978.[1] There is substantial growth in both series thereafter, with an acceleration—especially of income growth—in the 1990s. These are the trends that need to be explained. We begin with the Maoist period, when the determination of urban incomes and wages was essentially political and they were barely influenced by market forces.

2.2.1 The Maoist era, 1949–1977

In the era of centralized planning, the primary economic objective of the Chinese government was rapid industrialization, and the emphasis was placed on state-owned heavy industry located in cities. The price-scissors imposed by government on agriculture permitted high industrial prices in relation to agricultural prices and urban wages. Although it appears that industrial investment was financed from industrial profits, it is arguable that peasants ultimately paid for industrialization. The large gap between the income per capita of urban households reliant on wages and that of rural households suggests that it was the peasants rather than the workers who were required to make the sacrifice in consumption. Had the government considered that living standards generally should be kept down to finance capital accumulation, it could have kept urban incomes in line with rural incomes. It was crucially important to this outcome that rural–urban migration be rigidly restricted. Without the controls on migration that were put in place during the 1950s, urban workers would have had to compete with rural migrants. In that case, market forces would have depressed urban wages to reflect the supply price of rural labour.

After liberation the government adopted a system of bureaucratic allocation of labour and administered wages. The wage reform of 1956, which instituted a formal system of standardized wage scales in the state sector, was much influenced by the Soviet model. Only minor differences were allowed in the national wage scales: by region, according to the cost-of-living, and by industry, according to importance in the national economy and working conditions. Within enterprises, there were thirty wage grades for cadres, eighteen for technical staff, and normally eight for manual workers (Takahara 1992: 29–32).

The early 1950s saw substantial gains in urban real wages, which Howe (1973: 55) attributed to the need for the CCP to build up urban support. Between 1952 and 1955 the average real wage rose by 3.4 per cent per annum. The 1956 wage reform resulted in a further 14 per cent increase. This was partly due to the new wage scales, partly because work units handled conflicts over the increased wage differentials by means of unauthorized grade promotions and bonus payments, and partly through the wider use of the piece-rate system (Takahara 1992: 41). As this became clear, the view gained ground among the leadership that urban wages had risen too high. The call was for a 'rational, low-wage system' which linked urban unskilled wages to peasant incomes.

In 1957 Zhou Enlai acknowledged that 'in the wage reforms of the past, it was a big mistake that we determined the wages of unskilled workers ... at a relatively high level. We must correct this mistake ... Under the situation where the living standard of the peasants cannot be improved swiftly, workers should not demand too much to have their livelihood improved' (quoted in Takahara 1992: 45). Deng Xiaoping published a report in the same year stating that 'there should not be too large a gap between workers' and peasants' lives, and between urban and rural lives. In enhancing living standards, we must take into account the conditions of a good majority of the nation. For the time being, therefore, we must adhere to a rational, low-wage system' (quoted in ibid. 44). Another leader, Song Ping, also argued for curtailing the future growth of urban wages. In this way, peasant migration would be controlled and the larger surplus would generate more urban investment and employment (Song 1957).

Figure 2.3 shows the movement of wages over the period of centralized planning. We see that real wages fell in the four years after 1957, to a level below that of 1952. There are various reasons for this decline. Bonuses and piece-rates were abolished in 1957–8. The effect of the rational, low-wage policy was to freeze nominal wages in the state sector, and the entry of new workers into the lowest rungs of the wage ladder reduced the average wage. Moreover, the rural collapse in the wake of the Great Leap Forward raised

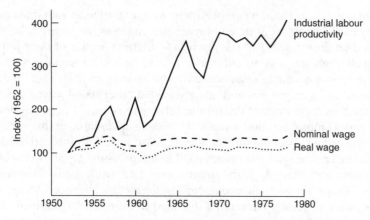

FIG. 2.3 *Average nominal and real wages and labour productivity*

the urban cost-of-living. Thereafter both nominal and real wages were very steady for a prolonged period. In 1977 they were 144 and 103 per cent respectively of their 1952 levels. Takahara (1992: 62, 66) described widespread unrest among workers in the years 1975–7, reflecting grassroots discontent at the stagnation of real wages. It is notable from Figure 2.3 that real wages did not respond to the rapid growth in labour productivity that took place during the period of centralized planning (here measured by gross output per employee in industry).

The government was as concerned with the distribution of urban wages as with their level. The span of incomes within enterprises was reduced from forty or fifty fold, reflecting scarcity and abundance in the market economy prior to 1949, to four or seven fold in the centrally planned economy of the mid-1950s (Howe 1973: 35–8). The wage reform of 1956 widened occupational differentials, reflecting a State Council document of that year: 'the phenomenon of egalitarianism is still relatively serious. . . . to be energetically overcome' (quoted by Korzec and Whyte 1981: 256). The wage adjustment of 1963 reversed the process, however, and during the Cultural Revolution wage policy was strongly egalitarian. Political activists exploited dissatisfaction created by income differentials and preferred social to technical criteria in wage-setting. The need for material incentives was played down, and premiums and bonuses based on work performance were abolished.

Of all aspects of planning in China, 'the allocation of labour resources is by far the furthest from the market mechanism' (White 1988: 14). After 1957 the State labour bureaux exercised a virtual monopoly over the allocation of urban labour, and the scope for individual expression of preferences was very limited. The initial assignment to a job was very important: the first job was often the last. Job rights were firmly entrenched. The security and human dignity provided by employment were regarded as valuable ends in themselves. Almost all State employees, and many in the larger collectives, enjoyed an 'iron rice bowl' (*tie fan wan*)—lifetime tenure of their job at a relatively high wage in an enterprise providing a mini welfare state. The enterprise was normally responsible for the housing, pensions, and medical treatment of its employees and often provided other social services as well.

There was an important dualism in urban employment between perma-nent state employees and others. This dualism created a hierarchy of preferences and consequent pressure for state jobs. Administrative labour allocation encouraged overmanning. Under pressure to alleviate urban unemployment, state labour bureaux expected work units (*danwei*) to accept labour above their economic requirements. The need to increase employment generally dominated the need to raise labour productivity by using it more efficiently. The State's response to urban unemployment was to allocate it away and to permit the practice of job inheritance (*ding ti*). The State was concerned with the socio-political consequences of urban unemployment.

We can summarize the urban labour situation during the period of cen-tralized planning as follows. The system was heavily directed, providing very little scope for individual preferences or responses to economic incentives. It was the plan, and not market wages, that governed labour supply and demand. The centralized control of enterprises provided no inducement for the efficient use of labour, and indeed surplus labour was imposed on enter-prises. Workers had few incentives to acquire human capital, to work efficiently, or to improve work methods. On the other hand, urban workers occupied a privileged position in Chinese society, enjoying higher income, greater security, and better social services than did the rural peasants. Moreover, because the State exercised great control over the system, it was able to pursue its various objectives—egalitarian and ideological.

2.2.2 The reform era, 1978–95

The reformist coalition gave first priority to agricultural and rural reform, which proved to be relatively easy, and only later turned seriously to indus-trial and urban reform, which was more difficult. The decentralization of decision-taking to state enterprises, and their powers to retain some of their profits, meant that wages were no longer completely in the control of gov-ernment. A second reason for diminution of state control over wages was the growth of the non-state sector—collective, private, and joint-partnership enterprises. In 1978 the state sector accounted for 78 per cent of urban employment; in 1995 this figure was down to 71 per cent, and the private sector employed 9 per cent of the total (Table 2.6). The loss of con-trol resulted in upward pressure on wages. Table 2.6 also shows that real wages grew annually by 4.8 per cent in the period 1978–85, and by 4.1 per

TABLE 2.6 *Wages in urban China, total and by ownership category, 1952–95*

	Total	State-owned	Urban collective	Other
Nominal wages (yuan p.a.)				
1952	445	446	348	
1962	551	592	405	
1978	615	644	506	
1985	1,148	1,213	967	1,436
1995	5,500	5,625	3,931	7,463
Nominal wages (state-owned = 100)				
1952	100	100	78	
1962	93	100	68	
1978	96	100	79	
1985	95	100	80	118
1995	98	100	70	133
Real wages (1952 = 100)				
1952	100	100	100	
1962	92	99	86	
1978	110	115	116	
1985	153	162	165	
1995	229	234	210	
Rate of change of real wages (% p.a.)				
1952–62	−0.8	0.0	−1.4	
1962–78	1.1	1.0	1.9	
1978–85	4.8	4.9	5.1	
1985–95	4.1	3.8	2.5	5.0
Rate of change of industrial labour productivity (% p.a.)				
1952–62	5.8			
1962–78	5.4			
1978–85	5.6			
1985–95	14.0			
Share of total employment (%)				
1952	100	98	2	
1962	100	77	23	
1978	100	78	22	
1985	100	73	27	0
1995	100	71	20	9

Notes: 1. The sector 'other', not reported before 1985 and negligibly small in that year, comprises (local and foreign) private and joint-partnership enterprises but not self-employed individuals.

2. Borensztein and Ostry (1996: 225) argue that industrial output is underdeflated, especially since 1989, implying exaggeration of the growth rate of industrial labour productivity.

Sources: PRC, SSB 1993: 110, 212; 1996: 117, 255.

cent in the period 1985–95, and that this outcome was similar across all forms of ownership.

Bonuses and piece-rates were reintroduced in 1978. The wage adjustment of 1979 stressed incentives and performance at both individual and enterprise levels. Enterprise profit retention (up to a low ceiling) was introduced in 1979: retained profits could be used for bonus payments. Ceilings on bonuses were abolished in 1984 but a progressive bonus tax was introduced to provide an indirect brake on wages (Takahara 1992: 139–40). Table 2.7 shows bonuses and their equivalent, above-norm piece-rate payments, rising from 2 to 16 per cent of total wages between 1978 and 1984. In the words of a prominent economist, Xue Muqiao: socialist managers 'tend to side with their workers, being ready to pay more wages and premiums in order to please their workers on the one hand and to benefit themselves indirectly on the other' (quoted in ibid. 115).

The major wage reform of 1984 introduced the 'structured wage system', which was intended to eliminate anomalies and to improve incentives and morale. A worker's remuneration now had four components: base wage, position wage (according to the job), seniority wage, and bonus. The wage reform also raised pay in the state non-enterprise sector by some 20 per cent to bring it into line with pay in the enterprise sector, which included bonuses.

Under the 'management responsibility system' state enterprises were generally able to raise wages according to economic performance, as judged by profits and tax payments. The bonus continued to rise both in absolute and relative terms until 1993, when it represented 22 per cent of the total wage. The average bonus fell as a result of the 1994 wage reform, when it was partly consolidated into the basic wage (Table 2.7). Generally, wage segmentation among enterprises increased as a result of the reforms, according to the productivity and profitability of enterprises.

We see from Figure 2.4, showing the annual rate of change in the average real wage, that its behaviour was erratic, with spurts in 1978–80, 1984–6, and 1990–4, and troughs in the intervening periods 1981–3 and 1987–9. The pattern is similar irrespective of forms of ownership. It is not amenable to statistical analysis, as real wages remained largely a matter of government policy, which was more exogenous than endogenous.

The rapid increase in real wages between 1977 and 1980 represented a policy change after the long stagnation during the Cultural Revolution. This was followed by three years of consolidation. The most rapid increase in real wages (averaging 15 per cent) occurred in 1984, as a result of the basic wage reform of that year and the enterprise reforms which partly decentralized wage-setting. The fall in real wages over the period 1987–9 represented tardy government response to the boom-induced inflation and government concern about the role of wages in increasing demand and costs. It is notable from the curve showing the rate of inflation that inflation

TABLE 2.7 *The bonus and above-norm piece-rate wage in real terms and as a percentage of the total wage per employee, 1978–95*

	Bonus and above-norm piece-rate wage	
	Real (1985 = 100)	As percentage of total wage
1978	9.1	2.0
1979	37.4	7.5
1980	48.6	9.1
1981	59.6	11.1
1982	67.5	12.4
1983	71.5	12.9
1984	96.6	16.4
1985	100.0	15.1
1986	105.6	14.6
1987	119.8	16.8
1988	139.5	19.2
1989	135.3	19.5
1990	136.9	18.2
1991	131.6	18.9
1992	156.4	20.8
1993	177.3	22.2
1994	152.8	17.9
1995	143.3	16.3

Source: PRC, MOL 1996: tables 1-10, 1-31, 1-32.

responded with a lag to the wage increase of 1984 and that real wages fell as demand-led inflation accelerated after 1986. Resumed real wage growth in 1989 may reflect a catching up, as inflation decelerated, and a political response to the events of 1989. In the 1990s expectations of inflation were incorporated into wage-setting: real wages continued to grow rapidly as inflation accelerated after 1990.

The growth of real wages over the reform period (averaging more than 4 per cent per annum) meant that staff and workers benefited from some, but not all, of the growth in industrial labour productivity (over 10 per cent per annum). Can we be confident that there was a causal relationship between them? This question requires an econometric analysis of the sort conducted by Hussain and Zhuang (1994). They used a panel dataset of over 500 state-owned enterprises covering the years 1986–91. They did not analyse labour productivity *per se* but instead profit per worker, which in the Chinese context can generally be expected to rise as labour productivity rises. Regular wages were found to be insensitive to profitability. By contrast, bonuses in profit-making enterprises increased with profitability. The

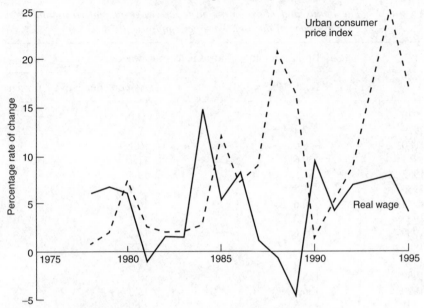

FIG. 2.4 *Annual percentage rate of change over previous year in the real wage and in the urban consumer price index*

marginal propensity for the bonus to increase with profit was 0.04 (Hussain and Zhuang 1994: table 5). However, bonuses in loss-making enterprises were predominantly positive, and bore no relationship to the scale of losses. Given soft budgets, bonuses are available to all, but workers are able additionally to wrest part of any quasi-rents from their employers.

The egalitarian wage policy of the Cultural Revolution was reversed after Mao's death. The wage reform of 1979 reinstated and enlarged performance-related payments by enterprises and the widening of differentials. Economic incentives for workers were now approved policy, and the official view was that 'egalitarianism is the arch-enemy of our wage readjustment' (quoted by Korzec and Whyte 1981: 259). Nevertheless, the period 1978–85 did not see a rise in occupational differentials (Hay *et al.* 1994). Rather, as the productivity and pay of production workers rose, so other workers were given the same absolute increases in the absence of market criteria and in the presence of egalitarian pressures within enterprises.

The perennial conflict between the claims of efficiency and of equality intensified as the wage reforms progressed. The attempts to reward effort and skills met with resistance from those who stood to lose, for instance older workers and workers in non-profit work units. Managers were responsive to these pressures, which were strengthened by the fact that enterprises were often social entities, i.e. communities based on residence. Managers recognized that morale was important for enterprise performance, and that wage differentiation could be counter-productive insofar as it caused grass-roots discontent (Takahara 1992: 115, 163, 176).

Walder (1987) presents a gloomy assessment of the attempt to introduce performance incentives into the pay structure: a web of factory interests gave rise to a fairly equal distribution of bonuses. With liberalization, work-ers became more calculative and more contentious; aided by their (intra-enterprise) workers' congresses, they could now influence management. Management therefore encouraged worker cooperation by maximizing bonuses and minimizing contention through the fairly equal distribution of rewards. If bonuses acted as incentives, they did so more at the enterprise than at the individual level.

During the 1980s the 'iron rice bowl' came under attack from pro-market reformers within the government. The reforms introduced elements of a labour market. The formal network of state labour bureaux was partly bypassed, so reducing administrative controls over recruitment. The greater responsibility given to managers in enterprises offered them greater power to hire, discipline, and dismiss. The contract labour system, intro-duced in 1983 and strengthened in 1986, gave new entrants to state employ-ment neither security of tenure nor all the welfare benefits of permanent employees. However, the new system encountered resistance. It was held to challenge the values of collectivism and loyalty to the firm, and to create unjustifiable inequalities. Many managers, being concerned to main-tain good labour relations, were reluctant to confront the iron rice bowl. Only in booming and efficient Shenzhen, where workers valued freedom and mobility, was most labour employed on contracts of limited duration (Korzec 1992: 29, 51). By 1990 only 12 per cent of employees were on contract terms. The State gave momentum to the policy only in 1995, when this proportion rose to 41 per cent, from 26 per cent in the previous year (PRC, SSB 1996: 107).

During the reform era, the expression of interests was institutionalized at the enterprise level (Takahara 1992: 181). This helps to explain why, despite the apparent abandonment of the right to work as the founda-tion of state employment policy, in reality little changed during the 1980s. Government continued to bear the cost of surplus employees, and no significant redundancies or dismissals occurred. The State was reluctant to implement market reforms that might undermine Communist Party power (Korzec 1992: p. viii).

The fiscal burden of some state-owned enterprises became more serious as marketization occurred and competition intensified. In 1985, the losses of loss-making enterprises represented 2 per cent of total pre-tax profits; in 1993, they came to 33 per cent (PRC, SSB 1996: 429). The attention of the State turned increasingly to reform of its failing enterprises. The 'optimal labour reorganization scheme', designed to reduce surplus labour in the state-owned enterprises, was extended nationwide in 1989. The selected enterprises were subjected to reorganization, redeployment, and retraining of labour. A combination of training and attrition, i.e. no recruitment, was used to limit urban unemployment. Nevertheless, as the pace of reform accelerated, redundancies became inevitable. In 1995 the national urban registered unemployment rate was a mere 2.9 per cent. However, to this could be added the *xia gang* workers (redundant workers no longer attending but nominally employed at a low wage by their relinquishing enterprises), representing another 3.1 per cent, as well as job-seeking rural–urban migrants (PRC, MOL 1996: tables 1–9, 8–1).

By the mid-1990s there was still not a properly functioning labour market in urban China. The move had instead been towards decentralization of labour management. The urban workforce was sharply segmented, both by employer and according to urban or rural registration. Real wages were continuing to rise rapidly. However, as a counter to this, the employment security accorded to urban workers by the iron rice bowl was being eroded. The State was forced into this policy, despite the potential urban discontent, by the deteriorating fiscal position. It was encouraged by the prospect of a sharp decline in the number of entrants to the urban labour force, a helpful legacy of the one-child family policy that had been introduced in 1980.

2.3 RELATIVE DEPRIVATION AND POLITICAL PRESSURES

It is an interesting issue whether urban workers and rural peasants possess the political power to influence government policies in China and, if so, which of these groups has the greater political power. The notion of 'relative deprivation' is relevant here. Relative deprivation is defined as a discrepancy between people's 'value expectations' (their aspirations to have things or lifestyles) and their 'value capabilities' (their capabilities to fulfil these aspirations) (Gurr 1970: 24). Gurr argued that the potential for people to rebel depends partly on the strength of the relative deprivation that they feel. The value expectations of a group may depend on the rate of value gain of the most rapidly gaining group of similar socio-economic status, or on the rate and duration of the group's past value gains. Thus, relative deprivation is likely to increase if a group feels left behind in the development process or if it experiences a halt after a period of sustained economic improvement.

Huntington (1968) argued that the simple correlation between poverty and political instability is weak: traditional societies are often stable and abjectly poor people are often conservative. Similarly, economically developed, modern societies tend to be stable. It is rapidly changing, modernizing societies that are politically unstable. Economic development increases value capabilities but it also increases value expectations, and it is possible for the latter to outpace the former. For instance, economic development creates new economic groups with their own group objectives, it can increase the capacity for group organization, it increases geographical and social mobility, it can increase corruption if political institutions do not match economic and social changes, it broadens people's horizons and creates new wants, and it can increase income inequality. With such changes come hope, envy, and rising confidence, and it is easy for value expectations to outpace value capabilities.

Huntington (1968: 55) traced the effect of modernization on political instability in three stages. First, the degree of modernizing change in relation to the pace of economic development determines the degree of relative deprivation. Secondly, the degree of relative deprivation in relation to opportunities for economic redress (such as economic improvement and mobility) determines the extent of political participation. Thirdly, the extent of political participation in relation to the political institutions available to accommodate it determines the extent of political protest and instability. He argued that most modernizing societies offer inadequate opportunities for improvement and mobility to prevent the growth of political participation, and that their political institutions lag too far behind to offer legitimate channels by which demands can be expressed and addressed. Hence the link between modernization and political instability.

Consider the relevance of this framework to China. Throughout the Communist period, in both urban and rural China, if discontent has been felt it has had either to be simply endured or to be expressed in political protest. It is arguable that in the Maoist period government had two important economic achievements: it carried out a popular land reform for the rural peasants and it gave urban workers a lifestyle that was better and more secure than that of the peasants. Beyond these, politics and not economics was in command. The State had sufficient control over society to be able to neglect economic achievements in favour of ideological objectives. It would be difficult to claim that the political power of urban workers or rural peasants, even in passive or latent form, had significant influence on government policies. The Communist Party dominated.

The reform period presents a different picture. We have seen how, once they perceived that change was possible, peasants took the lead in the rural reforms. Both value expectations and value capabilities are likely to have risen very rapidly in rural China up to 1984. Thereafter, the relative stagnation of agriculture probably increased perceptions of relative deprivation among those rural people who could not benefit from rural industrialization. Although the peasants' information is limited and they have restricted and localized orbits of comparison, it is likely that the growth of rural inequality contributed to feelings of relative deprivation. It is also likely, however, that the fragmented, localized, unorganized nature of peasant society meant that expressions of discontent were easily manageable and containable, and were not a serious political threat to the State.

The rapid growth of real wages during the 1980s should have raised the value capabilities of urban workers but, again, their value expectations could have grown even faster. The State's determination to protect urban residents from rising food prices suggests that it feared that the loss of urban privileges would generate protest. The growth of corruption and ostentatious consumption no doubt added to feelings of relative deprivation in the cities. In the early 1980s urban people had more reason to feel deprived than rural people but in the late 1980s the reverse was the case. Nevertheless, the government probably remained more sensitive to urban discontent because it was capable of being converted into damaging action. Townspeople are more concentrated, more interactive, better informed, and better organized than villagers.

The notion that urban-dwellers might feel relative deprivation in relation to rural-dwellers, despite the undoubted urban advantage, was advanced by Putterman (1993: 354): 'protection of urban workers was a constant source of political anxiety for the government because the initial gains of reform were enjoyed most by peasants, and to a disproportionate extent by precisely those peasants with whom urban-dwellers were likely to come into contact, the residents of the rural areas nearest the cities.'

The phenomenon of rural–urban migration has interesting implications for our analysis of political pressures. In the commune period the prohibition on movement from rural to urban areas or even within rural areas greatly curtailed information flows and limited the basis on which feelings of relative deprivation could be formed. The relaxation of controls in the reform period had two countervailing effects on rural people. On the one hand, by broadening their horizons it might have made poor rural people feel deprived. On the other hand, it could act as a safety valve for the desperate and the ambitious. As in-migration gained momentum in the 1990s, the effect on the urban areas was probably to increase the relative deprivation both of the city residents, whose lifestyles were threatened by the influx, and of the migrants, who were crowded into inferior positions and treated as inferiors.

This section has attempted to answer a limited question concerning the relative political power of workers and peasants. It has not attempted to provide a full analysis of the political pressures that enter policy formation. The structure of authority in China is also important, no less so because it is fragmented. Major policy changes require sufficient consensus among the top leaders and the cooperation of the bureaucracy at various levels and with various concerns, including the bureaucrats' own interests (Zhang and Yi 1994). Our analysis of relative deprivation thus provides only a partial explanation of government policies as they affect rural and urban people.

2.4 CONCLUSION

The task that we set ourselves in this chapter was to explain the broad trends in the movement of real income in rural and urban China, and in the ratio of these incomes. The most important point to emerge is that the ratio has been large throughout the period of Communist Party rule, generally having a value of between 2 and 3. This rural–urban income divide demanded an explanation, and the movements in the ratio helped to provide the explanation.

We recognized the overwhelming importance of politics. The retention of power was a predominant influence, and ideological objectives were a luxury to be pursued when power appeared to be secure. Often economic factors did not govern the economic outcomes directly. Their influence, such as it was, appeared indirectly, by affecting the interests of various political actors and provoking political responses. We attempted to analyse economic outcomes in terms of the interests of various institutions and groups in society, and the pressures—normally implicit rather than explicit, passive rather than active—that they could exert on a government whose primary objective was to stay in power. Underlying the 'urban bias' observable in state policies and institutions was 'state bias', to be explained in terms of the concerns and objectives of the Chinese leadership. We argued that there is no simple relationship between poverty and political pressure, as it is complicated by the notion of relative deprivation and by institutional and organizational strength.

During the period of centralized planning and the communes, the main economic policy objective was rapid urban industrialization. The capital required for industrialization was to be extracted from the peasantry. The communes can be seen partly as an institutional response to that need. This role, and the State's failure to solve the resultant incentive problems, help to explain the relative stagnation of rural income per capita up to 1978. Although the government espoused a 'rational, low-wage system' for urban workers during much of the planning period, real wages were set at a level which enabled urban households to maintain a much higher standard of living than their rural counterparts. The disparity was exacerbated by the job security and welfare benefits provided by urban (very largely, state) employers. There is a fine line between 'efficiency wage' and 'political pressure' explanations of the relatively high urban wage. Worker discontent, low morale, and threat to political stability are all aspects of the latent power which residentially concentrated, interacting workers appeared to possess. The urban–rural income and consumption ratios remained high but fairly constant throughout the planning period. The exception was a sharp rise in the ratio during the famine in the wake of the Great Leap Forward, which hurt peasants more than workers.

The period of decollectivization, 1978–84, was one of rapid growth in peasant incomes. The changes reflected a shift in the concerns of the Chinese leadership from the ideological to the economic. The rural reforms were that rare economic event, a Pareto improvement, as there were hardly any losers. It is interesting that the reforms went further and faster than was intended. A process of atomized peasant behaviour and cumulative causation pulled the leadership along behind. Urban real wages also rose in this period, reflecting the change in government objectives. Nevertheless, there was a sharp fall in the urban–rural income ratio.

In the mid-1980s government attention turned from rural to urban reform policies. The once-for-all nature of the gains from decollectivization and the policy reluctance to raise food prices produced agricultural stagnation for some years after 1984, ameliorated by rapid rural industrialization and an increase in temporary migration to the cities and towns. Government policy with regard to the procurement, producer prices, and consumer prices of grain and other necessities provides a good test of the relative political influence of workers and peasants. The tardy and tortuous dismantling of the price-scissors policy suggests that the urban minority were politically more important to government than the rural majority. Urban real wages continued to grow rapidly, in no small part due to the decentralization of powers to enterprises and managerial willingness— mainly for efficiency wage reasons—to share profits with their employees. The urban–rural income ratio grew rapidly after 1984.

This chapter has provided a broad-brush sweep of the main influences on the urban–rural income divide. However, it leaves various questions unanswered. For instance, to what extent can the income gap be justified in terms of differences in the productive characteristics of urban and rural workers? Is the gap as great for urban and rural wage-employees as for urban and rural households? Is the inequality of income within both urban and rural China so great as to make the comparison of averages misleading? These and similar questions can only be answered by means of a detailed microeconomic analysis of the sort to which we turn in Chapter 3.

NOTE

1. The fact that consumption exceeds income in various years, and consistently so after 1984, is probably due to the definitions of consumption and net income being used (consumption is not defined in the *Statistical Yearbooks*). Another consumption concept, 'household living expenditure', follows the same trend as consumption (for the years in which it is available) and would produce a positive saving rate in all years.

REFERENCES

Ash, Robert F (1993). 'Agricultural policy under the impact of reform', in Y. Y. Kueh and Robert F. Ash (eds.), *Economic Trends in Chinese Agriculture*, Oxford: Clarendon Press.

Aston, Basil, Hill, Kenneth, Piazza, Allan, and Zeitz, Robin (1984). 'Famine in China, 1958–61', *Population and Development Review*, 10 (Dec.): 613–45.

Aubert, Claude (1990). 'The agricultural crisis in China at the end of the 1980s', in Jorgen Delman, Clemens Ostergaard, and Flemming Christiansen (eds.), *Remaking Peasant China*, Aarhus: Aarhus University Press.

Borensztein, Eduardo, and Ostry, Jonathan D. (1996). 'Accounting for China's growth performance', *American Economic Review. Papers and Proceedings*, 86 (2): 224–8.

Drèze, Jean, and Sen, Amartya (1989). *Hunger and Public Action*, Oxford: Clarendon Press.

Gurr, Ted Robert (1970). *Why Men Rebel*, Princeton: Princeton University Press.

Hay, Donald, Morris, Derek, Liu, Guy, and Yao Shujie (1994). *Economic Reform and State-Owned Enterprises in China, 1979–87*, Oxford: Clarendon Press.

Howe, Christopher (1973). *Wage Patterns and Wage Policy in Modern China 1919–1972*, Cambridge: Cambridge University Press.

Howes, Stephen, and Hussain, Athar (1994). 'Regional growth and inequality in rural China', Development Economics Research Programme EF No. 11, STICERD, London School of Economics.

Hua Sheng, Zhang Xuejun, and Luo Xiaopeng (1993). *China: From Revolution to Reform*, London: Macmillan.

Huntington, Samuel P. (1968). *Political Order in Changing Societies*, New Haven: Yale University Press.

Hussain, Athar, and Zhuang Juzhong (1994). 'Impact of reforms on wage and employment determination in Chinese state enterprises, 1986–1991', Development Economics Research Programme EF No. 12, STICERD, London School of Economics.

Kelliher, Daniel (1992). *Peasant Power in China. The Era of Rural Reform 1979–1989*, New Haven: Yale University Press.

Korzec, Michael, and Whyte, Martin King (1981). 'Reading notes: the Chinese wage system', *China Quarterly*, 86 (June): 248–73.

——(1992). *Labour and the Failure of Reform in China*, London: Macmillan.

Kristoff, Nicholas D., and Wudunn, Sheryl (1994). *China Wakes*, London: Nicholas Brealey.

Lin Justin Yifu (1990). 'Collectivization and China's agricultural crisis in 1959–1961', *Journal of Political Economy*, 98 (Dec.): 1228–52.

——(1992). 'Rural reforms and agricultural growth in China', *American Economic Review*, 82 (1): 34–51.

——(1994). 'Chinese agriculture: institutional changes and performance', in T. N. Srinivasan (ed.), *Agriculture and Trade in China and India*, San Francisco: International Centre for Economic Growth.

Matsuda, Yoshiro (1990). 'Survey systems and sampling designs of Chinese household surveys, 1952–87', *The Developing Economies*, 28 (3): 329–52.

Nolan, Peter (1988). *The Political Economy of Collective Farms*, Cambridge: Polity Press.

——and White, Gordon (1984). 'Urban bias, rural bias or state bias? Urban–rural relations in post-revolutionary China', *Journal of Development Studies*, 20 (3): 52–81.

Oi, Jean C. (1989). *State and Peasant in Contemporary China*, Berkeley and Los Angeles: University of California Press.

——(1993). 'Reform and urban bias in China', *Journal of Development Studies*, 29 (4): 129–48.

Peoples' Republic of China, Ministry of Agriculture (PRC, MOA), Research Centre for Rural Economy (1993). 'Rural reform and development in China: review and prospect', theme report prepared for the International Conference on China's Rural Reform and Development in the 1990s, Beijing.

——, Ministry of Labour (PRC, MOL) (1996). *China Labour Statistical Yearbook 1996*, Beijing: China Statistical Publishing House.

——, State Statistical Bureau (PRC, SSB) (1986). *China Statistical Yearbook 1986*, Oxford: Oxford University Press.

——(PRC, SSB) (1991). *China Statistical Yearbook 1991*, Beijing: China Statistical Publishing House.

——(PRC, SSB) (1993). *China Statistical Yearbook 1993*, Beijing: China Statistical Publishing House.

——(PRC, SSB) (1995). *China Statistical Yearbook 1995*, Beijing: China Statistical Publishing House.

——(PRC, SSB) (1996). *China Statistical Yearbook 1996*, Beijing: China Statistical Publishing House.

——(PRC, SSB) (1996a). *Rural Statistical Yearbook of China 1996*, Beijing: China Statistical Publishing House (in Chinese).

Putterman, Louis (1993). *Continuity and Change in China's Rural Development*, New York: Oxford University Press.

Riskin, Carl (1987). *China's Political Economy. The Quest for Development since 1949*, Oxford: Oxford University Press.

Selden, Mark (1988). *The Political Economy of Chinese Socialism*, Armonk, New York: M. E. Sharpe.

Song Ping (1957). 'Why we must implement a rational, low-wage system', in Christopher Howe and Kenneth R. Walker (eds.) (1989), *The Foundations of the Chinese Planned Economy: A Documentary Survey, 1953–65*, London: Macmillan.

Takahara, Akio (1992). *The Politics of Wage Policy in Post-Revolutionary China*, London: Macmillan.

Taylor, Jeffrey R. (1988). 'Rural employment trends and the legacy of surplus labour 1928–86', *China Quarterly*, 116 (Dec.): 736–66.

Walder, Andrew G. (1987). 'Wage reform and the web of factory interests', *China Quarterly*, 109 (Mar.): 22–41.

Wen, Guangzhong James (1989). 'The current land tenure and its impact on long-term performance of the farming sector: the case of modern China', Ph.D. diss, University of Chicago.

White, Gordon (1993). *Riding the Tiger. The Politics of Economic Reform in Post-Mao China*, London: Macmillan.

—— (1988). 'Evolving relations between state and worker in the reform of China's urban industrial economy', in Stephan Feuchtwang, Athar Hussain, and Thierry Pairault (eds.), *Transforming China's Economy in the Eighties*, ii, Boulder, Color.: Westview Press.

Zhang Weiying, and Gang Yi (1994). 'China's gradual reform: an historical perspective', February, Oxford, processed.

Zhao Renwei (1993). 'Three features of the distribution of income during the transition to reform', in Keith Griffin and Zhao Renwei (eds.), *The Distribution of Income in China*, London: Macmillan.

3

The Rural–Urban Income Divide:
Microeconomics

In this chapter we again investigate and compare household incomes in
rural and urban China. The difference from Chapter 2 is that we generally
use micro-analysis and concentrate on one point in time. The year chosen
is 1988 because in that year a national household survey was conducted
by the Institute of Economics, Chinese Academy of Social Sciences (CASS)
to investigate income distribution in China.[1] The existence of a detailed,
nationally representative household survey, specially designed not only
to measure income but also to explain its determinants and the reasons
for income inequality, enables us to examine the causes of the urban–
rural income differential. A virtue of the survey was that it attempted to
encompass the various non-cash forms of income and subsidy which are
important in a socialist country.

In Section 3.1 the urban–rural income differential for China as a whole
is examined and its underlying sources are probed. The CASS survey results
are first compared and contrasted with the official household survey conducted by the State Statistical Bureau (SSB) in the same year. We measure
the net effect of fiscal transfers on rural and urban households to illustrate
the redistributive role of government. Income functions are estimated for
both rural and urban China, and are used to show how various characteristics affect household income. The income difference is then decomposed
into the part which is due to differences in measured characteristics and the
residual which is independent of characteristics. An overall comparison of
rural and urban incomes can be misleading. Section 3.2 disaggregates the
sample into provinces, so permitting an analysis of interprovince variation.
The hypothesis is that, because government polices tend to standardize
urban incomes across China, the urban–rural differential is greater in the
poorer provinces.

It would be misleading to concentrate on the intersector inequality
between rural and urban China if it were dwarfed by intrasector inequality. The chapter goes on to examine more generally the income inequality
within the urban areas (Section 3.3) and the rural areas (Section 3.4).
Section 3.3 is concerned with inequality of income from employment and
its determinants, and with how this wage structure relates to household
income distribution. Section 3.4 analyses rural income inequality, which has
always been considerable on account of China's great size and unevenly

distributed factor endowments. This inequality was exacerbated during the reform period as some households and some areas developed faster than others. The 1988 CASS survey and other surveys are used to examine the extent of economic polarization in rural China. An important source of rural inequality is the development of rural industry. Section 3.5 again uses the 1988 CASS survey to compare and explain the wage levels and structures of individual wage employees in rural and urban China. Light is thrown on the operation of rural and urban labour markets. Finally, Section 3.6 draws together this diverse evidence to place the rural–urban income disparity in the context of general income inequality in China.

3.1 THE RURAL–URBAN INCOME GAP: DECOMPOSITION

Our main source of information in this chapter is the 1988 CASS household income survey. We begin by explaining the nature of the income data collected in the survey and their relationship to the income data from the larger, official SSB household survey of that year. The intended advantage of the specially designed survey was that it would use more appropriate concepts of income and collect more ancillary information to help explain the determination of household incomes than did the SSB survey, which anyway is published only in descriptive and fairly aggregative form.

The CASS sample was selected in a stratified random way from the sampling frame used by the SSB for the national household survey and other surveys; it is therefore a subset of the national household survey sample. Like the larger survey, the rural and urban samples were selected separately. Whereas the rural survey covered all twenty-eight provinces (excluding Tibet) and contained 10,250 households, the urban survey covered ten provinces and contained 9,000 households. The number of households actually analysed is normally smaller owing to the elimination of households via consistency checks and incomplete reporting. The survey is described in the annexe to Griffin and Zhao (1993).

Table 3.1 provides a comparison of the two sources in 1988, beginning with the SSB survey. The mean income per capita of urban households was 2.19 times that of rural households. The corresponding ratio of household 'living expenditure' per capita (the best measure of household consumption) was 2.32. The ratio of mean household incomes (1.61) was smaller than that of its per capita equivalent because households were smaller in urban areas. It cannot be claimed, however, that the difference in mean household income per capita was due to this difference in household size (the mean urban household was 27 per cent smaller) because there were also fewer urban workers per household (31 per cent fewer).

The most important contrast between the two sources is that mean household income per capita is higher in the CASS survey: 44 per cent higher in

TABLE 3.1 *Summary statistics from the SSB and CASS household income surveys, 1988*

	SSB Survey				CASS Survey			
	National	Urban	Rural	Urban (rural = 100)	National	Urban	Rural	Urban (rural = 100)
No. of households surveyed	102,131	34,945	67,186	52	19,267	9,009	10,258	88
Mean persons per household	4.60	3.63	4.94	73	4.63	3.53	5.01	70
Mean workers per household	2.71	2.03	2.95	69	2.74	2.01	2.99	67
Mean household income per capita (yuan p.a.)	625.1	1,192.1	476.6	219	1,074.6	1,902.1	786.7	242
Mean household consumption per capita (yuan p.a.)	638.5	1,104.0	476.6	232	—	—	—	—
Mean household income (yuan p.a.)	2,878.2	4,327.2	2,692.0	161	4,713.1	6,748.1	4,005.1	168

Note: In the case of the CASS survey, the national mean statistics are weighted means of the urban and rural figures, the weights being the urban (0.258) and rural (0.742) shares of the population in 1988. In the case of the SSB survey, mean household income is derived from the figures for mean household income per capita and mean persons per household. Workers are defined as persons aged 16 to 65.

Sources: SSB survey: PRC, SSB 1991, sect. 8. CASS survey: basic data.

the rural sample and 60 per cent higher in the urban sample. In a sense, this was deliberate. One of the purposes of the CASS survey was to provide a comprehensive measure of income, encompassing elements that appear to be inadequately covered in the official estimates. These include forms of income-in-kind and subsidy that are important in China.

The difference in rural income per capita estimated from the two surveys is almost entirely attributable to differences in definition rather than in measurement. In particular, it is due to the inclusion of the rental value of housing, the more comprehensive coverage of net direct subsidies, and the valuation of income-in-kind at market prices rather than at state purchase prices for farm products. By contrast, the SSB used the contract purchase prices at which the State purchased a major proportion of marketed farm products, which in 1988 were below market prices.

The even larger difference in the two estimates of urban income per capita is due mainly to the housing subsidy enjoyed by most urban households, which the SSB ignored. The replacement value of a household's dwelling unit was calculated from information on its size and amenities, and the rental value was estimated at 8 per cent of the replacement cost; from which a net subsidy could be derived. The CASS survey had a more comprehensive coverage and a more appropriate valuation of subsidies and of incomes-in-kind. Other direct subsidies and payments-in-kind, such as ration coupons, were valued by means of the relevant market prices, and rents of owner-occupied housing were imputed.

The urban–rural income ratio was higher in the CASS survey (2.42) than in the SSB survey (2.19) because its proportionate revision of the urban estimate exceeded that of the rural estimate. In either case there is a huge urban–rural income gap to be explained, but the CASS estimate is likely to be a better guide to relative welfare levels.

A remarkable finding of the CASS survey is the urban–rural contrast in net subsidies (subsidies minus direct taxes). These are shown in Table 3.2. An extremely high proportion of urban income, 38 per cent, is provided by the State or its enterprises in the form of net subsidies. This is generally income-in-kind for which little charge is made, in particular housing and ration coupons. Rural households are treated very differently: the average rural household makes a net payment, equal to 2 per cent of its income, to the government. Thus fiscal intermediation via direct taxes and subsidies seriously exacerbates urban–rural inequality. If government subsidies and direct taxes were not in place, the ratio of income per capita would fall from 2.42 to 1.48. In fact, the total urban net subsidy of 720 yuan is over 90 per cent of the total rural income of 787 yuan (Khan *et al.* 1993: 34).

Table 3.3 and Figure 3.1 illustrate the rural and urban distributions of household income per capita in the 1988 CASS survey. The figure gives the percentage of each sample in each 100-yuan income class. The difference in the means is reflected in the frequency distributions. The rural distribution

TABLE 3.2 *Net subsidies to rural and urban households: 1988 CASS survey*

	Yuan per capita p.a.	
	Rural	Urban
Net subsidy	−14.4	719.9
of which: housing subsidy		334.1
ration coupon subsidy		97.0
other net subsidies		288.8
Income	786.7	1,902.1
Income before direct taxes and subsidies	801.1	1,182.2
Net subsidy as a proportion of income (%)	−1.8	37.8

Sources: Table 3.1; Khan *et al.* 1993: 30–7.

TABLE 3.3 *Rural and urban household income distributions, measures of central tendency and dispersion: 1988 CASS survey*

	Income per capita (yuan p.a.)		
	Rural	Urban	Urban (rural = 100)
Mean	801	1,902	237
Median	668	1,687	252
Mode	625	1,425	228
Standard deviation	601	978	163
Coefficient of variation (%)	75.0	51.5	68
Gini coefficient (%)	33.5	23.7	71
No. of observations	9,417	8,930	

Note: Some rural households reported negative net income after deduction of inputs; these were excluded from the analysis.

is to the left of the urban; it is also more peaked. The median is 83 per cent of the mean in the rural sample and 89 per cent in the urban: hence the higher ratio for the medians than for the means. The urban distribution, having a higher standard deviation, is more widely dispersed in absolute terms. However, the rural relative dispersion is greater: both the coefficient of variation and the Gini coefficient are larger for the rural sample. The urban Gini is low by international standards (23 per cent) and the rural Gini less atypical (34 per cent).

The CASS survey can be used to examine the reasons for the income gap between urban and rural China. How far is it attributable to differences in the characteristics of urban and rural workers and how far to urban–rural

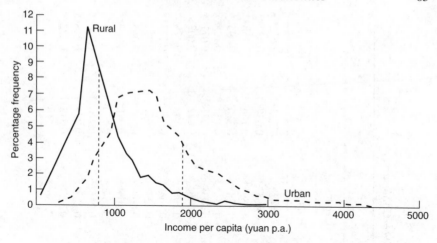

FIG. 3.1 *Frequency distribution of urban and rural household income per capita,*
1988

differences in the income-generation process? In a combined urban and rural sample the coefficient on urban location (rural location being the omitted category) is highly significant and large in the specification yielding the highest value of adjusted R^2. It implies that, holding all other characteristics constant, the urban/rural income ratio is 2.12.

Specifications that pool the samples and allow for urban–rural differences in the income-generation process solely by means of an urban dummy variable are too simple. This is established by a Chow test and by the estimation of the regressions in Table 3.4 using the pooled samples and a full set of interaction terms (interacting urban location with the other explanatory variables). The majority of the interaction terms are significant in each case, indicating that most coefficients are significantly different in the two samples. For that reason only the separate functions are presented in Table 3.4.

Regressions (1) and (2) contain the full rural sample, the difference being that (1) contains no location terms and (2) distinguishes eastern, middle, and western China. In (3) the rural sample is confined to the provinces contained in the urban sample and there is a set of province dummy variables. The dependent variable is in every case the logarithm of household income per capita ($y = \ln Y$). The independent variables are a set of characteristics (X) of the household or its head.

Surprisingly, female-headed households have significantly higher income per capita in both rural and urban areas, and particularly in the former. This might reflect compositional effects and, in the former case, the presence of husbands in the urban areas. Rural income is raised substantially if the household head has education to primary grade 3 but additional education

TABLE 3.4 Income functions for rural and urban households: 1988 CASS survey

Independent variable		Coefficient					
		Rural			Urban		
		Eq. (1)	Eq. (2)	Eq. (3)	Eq. (1)	Eq. (2)	Eq. (3)
Intercept		6.359**	6.556**	6.204**	7.542**	7.733**	7.632**
Female household head	S_2	0.221**	0.209**	0.204**	0.065**	0.058*	0.024*
College and above	E_1	0.144	0.092	−0.033	0.189**	0.166**	0.158**
Technical high school	E_2	0.213**	0.153**	0.179*	0.124**	0.110**	0.095**
Upper-middle school	E_3	0.217**	0.153	0.190**	0.156**	0.134**	0.105**
Lower-middle school	E_4	0.188**	0.140**	0.162**	0.093**	0.071**	0.071**
4–6 years of primary school	E_5	0.175**	0.135**	0.103**	0.046**	0.022	0.002
Age: 16–20	A_1	−0.008	0.010	0.021	0.206**	0.193**	0.228**
21–5	A_2	0.013	0.045	0.037	0.166**	0.154**	0.147**
31–5	A_4	0.106**	0.085**	0.082*	0.033**	0.031*	0.024*
36–40	A_5	0.191**	0.145**	0.150**	0.067**	0.069**	0.045**
41–5	A_6	0.225**	0.183**	0.223**	0.105**	0.096**	0.069**
46–50	A_7	0.216**	0.168**	0.185**	0.164**	0.156**	0.143**
51–5	A_8	0.222**	0.164**	0.198**	0.235**	0.240**	0.212**
56–60	A_9	0.165**	0.126**	0.163**	0.288**	0.276**	0.248**
61–5	A_{10}	0.216**	0.150**	0.234**	0.315**	0.313**	0.272**
66–	A_{11}	0.226**	0.155**	0.200**	0.186**	0.164**	0.138**

		(1)	(2)	(3)	(4)	(5)	(6)
Ethnic minority	R_2	-0.142**	-0.098*	-0.001	0.009	-0.011	0.014
Not Party member	CP_2	-0.154**	-0.131**	-0.129**	-0.062**	-0.077**	-0.075**
No. of household members = 2	N_2	0.010	0.059	0.247*	-0.123**	-0.123**	-0.141**
= 3	N_3	-0.051	-0.026	0.224*	-0.414**	-0.405**	-0.436**
= 4	N_4	-0.283**	-0.223**	0.002	-0.632**	-0.605**	-0.650**
= 5	N_5	-0.440**	-0.359**	-0.115	-0.801**	-0.761**	-0.814**
= 6	N_6	-0.559**	-0.465**	-0.236*	-0.965**	-0.904**	-0.978**
= 7	N_7	-0.675**	-0.574**	-0.364**	-1.007**	-1.000**	-1.059**
= 8	N_8	-0.697**	-0.584**	-0.358**	-1.176**	-1.140**	-1.258*
No. of household workers = 2	W_2	0.248**	0.252**	0.277**	0.215**	0.207**	0.198**
= 3	W_3	0.360*	0.363**	0.372**	0.364**	0.350**	0.346**
= 4	W_4	0.456**	0.447**	0.442**	0.504**	0.478**	0.488**
= 5	W_5	0.494**	0.484**	0.469**	0.598**	0.550**	0.544**
= 6	W_6	0.522**	0.495**	0.521**	0.741**	0.650**	0.749**
= 7	W_7	0.540**	0.513**	0.475**	0.334	0.471	0.588**
Beijing	P_1			0.318**			0.228**
Shanxi	P_4			-0.396**			-0.230**
Liaoning	P_8			-0.080*			-0.016
Anhui	P_{12}			-0.231**			-0.149**
Henan	P_{16}			-0.443**			-0.183**
Hubei	P_{17}			-0.028			-0.051**
Guangdong	P_{19}			-0.457**			0.531**

TABLE 3.4 *Continued*

Independent variable		Coefficient					
		Rural			Urban		
		Eq. (1)	Eq. (2)	Eq. (3)	Eq. (1)	Eq. (2)	Eq. (3)
Yunnan	P_{23}			-0.470**			-0.000
Gansu	P_{26}						0.085**
Area 2: middle China	L_2		-0.336**			-0.330**	
Area 3: west China	L_3		-0.356**			-0.143**	
No. of observations		9,500	9,500	3,605	9,017	9,017	9,004
Dependent mean		6.488	6.488	6.467	7.458	7.458	7.459
Adjusted R^2		0.102	0.166	0.268	0.244	0.376	0.516
F-value		35.693	58.424	33.915	95.062	165.368	240.819

Notes: 1. ** denotes statistical significance at the 1% and * at the 5% level.

2. The omitted categories in the dummy variable analysis are male (S_1), illiterate or primary school grades 1–3 (E_6), age 26–30 (A_3), Han (R_1), Party member (CP_1), one household member (N_1), one household worker (W_1), east China (L_1), Jiansgu (P_{10}).

3. $L_1 = P_1, P_2, P_3, P_6, P_9, P_{10}, P_{11}, P_{13}, P_{15}, P_{19}, P_{20}$;
   $L_2 = P_4, P_5, P_7, P_8, P_{12}, P_{14}, P_{16}, P_{17}, P_{18}$;
   $L_3 = P_{22}–P_{29}$, in the notation of Table 3.3.

4. The dependent variable is the logarithm of household income per capita.

has negligible effects, whereas urban income rises almost monotonically with the education of the head. In both sectors household income rises fairly continuously with the age of the head, peaking beyond age 60. Minority ethnic status reduces rural income significantly but has no effect in urban China. According to the characteristics of their heads, therefore, different households face different urban–rural income gaps.

Income per capita is seen to fall sharply as the number of household members rises, beyond two or three members in rural areas and from the start in urban areas. The effect is much more powerful in the urban sample. For instance, income per capita in a seven-member is only 28 per cent of that in a one-member urban household, *ceteris paribus*; the equivalent rural figure being 69 per cent (regression 3). Income per capita rises strongly with the number of household workers. Comparing households having four workers with those having one, the urban increase is 63 per cent and the rural increase 56 per cent (regression 3). Of course, members and workers tend to vary together although the average worker/member ratio falls as household size rises. The net effect is to temper the negative relationship between household size and income per capita. It is clear that the worker/dependant ratio (the number of household members aged 16–65 relative to the number outside that age range) is extremely important to household welfare.

Rural income varies significantly among the three regions of China. The area coefficients imply that the urban/rural income ratio is greater in western and smaller in middle than in eastern China. The province variables are generally significant and large, being more dispersed in rural areas. These issues are deferred to the province analysis of Section 3.3.

To probe the sources of the urban–rural income gap, it is appropriate to apply 'decomposition' analysis of the sort used in the study of sex or race discrimination. Where y is the logarithm of household income, Y, and the urban income function is $f_u(X_u)$, then $\overline{y_u} = f_u(\overline{X_u})$; similarly, $\overline{y_r} = f_r(\overline{X_r})$ for the rural sample. The logarithmic income differential, D, can be decomposed as follows:

$$
\begin{aligned}
D = \overline{y_u} - \overline{y_r} &= f_u(\overline{X_u}) - f_r(\overline{X_r}) \\
&= f_u(\overline{X_u} - \overline{X_r}) + [f_u(\overline{X_r}) - f_r(\overline{X_r})] \\
&= E + R,
\end{aligned}
\tag{3.1}
$$

where E is that part of the differential which can be 'explained' by differences in mean characteristics and R is the 'residual' attributable to differences in the income-generation process. E effectively answers the counterfactual question: how would the mean income of urban people change if they had the mean characteristics of rural people? There is an analogous question answered by E': how would the mean income of rural people change if they had the mean characteristics of urban people?

$$D = [f_u(\overline{X}_u) - f_r(\overline{X}_u)] + f_r(\overline{X}_u - \overline{X}_r).$$
$$= R' + E' \tag{3.2}$$

Table 3.5 presents the results of the decomposition analysis. The first four columns are based on regression (2) of Table 3.4 (the full samples with area dummy variables) and the last four on regression (3) (the ten-province samples with province dummy variables). With decomposition 3.1 (corresponding to equation 3.1), differences in mean characteristics (E) account for 18 per cent (full samples) and 22 per cent (ten provinces) of $D = \overline{y}_u - \overline{y}_r$. The residual ($R$), due to differences in the income-generation process, therefore accounts for 82 or 78 per cent of D respectively.

The main contributions to E are the lower education and the larger households of the rural sample, partly offset by their having more workers. The main contribution to R is the intercept term, i.e. there is a large predicted difference ($\hat{y}_u - \hat{y}_r$) for households with the characteristics of the omitted categories (household head male, Han, age 26–30, education less than primary grade 4, Party member; household with one member, one worker and living in eastern China/Jiangsu province). Two offsetting influences are the stronger returns to education (except at college level) in rural areas and the more weakly depressing effect of bigger households in rural areas—probably because land is generally allocated to peasant households according to the number of people they contain (Knight and Song 1993a: 208). In the ten-province sample the province coefficients also contribute to R: the overall urban–rural income gap is greater than in Jiangsu province with its rural prosperity. Decomposition 3.2 (based on equation 3.2) again places less weight on characteristics than on coefficients, the contribution of E' being 17 (full samples) or 20 per cent (ten provinces).

Thus only a minor part of the urban–rural income gap can be explained by differences in the productive characteristics of the two samples. The great majority is attributable to differences in the income-generation process. The unstandardized ratio of urban and rural (geometric) mean incomes in the full samples used for the decomposition analysis is 2.64. By contrast, the standardized ratio implicit in decompositions 3.1 and 3.2 are 2.21 and 2.25 respectively.[2]

3.2 THE RURAL–URBAN INCOME GAP BY PROVINCE

The 1988 CASS survey permits an examination of the urban–rural income gap by province in the ten provinces from which urban samples were drawn (Table 3.6). The urban/rural ratio of household income per capita was 2.52 in the case of these ten provinces, but it varied from 1.85 in Beijing to 3.98 in Gansu. This is not a peculiarity of the CASS survey: the 1994 SSB household survey of 29 provinces yielded an overall income ratio of 2.55 which

TABLE 3.5 *Decomposition of the urban-rural difference in the logarithm of household income per capita: 1988 CASS survey*

	Full samples				Ten provinces			
	Decomposition 3.1		Decomposition 3.2		Decomposition 3.1		Decomposition 3.2	
	Characteristics	Coefficients	Characteristics	Coefficients	Characteristics	Coefficients	Characteristics	Coefficients
Intercept	—	1.1767	—	1.1767	—	1.4288	—	1.4288
Sex	0.0017	-0.0088	0.0060	-0.0131	0.0006	-0.0111	0.0052	-0.0157
Education	0.0485	-0.0670	0.0190	-0.0375	0.0477	-0.0732	0.0153	-0.0409
Age	0.0019	-0.0054	0.0001	-0.0037	-0.0006	-0.0439	-0.0011	0.0434
Ethnicity	0.0003	0.0058	0.0028	0.0033	-0.0003	0.0009	0.0000	0.0006
Party membership	0.0182	0.0462	0.0310	0.0345	0.0186	0.0472	0.0321	0.0338
No. of household members	0.2326	-0.4046	0.1888	-0.3607	0.2597	-0.6933	0.1969	-0.6305
No. of household workers	-0.1205	-0.0055	-0.0974	-0.0287	-0.1318	-0.0119	-0.0918	-0.0519
Province/area	-0.0045	0.0551	0.0113	0.0393	0.0266	0.1293	0.0416	0.1143
Total	0.1782	0.7925	0.1617	0.8090	0.2204	0.7728	0.1981	0.7951
Proportion of difference explained	0.184	0.816	0.167	0.833	0.222	0.778	0.199	0.801

Notes: 1. In the full sample case the difference in the logarithm of household income per capita is 0.9707, the (geometric) mean values of Y_u and Y_r being 1735 and 657 yuan per annum respectively. In the ten-province case the corresponding figures are 0.9932, 1734, and 643 respectively.

2. Each figure indicates that part of the difference which is due to the coefficients (column) or the characteristics (column) of the variable or set of variables (row).

TABLE 3.6 *Household income per capita in urban and rural areas and the urban/rural income ratio, by province: 1988 CASS survey, provinces in the urban sample*

	Income per capita (yuan p.a.)		
	Urban	Rural	Urban (rural = 100)
Beijing	205	111	185
Shanxi	117	50	234
Liaoning	148	72	206
Jiangsu	154	82	188
Anhui	130	55	236
Henan	127	45	282
Hubei	145	65	223
Guangdong	264	111	238
Yunnan	107	54	198
Gansu	163	41	398
All ten provinces	159	63	252

varied from 1.58 in Shanghai and 1.88 in both Beijing and Tianjin to 3.93 in Yunnan and 3.99 in Guizhou. How are these discrepancies among provinces to be explained?

A regression analysis was conducted at the province level to examine the relationship between mean urban and rural income per capita:

$$Y_u = a + bY_r,$$
(3.3)

where Y_u is urban and Y_r rural income per capita. The results for the ten provinces of the 1988 CASS survey and the 29 provinces of the 1994 SSB survey are presented in Table 3.7. In both cases the coefficient on Y_r and the intercept are significantly positive (at the 1 per cent level). The positive intercept implies that the income ratio declines as rural income rises. In the ten-province survey, we have:

$$Y_u/Y_r = 1.523** + 51.527**/Y_r$$
(3.4)

and in the twenty-nine-province survey:

$$Y_u/Y_r = 1.189** + 114.729**/Y_r.$$
(3.5)

In the logarithmic form (not shown), the coefficient on y_r ($= \ln Y_r$) in 1994 is 0.487**, which implies an elasticity of response of urban to rural income of just under one-half.

Why is the urban/rural income ratio higher in the poorer provinces? In a country as large as China it is inevitable that there are significant regional disparities in farm productivity and in rural income per capita. These

TABLE 3.7 *Regression analysis: the relationship between province urban and rural mean income per capita: 1988 CASS survey and 1994 SSB survey*

Independent variable	Coefficient	
	1988 CASS	1994 SSB
Intercept	51.527*	114.729**
Rural mean income per capita (Y_r)	1.523**	1.189**
$\bar{R}_2$	0.65	0.68
F-value	17.70	60.25
Mean of dependent variable $(\bar{Y}_u)$	156.00	214.98
Mean of independent variable $(\bar{Y}_r)$	68.60	84.40
$\bar{Y}_u/\bar{Y}_r$	2.27	2.55
No. of observations	10	29

Notes: 1. * denotes significance at the 10% and ** at the 1% level.
2. The dependent variable is province urban mean income per capita (Y_u).

Source: PRC, SSB 1994: 265, 278.

disparities would be reflected in local labour supply prices, and thus in local wages if they were determined in competitive labour markets. Moreover, such wage differences would be exacerbated by the presence of artificial restrictions on non-local labour mobility.

In 1956 the government introduced a common wage system for the state sector throughout China. This largely eliminated regional wage disparities in the state sector. Apart from a few regional supplements applicable to specific sectors and areas, the only regional differences in the standard wage tables should have reflected regional differences in the cost of living, i.e. real wages were standardized across regions. In 1987 province urban consumer price levels (with China = 100) ranged from 92 in Henan to 106 in Shanghai (Howes and Lanjouw 1991: table 5). Thus nominal wage levels varied only little among provinces.

This inference is borne out by an earnings function analysis conducted on the sample of 18,000 urban workers in the 1988 CASS survey (Knight and Song 1993b: table 2). As Table 3.8 shows, when province dummy variables were added to the set of personal and employer characteristics used to explain regular earnings $(y_2 = \ln Y_2)$, their coefficients ranged only from 10 per cent below to 8 per cent above the omitted province (Jiangsu).

During the period of economic reform non-regular earnings (such as bonuses and subsidies) became increasingly important as the planning system was dismantled, decision-taking was decentralized, and enterprises were permitted to retain profits and exercise greater initiative over remuneration. Between 1978 and 1988 the basic 'time-wage' fell from 85 to 49

TABLE 3.8 *Coefficients on province dummy variables in the earnings function: 1988 CASS survey, sample of urban workers*

Independent variable	Coefficient		
	Total cash income	Regular income	Other cash income
Beijing	0.0006	−0.0385**	0.0183
Shanxi	−0.1978**	−0.1000**	−0.4247**
Liaoning	−0.0228**	−0.0012	−0.0604**
Anhui	−0.0852**	−0.0931**	−0.1210**
Henan	−0.2174**	−0.0328**	−0.6256**
Hubei	−0.0935**	−0.0249**	−0.2124**
Guangdong	0.3083**	0.0801**	0.4673**
Yunnan	0.0188	0.0052	−0.0013
Gansu	−0.0684**	0.0402**	−0.2959**

Notes: 1. ** denotes statistical significance at the 1% level.
2. The omitted province is Jiangsu.
3. Other explanatory variables included in the regression but not reported in the table are sex, education, party membership, ethnicity, occupation and age of worker, ownership status and sector of employment.
4. Coefficients are converted into percentages in the text as exp. (coefficient—1).
5. The dependent variables are the natural logarithms of total cash income, regular income, and other cash income (y_1, y_2, and y_3 respectively).

Source: Knight and Song 1993*b*: table 7.3.

per cent of the total wage bill (PRC, SSB 1991: 107). The CASS survey showed the regular wage to be 56 per cent of the total in 1988 (Knight and Song 1993*b*: table 7.2). Non-regular income is much more sensitive to location: the coefficients on province in the earnings function analysis for 'other cash income' ($y_3 = \ln Y_3$) encompassed a wider range: from 47 per cent below to 60 per cent above the omitted province. The provincial variability of total cash income ($y_1 = \ln Y_1$; $Y_1 = Y_2 + Y_3$) is intermediate: ranging from 20 per cent below to 36 per cent above Jiangsu (Table 3.8). In each case the highest-paying among the ten provinces was Guangdong, the lowest-paying being Henan or Shanxi.

To what extent do urban wages in different parts of China reflect local economic conditions? Using province mean-income data, we attempted to explain urban total cash income (Y_1), regular wage (Y_2), and 'other cash income' (Y_3) in terms of income per working member of rural households (RY). The results are shown in Table 3.9. Rural income per worker, which varies much among provinces, has no significant effect on the regular wage, which varies little. However, RY does have a significant positive effect on Y_1 and Y_3, which are more variable than Y_2. A rise of 1 yuan in rural income raises 'other cash income' of urban workers in the same province by 0.52 yuan and the total cash income by 0.56 yuan.

There are two possible explanations for this relationship. One is that market forces operate in the labour market. If the surrounding rural areas are prosperous, urban employers need to pay well above the regular wage to attract and motivate workers. The other explanation relies on mutual interaction between local rural and urban economies. If prosperous rural economies boost neighbouring urban economies and vice versa, the high rural income is both cause and effect of successful urban economic activities, in turn giving rise to high profits which are partly distributed to workers in the form of bonuses and subsidies.

The collective sector is not subject to the government-imposed national scale for regular wages, and indeed some collectives are effectively private businesses. Does the urban collective sector behave in the same way? A corresponding analysis was conducted for urban collective employees, and the results are also shown in Table 3.9. As expected, total pay is even more sensitive to rural income per worker: a rise of 1 yuan in rural income per worker raises total cash income per urban collective worker by no less than 0.84 yuan. Moreover, it is the regular wage equation which is well determined and has the high regression coefficient (0.71), not the 'other cash income' equation (0.13). It also has the higher coefficient of variation. Since the regular wage is not imposed from above, there is no need to use other cash income as the means of adjustment to local conditions.

The ratio of urban to rural income per worker implicit in Table 3.9 (based on province data for the provinces included in the urban survey) is considerable. The mean value among the provinces of rural income per worker (RY) is 921 yuan (with standard deviation 353 yuan), whereas the mean value of urban total cash income per employee (Y_1) is 1789 yuan (with standard deviation 317 yuan). The ratio of urban to rural income is thus 1.94, and even comparing RY with urban collective Y_1 (1492 yuan, with standard deviation 425 yuan) it is 1.62.

The positive intercepts in Table 3.9 again indicate that the urban/rural income per worker ratio declines as rural income rises. Both the prevalence of an urban–rural income gap in all provinces and its greater size in the poorer provinces suggest that rural–urban migration is not occurring adequately and market forces are not operating effectively to equalize urban and rural incomes within provinces. It seems that such urban wage differences as exist among provinces are less likely to reflect local market forces than informal profit-sharing between enterprises and their employees.

3.3 INEQUALITY OF URBAN INCOME

Given the high labour force participation of urban adults and the predominance of wage employment, the urban wage structure is the major deter-

TABLE 3.9 *Explaining urban wages in terms of rural incomes, by province: 1988 CASS survey*

Independent variable	Coefficient		
	Total cash income	Regular wage	Other cash income
All sectors			
Intercept	1,275.91**	977.58**	298
Rural income per worker (*RY*)	0.56*	0.04	0.52*
Adjusted R^2	0.30	−0.10	0.38
F-value	4.35	0.28	5.90
Standard error of the estimate (%)	13	7	27
No. of observations	9	9	9
Dependent variable:			
mean	1,789.02	1,015.30	773.71
standard deviation	317.40	73.10	269.15
coefficient of variation (%)	17	7	34
Collective sector			
Intercept	736.89	52.25	684.62**
Rural income per worker (*RY*)	0.84*	0.71*	0.13
Adjusted R^2	0.45	0.49	0.16
F-value	6.77	7.71	2.31
Standard error of the estimate (%)	21	36	11
No. of observations	8	8	8
Dependent variable:			
mean	1,491.68	687.02	804.65
standard deviation	424.80	346.87	93.34
coefficient of variation (%)	28	50	12

Notes: 1. **denotes statistical significance at the 1% level and * at the 5% level.
     2. The dependent variable is province urban mean income per worker: total cash income, regular wage, and other cash income (Y_1, Y_2, and Y_3 respectively).

minant of urban household inequality. The absence of an effective labour market in urban China—reflected in bureaucratic allocation of labour and administered wages—gives the Chinese government redistributive instruments not available in a market economy. Intervention on wages is likely to be central to policy directed at urban income inequality.

The urban sample of the 1988 CASS survey permits an analysis of the determinants of urban wages. We analyse the 18,000 workers in the sample of 9,000 households, using three main concepts of income: Y_1 (total cash income of the working member), Y_2 (regular wage), and Y_3 (other cash income), where $Y_1 = Y_2 + Y_3$. The variable Y_2 excludes, and thus Y_3 comprises, irregular payments, bonuses, cash subsidies, and income from other jobs. Our analysis is generally confined to cash income, i.e. excluding payments in kind. However, the non-cash payments made by employers and recorded in the survey are either negligible or not attributable to particular members of the household. For instance, housing—the subject of Chapter 5—which in urban areas is heavily subsidized by employers, has to be analysed at the household and not the worker level.

The potentially relevant determinants can be classified as exogenous or endogenous, and personal or environmental in the sense that they pertain to the job rather than the person. The exogenous personal characteristics are age, sex, and ethnicity. The personal characteristics that are in principle choice variables are educational level, occupational group, nature of employment, and party membership, but in practice these may be beyond the control of the individual. The potentially relevant characteristics of the environment, all possibly choice variables but probably not fully so, are ownership form of employer, economic sector of employment, and province.

Table 3.10 reports income functions for the three concepts of income: where $y_i = \ln Y_i$, the three dependent variables are y_1, y_2, and y_3. All three equations have fairly high F and adjusted R^2 values. However, the best determined equation is that for the regular wage (y_2) and the least-well determined equation is that for other cash income (y_3). Most of the individual coefficients are significant in each of the three equations. Concentrating on the total cash wage (y_1), we examine the more interesting explanatory variables in turn.

The familiar inverted U-shaped age-earnings profile is found in this sample, as in many others. Income rises monotonically to a peak for workers in their fifties (A_8 and A_9), when it is 90 per cent higher than for workers in their teens, and thereafter declines slightly. It is difficult to interpret the Chinese result in the familiar way, i.e. human capital acquired through employment experience is rewarded with its marginal product in competitive labour markets. Nor can it be seen as a means of recouping firm-specific training by means of seniority payments: the absence of voluntary mobility in China means that seniority payments are unnecessary for maintaining internal labour markets. The old have power in China—an outcome both of its culture and of its bureaucracy. Great weight has been placed on length of service within the employment unit throughout the period in which the system of wage grades has operated: seniority is a central aspect of the Chinese wage system.

The contrast between regular and other income helps to explain why age is rewarded. Regular income is more responsive to age, whereas other income peaks early (in the age-group $A_6 = 41$–5 years) and then declines sharply. The former is likely to be governed by the centrally imposed system of wage grades whereas the latter depends more on the policy and resources of the employer: concepts of fairness (for example, everyone

TABLE 3.10 Income function analysis of urban workers: 1988 CASS survey

Independent variables		Coefficients			Proportion of sample (%)
		Y_1	Y_2	Y_3	
Constant term		7.0567**	6.5435**	5.8716**	100.00
Female	S_2	−0.0814**	−0.0662**	−0.0963**	47.72
College graduate or above	E_1	0.1810**	0.2022**	0.1741**	6.17
Community college graduate	E_2	0.1277**	0.1357**	0.1363**	6.24
Professional school graduate	E_3	0.1121**	0.1197**	0.1362**	11.07
Upper-middle school graduate	E_4	0.0978	0.0982	0.1234**	24.89
Lower-middle school graduate	E_5	0.0914**	0.0996**	0.0984**	38.61
Primary school graduate	E_6	0.0379	0.0567**	0.0112	10.32
Three years or more of primary school	E_7	0.0062	0.0355	−0.0391	1.07
Communist Party member	C_1	0.0675**	0.0595**	0.0842**	23.44
National minority	M_1	−0.0061	−0.0028	−0.0267	3.67
Other publicly-owned sector	Ow_2	−0.0789**	−0.0821**	−0.0745**	39.05
Collective sector	Ow_3	−0.1747**	−0.1399**	−0.2658**	20.45
Private or individually-owned sector	Ow_4	−0.3383**	−0.2707**	−0.5893**	0.23
Sino-foreign joint venture	Ow_5	0.1919**	0.3109**	−0.0802	0.31
Foreign-owned sector	Ow_6	0.0219	0.1341	−0.1123	0.05
Other	Ow_7	−0.1239*	−0.0712	−0.2748**	0.58
Multiple ownership	Ow_8	−0.3916	−0.1321	−1.0037**	0.01
Owner of private or individual enterprise	Oc_1	0.0291	0.0342	−0.0033	0.57
Owner and manager of private or individual enterprise	Oc_2	0.0803**	0.0911	−0.0652	0.11
Professional or technical worker	Oc_3	0.0727**	0.0753**	0.0919**	16.00
Responsible official of government	Oc_4	0.0855**	0.1098**	0.0792**	4.71

Factory director or manager	Oc_5	0.1422**	0.1362**	0.1506**	1.79
Office worker	Oc_6	0.0365**	0.0428**	0.0468***	23.63
Agriculture, forestry, animal husbandry	Es_1				
Fishing, water conservancy		−0.0223	−0.0420*	0.0457	0.97
Mining	Es_2	0.0754**	0.0746**	0.1055**	3.18
Geological prospecting	Es_4	−0.0646**	−0.0357	−0.0879	0.88
Construction	Es_5	0.0187	0.0029	0.0347	3.46
Transport, communication, post and telecommunications	Es_6	0.0144	0.0128	0.0262	6.78
Trade, restaurants, catering material supplying and marketing	Es_7	−0.0189**	−0.0504**	0.0057	14.25
Real estate and public utilities	Es_8	−0.0684**	−0.0683**	−0.0790*	1.43
Personal services and consulting services	Es_9	−0.0780**	−0.0968**	−0.1589**	0.97
Health, sport, and social welfare	Es_{10}	−0.0333**	−0.0399**	−0.0113	4.63
Education, culture, and the arts	Es_{11}	−0.0419**	−0.0284**	−0.0442*	7.32
Scientific and technical services	Es_{12}	−0.0263	−0.0280	−0.0068	2.07
Finance, insurance	Es_{13}	−0.0606**	−0.0517**	−0.0300	1.55
Party, government, or social organs	Es_{14}	−0.0933*	−0.0432**	−0.1582**	8.53
Other	Es_{15}	−0.0929**	−0.1113**	−0.1258**	0.70
Permanent worker	J_1	0.2279**	0.1246**	0.5678**	97.64
Temporary worker	J_2	−0.1144**	−0.0199	−0.3189**	1.84
Other	J_4	−0.2006*	0.2371**	−0.0625	0.20
Age below 20	A_1	−0.3294**	0.3190**	−0.4171**	6.29
21–5	A_2	−0.2048**	−0.1806**	−0.2717**	10.85
31–5	A_4	0.1505**	0.1211**	0.1836**	17.25
36–40	A_5	0.1996**	0.2008**	0.2118**	17.67
41–5	A_6	0.2613**	0.2885**	0.2289**	12.62
46–50	A_7	0.2902**	0.3516**	0.1902**	12.19
51–5	A_8	0.3173**	0.4190**	0.1631**	7.63

TABLE 3.10 *Continued*

Independent variables		Coefficients			Proportion of sample (%)
		Y_1	Y_2	Y_3	
56–60	A_9	0.3167**	0.4645**	0.0860**	3.37
61–5	A_{10}	0.2926**	0.4074**	0.1244	0.49
66+	A_{11}	0.2749**	0.4005**	0.0362	0.21
Beijing	P_1	0.0006	−0.0385**	0.0183	4.95
Shanxi	P_4	−0.1978**	−0.1000**	−0.4247**	10.90
Liaoning	P_8	−0.0228*	−0.0012	−0.0604**	10.37
Anhui	P_{12}	−0.0852**	−0.0931**	−0.1210**	9.78
Henan	P_{16}	−0.2174**	−0.0328**	−0.6256**	11.78
Hubei	P_{17}	−0.0935**	−0.0249**	−0.2124**	10.82
Guangdong	P_{19}	0.3083**	0.0801**	0.4673**	11.79
Yunnan	P_{23}	0.0188	0.0052	−0.0013	10.13
Gansu	P_{26}	−0.0684	0.0402**	−0.2959**	6.67
F-value		246.041	299.785	127.687	
$\bar{R}^2$		0.461	0.510	0.307	
$\bar{y}_1 \, \bar{y}_2 \, \bar{y}_3$		7.3903	6.8417	6.3961	
No. of observations		17,480	17,480	17,480	

Notes: 1. ** denotes statistical significance at the 1% level and * significance at the 5% level.

2. The omitted categories in the dummy variable analysis are male (S_1), less than three years of primary school (E_8), not Communist Party member (C_2), Han (M_2), state-owned sector (Ow_1), manual worker (Oc_7), manufacturing (Oc_7), management of private or individual enterprise (Es_3), age 26–30 (A_3), and Jiangsu (P_{10}).

3. The dependent variables are the logarithms of total cash income, regular wage, and other cash income income of urban workers.

Source: Knight and Song 1993b: 222–4.

should receive the same) or productivity (for example, rewards for individual efficiency) are more likely to apply than seniority *per se.*

There is some tendency for the returns to age to increase with educational level, and to be greater for non-manual than manual workers, but these results are open to both human capital and institutional interpretations. The least ambiguous evidence is to be found by comparing ownership sectors. In the public sector (Ow_1 and Ow_2) wages peak in the age-group 66 and over, the highest-paid group earning respectively 117 and 118 per cent more than the lowest-paid. In the collective sector (Ow_3) and in the other sectors (Ow_4–Ow_8), the corresponding figures are 69 and 67 per cent and the peak age-groups are 56–60 and 41–50 respectively. In the public sector wage structures are laid down by the State whereas in the other sectors employers have more autonomy. This suggests that a major part of the returns to age or employment experience stems from the standardized wage scales imposed from above. However, that only raises the deeper question: why does the system of wage grades reward seniority? It might reflect a culturally based respect for age or it might represent an underlying concern to reward human capital in the absence of a labour market.

Historically, much value was placed on education in China. Entrance to the bureaucracy, offering high status and wealth positions, was by means of competitive examinations. The Confucian stress on education lives on in Chinese culture but the economic motive may dominate: is education rewarded in the labour market? Respondents were classified into eight educational levels, their mean length of education running from one (E_8, the omitted category) to fifteen years (E_1). College graduates (E_1) receive 20 per cent more income than the 'uneducated' base group. The premium on education, as measured by the coefficients in Table 3.10, increases almost monotonically with education. The premium is not consistently higher for regular wages than for other income. More education does mean more income in urban China, but the effect of education on income is remarkably slight by comparison with other countries.

It might be hypothesized that education, if it is productive, will be rewarded more by collective and by private sector employers than by the State if the latter has weaker profit and efficiency goals and stronger equity goals. The regression results for the different ownership subsamples are consistent with this hypothesis. Only one education term (E_1) has a significant coefficient in the state-owned sector whereas at least five have significant positive coefficients in the other publicly owned and collective sectors. Moreover, their coefficients are in each case larger than in the state-owned sector, and rise consistently with educational level. The evidence suggests that education is better rewarded where employers have greater autonomy, and that the State, where it can, compresses the educational wage structure by comparison with a free market outcome.

In principle the occupation-based wage system and lack of occupational mobility should make occupation the most important determinant of wages in China. However, there is a sense in which wages are attached to individuals rather than to jobs. For instance, most manual workers can rise through the manual grades as their years of service increase, irrespective of the precise occupation or its skill level. This suggests that the determinants of initial allocation to the manual, technical, or administrative groups, and their corresponding wage systems, can be important determinants of pay. That is a way in which education can influence pay.

In the absence of a labour market, however, relative pay between the different wage systems is influenced by concepts of fairness, in turn moulded by political and social values and by the employers' practice of creating housing communities of their workers. Occupational wage distinctions are therefore likely to be muted. Seven occupations were distinguished in the survey and are shown in Table 3.10, manual labourer (Oc_7) being the omitted category. The coefficients on each of the non-manual occupations are positive and significant, although not large. The greatest wage difference, *ceteris paribus*, between a factory director or manager and a labourer, is only 15 per cent. It is probable that technically qualified workers are not paid well enough to provide workers with incentives to acquire qualifications or employers with incentives to economize on the use of qualified labour.

There is a powerful, statistically significant relationship between education and occupation. For instance, the proportion of workers in manual occupations rises monotonically, from 2 per cent in the case of college graduates to 88 per cent in the case of those with less than three years of primary education. Education has indeed been an important criterion for allocating workers to occupations, although less so during the Cultural Revolution decade. Education thus raises the income of a worker not only directly but also indirectly by improving his chance of allocation to a well-paid occupation. The omission of the occupation terms from the income function therefore shows the combined effect of education on income. The spread of earnings is widened from 20 to 34 per cent but the premium on education remains low in comparison with most developing countries.

It has been government policy in China to remove gender discrimination in both jobs and wages. Labour allocation and administrative wage-setting gave government the power to correct the inequalities of the past. There are few 'housewives' in China: in the urban sample women constituted no less than 47 per cent of employees. Female employees are thus not a select group. Nevertheless, women receive on average 16 per cent less income than men, both in their regular wage and in their other income. How is the difference to be explained?

Women tend to be 'crowded' into the lower-paying collective sector, despite pressures from labour bureaux and Party branches to overcome managers' prejudices. Since liberation government has also pursued a policy of providing equality of educational access for boys and girls. Equality has not been achieved, however, except for the youngest age-groups in the urban areas. A regression analysis of educational attainment shows that urban women have 1.8 years of education fewer, *ceteris paribus*, than men (Knight and Li 1993: 295). In the urban worker sample, 20 per cent of women had gone beyond upper middle school and 52 per cent had not reached it, the corresponding figures for males being 28 and 47 per cent respectively.

How much of the gender difference in mean wages is due to such differences in characteristics and how much to differences in the income-generation process itself? The coefficient on female sex in the income function (Table 3.10) implies that women are paid 9 per cent less, *ceteris paribus*. A decomposition analysis shows that differences in characteristics account for some 45 per cent of the wage difference. Men have more favourable education, age, and occupation structures, and a higher proportion of them are state employees. Residual differences in coefficients account for some 55 per cent of the wage difference. Do they represent discrimination against women?

We can learn about the nature of the residual component by examining its incidence. The coefficient on female sex is larger for less educated women. There is very little difference in wage income between men and women with high education at all ages and between young men and women with low education, but the difference emerges and grows consistently from the late twenties onwards for those with low education. It appears that gender is largely irrelevant in the early stages of the working life but becomes important in the later stages. This may be the result of labour market discrimination against women: for instance, men may receive preference in promotion to better-paid jobs and grades. Similarly, the facts that the sex difference is small in the private and individual ownership sector (much self-employment) and in temporary employment (much piecework) are consistent with the discrimination explanation applying where the sex difference is large, i.e. among older, less educated employees. Possession of education protects women against discrimination, apparently because it gives them access to jobs in which there is less discrimination.

Labour market segmentation among employing enterprises has been growing and is now substantial. No less than 78 per cent of urban workers are employed by publicly owned enterprises, 39 per cent by the national government, and 39 per cent by subnational governments. The wage difference is minor: the latter are paid 8 per cent less, *ceteris paribus*, than the former. Some state units—the industrial enterprises—earn profits and are therefore in a better position to pay bonuses and other supplements to the basic wage. The collective sector pays 16 per cent less than the state sector, perhaps reflecting their weaker political position and 'hard' budgets. Collective employees tend to be younger, less well educated, and more frequently female than state employees: collectives are rarely the preferred sector. The lowest-paying sector is local private or individually owned enterprises, and the highest-paying is sino-foreign joint ventures. It is the growing number of small firms that are most likely to pay no more than the supply price of rural labour. Moreover, it is within this group that exploitative relationships are most likely to be found: some employers can take advantage of poorly informed workers coming from a distance on fixed-term contracts. The urban private sector is still small and heterogeneous, having both high- and low-paying segments, one capable of attracting good workers and the other absorbing the disadvantaged. As the size of both segments grows, so their influences are likely to be felt in the labour market.

Being a cross-section dataset, the 1988 survey does not permit an analysis of the effects of the enterprise reforms that took place during the 1980s. It is nevertheless possible to examine predictions of the likely effects of the reforms. During the Cultural Revolution there was little relationship between pay and work. Afterwards there was a continuous call to tie pay to individual performance. Enterprise-specific determinants of pay grew in importance during the 1980s as state enterprises were given more autonomy and profit-related bonuses were allowed to grow. As we have seen in Chapter 2, real wages increased rapidly if sporadically, and the composition of pay moved away from time-wages towards performance pay (piece-rates and bonuses) and subsidies.

Can we expect individual differences in non-basic pay to represent differences in productivity, i.e. to reflect economic rationality? There is little sign that non-basic pay, being less subject to government control and duration, has an economically more rational structure. On the contrary, compared with basic income, Communist Party members are proportionately more and women proportionately less rewarded, and state ownership yields a large premium. The returns to education and the pattern of occupational pay are on a par with those for basic income, yet education- and occupation-based skills are surely too little rewarded for economic efficiency. These results for 1988 are consistent with the view that a web of factory interests gave rise to a distribution of bonuses unrelated to the productivity of individual workers (Walder 1987). Management encouraged worker cooperation by maximizing bonuses, and distributed the rewards so as to minimize contention. If bonuses improved incentives, they did so more at the enterprise level than at the individual level.

We would expect the compressed wage structure to generate a low degree of personal income inequality among urban workers. According to the 1988 CASS survey, the Gini coefficient of income among workers in urban China is indeed low by international standards. It is lower for basic pay (0.20) and higher for other income (0.34) than for total income from employment (0.24). More interesting are the inequality measures for worker income 'inside the plan' and 'outside the plan' (Zhao 1993: 76–7).

The Gini coefficient of the former (state, other public, and collective enter-prises) is 0.23; that of the latter (the other ownership-forms) is twice as high: 0.49. As this small sector grows in importance, so overall inequality of wage incomes will rise.

The low inequality of income among the urban employed should in turn help to keep inequality low among urban households. However, the trans-lation from personal to household inequality introduces additional vari-ables. Each household comprises a number of employed persons: 12 per cent of households in the urban sample have only one worker, 69 per cent have two, 14 per cent three, and the mean number is 2.14. As expected, mean household income increases systematically with the number of work-ers in the household (Tables 3.4 and 3.11). However, mean household income per worker declines as the number of workers rises; and per capita it is fairly constant (Table 3.11). Owing to a positive correlation between the number of workers and members of a household, mean house-hold income also increases with household size (Table 3.12). However, the tendency for the worker/member ratio to fall as household size rises helps to explain why mean income per capita moves inversely with household size. The contribution that household size (raising income) makes to the inequality of household income equals its contribution (lowering income per capita) to the inequality of household income per capita (Table 3.13). The table shows that, using four different concepts of urban income, the Gini coefficient is in each case 0.24. Moreover, there is only a negligible dif-ference in the degree of income inequality across the different concepts when other measures of inequality are used.

The inequality of urban household income per capita in China is remark-ably low compared with that found in most urban household income sur-

TABLE 3.11 *Urban household mean income by number of persons employed: 1988 CASS survey*

No. of persons employed	Percentage of cases	Mean income of household (yuan p.a.)		
		Total	Per employed person	Per capita
1	11.7	5,337	5,337	2,011
2	69.1	6,199	3,099	1,834
3	13.8	8,173	2,724	1,974
4	4.4	9,701	2,425	1,999
5	0.9	11,075	2,715	1,956
6–	0.1	12,738	2,099	1,777
All households	100.0	6,573	3,271	1,903

TABLE 3.12 *Urban household mean income by number of household members: 1988 CASS survey*

No. of members	Percentage of cases	Worker/member mean ratio	Mean income (yuan p.a.)	
			Total	Per capita
1	0.4	0.97	2,839	2,839
2	6.8	0.61	5,146	2,573
3	45.4	0.62	5,872	1,957
4	30.9	0.54	6,947	1,737
5	12.0	0.49	7,937	1,587
6	3.6	0.47	8,716	1,453
7	0.7	0.46	9,943	1,420
8+	0.2	0.47	11,231	1,378
All households	100.0	0.58	6,573	1,867

TABLE 3.13 *Measures of urban income inequality: 1988 CASS survey*

	Income variable			
	Worker		Household	
	Income per worker	Total income	Income per employee	Income per capita
Gini coefficient	0.240	0.240	0.248	0.238
Share of poorest 40%	25.0	25.6	25.5	25.7
Standard deviation of ln income	0.48	0.42	0.42	0.41
Coefficient of variation of income	1.84	1.95	1.83	1.95

veys in developing counties. For instance, instead of 0.24, the comparable urban Gini coefficient for India in 1975 was 0.42 (Mills and Becker 1986: table 8-1), and for Malaysia in 1976 it was 0.51 for metropolitan towns and 0.46 in towns (Anand 1983: table 3-11). Urban income is more equally distributed in China than elsewhere not only because of the compressed wage structure but also because of the lack of income from wealth and the very limited size of the self-employment sector. Restrictions on rural–urban migration have limited the growth of urban informal employment and of urban unemployment, so keeping serious poverty out of urban China.

3.4 INEQUALITY OF RURAL INCOME

The 1988 CASS survey found a household mean income per capita in rural China of 787 yuan. However, the dispersion around the mean was considerable, the standard deviation being 614 yuan, the coefficient of variation 78 per cent, and the Gini coefficient 34 per cent. It is important, therefore, to examine and explain the variation in rural incomes.

After 1949 the Chinese government pursued its egalitarian objectives in the rural areas by means of state confiscation of land and the formation of people's communes. Income-sharing took place at the commune level and at lower organizational levels. Even with the disbanding of the commune system and the restoration of the household as the rural production and income accounting unit after 1978, private ownership was anathema and the allocation of land to households was made on egalitarian principles. The communes were replaced by township organizations. At the township level and at the lower, village level, therefore, we still expect little income inequality among households by comparison with most developing countries.

There are nevertheless reasons to expect considerable spatial income inequality in rural China, even during the commune period. China had a rural population in 1988 of no less than 824 million people, the average population per province being 28 million (PRC, SSB 1991: 61). Yet only twelve out of 101 developing countries had a rural population larger than 28 million (World Bank 1988: 222, 284–5). The different regions of rural China are at very different levels of development, despite forty years of egalitarian regional policy (Lardy 1978; Riskin 1987; Aguignier 1988). These differences stem from the sheer size of the country, giving rise to differences in natural endowments, population density, and rural industrialization as well as the human capital, attitudes, and enterprise of their people. Moreover, one aspect of Chinese policy would have exacerbated spatial inequality. The draconian restrictions on the mobility of rural people to the urban areas and the more developed rural areas will until recently have prevented poor people from attempting to migrate out of their poverty.

It is in principle possible to conduct a spatial analysis of rural income inequality at various levels of aggregation. These levels might correspond to the province, the county (*xian*), the township (formerly commune), and the village (formerly production team). They vary greatly in group size: in 1988 the rural population per province averaged 28 million, per county 364,000, per township 15,500, and per village 1,170 people. Once the various constraints had been removed by the economic reforms, it was to be expected that differential enterprise, access to resources, and capital accumulation would create and foster income inequalities at all levels. Differentiation is likely to have grown among provinces, counties, villages, and households. We structure this section by examining the extent of, and the change in, inequality at each of these levels.

3.4.1 Inequality among provinces

Table 3.14 shows rural net income per capita (Y) by province for 1980 (at the start of the reforms, and the earliest year for which a near-complete set of province incomes is available) and for 1993. The same information is provided from the CASS survey of 1988. The table also shows measures of dispersion among provinces. Interprovince inequality was high in both 1980 and 1993, but it rose on every measure. For instance, the coefficient of variation of Y rose from 28 per cent in 1980 to 47 per cent in 1993.

Equation (3.6) presents the interprovince relationship between y_{80}, the logarithm of Y in 1980, and Δy between 1980 and 1993:

$$\Delta y = -0.7720 + 0.4395 * y_{80} \tag{3.6}$$

($\overline{R^2} = 0.196$, F-value $= 7.346$, $\overline{\Delta y} = 1.554$, $N = 27$ and * indicates statistical significance at the two per cent level). Although the equation is not well determined, suggesting that other influences were also important, the coefficient on y is significantly positive. Moreover, any errors in the reporting of income in 1980 would bias the coefficient downwards.[3] The equation shows that, if the rural income per capita of a province were higher by 10 per cent, its growth rate of rural income per capita would be increased by 4.4 percentage points over the thirteen years. Not only did the dispersion of rural income per capita among provinces increase over the period of rural reform but also it was, on average, the better-off provinces that enjoyed the relative improvement.

3.4.2 Inequality among counties

Counties being by definition rural areas, it is possible to examine the spatial contribution to rural income inequality by means of the data on the 2,400 counties of China (PRC, SSB 1989). This publication provides a table of statistics for each county in 1987, including population and 'gross social output', i.e. the gross rural output measured in value terms. A net output estimate is given for agriculture but not for the rural activities as a whole. Net output—corresponding to income—is the relevant concept in the analysis of income distribution. The use of gross output will exaggerate the relative income of those counties which use a high proportion of intermediate inputs. Since these are likely to be the more industrialized counties, the bias implicit in this procedure is potentially misleading. Accordingly, we use an approximation to construct the net output of each county (see Knight and Song 1993c: 196). This forms the basis of our analysis; we use the terms output and income interchangeably.

The overall mean annual output per person in 1987 was 627 yuan but the standard deviation among the counties was remarkably large (1068 yuan), exceeding the mean. Intercounty income disparities are considerable. The

TABLE 3.14 *Rural household net income per capita by province, 1980, 1988, and 1993*

	1980 (SSB)	1988 (CASS)	1993 (SSB)
Beijing	290.5	1,275	1,882.6
Tianjin	227.9	1,487	1,473.1
Hebei	175.8	784	803.8
Shanxi	155.8	603	718.3
Inner Mongolia	181.3	535	778.0
Liaoning	273.0	858	1,161.0
Jilin	236.3	661	891.6
Heilongjiang	205.4	446	1,028.4
Shanghai	397.4	1,763	2,727.0
Jiangsu	217.9	946	1,266.9
Zhejiang	219.2	1,392	1,745.9
Anhui	184.8	640	724.5
Fujian	171.7	849	1,210.5
Jiangxi	180.9	728	869.8
Shandong	194.3	733	952.7
Henan	160.8	549	695.9
Hubei	169.9	761	783.2
Hunan	219.7	881	851.9
Guangdong	274.4	1,270	1,674.8
Guanxi	173.7	699	892.0
Hainan	—	1,071	992.0
Sichuan	187.9	689	698.3
Guizhou	161.5	524	579.7
Yunnan	150.1	631	674.8
Tibet	—	—	889.5
Shaanxi	142.5	522	653.0
Gansu	153.3	474	550.8
Qinghai	—	607	672.6
Ningxia	178.1	611	636.4
Xinjiang	198.0	—	777.6
No. of observations	27	28	30
Measures of income			
mean	204.9	821.0	1,007.4
standard deviation	56.7	334.9	477.2
coefficient of variation (%)	27.7	40.8	47.4
Measure of ln *income*			
standard deviation	0.24	0.36	0.38

Note: The income concept is net income; the definitions differ for the CASS and the SSB surveys.

Sources: 1980: PRC, SSB 1986: 586. 1988: CASS survey, rural sample. 1993: PRC, SSB 1994: 279.

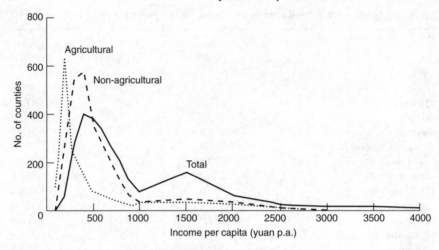

FIG. 3.2 *Frequency distribution of agricultural and non-agricultural income per capita of counties, 1987*

extent of spatial inequality is explored in Figure 3.2, which shows a frequency distribution of income (strictly net output) per capita by county. It indicates a fair concentration in the range 300–700 yuan, but a large right-hand tail. The frequency distribution of agricultural income per capita is less dispersed, and that of non-agricultural income per capita is more skewed to the right than their combination. Counties differ greatly in their degree of rural industrialization.

With the county as the unit of analysis, the Gini coefficient of inequality in income per capita is no less than 35 per cent. To what extent is spatial income inequality due to differences among provinces rather than among counties? A decomposition of inequality into 'within' and 'between' components is not possible for the Gini coefficient, but it is possible for the Theil index of inequality. According to the Theil measure, within-province inequality is responsible for 39 per cent and among-province inequality for 61 per cent of total inequality among counties.

To throw a light on the determinants of spatial income inequality we conduct an income function analysis by county. Table 3.15 reports the mean values of the variables, the mean values of income per capita by dummy variable category, and the regression coefficients in the various equation specifications.

In the most general equation (equation 1) the dependent variable is the natural logarithm of the income per capita ($\ln Y = y$) and the independent variables available are province ($P_1, \ldots, P_{29}$), type of terrain ($G_1, \ldots, G_3$), type of farming activity ($F_1, \ldots, F_3$), gross non-agricultural output as a percentage of gross social output (A), whether the county is a suburb (S_0, S_1),

TABLE 3.15 Income function analysis of income per capita by county, 1987

Independent variables		Mean value (%)	Mean value of income per capita	Coefficients Dependent variable			
				ln Y Eq. 1	ln Y_a Eq. 2	Y_a Eq. 3	Y_n Eq. 4
Constant term		—	—	6.371**	6.123**	-384.20**	297.03**
Agricultural income per capita	Y_a	—	—	—	—	—	0.28**
Non-agricultural income per capita	Y_n	—	—	—	—	1.90**	—
Beijing	P_1	0.345	1,383	0.524**	0.382**	-494.33**	330.05**
Tianjing	P_2	0.215	984	-0.016	0.033	244.26	-141.40
Hebei	P_3	6.430	576	-0.362**	-0.305**	336.84**	-184.03**
Shanxi	P_4	4.574	376	-0.750**	-0.746**	280.65**	-176.16**
Inner Mongolia	P_5	3.495	840	-0.239**	-0.050	929.57**	-428.14**
Liaoning	P_6	2.503	1,663	0.022	0.115	603.28**	-153.85**
Jilin	P_7	2.028	811	0.155*	0.297**	614.01**	-263.04**
Heilongjiang	P_8	3.409	994	0.279**	0.449**	869.58**	-350.34**
Shanghai	P_9	0.431	1,959	0.437**	0.027	-1551.91**	803.57**
Jiangsu	P_{10}	3.245	1,067	—	—	—	—
Zhejiang	P_{11}	3.323	874	-0.044	0.023	282.12**	-135.06**
Anhui	P_{12}	3.496	556	-0.258**	-0.111	528.84**	-264.96**
Fujian	P_{13}	2.891	616	-0.134*	0.039	647.09**	-322.84**
Jiangxi	P_{14}	3.884	485	-0.277**	-0.107	575.40**	-286.20**
Shandong	P_{15}	4.790	743	-0.043	0.119**	579.29**	-276.14**
Henan	P_{16}	5.567	493	-0.464**	-0.396**	-368.57**	-205.14**
Hubei	P_{17}	3.193	618	-0.096	0.073	576.75**	-267.16**
Hunan	P_{18}	4.445	503	-0.260**	-0.091	567.40**	-281.45**
Guangdong	P_{19}	4.747	817	-0.096	0.082	597.68**	-290.40**
Guangxi	P_{20}	3.711	380	-0.468**	-0.257**	616.02**	-321.99**
Sichuan	P_{21}	8.243	457	-0.384**	-0.286**	430.67**	-228.85**

Guizhou	P_{22}	3.539	305	−0.625**	−0.466**	489.77**	−266.11**
Yunnan	P_{23}	5.351	384	−0.430**	−0.274**	507.54**	−261.28**
Tibet	P_{24}	2.632	547	−0.036	0.137	707.49**	−336.23**
Shaanxi	P_{25}	4.186	405	−0.636**	−0.542**	382.93**	−220.43**
Gansu	P_{26}	3.452	437	−0.634**	−0.517**	458.47**	−250.49**
Quinghai	P_{27}	1.640	710	−0.126	0.022	712.01**	−359.39**
Ningxia	P_{28}	0.776	510	−0.649**	−0.510**	513.04**	−272.64**
Xinjiang	P_{29}	3.495	769	−0.079	0.101	748.38**	−362.68**
Hilly area	G_1	26.370	616	−0.164**	−0.157**	27.32	−36.72**
Mountainous area	G_2	39.792	476	−0.252**	−0.213**	61.50*	−59.74**
Plain area	G_3	33.838	809	—	—	—	—
Agricultural area	F_1	89.384	621	—	—	—	—
Livestock area	F_2	4.704	864	0.522**	0.561**	214.95**	—
Mixed farming area	F_3	5.912	512	−0.064	−0.029	23.20	—
Non-agricultural output as a percentage of total output	A	27.158	—	0.804**	—	—	—
Suburb	S_1	14.069	866	0.223**	0.096**	−367.71**	192.29**
Non-suburb	S_0	85.931	587	—	—	—	—
Special economic zone	Z_1	12.170	1,166	0.161**	0.055**	−321.85**	210.10**
Non-special economic zone	Z_0	87.930	551	—	—	—	—
Adjusted R^2		—	—	0.4873	0.3826	0.5603	0.6611
F-value		—	—	63.88	43.22	85.312	137.899
No. of observations		2,317	—	2,316	2,316	2,316	2,316
Mean value of dependent variable		—	—	6.242	5.890	434.298	192.324

Notes: 1. ** denotes significance at the % and *at the 5% level.
2. The omitted categories in the dummy variable analysis are P_{10} (Jiangsu province), G_3 (plain area), F_1 (agricultural area), S_0 (non-suburb), and Z_0 (non-special economic zone).
3. The superior of the specifications using the logarithmic or the actual value of the dependent variable is reported in each case.
4. Other potential explanatory variables in the dataset were not included owing to their possible endogeneity, e.g. counties in receipt of special assistance.
5. Eqs. 3 and 4 are estimated simultaneously using 2SLS. However, the 2SLS results are not substantively different from those using OLS.

Source: PRC 1989.

and whether it is in a Special Economic Zone (Z_0, Z_1). County per capita income can be explained reasonably well: R^2 is no less than 0.49, $F = 64$, and each set of dummy variables is significant according to the relevant F-test. Income per capita is significantly lower in hilly and in mountainous areas than in plain areas. Similarly, livestock areas have significantly greater income per capita than cultivated areas. The greater the share of non-agricultural output in total output in a county, the higher is its income per capita: rural industrialization thus appears to be important in raising incomes. Suburban counties, being close to urban markets, have significantly higher income per capita, as do those located in Special Economic Zones (SEZs) and thus benefiting from investment incentives. There is a great range of incomes by province: the, predictably prosperous, counties around the two main cities, Beijing and Shanghai, have income per capita respectively 69 and 55 per cent higher than those in the omitted province, Jiangsu, and Guizhou, Shanxi, and Gansu have income per capita respectively 46, 53, and 47 per cent lower. Counties are spatially clustered in their levels of development. Equation 2 shows that agricultural income per capita can be predicted almost equally well as total income per capita, using the province, land-type, agriculture-type, and location variables.

It is relevant to inquire whether agricultural and non-agricultural activities are complements or substitutes in production. Each activity could either compete with the other for resources or provide the other with resources and a market. On the one hand, poor agricultural areas might have more labour available, and a greater incentive to develop rural industry, and government might wish to assist them. On the other hand, prosperous agricultural areas provide both the demand and the saving for local industrialization. The relationships can be examined using the county data. Defining Y_a and Y_n as net output per capita in the agricultural and non-agricultural sectors respectively, we hypothesize that Y_a is a function of Y_n and Y_n a function of Y_a. Each is introduced as a variable explaining the other (equations 3 and 4). To avoid simultaneous equation bias, the equations are estimated simultaneously using two-stage least squares. Both coefficients are positive and significant. With Y_a as the dependent and Y_n the independent variable (equation 3), the response of Y_a to a unit increase in Y_n is 1.90. Equation 4 implies that a one yuan increase in Y_a raises Y_n by 0.28 yuan. The fact that causation runs both ways merely strengthens the conclusion: 'Unto him that hath shall be given.'

Some of the correlation observed between Y_n and Y_a might be non-causal and reflect the dependence of both variables on third factors such as proximity to markets, access to transport facilities, provincial government policies, or the human capital and attitudes of the people. The data permit partial standardization for such factors. Both equations 3 and 4 include relevant province, terrain, and location dummies as explanatory variables, and their inclusion adds significantly to the power of the equations. In the equation for Y_n, almost all the province variables are significant. If a county is a suburb or in an SEZ, its non-agricultural income per capita is raised significantly. Since the positive relationship holds even within provinces and areas of similar terrain and location, it seems likely that rural industrialization has indeed had a disequalizing effect on rural incomes.

The county data are available for the years 1985 through to 1991. Howes and Hussain (1994) have analysed the time-series to discover whether inter-county inequality increased over the six years. Real mean net output per capita of the counties rose by 6.4 per cent per annum over the period, while the Gini coefficient rose by 5.4 per cent per annum—from 24.4 to 33.5 per cent (Table 3.16). The main reason for the increase in inequality was the growing importance of non-agricultural output, which was very unequally distributed among counties. Table 3.16 shows that the non-agricultural Gini coefficient exceeded 50 per cent whereas the agricultural Gini fell short of 25 per cent. Non-agricultural activities grew from 27 per cent of net output in 1985 to 45 per cent in 1991. This change in sectoral composition accounted for 55 per cent of the increase in inequality among counties. In addition, 33 per cent of the increase was due to greater inequality of agricultural output, and 11 per cent to greater inequality of non-agricultural output (Howes and Hussain 1994: 10). It is interesting that the intercounty distribution of rural industry, although highly unequal, did not become substantially more unequal over this period of rapid industrial growth.

TABLE 3.16 *Decomposition of net output inequality among counties, 1985 and 1991*

	1985	1991	Percentage increase p.a. 1985–91
Total output			
Mean real output per capita	330	479	6.4
Gini coefficient	24.4	33.5	5.4
Non-agricultural output			
Mean real output per capita	89	213	15.6
Share of net output	27.0	44.5	—
Gini coefficient	52.6	55.9	1.0
Agricultural output			
Mean real output per capita	241	266	1.7
Share of net output	73.0	55.5	—
Gini coefficient	18.9	23.3	3.6

Notes: 1. Output per capita is measured in 1980 prices and is an annual figure.
         2. The Gini coefficient is expressed as a percentage, and output in yuan.

Source: Howes and Hussain 1994: tables 3,4.

3.4.3 Explaining the growth of spatial inequality

We turn to the possible causal relationships which might contribute to the growing spatial inequality that is suggested by the two previous sections. First, it is plausible to expect that an area's industrialization is assisted by its agriculture. Credit markets are imperfect: communities may have to rely on their own funds to develop rural industry. Thus, in its early stages, before it can be self-financed, rural industrialization may depend heavily on local agricultural savings. A case study of four counties found that in the two counties with advanced agriculture rural industrialization started early and proceeded rapidly, whereas in the two with backward agriculture it was belated and slow; the difference was explained in terms of access to local finance (Wang 1990: 222).[4] The initial source of funds for a sample of rural enterprises was found to be mainly bank loans or grants from community governments, which in turn were largely determined by local bank deposits and local revenue-raising (Byrd and Lin 1990: 200–1, 222, 364). Those counties with relatively high and fast-growing levels of agricultural output per capita were thus better able to industrialize.

The reverse causation—rural industry promoting agriculture—is also supported in the literature. After decollectivization, agriculture became increasingly dependent on rural industry for funds as state funding of agriculture declined (PRC 1990). In arguing for the simultaneous development of industry and agriculture, Bao (1991) calculated that over the decade 1978–88 the rural township and village enterprises transferred funds into the agricultural sector and rural community services equal to 34 per cent of state agricultural investment. Bao reported that 70 million workers were transferred from agriculture into rural industry over the decade. On his assumption that each worker would otherwise require 3.5 mu to farm, rural industrialization effectively created 245 million mu of farming land—an increase of 17 per cent—so relieving the poverty attributable to land scarcity. The counties which industrialized fastest would have benefited most.

There is a third reason to expect inequality among counties and among provinces to grow after 1978. Before then, restrictions on the choice of agricultural crops and on many types of economic activity and ceilings on consumption blunted incentives and meant that well-located areas could not capitalize fully on their advantages. After the reforms, areas suited for specialization in high-value crops, or close to city markets, or with good transport links, or with better human capital, or larger investible surpluses per capita, were able to grow relatively fast.

A fourth disequalizing factor was the redirection of regional policy in the post-Mao period. Under Mao, the Chinese government pursued an egalitarian regional policy, using its budget to transfer resources from the richer to the poorer regions. The policy appeared to prevent a widening of rural inequality: the coefficient of variation of the gross value of agricultural output per capita among provinces was 0.22 in 1957 and 0.19 in 1979 (Riskin 1987: 232). After 1978 the emphasis was switched from regional equality to regional comparative advantage—a change that benefited the relatively prosperous eastern seaboard. Thus, the twelve coastal provinces were to have 50 per cent of state investment in the Sixth Plan (1981–5) compared with 40 per cent in the Fourth (1971–5) and 30 per cent in the Third (1966–70) (Yang 1990: 235). The government wanted this region to become internationally competitive, and located all the Special Economic Zones on the coast. The coastal provinces secured 92 per cent of foreign investment over the period 1979–87 (ibid. 248). Even if much of this state and foreign investment was urban, it may have benefited industry and agriculture in the surrounding areas by expanding their markets and by altering people's values and attitudes.

The state budget continues to redistribute revenue from the rich to the poor provinces. Knight and Song (1993c: 206–9) were able to quantify the extent of redistribution through the state budget and its relation to province income per capita. By contrast, provinces themselves spend all their extra-budgetary revenue. We estimated the marginal propensity of central government to tax provincial governments in order to effect a redistribution of revenue among them. This marginal propensity to tax province mean household income per capita fell from 0.47 in 1983 to 0.27 in 1987 to 0.12 in 1990 (Knight and Li 1995: table 8). The power of central government to redistribute funds among the provinces was weakened by the growth of extra-budgetary revenue, which rose from 24 per cent of total revenue in 1978 to 45 per cent in 1987. The same analysis was conducted for counties within two provinces (Knight and Song 1993c: 209). It showed that the state budget does not permit important differences in budgetary expenditure per capita as between the rich and the poor counties of a province. However, the increasingly large extra-budgetary revenues and expenditures of counties are likely to have generated growing intercounty inequality in public provision.

Fifthly, the mechanism of divergence is partly to be found in the spatial distribution of rural investment. We have data by province on investment by individuals and collectives in the rural areas. Where I is 'productive' investment per capita (excluding housing investment) and Y is rural income per capita, we estimated I as a function of Y in 1988. The coefficient on Y (the rural marginal propensity to invest) is highly significant and no less than 0.64 (Knight and Song 1993c: 203–5 and table 2). As the rural income per capita of a province rises, it would seem that almost two-thirds of the additional income is invested productively.

Sixthly, although agriculture may have provided the initial funds for investment in rural industry, increasingly the source of funds became rural industry itself. We can see this from an analysis of time-series data for the rural areas by province (equation 3.7). We take the absolute change in industrial output per capita at constant prices between 1982 and 1988 (ΔY_m)

as the dependent variable.[5] The explanatory variables are industrial output per capita in 1982 (Y_m), agricultural output per capita in 1982 (Y_a), and change in that variable at constant prices (ΔY_a).[6] An OLS regression yields:

$$\Delta Y_m = 58.162^{**} + 3.685^{**}Y_m - 0.086Y_a + 0.010\,\Delta Y_a \tag{3.7}$$

(adjusted $R^2 = 0.940$, $F = 126.9$, mean $\overline{\Delta Y_m} = 466.9$, $N = 27$ and ** denotes significance at the 1 per cent level). The equation implies that rural industrialization is not significantly related to the initial level of agricultural output nor to its growth. However, it is strongly, significantly, and positively related to previous industrialization. If the initial value of industrial output per capita is 1 yuan higher, the increase in the constant price level of industrial output per capita is higher by 3.7 yuan over the six years.

This result is not surprising. By 1986, the dominant source of funds for the sample of rural enterprises in the four counties referred to above had become the enterprise itself or other local enterprises (Byrd and Lin 1990: 201, 376–9). The Chinese government's policy is to encourage self-reliance in the financing of local services in rural areas. This means that in the poor counties with little industry, the profits and taxes of enterprises were used by local governments to fund their expenditures. By contrast, in counties already endowed with local industry, a much higher level and proportion of profits was available to industrialize further. Past industrial success breeds further industrial success.

3.4.4 Inequality among villages

There is reason to expect that the processes of growing rural inequality which are observable at the province and county levels are also found among townships and villages within a county. Here we report in a qualitative way on a case study of seven villages in the Handan area of Hebei Province, which we conducted in 1993 (see Knight and Li 1997).

The village is an important unit in rural China. The administrative village (formerly the brigade) is where the State meets society, and the natural village (formerly the production team) involves considerable sharing of resources. Often a village comprises very few clans, giving rise to extensive social networks and social cohesion. Informal income redistribution among households of the village is therefore likely to occur. Village land is normally allocated among households on an equal per capita basis (Knight and Song 1993a: 208). Almost all revenue for village investment and village welfare provision must come from the village itself—in the forms of taxes on village people and production, the rent of land or factories, and the profits of village collective enterprises. Particularly where ownership is collective rather than private, village members receive priority in access to industrial employment. Those with a right to live in the village are effectively 'shareholders' in the resources of the village.

Before the village reforms the main source of income differences among villages was the quantity and quality of agricultural land and other natural resources available to each village. The development of rural industry produced a new source of income stratification among villages. Some villages were more successful than others in establishing industry, and some could not industrialize at all. This process of differentiation occurred both where rural industrialization was mainly organized in collectives and where it was mainly left to private initiative. Even within the same county, the varying success of villages in setting up non-agricultural activities depends on the initiative of the village leaders in forming collective enterprises or attracting private investors from outside or forming links with city enterprises, on the degree of enterprise, skill and initiative displayed by the villagers themselves, on village location, infrastructure and transport facilities, and on access to funds.

It seems that a process of cumulative causation is operating, with some villages being launched into virtuous circles of economic growth while others are trapped in vicious circles. For instance, entrepreneurial skills are often acquired through experience, in a process of learning-by-doing, and there can be externalities within a community because the success of one entrepreneur provides an example, information, contacts, and skills for others (Lall 1987); training on-the-job can raise the quality of workers, and village success can improve their attitudes and aspirations; additional village revenues can improve welfare services such as education and health with consequent effects on labour quality, and can raise investment in infrastructure such as irrigation, communications, and transport. Profits are available for the expansion of the enterprise or the establishment of new enterprises. If social welfare is not collectively provided in the industrialized villages, village households can afford to buy their own welfare and security, whereas in unindustrialized villages adequate provision cannot be made either collectively or individually.

Industrialization eventually creates a shortage of labour, and this draws in labour from neighbouring villages or from further afield. The migrants often work for low pay on the farms leased by village industry workers or in the least pleasant, most arduous jobs in village industry such as brick factories. Normally they cannot share, or have to pay fully for, village welfare services. Such in-migration can only be temporary as it is generally impossible for workers and their families to change their place of household registration. Rural labour markets are not competitive but are segmented as between village 'insiders' and 'outsiders'. Thus 'trickle down' effects do occur among villages but they tend to be diluted by vested interests and restrictions on labour mobility, and consequent lack of open competition.

This scenario can be illustrated by comparing two villages in our sample from the Handan area. Handan county had a mean income per capita in 1991 of 657 yuan. Both villages were within 20 kilometres of Handan city, yet one was among the richest in the county (mean income per capita, 1,080 yuan in 1991) and the other among the poorest (380 yuan). Both villages had progressed rapidly since 1978 but the ratio of their mean per capita incomes had doubled, from about 1.4 to 2.8. The greatest visual contrast between the two villages was in the quality and modernity of their housing.

The rich village contained six collectively owned enterprises, all effectively begun since 1985. Village revenue per capita (86 per cent of it coming from industry) actually exceeded household income per capita. The revenue was used for agriculture (e.g. irrigation), infrastructure (e.g. a new primary and middle school), welfare (e.g. educational and medical expenses), and for further investment in industry. The village made no fiscal contribution to the township or the county government. Migrant workers were employed in unpleasant jobs (which village people would not do) and as technicians (which the village lacked).

In the poor village, by contrast, agriculture was the main source of domestic income. Although a factory was planned, there was still no industry. No less than half of its labour force worked outside the village, for instance as construction workers and petty traders, in villages near by, or in Handan city. Yet there was still said to be a surplus of labour. Village revenue, mainly from agriculture, amounted to only 17 yuan per capita, and infrastructural investment and welfare services were very limited. The township government had provided only meagre financial assistance, for instance by acting as a guarantor of a bank loan for the proposed factory and by building a connecting road to the village. The economic progress of the village had been held back by limited and poor agricultural resources—the soil being dry and sandy—by conservative village leadership, and by weak infrastructure and transport facilities.

It is possible that in the next few years the poor village will industrialize and narrow the gap which widened during the 1980s. Nevertheless, it is the rich village that is in the better position to respond to new opportunities. The weak interventionist role played by the township and county governments would not be sufficient to prevent intervillage inequalities from continuing to grow in the future.

3.4.5 Inequality among households

How much income inequality exists among the households of a village, and how does it arise? The egalitarian allocation of farming land within a village implies that farm income will be fairly equal among households that choose to continue farming. Moreover, village revenues from rent of its natural resources and common property and the profits of village collective enterprises are likely to be allocated in an egalitarian way or spent on the common good. Because many households are related, villages tend to be cohesive communities.

We expect inequality within villages to grow as they industrialize, especially in the villages where industry is privately owned. Entrepreneurial and wage incomes in rural industry are higher than incomes from farming. The new power structure within villages may accentuate income inequalities because it reflects the economic success of households. Powers of patronage are in the hands of those with access to resources, or with human capital, or with good contacts. Economic and political power go hand-in-hand and they can interact, e.g. village cadres were in a good position to become economic leaders.

The CASS national household income survey of 1988 affords an opportunity to analyse both household and spatial determinants of rural income inequality by means of an income function analysis (Table 3.17). Some of

TABLE 3.17 *Income function analysis of rural households: 1988 CASS survey*

Independent variable	Mean values (%)	Coefficients	
		Y	y
Intercept	—	907.729**	6.5379**
Suburb area	1.4	−27.653	−0.0741
Hilly area	30.5	−32.706*	−0.0222
Mountainous area	20.5	−67.806**	−0.519**
Lake area	1.3	−128.58*	0.0164
Inland	96.7	−65.259	0.0112
National minority region	8.3	−83.772**	−0.1491**
Old revolutionary area	14.6	−33.736	−0.0243
Impoverished area	19.9	−107.07**	−0.1579**
Beijing	1.1	280.889**	0.1593*
Tianjin	1.1	444.794*	0.1959**
Hebei	6.8	−237.36**	−0.2234**
Shanxi	3.8	−432.79**	−0.5805**
Inner Mongolia	3.1	−408.16**	−0.4784**
Liaoning	3.1	−232.39**	−0.2484**
Jilin	2.6	−424.21**	−0.5876**
Heilongjiang	3.7	−629.80**	−1.0441**
Shanghai	1.1	740.835**	0.5959**
Zhejiang	4.7	434.681**	0.1600**
Anhui	5.3	−301.10**	−0.2820**
Fujian	3.2	−102.42**	−0.0689
Jiangxi	3.8	−153.74**	−0.1068**
Shandong	6.9	−222.90**	−0.1590**
Henan	6.9	−382.92**	−0.4485**
Hubei	5.2	−156.64**	−0.0962**
Hunan	5.7	−59.355	−0.0260
Guangdong	4.1	325.927**	0.3119**
Guanxi	3.7	−185.08**	−0.1758**

TABLE 3.17 *Continued*

Independent variable	Mean values (%)	Coefficients	
		Y	y
Sichuan	8.5	−85.854**	−0.0381
Guizhou	3.3	−212.54**	−0.2707**
Yunnan	3.7	−96.453*	−0.0112
Shaanxi	3.7	−446.14**	−0.6112**
Gansu	3.2	−292.71**	−0.2878**
Ningxia	1.1	−265.78**	−0.2317**
Hainan	1.4	147.27**	0.1719**
Farming land	4.54	−0.0298	−0.0004**
Household labourers (L)	3.00	75.7608**	0.0881**
L^2	—	−10.918**	−0.0126**
Average years of education of adults (E)	4.70	−3.2584	−0.0020
E^2	—	1.1426**	0.0010*
Average age of adults:			
16–20	0.2	35.445	−0.3579**
21–5	14.2	−33.651	−0.0574
26–30	31.9	−34.073*	−0.0359*
36–40	23.8	41.525**	0.0487**
41–5	10.7	115.869**	0.1155**
46–50	6.7	98.684*	0.1526**
51–5	4.2	221.300**	0.2098**
56–60	3.3	193.795**	0.2186**
61–5	2.6	208.957**	0.2381**
Communist Party member	0.2	102.539**	0.1145**
Five guarantees household	0.2	51.74	0.0033
Household with cadre	7.5	182.63**	0.1899*
Household with wage employee	4.5	283.31**	0.3289*
Household with urban resident	4.2	35.2816	0.0332
F-value		50.958	66.230
Adjusted R^2		0.2134	0.2618
Mean of dependent variable		812.721	6.509
No. of observations		9762	9749

Notes: 1. ** denotes that the coefficient is significant at the 1% level and * at the 5% level.
2. The dependent variables are rural household income per capita (Y) and its logarithm (y).
3. The omitted categories in the dummy variable analysis are non-suburb area, flat area, coastal area, not old revolutionary area, non-minority area, not officially designated 'impoverished' area, Jiangsu province, peasant household.
4. The definition of income is that used in the CASS survey rather than the official SSB definition.

Source: 1988 CASS survey, rural sample.

the location variables are large and significant in the equations, both with household income (Y) and the logarithm of income ($y = \ln Y$) as the dependent variable. Areas with minority populations and officially designated 'impoverished' areas have lower income, and flat areas have higher income. The province coefficients are generally large and almost all are significantly different from the omitted province, Jiangsu. They range from (rural) Shanghai and Guangdong (81 and 37 per cent above Jiangsu) to Heilongjiang and Shaanxi (65 and 46 per cent below). The location and province variables represent the spatial contribution to income differentiation among households. The size and significance of many of their coefficients suggest that the spatial contribution is large. Indeed, an equation confined to the spatial variables produces values of adjusted R^2 in the range 0.18–0.25, compared with the range 0.21–0.28 when all the independent variables are included.

It was possible to use the sample to examine the influence of the size of an area on the degree of household income inequality within it. Information was available on 161 counties in which at least ten sampled households are included, giving an average number of households per county of sixty-seven. The Gini coefficient for rural income per capita at the national level was 34 per cent. The mean Gini coefficient for twenty-eight provinces was 31 per cent, and for the 161 counties 27 per cent. The smaller the area under consideration, the lower the inequality within it. However, the Gini coefficient cannot be neatly decomposed: our spatial decompositions are based on the Theil index. When the province is the unit, we find that 78 per cent of income inequality occurs within provinces and 22 per cent among provinces. By contrast, when the county is the unit, we find that only 30 per cent of income inequality occurs within counties and as much as 70 per cent among counties. The implication is that much income is spatial and occurs among areas as large as or larger than counties.

How does the degree of inequality of household income per capita within an area relate to its level of income per capita? As rural development takes place, there may be greater scope for income differentiation among households: opportunities for increasing income are limited. However, rural development may generate labour shortages and market demands: especially if inward migration were restricted, the 'trickle-down' effects could spread prosperity to all households within an area. Which of these outcomes would emerge might depend on the pace and extent of development in the area. The former outcome might in time give way to the latter.

Table 3.18 shows the relationship between the inequality of income and its level, both among counties and among provinces. An attempt to introduce a non-linear specification, i.e. testing for the well-known inverted U-shaped relationship, was not successful. The interesting result is that, among counties, the relationship is negative and significant whereas, among provinces, it is positive and significant. There is a plausible explanation for

TABLE 3.18 *The relationship between inequality and level of income per capita in counties and provinces: 1988 CASS survey, rural sample*

	Gini coefficient (%)	
	County	Province
Intercept	28.007**	30.635**
County mean income per capita	−0.004**	
Province mean income per capita		0.016**
Adjusted R^2	0.030	0.312
F-value	5.915	12.318
Dependent mean	27.070	31.166
No. of observations	161	26

Notes: 1. ** denotes statistical significance at the 1% and *at 5% level.
2. The dependent variables are the Gini coefficient within the county and within the province.

these contrasting results. The reason why inequality might on average fall as income rises within a county (mean rural population 364,000) is that there is sufficient mobility of resources and labour for the benefits of economic growth to be spread widely. For a province (mean rural population 28 million), however, the size of the provincial economy and the immobility of resources and labour prevent widespread trickle-down throughout the province; hence the finding that the provinces that have become prosperous display higher inequality.

Returning to Table 3.17, we examine the characteristics of individual households as opposed to the places where they live. Whereas in many poor countries the amount of farming land is an important determinant of rural household income, in China the relationship is weak and not significant (see also Khan 1993: 97). This may represent inadequate standardization for land quality in the survey: owing to historically equilibrating settlement patterns and equalizing land policies, the quantity and quality of land tend to be inversely related. One might expect the addition of family labourers to raise income per capita (as the worker/dependant ratio rises) but the effect is surprisingly weak and non-linear: the optimal number of family labourers is three. Beyond this number, more labourers mean more underemployment. There is some tendency for income per capita to rise with the average age of adults, the peak occurring for adults in their fifties. There is also a significant tendency for income per capita to rise with the mean years of education that adult members of the household possess. For instance, those households which average more than twelve years of education have 12–16 per cent more income than those which average less than four years. The most important income-raising characteristics are whether the household contains cadres, or wage employees, or Communist Party members.

The effect of wage employment on rural household income is of particular interest. For instance, is wage income from rural industry obtained at the expense of the household's farm income? In the 1988 CASS survey, 16 per cent of rural households reported wage income. Most of these households also reported farm income. There may be good economic reasons for the lack of household specialization. The limited land available to a household often means that household farm production is not reduced on account of non-farm employment. Households containing wage employees are likely to be less underemployed and less dependent on the vagaries of farming.

In Table 3.19 we compare households with and without wage income in the 1988 CASS rural sample. Households with wage income (call them group one) have a mean income per capita 60 per cent higher than that of households without wage income (group two), and a mean income per worker 43 per cent higher. The income of group one is roughly equally divided between the two sources. Non-wage income per worker in group one is 72 per cent of (non-wage) income per worker in group two. The group differences arise partly because the wage per employee in group one exceeds (by 31 per cent) the income per worker in group two. The other reason is that the non-wage income per non-wage worker in group one exceeds (by 26 per cent) the income per worker in group two.

Group-one households appear to sacrifice little of their non-wage income in order to earn wages. There are various explanations for this apparent low opportunity cost of wage employment. One is that wage employment tends to be concentrated in high-income areas: prosperous farmers thus have better opportunities to get wage income. Supporting evidence is found in a province-level analysis which explains group one household behaviour in terms of household income per worker in group two. The wage per employee, the income per worker, the wage income per worker, and the number of wage employees per household in group one are all positively and significantly related to the income per worker in group two (Knight and Song 1993a: table 6.9).

A second explanation is that many rural households are characterized by a shortage of land, on one hand, and by a surplus of labour, on the other: labour can be released to rural industry without damaging farm production. Table 3.19 also shows the land available to the two household groups. The amount of land cultivated by the household is greater, per household and per worker, in group two households. However, group-one households have 29 per cent more cultivated land per non-wage worker. This helps to maintain their farm income.

TABLE 3.19 *Income and other characteristics of rural households with and without wage income: 1988 CASS survey, rural sample*

	Households with wage income	Households without wage income
No. of households	1615	8419
Mean number in household		
Members	4.89	5.03
Workers	3.08	2.94
Wage employees	1.47	0
Other workers	1.61	2.94
Per household		
Total income	3838	2538
Wage income	1885	0
Other income	1954	2538
Per capita		
Total income	838	524
Per worker		
Total income	1377	960
Wage income	684	0
Other income	693	960
Per employee		
Wage income	1254	0
Per non-wage worker		
Non-wage income	1214	960
Cultivated land per household		
Per household	9.19	12.57
Per worker	3.16	4.80
Per non-wage worker	6.17	4.80

Note: Income is expressed in yuan p.a.

Thirdly, wage employment may be more remunerative than other activities. The rural wage per employee is generally higher than (non-wage) income per (non-wage) worker, especially in the poorer provinces. An income function analysis of rural households receiving wage income in the 1988 CASS survey showed:

$$Y = 2328.83** + 938.09**E + 178.94**NE + 1.857L \qquad (3.8)$$

($\bar{R}^2 = 0.30$, F-value = 21.47, $\bar{Y} = 3848.57$, $N = 1470$, ** denotes statistical significance at the 1 per cent level, Y is household income, E and NE represent wage employees and other workers, and L is household land measured in mu). Both marginal products of labour are positive and significant, but the coefficient on the number of wage employees is over five times that on the number of other workers. There are two implications. First, wage employment has an opportunity cost in terms of income forgone as labour is withdrawn from other activities. Secondly, a unit of wage employment makes a greater contribution to income than does a unit of other labour, and is much to be preferred: its opportunity cost is relatively low.

It is notable that income from wages accrues largely to the richer rural households. In the 1988 CASS rural sample, the lowest decile of households, classified by income per capita, received only 1 per cent of wage income whereas the highest decile received 62 per cent; the poorest 30 per cent received only 3 per cent of wage income and the richest 30 per cent received 84 per cent (Khan *et al.* 1993: table 1.4). These authors also showed that wage income was the most disequalizing source of rural income.

In summary, two things are crucial for rural household income. The first is for the household to be in the right place, which, given restrictions on households' mobility, often means being born in the right place. The second is for household members to have access to the scarce income-earning opportunities. Households fortunate enough to have access to the limited number of jobs in rural industry will grab them and hold onto them. The spatial pattern of rural industrialization and the system by which industrial jobs are distributed are therefore important issues.

Knight and Song have conducted logit analyses of the determinants of rural workers' and households' access to wage employment. Education, male sex, and Communist Party membership each facilitate entry to wage employment, and the province coefficients are generally important (Knight and Song 1993*a*: table 6.11). Households are assisted by suburban location and hindered by mountainous location. Having less land and more workers in the household assists access, reflecting greater effort on the part of members or the equalizing allocation policies of village governments (ibid.: table 6.14). This is one piece of evidence to suggest that rural industry can have an equalizing effect on household incomes. Unfortunately, the other personal and the spatial determinants of industrial employment suggest, on the contrary, that rural industrialization is disequalizing.

3.5 RURAL AND URBAN WAGES FROM EMPLOYMENT

In their productive characteristics and in the factors that govern their incomes, 'township, village, and private' (TVP) enterprise workers are the rural group most comparable to urban workers. Section 3.4 showed that they constitute a rural élite. Can they also be viewed as a disadvantaged group of wage employees? Insofar as their wages differ from those of their urban worker counterparts, is it the large or small size of the difference that requires explanation?

In this section we contrast employees in rural and urban enterprises. How does the cash income of the two groups compare, and how do their income functions differ? Table 3.20 presents comparative regression results both for the full samples and for the industry subsamples, the latter being probably more comparable. The independent variables are chosen and defined to be the same for rural and urban workers alike. Column 1 shows the rural regression, column 2 the urban regression, column 3 the combined regression with an urban dummy variable but with the other coefficients constrained to be the same for rural and urban areas, and column 4 the combined regression with a full set of interaction dummy variables (rural residence being the base and urban being the interacted). Column 4 corresponds to the difference between columns 1 and 2 but has the advantage of indicating whether the coefficients are significantly different as between rural and urban areas.

The geometric mean of urban wages is 36 per cent higher than that of rural wages in both the full samples and the industry subsamples. How much of this is due to the location being rural or urban? The pooled but constrained regression (column 3) yields a significantly positive coefficient on the dummy variable in both cases. *Ceteris paribus*, urban wages are 12 per cent higher than rural wages in the former case and 5 per cent higher in the latter. However, this method of isolating the effect of location is unreliable because—as column 4 shows—many of the coefficients of the rural and urban samples are significantly different.

Consider the differences in coefficients that are interesting and significant. The negative coefficient on female sex is nearly twice as large in the rural sector, whether we consider the full samples or the industrial subsamples. Given the rural importance of piecework payments, this result is at first sight surprising. However, it might be explained by job discrimination in rural enterprises and relatively successful anti-discrimination policy in the urban state-owned sector. Oddly, membership of the Communist Party adds to the wage of urban employees but reduces that of rural employees, *ceteris paribus*. However, the different characteristics of rural and urban party members might explain this discrepancy. Rural party members were concentrated in the 'ordinary cadre' occupation category. It seems that most of them were village leaders, who might have had additional sources of income such as farming.

Compared with the lower-middle school level (E_4), the returns to education, although consistently significant only in the urban sector, are higher in rural enterprises, some coefficients significantly so. This could reflect greater rewards for human capital in the less institutionalized labour market. By contrast, the returns to age, which might also represent payments for human capital in the form of employment experience, are higher and more consistent in urban enterprises. This could reflect institutionalized stress on seniority in the centralized wage system.

TABLE 3.20 Income functions of wage employees and of industrial wage employees in rural and urban areas: 1988 CASS survey

Independent variables		All sectors				Industry sector			
		Coefficients							
		Rural	Urban	Combined (constrained)	Combined (interaction terms)	Rural	Urban	Combined (constrained)	Combined (interaction terms)
		(1)	(2)	(3)	(4)	(1)	(2)	(3)	(4)
Constant		7.159**	7.371**	7.248**	0.212**	7.205**	7.334**	7.275**	0.129*
Female	S_2	-0.131	-0.082**	-0.081**	0.049**	-0.176*	-0.079**	-0.084	0.098
Age									
-20	A_1	-0.253**	-0.360**	-0.327**	-0.107**	-0.212*	-0.364**	-0.323**	-0.152
21-5	A_2	-0.085*	-0.193**	-0.173**	-0.108**	-0.080	-0.183**	-0.165**	-0.103*
31-5	A_4	0.123**	0.157**	0.155**	0.034	0.159*	0.165**	0.165**	0.005
36-40	A_5	0.184*	0.199**	0.196**	0.150	0.227*	0.209**	0.206**	-0.018
41-5	A_6	0.143**	0.256**	0.246**	0.113**	0.187	0.267**	0.259**	0.081
46-50	A_7	0.204**	0.286**	0.276**	0.082*	0.168	0.278**	0.271*	0.110
51-5	A_8	0.043	0.312**	0.296**	0.269**	0.005	0.313**	0.291**	0.308*
56-60	A_9	0.266**	0.316**	0.311**	0.050	0.358**	0.325**	0.323**	-0.033
61-5	A_{10}	0.111	0.294**	0.274**	0.182	0.100	0.326**	0.257**	0.226
66+	A_{11}	-0.021	0.250**	0.190**	0.270	-0.782	0.285	0.078	1.067
College graduate or above	E_1	0.010	0.059**	0.064**	-0.041	-0.157	0.077**	0.074**	0.234
Professional school graduate	E_2	0.125*	0.020*	0.023*	-0.106*	-0.092	0.025	0.022	0.116
Upper school graduate	E_3	0.042	0.008	0.003	0.034	0.112*	0.013	0.012*	-0.099*
Primary school graduate	E_5	-0.072**	-0.063**	-0.063**	0.009	-0.043	-0.050**	-0.050**	-0.007

3 years or more of primary school education	E_6	-0.208**	-0.094**	-0.116**	0.114*	-0.172	-0.121**	-0.135**	0.051
Less than 3 years of primary school education	E_7	-0.127**	-0.206**	-0.206**	-0.079	-0.192	-0.164**	-0.198**	0.028
Communist Party membership	Cp_1	-0.098**	0.058**	-0.051**	0.156**	-0.179*	-0.070**	0.061**	0.249*
Minority nationality	M_1	-0.116**	-0.004	-0.013**	0.112**	-0.041*	-0.019	-0.020	0.022
Collective ownership	Ow_2	-0.039	-0.131**	-0.125	-0.092**	-0.052	-0.127**	-0.124**	-0.074
Private or individual ownership	Ow_3	-0.087	-0.568**	-0.159**	-0.481**	-0.121	-0.527	-0.141**	-0.406
Foreign or Sino-foreign joint venture	Ow_4	0.542**	0.205**	0.261**	-0.337*	0.584	0.151**	0.231**	-0.433**
Other ownership	Ow_5	-0.131**	-0.236**	-0.229**	-0.105	-0.147**	-0.217**	-0.027	-0.070
Government official	Oc_1	0.151	0.091**	0.102**	-0.060	0.068	0.100**	0.111**	0.032
Professional	Oc_2	0.004	0.081**	0.086**	0.077	0.232	0.053**	0.066**	-0.179
Ordinary cadre	Oc_3	0.133**	0.031**	0.033**	-0.102**	0.364**	0.047**	0.057**	-0.318**
Owner or manager in private sector	Oc_5	0.088	0.043	0.048**	-0.045	-0.008	0.029	0.008	0.037
Secondary sector	Es_2	0.057*	-0.015	-0.000	-0.072	—	—	—	—
Tertiary sector	Es_3	-0.067	-0.065**	-0.060**	0.001	—	—	—	—
Beijing	P_1	0.095**	0.063**	0.069**	0.032	0.113	0.080**	0.087**	-0.033
Shanxi	P_4	0.195**	-0.157**	-0.153**	0.039	-0.097	-0.164**	-0.153**	-0.067
Liaoning	P_6	0.365**	-0.000	0.010	0.365**	0.252*	-0.005	0.009	-0.256
Anhui	P_{12}	-0.250**	-0.059**	-0.060**	0.191**	-0.057	-0.028*	-0.021	0.029**
Henan	P_{16}	-0.035	-0.184**	-0.177**	-0.150**	-0.084	-0.172**	-0.162**	-0.088
Hubei	P_{17}	-0.285**	-0.084**	-0.085**	0.200**	-0.421**	-0.062**	-0.059**	0.360
Guangdong	P_{19}	0.408**	0.319**	0.329**	-0.089**	0.483**	0.297**	0.320**	-0.186**

TABLE 3.20 *Continued*

Independent variables		Coefficients							
		All sectors				Industry sector			
		Rural	Urban	Combined (constrained)	Combined (interaction terms)	Rural	Urban	Combined (constrained)	Combined (interaction terms)
		(1)	(2)	(3)	(4)	(1)	(2)	(3)	(4)
Yunnan	P_{23}	0.34	0.020*	0.027**	-0.014	-0.095	0.064**	0.076**	0.160**
Gansu	P_{26}	-0.022**	-0.002**	-0.002**	-0.020**	—	-0.002**	-0.002*	—
Urban				0.109**				0.050**	
F-value		8.562	357.518	328.124		6.814	193.945	183.577	
Adjusted R^2		0.147	0.441	0.4038		0.162	0.431	0.398	
No. of observations		1,670	17,165	18,836		1,050	9,175	10,226	
Mean of ln Y_1		7.1277	7.4323	7.4053		7.1084	7.4132	7.3819	
Variance of ln Y_1		0.3699	0.1694	0.1947		0.3512	0.1692	0.1965	

Notes: 1. ** denotes statistical significance at the 10% level; * denotes statistical significance at the 5% level.

2. The dependent variables are ln wage in rural areas (col. 1), urban areas (col. 2), and rural and urban areas combined (col. 3). Col. 4 is col. 1 minus col. 4, and provides a significance test of the difference between urban and rural coefficients.

If we regard the wage in local private and individually owned enterprises as the best indicator of the market wage, then foreign ownership pays vastly above the market wage in both sectors. The State is not only more important but also more interventionist in urban areas: the wage superiority of state over private and individual ownership is far greater in the urban than in the rural context. The coefficients on the ten-province dummy variables in the all-sector equations are more dispersed in rural areas (standard deviation 0.242) than in urban areas (0.140). This result is suggestive of greater market flexibility in rural areas.

Our final rural–urban comparison is to conduct a decomposition analysis of the difference between urban and rural mean wages. Where W_r and W_u are wages in rural and urban areas respectively, F_r and F_u are income functions, X_r and X_u are vectors of explanatory variables, and a bar indicates a mean value, the mean wage difference, $D = \overline{W}_u - \overline{W}_r$, can be decomposed as:

$$D = F_u(\overline{X}_u - \overline{X}_r) + [F_u(\overline{X}_r) - F_r(\overline{X}_r)]. \tag{3.9}$$

The former term is the part owing to differences in mean characteristics and the latter the part owing to differences in income functions. The alternative decomposition is:

$$D = [F_u(\overline{X}_u) - F_r(\overline{X}_u)] + F_r(\overline{X}_u - \overline{X}_r), \tag{3.10}$$

where the first term represents the difference attributable to functions and the second term the difference attributable to characteristics.

Table 3.21 presents the results of the decomposition analysis, both for all the wage employees and for industrial wage employees. The difference in geometric means ($\overline{W}_u - \overline{W}_r$) is 443 yuan in one case 435 yuan in the other. Decomposition (3.10), using $F_r(\overline{X}_u)$, attributes roughly equal importance to the difference in income-generating processes and the differences in mean characteristics. The difference in intercepts (−0.212) more than fully explains the fall in the urban mean wage that results from substituting the rural for the urban function, i.e. $F_u(\overline{X}_u) - F_r(\overline{X}_u)$. By contrast, decomposition (3.9), using $F_u(\overline{X}_r)$ attributes over 80 per cent of the difference in mean wages to different characteristics. There are two main reasons for this result. First, a comparatively high proportion of rural employees (46 per cent) are under 26 and the urban income function has high negative coefficients for these age-groups. Secondly, collective and private ownership together account for 79 per cent of rural wage employees and, with state ownership as the omitted category, their coefficients are large and negative in the urban sample.

By this test, it is the role of the State as the major employer and a high and age-related payer in the urban areas and the tendency for rural enterprises to employ young people that explain much of the difference in mean

TABLE 3.21 *Decomposition of the difference between rural and urban mean wages: 1988 CASS survey*

	All wage employees		Industrial wage employees	
	yuan p.a.	%	yuan p.a.	%
Mean difference (D)	443	100.0	435	100.0
Due to (using 3a):				
difference in income functions	88	19.9	5	1.1
difference in mean characteristics	355	80.1	430	98.9
Due to (using 3b):				
difference in income functions	239	54.0	220	50.6
difference in mean characteristics	204	46.0	215	49.4

wages. The use of the rural income function, however, suggests that the compositional differences are less important, so leaving a larger residual suggestive of rural disadvantage in wage payments.

Although their standardized mean wages are not very different, it is clear that wages are more widely dispersed in rural than in urban areas. The final row of Table 3.20 shows the variance of log wages. According to this inequality measure, rural inequality is twice as great, whether we consider wage employment as a whole or the industrial sector alone. This result is repeated when we use the Gini coefficient as the measure of wage inequality: the Gini coefficients are 0.46 and 0.23 in rural and urban areas respectively. Figure 3.3 suggests that the greater inequality among rural wage-earners is due to the fact that, whereas their modal wage is lower, their distribution has a long right-hand tail and some very high wages.

There are numerous pieces of evidence to suggest that the rural wage labour market is freer and more subject to market forces than its urban counterpart. For instance, piecework payments are important in TVPs. In a survey of TVP enterprise systems in three counties, Wu *et al.* (1990: table 15.7) found that piece-rates were the primary wage system in more than 60 per cent of enterprises in each county. We would therefore expect individual productive characteristics to influence pay. Consistent with this expectation, education is better rewarded in the rural than in the urban areas but age is less well rewarded.

Location also influences rural wages—more so than in urban China. Many of the province dummy variables are significantly different from

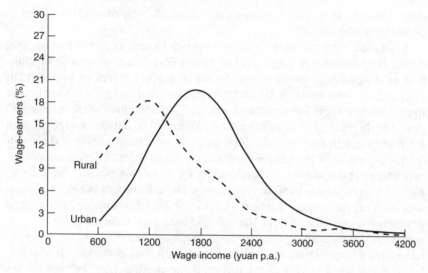

FIG. 3.3 *Frequency distributions of urban and rural wages, 1988*

Jiangsu, the omitted province. Searching for a pattern, we regressed p_i, the coefficient of the province dummy variable, on y_i, the equivalent measure of province rural income per capita ($y_i = \ln Y_i - \ln Y_j$, where i denotes province i and j Jiangsu):

$$p_i = 0.174^{**} + 0.413^{**} y_i \qquad (3.11)$$

(adjusted $R^2 = 0.246$, F-value $= 9.80$, $SEE = 22$ per cent, mean $p_i = 0.032$, $N = 28$, and ** denotes statistical significance at the 1 per cent level). The equation implies that a 10 per cent increase in the rural income per capita of a province raises the enterprise wage in the province by 4.1 per cent. This positive relationship (albeit less than unity) suggests that labour market forces are part of the story.

But not the whole story. Regression analysis of annual data at 1980 prices over the period 1978–89 yielded the following equation at the national level:

$$W_r = -517.11^{**} + 0.84^{**} Y_r + 0.70^{**} W_u \qquad (3.12)$$

(adjusted $R^2 = 0.939$, F-value $= 74.48$, $SEE = 7.3$ per cent, mean $W_r = 529.36$, $N = 11$, and ** denotes statistical significance at the 1 per cent level, and W_r = average rural wage, Y_r = average rural income per capita, and W_u = average urban wage). The implication is that W_r is positively and significantly responsive to both Y_r and W_u. An increase in Y_r (our best measure of the rural supply price) by 1 yuan raises W_r by 0.84 yuan, whereas an increase in W_u (the best available urban wage comparator) by 1 yuan raises W_r by 0.70 yuan. These results suggest an interpretation of wage determination in rural enterprises in terms of both market and institutional influences.

A detailed 1986 survey of TVP enterprises in four counties throws light on the determinants of wage levels (Meng 1990). The counties can be characterized according to the extent to which market forces or government intervention prevailed in the labour market and according to whether there was a scarcity or surplus of labour. Thus Nanhai (market, scarcity) paid the highest wages, followed by Wuxi (intervention, scarcity), with Jieshou (market, surplus) and Shangrao (intervention, surplus) the joint-lowest payers. In both the labour-scarce counties, industrial wages and agricultural incomes had risen closely together as labour became scarce, and had overtaken wages in state enterprises. The differences between Nanhai and Wuxi lay in the importance of the private sector, as opposed to the local government-owned sector, in Nanhai. The local governments in Wuxi intervened on wages, curbing them despite the shortages of labour, in order to redistribute income between industrial and agricultural workers. In Nanhai, by contrast, local governments followed the predominant market forces. The two labour-surplus counties differed in that Jieshou had a large private sector and a corresponding labour market, in which wages were well below those in state enterprises, whereas Shangrao's local governments required their enterprises to imitate the wage-setting practices of state enterprises.

The 1988 CASS survey shows urban wages to be 36 per cent higher than rural wages. Moreover, at least one-half, and possibly 80 per cent, of the difference can be explained by differences in the income-earning characteristics. At least some of this 'explanation' is merely a reflection of institutional differences between rural and urban areas. Thus, for instance the higher-paying public-sector employment is prevalent in urban but not in rural China. Nevertheless, by comparison with the high standardized urban/rural ratio of household income per capita, the standardized urban/rural ratio of wage income appears small.

The difference is surprisingly small given the rural–urban difference in openness to market forces and in methods of production. There are at least five possible reasons why the observed wage difference is not larger. One concerns measurement. We were unable to quantify the extent to which urban employers, by contrast with rural, provide a mini-welfare state for their employees. Subsidized benefits-in-kind (housing, health care, and pensions) could greatly increase the reported wage difference. Nor were we able to standardize for labour hours and effort. Both are likely to be greater in rural China, so causing the true wage difference to be understated. Turning to substantive reasons, we note, secondly, the high proportion of TVPs that are owned by township and village governments, which are prone to imitate the state wage system. The degree of intervention by governments is variable but can be important. Thirdly, the relation between market and local government wages depends on whether local labour is scarce or abundant. TVP employment is disproportionately located in the prosperous rural areas, in which local labour market scarcities and constraints on in-migration drive wages up. Fourthly, efficiency wage considerations may be more important in rural than in urban China insofar as TVPs are more profit-maximizing. Finally, the rents associated with supernormal profits in the disequilibrium stages of TVP expansion might well have been shared with TVP workers, especially in enterprises owned by local governments or involving ties of kinship between owners and workers within a village.

3.6 RURAL–URBAN INCOME INEQUALITY IN PERSPECTIVE

In this section we draw together the various strands of argument of the chapter in order to view rural–urban income inequality in perspective. The rural–urban divide is important but it is by no means the only source of income inequality in the Chinese economy. We obtain an idea of its relative importance from the following statistics, taken from the 1988 CASS survey. The Gini coefficient of income per capita was 24 per cent for urban China and 34 per cent for rural China. When the two sectors were combined, the rural–urban income gap spread out the frequency distribution of income per capita: the Gini coefficient for the full sample rose to 38 per cent (Khan *et al.* 1993: tables 1.5, 1.7, 1.10). The Theil index of inequality can be decomposed into between-sector and within-sector components. According to this measure, income differences between the rural and the urban sector accounted for no less than 43 per cent of total inequality in income per capita, and income differences within the sectors for 57 per cent.

The ratio of urban to rural mean income per capita in the 1988 CASS survey was 2.42. This ratio was higher than the official estimate, and it was accentuated by fiscal interventions. Decomposition of the difference showed that it was largely due to differences in the income-generation process rather than to differences in income-earning characteristics. The ratio was higher in the poorer provinces because provinces differ greatly in their rural income levels whereas urban wages tend to be standardized across the country. Urban wages also exceed rural wages from employment. However, the lower value of this ratio suggests that rural labour market forces are tempered by institutional or efficiency wage considerations.

The inequality of reported income in urban China is remarkably low by international standards, both spatially and among households. It reflects the compressed nature of the administratively determined wage structure. Apart from employment experience, productive personal characteristics are little rewarded in China. There is scant indication that market forces influence urban wages. The enterprise reforms have given enterprises greater control over wages, but the main result has been wage segmentation by ownership type and by profitability of enterprise.

By contrast, there is great inequality of rural income per capita. Much of this is spatial in character, reflecting the vast size and diversity of the country. Spatial inequality existed even under the egalitarian policies of the pre-reform period, but both spatial and household inequalities have increased during the reform period. We examined the extent and growth of inequality at the province, county, and household levels, and found reasons to expect that processes of cumulative causation are at work. In some areas rural industrialization has proceeded rapidly, labour shortages have emerged, and rural incomes have risen towards urban incomes. In other areas, rural development is limited, surplus labour is chronic, and the potential economic gain from rural–urban migration is very great.

Two general conclusions emerge from this chapter. First, rural–urban income differences are sufficiently great to warrant economic analysis and policy attention, and cannot be dismissed as insignificant by comparison with other dimensions of income inequality in China. Secondly, rural China is sufficiently vast and diverse generally to require analysis of the incomes of particular rural spatial categories or household types rather than analysis of *the* rural–urban income gap.

NOTES

1. The authors were part of the international team engaged in the research project, and contributed to the volume which was the major English-language product of the research (Knight and Song 1993a, 1993b, in Griffin and Zhao 1993).
2. Based on $f_u(\overline{X}_r)/f_r(\overline{X}_r)$ and $f_u(\overline{X}_u)/f_r(\overline{X}_u)$ respectively.
3. Errors-in-variable bias in a downwards direction occurs because under-reporting of the initial value of y implies over-reporting of Δy.
4. However, it is difficult to discriminate between lack of funds and lack of enterprise (see Byrd 1990: 216, on the same case study).
5. Predictions of the proportionate rate of growth of this variable are meaningless because some provinces had negligible rural industry in 1982.
6. Industry is defined as industry, construction, and transportation. 1982 is the earliest year for which data are available.

REFERENCES

Aguignier, P. (1988). 'Regional disparities since 1978', in S. Feuchtwang, A. Hussain, and T. Pairault (eds.), *Transforming China's Economy in the Eighties, ii*, London: Zed Books.

Anand, Sudhir (1983). *Inequality and Poverty in Malaysia. Measurement and Decomposition*, New York: Oxford University Press.

Bao Youdi (1991). 'Township and village enterprises should be developed together with agriculture', *China's Industrial Economic Research*, 2: 55–6 (in Chinese).

Byrd, William (1990). 'Entrepreneurship, capital and ownership', in Byrd and Lin (1990).

——and Lin Qingsong (1990). *China's Rural Industry. Structure, Development and Reform*, Washington, DC: World Bank and Oxford University Press.

Griffin, Keith, and Zhao Renwei (1993). *The Distribution of Income in China*, London: Macmillan.

Howes, Stephen, and Hussain, Athar (1994). 'Regional growth and inequality in rural China', Development Economics Research Programme EF No. 11, STICERD, London School of Economics.

——and Lanjouw, Peter (1991). 'Regional variations in living standards in urban China,' *Development Economics Research Programme CP No. 17*, London: STICERD, London School of Economics.

Khan, Azizur Rahman (1993). 'The determinants of household income in rural China', in Griffin and Zhao (1993).

——Griffin Keith, Riskin, Carl, and Zhao Renwei (1993). 'Household income and its distribution in China', in Griffin and Zhao (eds.), *The Distribution of Income in China*, London: Macmillan.

Knight, John, and Li Shi (1993). 'The determinants of educational attainment in China', in Griffin and Zhao (1993).

——––(1995). 'Fiscal decentralization, redistribution and reform in China', *Applied Economics Discussion Paper No. 168*. Oxford: Institute of Economics and Statistics, University of Oxford.

——––(1997). 'Cumulative causation and inequality among villages in China', *Oxford Development Studies*, 25 (2): 149–72.

——and Song, Lina (1993*a*). 'Workers in China's rural industries' in Griffin and Zhao (1993).

——––(1993*b*). 'Why urban wages differ in China', in Griffin and Zhao (1993).

——––(1993*c*). 'The spatial contribution to income inequality in rural China', *Cambridge Journal of Economics*, 17: 195–213.

——––(1993*d*). 'Income inequality in rural China: communities, households and resource mobility', *Applied Economics Discussion Paper No. 150*, Oxford: Institute of Economics and Statistics, University of Oxford.

Lall, Sanjaya (1987). *Learning to Industrialize: The Acquisition of Technological Capabilities in India*, London: Macmillan.

Lardy, Nicholas R. (1978). *Economic Growth and Distribution in China*, Cambridge: Cambridge University Press.

Meng Xin (1990). 'The rural labour market' in Byrd and Lin (1990).

Mills, Edwin, and Becker, Charles (1986). *Studies in Indian Urban Development*, New York: Oxford University Press.

Peoples' Republic of China (PRC) (1990). 'Rural industry and agricultural relations', *Problems of Agricultural Economics*, 11 (13–17) (in Chinese).

——State Council (PRC, SC) (1988). *Industrial Census 1985*, vol. 7, Beijing (in Chinese).

——State Statistical Bureau (PRC, SSB) (1986). *Statistical Yearbook of China 1986*, Oxford: Oxford University Press.

——––(PRC, SSB) (1989). *Chinese Rural Economic Statistics, Summary by Counties 1980–1987*, Beijing: State Statistical Bureau (in Chinese).

————(PRC, SSB)(1991). *Statistical Yearbook of China 1991*, Beijing: China Statistical Publishing House.

————(PRC, SSB)(1994). *Statistical Yearbook of China 1994*, Beijing: China Statistical Information and Consultancy Center.

Riskin, Carl (1987). *China's Political Economy. The Quest for Development since 1949*, Oxford: Oxford University Press.

Walder, Andrew G. (1987). 'Wage reform and the web of factory interests', *China Quarterly*, 109 (Mar.): 22–41.

Wang Xiaolu (1990). 'Capital formation and utilization', in Byrd and Lin (1990).

World Bank (1988). *World Development Report 1988*, Washington, DC: World Bank.

Wu Quhui, Wong Hansheng, and Xu Xinxin (1990). 'Non-economic determinants of workers' incomes', in Byrd and Lin (1990).

Yang Dali (1990). 'Patterns of China's regional development strategy', *China Quarterly*, 122 (June): 230–57.

Zhao Renwei (1993). 'Three features of the distribution of income during the transition to reform', in Griffin and Zhao (1993).

PART III

RURAL–URBAN COMPARISONS OF WELFARE

4

Education

Between rural and urban China there are great differences not only in incomes but also in welfare levels and opportunities for self-fulfilment. These disparities include educational provision and attainment. The object of this chapter is to examine rural–urban educational inequalities, their causes and implications. Our main source will again be the national household survey designed and conducted by the Institute of Economics, Chinese Academy of Social Sciences (the 1988 CASS survey) reported in Griffin and Zhao (1993).

The analysis of educational attainment in developing countries has received little attention from economists. Among the exceptions are Behrman and Wolfe (1984), Birdsall (1985), and Knight and Sabot (1990: part IV). Yet education is an important determinant of individual income in many developing economies, as reflected in the coefficients of education terms in earnings function analysis and in estimated private rates of return (see Psacharopoulos and Woodhall (1985: ch. 3) for a review of the evidence). The role of education in promoting growth has received confirmation from the experience of the high-performing East Asian countries (World Bank 1993). It has been argued that education was important both in promoting economic growth and in contributing to social equity in these countries (Birdsall and Sabot 1994). Schooling can raise welfare not only by increasing income and fostering innovation but also through its 'non-market' effects, such as improvements in health, nutrition, family size, upbringing of children, and opportunities for self-fulfilment and enjoyment, and its development of individual capabilities (Haveman and Wolfe 1984). Education may thus contribute even more to the inequality of welfare than to the inequality of income.

4.1 THE SETTING AND THE HYPOTHESES

Education is available more widely in the urban than in the rural areas of many developing countries. In part this may reflect higher private and social rates of return to education in an urban economy, although the possibility of rural–urban migration should make that irrelevant. The rural educational system may be demand-constrained by low benefits and high opportunity costs of schooling. It may alternatively be supply-constrained, reflecting the phenomenon of 'urban bias' in government policies, which allows urban people preferential access to education and other subsidized services.

The effects of urban and rural location on educational attainment cannot be isolated and understood without also analysing the other explanatory factors. When education is publicly funded and funding is regionally decentralized, we would expect the extent of educational provision in a region to depend on its income. A prosperous region can afford to devote more resources to education; unless it is cross-subsidized, a poor region can afford less. Given a high urban–rural income disparity, the more rural regions are at an educational disadvantage.

The children of poor, uneducated households are often at a disadvantage in the competition for school places, whether it be market competition or meritocratic competition. Within a market economy in which government provision of goods and services is limited, household income is an important determinant of the demand for education. First, households with more income demand more education as a consumption good. Secondly, given capital-market imperfections richer households can better afford to invest in education. Thirdly, richer households may have the knowledge, the contacts, or the complementary resources which raise the rate of return to education for them. For these reasons we expect household income and the educational attainment of children to be positively related in countries with predominantly private educational systems. Thus, rural–urban income disparities can also generate educational disparities.

In state-financed educational systems which are meritocratic in the sense that promotion to higher educational levels depends on success in competitive examinations, we expect educational attainment to depend on natural ability and on prior human capital acquisition. The children of educated parents may be at a competitive advantage not only because they tend to inherit greater natural ability but also because they have better opportunities to acquire out-of-school human capital. For instance, they may receive more stimulus from the household environment, absorb more favourable attitudes, and have better access to books or to electric light for evening study. In this way educational inequalities can be transmitted from one generation to another. If urban-dwellers are more educated than rural-dwellers, their children, also, are placed at an advantage.

A further determinant of educational attainment is time—the date at which a person is of school-going age. In many developing countries income per capita has risen over the last few decades, and with it the demand for education and the ability to finance it. Of no less potential importance has been the growing willingness and determination of governments to supply education, often in response to the perceived needs of the modernizing urban economy.

Where there is economic discrimination against women, girls have less incentive to acquire education than boys; where there is social discrimination against them, girls have less opportunity to acquire education. These are common phenomena in less developed countries, especially with male-dominated societies. Where there is discrimination against a minority group, this too can reduce the opportunities or the incentives for such people to receive education. It is common for such forms of discrimination to be stronger in the more tradition-bound rural society than in urban society with its modernizing values.

We turn now to the institutional setting. People in China have tradition-ally placed a high value on education. The reason may be found not only in Confucian attitudes but also in the potential economic benefits. In Imperial China the highest status and wealth positions were occupied by high officials in the bureaucracy. Entrance into the bureaucracy was by way of competitive examinations. The returns to the select few who secured entry were very great, stemming from the powers accorded to their posts. It would be misleading, however, to regard pre-liberation Chinese society as generally well educated. For instance, 62 per cent of people born in 1930, and 74 per cent of people born in 1920, were 'illiterate or semi-literate' (PRC, SSB 1988: 728). To a considerable extent education—and particu-larly higher education—was the preserve of the rich classes. With weak gov-ernment provision, educational opportunities for the poor majority were very limited. After the Communist Party took power in 1949 the private schools were nationalized, and government greatly expanded education at all levels. Moreover, education was heavily subsidized, so providing oppor-tunities for the children of poor families.

The system of education in China comprises primary (normally six years), secondary (normally three years of lower and three years of upper-middle school), and higher (or college) education (varying between two and five years). In 1960, according to the *World Development Report*, China had primary, secondary, and tertiary enrolment rates of 109, 21, and near 0 per cent (World Bank 1984: table 25). The Cultural Revolution of 1966–76 had a traumatic effect on education, as on other spheres of life: colleges were closed for the first four years, middle school enrolments were expanded remarkably, the primary cycle was reduced to five years, entrance exami-nations for admission to education were abolished at all levels, lowly fam-ily background and political acceptability became important criteria for college entrance, and the quality of education generally suffered. In 1988 the primary, secondary, and tertiary enrolment rates were 134, 44, and 2 per cent respectively (World Bank 1991: table 29). By comparison with other poor countries, enrolment rates were high at the lower and low at the upper levels.

The public subsidy per pupil escalates up the educational pyramid, from 60 yuan per annum in primary school, 141 yuan in middle school, and 2,315 yuan in college in 1987 (PRC, SSB 1989: 115). Tuition fees are low (aver-aging 10 yuan per pupil per annum at primary and middle school in 1988) or non-existent (at college). In 1988 the proportion of private fees in total educational expenditure was only 3.6 per cent (ibid. 116). The main private costs are expenditure on books and materials and earnings forgone. Students at college may receive grants towards their living expenses according to the income of their families.

Even in 1988 only 66 per cent of primary graduates, 29 per cent of lower-middle graduates, and 27 per cent of upper-middle graduates were able to continue their education to the next level (PRC, SSB 1989: 364–7). The broad base and narrow top of the educational pyramid, combined with heavy and escalating subsidies, produced excess demand for places. Within the framework developed above it is likely that educational provision in China has been supply-constrained at the upper levels. The rationing of scarce places has generally been on the basis of academic competition rather than ability to pay.

There is considerable administrative and fiscal decentralization in China. The emphasis placed on self-reliance, especially in the rural areas, contributes to regional disparities in educational provision. The 'plan budget' negotiated and approved by central government involves fiscal redistribution from richer to poorer areas (Knight and Song 1993*a*). However, 'extra-budgetary' revenue and expenditure are dependent on local revenue-raising capacities and can thus give rise to spatial inequalities in educational expenditures. In particular, the dualistic system of financing education as between urban and rural areas gives rural residents poorer educational opportunities in respect of both quantity and quality. Educational rationing is thus tighter in the rural areas.

This discussion gives rise to the following hypotheses that will be tested:

(1)   There has been a rural–urban divide in educational provision in China: urban people have much higher educational attainment than rural people (Section 4.2).

(2)   The reasons for this difference are to be found in both supply and demand considerations: spatial differences in income, in attitudes, and in subsidized educational provision associated with different administrative and funding arrangements (Sections 4.3–4.6).

(3)   In urban China educational opportunities have improved with time, the crucial factor being the increased availability of heavily subsidized education. The modernizing influence of cities may have eliminated race and sex discrimination but we expect social class—in the form of parental education—to play an important role (Section 4.3).

(4)   Ethnic and gender discrimination may have persisted in rural China. Owing to the decentralized method of funding rural services, rural income levels should be important in determining variation in educational attainment among provinces. Parental education may improve demand for and access to rural education (Section 4.4).

(5) We expect to find interesting urban–rural differences in the determinants of current educational enrolment. We hypothesize that in urban
areas educational aspirations are generally high and there is excess
demand for education, whereas demand—as governed by the income
benefits and by the direct and opportunity costs of education—may
be more decisive in rural areas. Higher rural incomes of both households and provinces should help to overcome funding constraints. We
examine the hypothesis that the rural educational system is demand-
constrained rather than supply-constrained (Sections 4.5 and 4.6).

4.2 THE RURAL–URBAN DIVIDE IN EDUCATION

We use a small subset of the characteristics of households and individuals
reported in the 1988 CASS survey. These include education, gender, age,
province, majority/minority status, rural/urban residence, and city size.
Table 4.1 shows each independent variable to be used in the estimation of
educational attainment functions, its notation, its frequency distribution,
and its mean years of education.

Education, being the dependent variable in our analysis, deserves
detailed explanation. In the urban questionnaire the educational attainment of individuals was classified into eight levels (Table 4.1). Since our
dependent variable in the estimation of educational attainment functions
is years of education completed, it is necessary to assume a mean value of
years of education corresponding to each of these levels: their assumed
mean values are shown opposite. Owing to the more limited education of
rural people, somewhat different categories were used in the rural survey;
these levels and corresponding mean values are also set out in the table. It
is notable that 61/19 per cent of the sample of rural/urban persons aged 16
and over who had completed their education had no more than primary
education, 30/37 per cent were lower-middle school graduates, 8/33 per cent
upper-middle or professional school graduates, and only 0.5/12 per cent
college graduates.

Educational attainment functions were estimated for three samples:
rural, urban, and national (rural and urban combined). In each case the
dependent variable is the number of years of education of individuals aged
16 and over who had completed their formal education. The explanatory
variables differ slightly among the samples but three sets are common: sex,
age, and minority status. Because almost all provinces were covered in
the rural survey and only some in the urban survey, there are 28 province
variables in the rural and national functions and only 10 in the urban
function. City size is a variable available only to the urban function.
Finally, the national function contains rural or urban residence as an
additional regressor.

TABLE 4.1 *The variables: definitions, notation, proportion of observations, and mean values: 1988 CASS survey*

Variable	Notation	Proportion of observations			Mean value of education in years (E)		
		National	Urban	Rural	National	Urban	Rural
a. Education							
Illiterate		0.176		0.226			0
1–2 years of primary school		0.028	0.038	0.029		2	2
Less than 3 years of primary school			0.021	0.033			
3–5 years of primary school		0.248	0.135	0.325		4	4
Primary school graduates		0.325	0.365	0.298		6	6
Lower-middle school graduates		0.136	0.225	0.075		9	9
Upper-middle school graduates		0.046	0.100	0.009		12	12
Professional school graduates			0.060	0.005		13	13
2–3 years college graduates		⎫	0.057			17	
2–4 years college graduates		⎬ 0.027				17	15
4 years college graduates & above		⎭				17	
b. Gender							
Male	S_1	0.4927	0.4878	0.4958	8.50	10.50	6.69
Female	S_2	0.5073	0.5122	0.5042	6.03	8.73	4.22
c. Age-group							
16–20	A_1	0.1115	0.0449	0.1553	7.40	10.20	6.87
21–5	A_2	0.1253	0.0892	0.1489	8.54	11.25	7.47
26–30	A_3	0.0884	0.0969	0.0826	9.11	11.19	7.49
31–5	A_4	0.1240	0.1438	0.1108	8.29	10.59	6.32
36–40	A_5	0.1277	0.1471	0.1146	7.57	9.96	5.54
41–5	A_6	0.1002	0.1075	0.0951	7.39	10.20	5.30

46–50	A_7	0.0928	0.1132	0.0792	7.19	9.89	4.65
51–5	A_8	0.0755	0.0927	0.0641	6.16	8.98	3.47
56–60	A_9	0.0561	0.0655	0.0498	4.86	7.77	2.33
61–5	A_{10}	0.0377	0.0392	0.0366	3.61	6.47	1.59
66 and over	A_{11}	0.0609	0.0592	0.0619	1.91	4.01	0.58
d. Province							
Beijing	P_1	0.0269	0.0551	0.0083	9.19	9.90	6.01
Tianjin	P_2	0.0053		0.0088	6.34		6.32
Hebei	P_3	0.0369		0.0613	6.40		6.40
Shanxi	P_4	0.0610	0.1054	0.0318	8.70	9.80	6.26
Inner Mongolia	P_5	0.0171		0.0284	5.63		5.63
Liaoning	P_6	0.0555	0.0982	0.0274	8.85	9.29	6.23
Jilin	P_7	0.0143		0.0237	6.43		6.42
Heilongjiang	P_8	0.0188		0.0311	6.01		6.00
Shanghai	P_9	0.0052		0.0087	7.29		7.29
Jiangsu	P_{10}	0.0824	0.1345	0.0479	8.02	9.39	5.48
Zhejiang	P_{11}	0.0250		0.0416	5.59		5.59
Anhui	P_{12}	0.0712	0.0972	0.0540	7.09	9.23	4.55
Fujian	P_{13}	0.0181		0.0301	4.94		4.93
Jiangxi	P_{14}	0.0205		0.0341	5.08		5.08
Shandong	P_{15}	0.0397		0.0659	5.70		5.70
Henan	P_{16}	0.0860	0.1164	0.0659	7.60	9.70	5.13
Hubei	P_{17}	0.0725	0.1075	0.0493	8.18	10.08	5.45
Hunan	P_{18}	0.0285		0.0473	6.07		6.07
Guangdong	P_{19}	0.0733	0.1184	0.0436	8.31	9.55	6.07
Guangxi	P_{20}	0.0232		0.0384	5.67		5.67
Hainan	P_{21}	0.0078		0.0130	6.06		6.04
Sichuan	P_{22}	0.0471		0.0781	5.46		5.46
Guizhou	P_{23}	0.0183		0.0304	3.81		3.80

TABLE 4.1 *Continued*

Variable	Notation	Proportion of observations			Mean value of education in years (E)		
		National	Urban	Rural	National	Urban	Rural
Yunnan	P_{24}	0.0626	0.0991	0.0387	7.23	9.10	4.05
Shaanxi	P_{25}	0.0210		0.0348	5.51		5.51
Gansu	P_{27}	0.0452	0.0667	0.0309	7.05	9.26	3.90
Qinghai	P_{28}	0.0074		0.0122	3.42		3.42
Ningxia	P_{29}	0.0063		0.0104	4.22		4.22
e. Nationality							
Han	M_1	0.9442	0.9649	0.9305	7.52	9.57	5.98
Minority	M_2	0.0558	0.0351	0.0695	6.32	10.21	5.03
f. Residence							
Urban	R_1	0.3976			9.59		
Rural	R_2	0.6024			5.45		
g. City size							
Large cities	C_1		0.2669			10.01	
Middle cities	C_2		0.1669			9.43	
Small cities and towns	C_3		0.5725			9.42	

The regression results are shown in Table 4.2. In all three equations every included coefficient is significant, apart from the province dummy variables, the great majority of which in the national and rural samples, and a minority of which in the urban sample, are significantly different from Beijing.

TABLE 4.2 *Regression analysis: the determinants of educational attainment: 1988 CASS survey*

Independent variables		Coefficients		
		National	Urban	Rural
Intercept		7.877**	12.123**	8.014**
Female	S_2	−2.218**	−1.787**	−2.499**
16–20	A_1	0.600**	−0.302**	0.791**
21–5	A_2	1.097**	0.692**	1.273**
26–30	A_3	1.001**	0.691**	1.278**
36–40	A_5	−0.710**	−0.616**	−0.752**
41–5	A_6	−0.721**	−0.338**	−0.973**
46–50	A_8	−2.338**	−1.700**	−2.906**
56–60	A_9	−3.523**	−2.979**	−3.949**
61–5	A_{10}	−4.563**	−4.275**	−4.749**
66 and over	A_{11}	−5.884**	−6.455**	−5.521**
Tianjin	P_2	0.468*		0.535*
Hebei	P_3	0.464**		0.535**
Shanxi	P_4	−0.321**	−0.005	0.444*
Inner Mongolia	P_5	−0.529**		−0.435*
Liaoning	P_6	−0.180*	−0.202	0.566**
Jilin	P_7	0.368*		0.461*
Heilongjiang	P_8	−0.130		−0.109
Shanghai	P_9	1.241**		1.310**
Jiangsu	P_{10}	−0.602**	−0.050	−0.480**
Zhejiang	P_{11}	−0.354**		−0.307
Anhui	P_{12}	−1.349**	−0.373**	−1.524**
Fujian	P_{13}	−0.949**		−0.918**
Jiangxi	P_{14}	−0.957**		−0.945**
Shandong	P_{15}	−0.313**		−0.263
Henan	P_{16}	−0.655**	−0.012	−0.688**
Hubei	P_{17}	−0.295**	0.723**	−0.561**
Hunan	P_{18}	−0.051		0.018
Guangdong	P_{19}	−0.384**	−0.070	0.171
Guangxi	P_{20}	−0.345**		−0.224
Hainan	P_{21}	0.298		0.398
Sichuan	P_{22}	−0.561**		−0.520**
Guizhou	P_{23}	−2.226**		−2.079**
Yunnan	P_{24}	−1.345**	−0.691**	−1.528**
Shaanxi	P_{25}	−0.526**		−0.503**

TABLE 4.2 *Continued*

Independent variables		Coefficients		
		National	Urban	Rural
Gansu	P_{27}	−1.496**	−0.228	−2.193**
Qinghai	P_{28}	−2.477**		−2.354**
Ningxia	P_{29}	−1.796**		−1.732**
Minority status	M_2	−0.216**	0.613**	−0.545**
Urban	R_1	4.578**		
Middle cities	C_2		−0.690**	
Small cities and towns	C_3		−0.820**	
Adj. R^2		0.4578	0.2579	0.3857
F-value		1,171.13	334.00	538.85
Percentage standard error of the estimate		47	36	58
No. of observations		55,427	22,041	33,404

Notes: 1. ** denotes significance at the 1% and * at the 5% level.
2. The dependent variables are the educational attainment, measured in years of education (E), of individuals in the national, urban, and rural samples.

The proportion of the variance explained is 26 per cent in urban areas, 39 per cent in rural areas, and as high as 46 per cent nationally.

On average, urban residents had 9.6 years of education in 1988 and rural residents 5.5 years, a difference of 4.1. The standardized mean difference, taken from the national regression, is 4.6 years (Table 4.2). As we show in Figure 4.1, urban educational attainment consistently exceeds rural attainment over time: there has been only a slight narrowing in the mean difference over four decades.

A caveat is in order: the survey shows where educated people are now, not where they originated. It is thus a guide to the location of employment opportunities, and not to the location of educational opportunities, as between rural and urban areas. The problem is only a minor one because the opportunities for rural people to settle in the cities have been negligible. There is one exception: since rural people who reach higher education are likely to attend college in urban areas and be assigned to jobs in urban areas, the bias is liable to be important for college graduates.

The coefficient on urban residence in the regression equation for the national sample is potentially misleading as there are significant differences in the separate equations for rural and urban educational attainment.[1] A

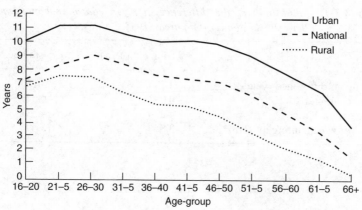

Fıg. 4.1 *Average years of eduction of adults: national, urban, and rural, 1988*

decomposition analysis was therefore conducted in order to distinguish that part of the gross difference in mean education which is due to differences in characteristics from that part which is due to differences in functions. The gross mean difference:

$$G = \overline{E}_u - \overline{E}_r = F_u(\overline{X}_u) - F_r(\overline{X}_r), \tag{4.1}$$

where $\overline{E}_i$ = the mean years of education in location i; $i = u, r$ = urban, rural location; F_i = the educational attainment function in location i; and $\overline{X}_i$ = a vector of mean values of explanatory characteristics in location i. Eq. (4.1) can be rewritten as:

$$G = [F_u(\overline{X}_u) - F_u(\overline{X}_r)] + [F_u(\overline{X}_r) - F_r(\overline{X}_r)] \tag{4.2a}$$

or

$$G = [F_u(\overline{X}_u) - F_r(\overline{X}_u)] + [F_r(\overline{X}_u) - F_r(\overline{X}_r)]. \tag{4.2b}$$

The first term in equation (4.2*a*) represents the contribution of character-istics and the second term the contribution of coefficients; the reverse is the case in (4.2*b*).

The results of this exercise, using a common set of variables and those provinces included in the urban sample, are set out in Table 4.3. Both equa-tions show the contribution of differences in characteristics to be slightly negative and that of differences in coefficients other than the intercept term slightly positive. It is the difference in intercept terms that is crucial. These results suggest the need for an explanation of the rural–urban disparity that is unassociated with the extent or effects of sex, age, minority status, or province.

TABLE 4.3 *Decomposition of the difference in mean educational attainment as between rural and urban areas: 1988 CASS survey*

	Using eq. (4.2a)	Using eq. (4.2b)
Gross mean difference (years)	4.183	4.183
Due to: characteristics	−0.093	−0.347
coefficients	4.276	4.531
of which: intercept term	3.896	3.896

4.3 URBAN EDUCATIONAL ATTAINMENT

Let us examine the urban sample more closely. The coefficients on the age dummy variables in Table 4.2 reveal a clear pattern of improvement over time. All coefficients are significantly different from the omitted category (age-group 31–5). Those in the age-group 21–5 have over seven more years of schooling, *ceteris paribus*, than those in the oldest group, 66+. The pattern is broken in the age-group 16–20 because those who had not completed their education were excluded from the sample, so reducing the reported education of that cohort. The monotonic pattern is also broken for the age-group 36–40 in 1988, which was affected by the Cultural Revolution. Young urban people were sent to the countryside and colleges were closed from 1966 to 1969. Consequently, many in this cohort missed the opportunity to complete their education.

On average, urban men have received more years of education than urban women, both the unstandardized and the standardized difference being 1.8 years (Tables 4.1 and 4.2). In Figure 4.2 we show that the sex difference by age-group rises consistently with age in the urban areas but is negligible for those under thirty. It would appear that traditional values favouring the education of boys rather than girls have been gradually eroded over forty years in the urban areas of China.

Tables 4.1 and 4.2 show that, contrary to our expectations, minority people in urban areas have more education than Han people, both their standardized and their unstandardized means being 0.6 years greater. This could be the result of affirmative action in favour of the education of minorities but it could also be owing to a process of self-selection whereby successful minority people have spread to cities throughout China.

Three sizes of city can be distinguished in the urban sample: large (with population exceeding 1,000,000), middle (500,000–1,000,000), and small (fewer than 500,000). Table 4.2 shows that middle-size cities have an average educational attainment 0.7 years less, and small cities 0.8 years less than large cities, *ceteris paribus*. There are two possible explanations: that educational opportunities increase with city size, or that larger cities attract

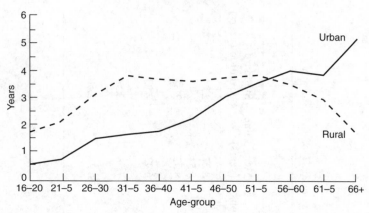

Fɪɢ. 4.2 *Difference in years of education between males and females: urban and rural, 1988*

more educated people. It is mainly only at the college graduate level that workers have an opportunity to move from their original place of residence. The latter hypothesis would imply that the city sizes will differ considerably in the proportion of college graduates in their adult populations. College graduates accounted for 14.4 per cent of the adult population of large cities, 10.8 per cent in the case of middle-size cities, and 9.6 per cent in the case of small cities. Assume that the alternative to being a college graduate (16 years of education, taking the average of two categories) was to have the mean years of education of the relevant subsample (9.43 years for middle-size and 9.42 years for small cities). Since college education adds 6.58 years to an additional 4.8 per cent of the population, it can explain only 0.31 years of the difference (0.82 years) between large and small cities. The implication of this exercise is that the majority of the difference in mean educational attainment between large and small cities is due to differences in educational provision rather than migration.

The 1988 survey is a household survey containing information on all household members. It does not provide information on persons who are not living in the household. However, there is a subset of over 5,000 households in which two generations are to be found. This subsample provides an opportunity to examine the role of family background—to be specific, the education of parents—on educational attainment.

We use the following variables: father's education, in years (*FED*), mother's education (*MED*), parents' mean education (*PED*), son's education (*SED*), daughter's education (*DED*), and child's education irrespective of gender (*CED*). We define these variables and provide their descriptive statistics in Table 4.4. Our object is to predict the educational attainment of the second generation from that of the first. There could be

TABLE 4.4 *Parent and child education variables: notation, frequency, and descriptive statistics, 1988 CASS survey*

Variable	Notation	Urban			Rural		
		No. of observations	Mean value (years)	Standard deviation (years)	No. of observations	Mean value (years)	Standard deviation (years)
Education of child	CED	2,464	11.27	2.26	3,001	8.27	2.24
Education of son	SED	1,265	11.26	2.29	1,448	8.54	2.12
Education of daughter	DED	1,197	11.28	2.22	1,553	8.02	2.33
Average education of parents	PED	2,464	8.84	3.14	3,001	6.92	2.23
Education of father	FED	2,464	9.76	3.56	3,001	7.58	2.59
Education of mother	MED	2,464	7.92	3.56	3,001	6.27	2.56

TABLE 4.5 *Regression analysis explaining the education of children by that of their parents: urban sample: 1988 CASS survey*

Equation	Independent variables	Coefficients		
		CED	SED	DED
1	PED	−0.1700**	−0.2180*	−0.1308
	PED^2	0.0220**	0.0250**	0.0196**
	Intercept	10.8396**	10.9931**	10.7136**
	$\bar{R}^2$	0.1226	0.1304	0.1160
	F-value	173.02	95.77	79.46
	No. of observations	2,646	1,265	1,197
2	FED	0.1429**	0.1543**	0.1313**
	MED	0.0929**	0.0884**	0.0992**
	Intercept	9.1435**	9.0659**	9.2090**
	$\bar{R}^2$	0.1084	0.1122	0.1046
	F-value	150.78	80.85	70.89
	No. of observations	2,646	1,265	1,197
3	FED	−0.0556	−0.0697	−0.0450
	FED^2	0.0094**	0.0107*	0.0083*
	MED	−0.1112*	−0.1408*	−0.0901
	MED^2	0.0125**	0.0140**	0.0117**
	Intercept	10.7375**	10.8528**	10.6580**
	$\bar{R}^2$	0.1236	0.1315	0.1159
	F-value	87.83	48.83	40.19
	No. of observations	2,646	1,265	1,197

Notes: 1. ** denotes statistical significance at the 1% and * at the 5% level.
2. The dependent variables are the values of *CED*, *SED*, and *DED*.

a positive correlation between the education of parents and children which arose simply from the passage of time: both younger children and younger parents may have had greater educational opportunities. However, this is not the case within our two-generation national sample, in which the child is aged between 16 and 30. Among the fifteen child-ages (16 . . . 30), we find a negative correlation between mean *PED* and mean *CED* (−0.30), whereas within each child-age, we find the correlation between *PED* and *CED* in each case to be positive (ranging from +0.20 to +0.59).

We concentrate on the 2,464 urban households which contain parents and their children aged 16 to 30 who have completed their schooling. The urban results are set out in Table 4.5. Equation 1 relates *CED* to *PED* and *PED^2*. Both coefficients are significant but only the squared term is positive: the education of parents has a progressively stronger marginal effect on that of their children. In the linear version (eq. 2) the education of fathers is more important than the education of mothers, a result that holds good for *CED*, *SED*, and *DED* alike. Mother's education is only slightly more important for daughters than for sons. When squared terms are introduced (eq. 3), it is the squared terms that are significant. We show these relationships graphically in Figure 4.3. The first six years—corresponding to primary school— of parental education are ineffective but thereafter parental education has an increasingly important effect on educational attainment. The extent of the non-linearity is similar in all six cases (corresponding to eq. 3) represented. To summarize: the educational attainment of parents does assist the educational attainment of their children, and the relationship appears to be non-linear, implying increasing marginal returns to parental education.

Further evidence of a close relation between the educational levels of two generations is provided by a survey of secondary-school pupils conducted in Haidian District, Beijing (Fang *et al.* 1990). The schools varied in the quality of teachers and equipment. Three categories of school were distinguished: high-quality ('key'), ordinary, and low-quality. Access to preferred schools depended almost entirely on scores in the entrance examination. Despite this meritocratic competition, there was a powerful relationship between the quality of school attended and the educational level of the pupil's mother. For instance, consider lower-middle schools: 71 per cent of key school pupils had mothers with college education and 6 per cent had mothers with lower-middle school education, the corresponding figures for low-quality schools being 12 and 41 per cent respectively. The quality of school attended in turn influences prospects for entrance to college.

The existence of non-linearities suggests that parents' education may be particularly important in determining urban access to post-secondary

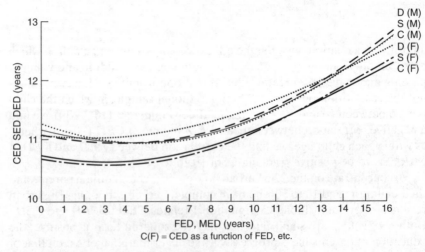

FIG. 4.3 *Relationship between children's and parents' education: urban survey, 1988*

education. We explore this hypothesis by conducting a logit analysis for the two-generation urban sample, the dependent variable being $E_{1,2} = 1$, i.e. 'attended college', and having a value of 0.178. The equation, presented in Table 4.6, predicts 74 per cent of the cases correctly. Although age and gender have the expected signs, their coefficients are not significant. All the province coefficients are negative (implying lower attendance than in Beijing), three significantly so. The most interesting results, however, concern parents' education. The coefficients on father's education rise

TABLE 4.6 *Logit analysis of college attendance: urban two-generation sample: 1988 CASS survey*

Independent variable	Notation	Coefficients
Education of father		
College	FED_1	2.5371**
Professional and upper-middle school	FED_2	1.7472**
Lower-middle school	FED_3	1.1736
Primary school	FED_4	0.8975
Education of mother		
College	MED_1	0.9794*
Professional and upper-middle school	MED_2	0.4627
Lower-middle school	MED_3	0.1763
Primary school	MED_4	−0.1283
Age, in years	A	−0.0120
Male	S_1	0.1675
Province		
Shanxi	P_4	−0.8232*
Liaoning	P_6	−0.0303
Jiangsu	P_{10}	−0.6884
Anhui	P_{12}	−0.4746
Henan	P_{16}	−0.6217
Hubei	P_{17}	−0.6264
Guangdong	P_{19}	−1.0385*
Yunnan	P_{24}	−1.3645*
Gansu	P_{27}	−0.5172
Intercept		−2.3697**
−2 log likelihood		−404
Mean of dependent variable		0.178
Cases predicted correctly (%)		74
No. of observations		986

Notes: 1. **denotes statistical significance at the 10% and *at the 5% level.
2. The omitted categories are 'did not complete primary school' (FED_5, MED_5), female (S_2), and Beijing (P_1).
3. The dependent variable is whether the individual attended college ($E_{1,2} = 1$).

TABLE 4.7 *Probability of college attendance, by mother's and father's education: urban two-generation sample: 1988 CASS survey*

Education of mother	Education of father				
	FED_1	FED_2	FED_3	FED_4	FED_5
MED_1	71	53	39	33	17
MED_2	60	41	28	23	11
MED_3	53	34	22	18	8
MED_4	45	27	17	14	6
MED_5	49	30	19	16	7

Notes: 1. The probabilities are calculated by standardizing the other explanatory variables, i.e. setting age and gender at their mean values ($A = 27, S_2 = 0.58$) and taking Beijing to be the province.

2. FED_1, MED_1 = 2 or more years of college education.
FED_2, MED_2 = professional or upper-middle school.
FED_3, MED_3 = lower-middle school.
FED_4, MED_4 = completed primary school (6 years).
FED_5, MED_5 = did not complete primary school.

monotonically; the highest two levels are significantly greater than the lowest. The coefficients on mother's education are smaller but again show a plausible pattern.

The probability of having a college education varies greatly over the matrix of parents' education (Table 4.7). The probabilities range from 71 per cent when both parents are college graduates to 7 per cent when neither completed primary education. Father's education has a more decisive influence than mother's. For instance, a comparison of the first row and the first column shows that the probability is highly sensitive to the level of father's education (the range being 54 percentage points) and less sensitive to the level of mother's education (22 percentage points).

4.4 RURAL EDUCATIONAL ATTAINMENT

Age is no less important a determinant of educational attainment in rural than in urban China (Table 4.2). The gender difference in years of education is greater in rural than in urban areas, both the unstandardized and the standardized difference being 2.5 years. Figure 4.2 above shows that the gender difference in educational attainment exceeds three years for all ages between 31 and 60. This might be explained by the higher opportunity cost (traditionally girls are family helpers) and a lower rate of return to the family (married daughters have less responsibility to support their parents in old age). The gap declines with age beyond 60 because the schooling even of boys had been very limited, and with youth under 30 either because attitudes began to change in the 1970s or policies of greater sexual equality in schooling were pursued.

Minority people have less education than Han people in rural China (their unstandardized and standardized means being 1.0 and 0.6 years lower respectively). This rural disadvantage occurs despite positive discrimination. There are special colleges for minorities, and lower minimum examination scores are required of minority candidates for college entrance. The explanation for their lower educational attainment may be cultural but it may also be economic. Most minority rural people live in mountainous and border areas in the economically backward parts of China, where the private rate of return to education may be low. Moreover, the provision of rural primary and middle-school education depends largely on the revenue raised by local government, so giving people living in poor areas fewer educational opportunities.

Provincial differences in educational attainment are considerable in rural China. At the extremes, (rural) Shanghai exceeds (rural) Beijing by 1.3 years and Qinghai falls short by 2.4 years (Table 4.2). There is reason to expect that these differences are related to differences in income levels. Rural areas are administered separately from urban areas, and greater emphasis is placed on self-reliance in revenue-raising. This hypothesis was tested by means of a regression analysis that attempted to explain the coefficients on the province dummy variables by province mean income per capita. Since it is the income level at the time of education (actual or potential) that is relevant, we explained the education of individuals aged 21–5 by income in 1980, that of individuals aged 26–30 by income in 1975, etc. The analysis was done separately for urban (ten provinces) and rural areas (twenty-eight provinces). The form of equation is:

$$P_i = a + bY_j + \varepsilon, \tag{4.3}$$

where P_i is the coefficient on the province dummy variable for age-group i, Y_j is the logarithm of province GNP per capita in year j, and ε is the error term with the usual properties assumed.

We find no relationship at all between P_i and Y_j in the urban areas but a powerful relationship in the rural areas (Table 4.8). In each of the four equations the coefficient on Y_j is significantly positive and has a value of approximately unity. These coefficients are large enough to have a substantial effect on the educational attainment of a province. For instance, if income per capita increases from that of the third poorest to that of the third richest province, equations 1 to 4 predict an increase in the mean length of education in the rural areas of 1.5, 1.9, 1.9, and 1.2 years respectively.

TABLE 4.8 *Regression analysis explaining the coefficients on province dummy variables by province income per capita, rural and urban: 1988 CASS survey*

Independent variables	Coefficients	
	Rural	Urban
Equation 1 ($i = 21$–$25, j = 1980$)		
Intercept	–5.780**	–1.195
Ln of GNP per capita (y_j)	0.912**	0.114
$\bar{R}^2$	0.249	–0.109
F-value	9.305	0.117
No. of observations	26	10
Equation 2 ($i = 26$–$30, j = 1975$)		
Intercept	–6.665**	–1.851
Ln of GNP per capita (y_j)	1.152**	0.231
$\bar{R}^2$	0.329	–0.061
F-value	13.297	0.483
No. of observations	26	10
Equation 3 ($i = 31$–$35, j = 1970$)		
Intercept	–7.746**	0.139
Ln of GNP per capita (y_j)	1.295**	–0.006
$\bar{R}^2$	0.347	–0.125
F-value	14.310	0.000
No. of observations	26	10
Equation 4 ($i = 36$–$40, j = 1965$)		
Intercept	–7.509**	–1.688
Ln of GNP per capita (y_j)	1.131*	0.282
$\bar{R}^2$	0.170	–0.077
F-value	6.111	0.356
No. of observations	26	10

Notes: 1. ** denotes statistical significance at the 1% and * at the 5% level.
  2. The subscript i represents the age-group for which the equation is estimated and j the year in which income per capita is measured.
  3. The dependent variables are the coefficients on the province dummy variable (P_i) in the rural and urban samples.

Sources: 1988 survey; PRC, SSB 1987.

The effects of family background on educational attainment in rural areas are presented in Table 4.9. Eq. 1 suggests that the relationship is again non-linear: there is an increasing marginal effect of parental education on the education of the child. Eq. 2 indicates that the mother's education has a greater influence than does that of the father, and that both mother and father have a greater influence on the education of the daughter than of the son. The education of parents, and particularly of mothers, may thus

TABLE 4.9 *Regression analysis explaining education of children by that of their parents: rural sample: 1988 CASS survey*

Equation	Independent variables	Coefficients		
		CED	SED	DED
1	*PED*	0.0852	0.0959	0.0944
	PED^2	0.0146**	0.0112	0.0169**
	Intercept	6.9066**	7.2994**	6.4555**
	$\bar{R}^2$	0.1014	0.0815	0.1245
	F-value	170.30	65.17	111.33
	No. of observations	3,001	1,448	1,553
2	*FED*	0.1212**	0.1134**	0.1416**
	MED	0.1945**	0.1569**	0.2209**
	Intercept	6.1331**	6.7116**	5.5449**
	$\bar{R}^2$	0.0994	0.0797	0.1216
	F-value	166.50	63.68	108.44
	No. of observations	3,001	1,448	1,553
3	*FED*	0.1178**	0.1098**	
	MED	0.0378	−0.0207	
	MED^2	0.0105**	0.0120**	
	Intercept	6.6618**	7.3033**	
	$\bar{R}^2$	0.1024	0.0839	
	F-value	115.07	45.17	
	No. of observations	3,001	1,448	

Notes: 1. **denotes statistical significance at the 1% and * at the 5% level.
2. The dependent variables are the values of *CED*, *SED*, and DED.

shape parental views about the education of girls. Eq. 3 suggest that the increasing marginal influence arises only on the mother's side.

We compare rural and urban China in Figure 4.4 by showing the best-fitting equation predicting child's education from mother's and from father's education. The $C_u(F)$ curve, for instance, shows *CED* as a function of *FED* in the urban areas, holding *MED* at zero; squared terms are dropped if they are not significant. The urban curves are both above their rural counterparts, reflecting greater educational attainment in cities. Whereas in the urban areas, the effects of *FED* and *MED* are little different, in the rural areas the effect of *FED* is linear and that of *MED* is powerful and strongly non-linear. This comparative analysis highlights the importance of rural mothers.

There are alternative explanations for the importance of mother's education in rural areas. One is attitudinal: more-educated women encourage and assist the education of their children, for instance by not expecting their daughters to do housework or farmwork. The other concerns selectivity:

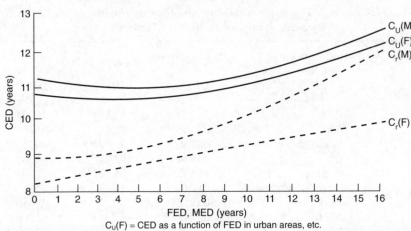

$C_U(F)$ = CED as a function of FED in urban areas, etc.

FIG. 4.4 *Relationship between children's and parents' education: comparison of rural and urban areas, 1988*

more-educated women may be found in richer rural households, either because they can more easily migrate to richer areas or because they are more acceptable to richer husbands. Rural areas and households with higher income can better afford education. Evidence consistent with this explanation is the significant positive correlation ($r = +0.17$) between mother's education and household income per capita, although the likely causal relationships are too complex for reliance on this result.

Many rural people (29 per cent of the sample) failed even to complete primary school whereas only 6 per cent of urban people were in this category. What are the characteristics of these unfortunate people who live in 'educational poverty'? We attempt to answer the question by conducting a logit analysis of the rural sample with dependent variable $NP = 1$, i.e. 'failed to complete primary school'. The independent variables are age-group, gender, minority status, and provincial income per capita in 1980 as a proxy for local income level at the time of withdrawal from school. All coefficients except the intercept term are significant at the 1 per cent level, and 79 per cent of cases are predicted correctly (Table 4.10).

With provincial income per capita set at its mean value (375 yuan in 1980) and other variables at their omitted categories (age 31–5, Han), 39 per cent of women were non-completers and 11 per cent of men: the gender disparity is enormous. Educational opportunities have improved greatly over time, the fall in the probability of non-completion being almost monotonic: 91 per cent of the oldest women were non-completers but only 21 per cent of the youngest age-group, the corresponding figures for men being 66 and 5 per cent respectively. Per capita income is also important, particularly for women. Moving from the income of the third poorest to that of the third

TABLE 4.10 *Logit analysis of educational disadvantage: rural sample: 1988 CASS survey*

Independent variable	Notation	Coefficient	Probability (%)	
			Women	Men
Age-group				
16–20	A_1	−0.8672**	21	5
21–5	A_2	−0.9767**	19	4
26–30	A_3	−0.6220**	26	6
31–5	A_4	0	39	11
36–40	A_5	0.2589**	45	13
41–5	A_6	0.3506**	48	14
46–50	A_7	0.8149**	59	21
51–5	A_8	1.4306**	73	33
56–60	A_9	2.0380**	83	47
61–5	A_{10}	2.3902**	88	56
66+	A_{11}	2.8040**	91	66
Gender				
Male	S_1	−1.6945**	0	11
Female	S_2	0	39	0
Minority status				
Minority	M_1	0.6694**	56	19
Han	M_2	0	39	11
Provincial income per capita	Y	−0.00143**		
Mean value			39	11
Mean + standard deviation			31	8
Third poorest province			43	13
Third richest province			14	3
Intercept		0.0869		
−2 log likelihood		−14,553		
Mean of dependent variable		0.287		
Cases predicted correctly (%)		79.4		
No. of observations		30,580		

Notes: 1. **denotes statistical significance at the 1% and * at the 5% level.
2. The dependent variable is 'did not complete primary education' ($P_6 = 1$).
3. Probabilities are calculated on assumption that Y is at its mean value (375 yuan in 1980, with standard deviation 60 yuan) and other independent variables are set at their omitted categories.

richest province reduces the probability of non-completion from 43 to 14 per cent for women, but from 13 to 5 per cent for men. Being old, female, having minority ethnic status, and living in a poor province—these are the characteristics of the educationally disadvantaged in rural China.

4.5 CURRENT SCHOOL ENROLMENT

In this section we use the 1988 CASS survey to examine the determinants of current school enrolment in both rural and urban areas. We concentrate on the age-group 14–19, who would normally be in middle school. No less than 75 per cent of this group in the urban sample, but only 45 per cent in the rural sample, were enrolled in 1988.

A logit analysis was conducted in which the dependent variable is binary—enrolment (E) as opposed to non-enrolment (NE)—and the independent variables are household income per capita (HY), provincial income per capita, rural or total (PRY or PY), age (in the range 14–19), gender, and minority status (Table 4.11). In both samples about 80 per cent of predictions are correct, and most of the coefficients are significant. That on age is large and negative in both cases, and that on male sex is positive: large and significant in the rural but small and not significant in urban areas. The coefficient on minority status is large and significantly negative in rural areas. With Beijing as the omitted category, there is a wide spread of coefficients on the twenty-eight province dummy variables (equation not

TABLE 4.11 *Logit analysis predicting the educational enrolment of youth aged 14–19: 1988 CASS survey*

Independent variables	Notation	Coefficients	
		Rural	Urban
Household income per capita	HY	0.0001	−0.0001
Provincial rural income per capita	PRY	0.0007**	
Provincial income per capita	PY		0.0005**
Age	A	−0.6866**	−0.8355**
Male	S_1	0.6948**	0.1490
Minority status	M_1	−1.7518**	
Intercept		10.3538**	15.0036**
−2 log likelihood		−4,694	−1,739
Percentage predicted correctly		79	82
Mean of dependent variable		44.5	75.1
No. of observations		8,638	3,968

Notes: 1. **denotes statistical significance at the 1% and *at the 5% level.
2. The omitted categories are female and (in the rural sample) Han.
3. Household income per capita in the urban sample is cash income only.
4. Information on minority status is not available for those without income in urban areas.
5. The dependent variables are enrolment of youth aged 14–19 in the rural and urban samples.

shown). Taking the extreme cases and setting other variables at their mean or omitted category values, the probability of rural youth attending middle school is 44 percentage points higher in Tianjin than in Zhejiang.

The coefficients on the income variables are of particular interest. Greater household income should help to fund the direct private cost of education but it can also raise the opportunity cost. Greater provincial income serves as a proxy for revenue-raising capacity, relevant to educational provision and the level of subsidy. In the rural areas the coefficient on *HY* is positive but small and significant only at the 10 per cent level. The coefficient implies that, when other variables are set at their mean or omitted category values, a rise in household income per capita by one standard deviation raises the probability of enrolment by only 1 percentage point. However, this result is sensitive to specification owing to co-linearity between the income variables: omission of the *PRY* variable raises it from 0.0001 to 0.0002** (equation not shown). Moreover, it is likely that the coefficient is biased downwards insofar as the enrolment itself reduces household income. The possible extent of bias can be gauged by deducting those enrolled from the number of household members, i.e. assuming that they would otherwise add to household income an amount equal to income per capita. The coefficient is indeed sensitive to this adjustment, rising from 0.0001 to 0.0012** (equation not shown). The implication is that a rise in *HY* by one standard deviation would raise the probability of enrolment by 13 percentage points. In the urban areas the coefficient on *HY* is actually negative but not significantly so (Table 2.11); again, it may be biased downwards.

The coefficient on provincial rural income per capita is significantly positive in the rural equation; likewise that on provincial income per capita in the urban equation. However, in neither case does a rise in the province income variable by one standard deviation raise the probability of enrolment, *ceteris paribus*, by more than 3 percentage points.

In summary, a conventional analysis provides limited evidence that income per capita at the household or the province level is important in increasing the chances of enrolment in middle school in either rural or urban areas. However, if we introduce the concept of opportunity cost and recognize that enrolment itself reduces household income per capita, we find that rural enrolment is sensitive to potential household income. It appears that provincial educational policies may have a more important effect on rural enrolment than provincial rural income per capita. Nevertheless, the coefficient on *PRY* is significantly positive and therefore consistent with our finding above that, in rural areas, educational attainment is positively related to provincial income per capita; the difference lies in degree.

It is not only the quantity of education that varies according to income levels within rural China but also the quality of education. The primary education of a (rural) county is subject to formal approval by its provincial education commission. In 1989, 72 per cent of the 2,170 counties had received such approval. In those counties with annual income per capita greater than 600 yuan ($y > 600$) the proportion was 87 per cent, in those with $300 \leq y \leq 600$, it was 73 per cent, and in those with $y < 300$, it was only 40 per cent (Hao *et al.* 1992: 36).

4.6 IS EDUCATION SUPPLY- OR DEMAND-CONSTRAINED?

In this section we examine first whether urban and then whether rural education is supply- or demand-constrained. The returns to education among urban employees, although positive, are low by comparison with other countries. An earnings function omitting occupation terms showed that college graduates earned only 34 per cent more income than the uneducated in 1988 (Knight and Song 1993*c*: 237). However, this understates the benefits of education because those with education have better access to agreeable occupations and to the state sector offering 'iron rice bowls' (Knight and Song 1993*c*: tables 7.7, 7.18).

Rates of drop-out (i.e. leaving school before graduating from the cycle) are relatively low in urban areas (see Table 4.14). Moreover, there is survey evidence that educational aspirations are high in urban China. One survey of lower- and upper-middle school pupils in a district of Beijing (Haidian) found that 90 per cent of lower and 95 per cent of upper-middle school pupils wished to continue their schooling, and even higher percentages of their parents wished them to continue (Fang, Chen, and Xi 1990: 70–1). Expectations depended on the type of school attended but even in the low-quality lower-middle schools 51 per cent expected to enter higher education, the corresponding figures for ordinary schools being 92 per cent and for high-quality ('key') schools 99 per cent. Admittedly, this is a well-off district, but about 30 per cent of the parents were manual workers. When upper-middle school pupils in the capital cities of Guangdong and Shaanxi provinces were asked what they would do if they failed their college entrance examination, only 26 and 8 per cent respectively proposed to enter the labour market rather than continue some form of study (Yang 1988: 42–3). When pupils in the same two cities were asked what they intended to do after graduating from lower-middle school, only 6 and zero per cent respectively planned to find a job. This evidence, limited though it be, suggests that urban education is generally limited by supply constraints.

In the case of rural education we apply the following tests. First, the educational behaviour of poor households is analysed to discover whether it reflects demand-based choices. Secondly, we measure the importance of school fees. Thirdly, we examine rates of drop-out from school. Fourthly, we attempt to measure the opportunity cost of schooling for rural youth. Fifthly, we consider the role that school quality might play in influencing attendance. Finally, an attempt is made to explain the fluctuations in secondary enrolment rates since the rural reforms began in 1978.

Are poor rural households caught in a poverty trap—a culture of poverty and a need to survive—which prevents them from responding to economic incentives? We address this question in a second logit analysis of current enrolment. The innovation here is to confine the analysis to poor households (the lowest quarter of households classified by income per capita) and to introduce measures of the opportunity cost and the benefit of education as explanatory variables. These measures were obtained by estimating household income functions for each county (counties with fewer than fifty observations were omitted). The dependent variable was the logarithm of household income and the independent variables included the number of workers with college or professional high-school education (E_1), upper-middle (E_2), lower-middle (E_3), primary (E_4), and no schooling (E_5). Thus, for instance, where the coefficients of the education terms are e_i, ($e_3 - e_4$) indicates the marginal returns to lower-middle schooling. By estimating coefficients of variables representing the number of workers in different age-groups, it was possible also to obtain the marginal product of a worker aged 16–20, our proxy for the opportunity cost of school attendance.

The dependent variable in the logit equation (Table 4.12) was the enrolment of children aged 10–18. As expected, girls and older children are significantly less likely to be in school. School fees and county income per capita are not important but have the right signs: school fees deter slightly and county prosperity (a proxy for public support) encourages enrolment. A rise in county income per capita by 50 per cent from the mean raises the probability of enrolment by 5 percentage points. Our measure of opportunity cost significantly reduces enrolment, as economic rationality requires, although the effect on the probability is small. The variables representing the income benefits of education are all positive, with the primary-school coefficient being the largest and the most significant. A rise of one standard deviation from the mean value of the returns to primary education raises the probability of enrolment by 16 percentage points. We conclude that the educational decisions of poor households are predictably responsive to economic variables and that the pattern of attendance or of provision may indeed reflect demand.

Why had more than half of the rural sample aged 14–19 dropped out of school? It is possible that a supply constraint is effective throughout the school system, with the rationing of places becoming tighter as children progress up the educational ladder. It is possible, however, that a demand constraint operates over at least part of the range, either because the perceived private rate of return on costs is too low or because the costs cannot be funded. We examine the private costs of rural education.

TABLE 4.12 *Logit analysis of school enrolment in poor households in rural China: 1988 CASS survey*

Independent variable	Notation	Coefficient
Intercept		8.3041***
Household income per capita	HY	−0.00054
County income per capita	CY	−0.00057
Male	S_1	0.7649***
Age	A	−0.5645***
Estimated income in county of workers aged 16–20	OC	−0.2770*
Average school fees in county	F	−0.00063
Marginal returns to education in county of:		
College and vocational school	e_1	0.2289
Upper-middle school	e_2	0.7747*
Lower-middle school	e_3	0.2936
Primary school	e_4	1.2379***
−2 log likelihood		2857.29
Percentage predicted correctly		82.8
Mean of dependent variable	E_1	63.9
No. of observations		2,184

Notes: 1. *denotes statistical significance at the 10%, ** at the 5%, and *** at the 1% level.
    2. Poor households are the bottom quarter of households classified by income per capita.
    3. The dependent variable is whether a child aged 10–18 is enrolled in school (enrolment = E_1 = 1).

Our rural sample shows that almost 6,000 rural households paid school fees, the average annual fee being 67 yuan per paying household. A regression analysis was conducted in which the dependent variable was expenditure on school fees by the household (SF). The independent variables were household income per capita (HY), the rural income per capita of the province (PRY), minority status, the number of pupils aged 6–13 in the household (representing primary school attendance), the number aged 14–19 (middle-school pupils), and the number aged 20 or above (college students). The results are presented in Table 4.13. Almost all the coefficients are significantly different from zero and have the expected sign. Both coefficients on the income variables are positive: an additional 100 yuan of household income per capita increases expenditure on school fees by 1.2 yuan, *ceteris paribus*; and an additional 100 yuan of provincial rural income per capita increases it by 3.2 yuan. However, these propensities will understate the full effect of income if the children of richer households or of households in richer areas are more likely to attend school. There are three possible reasons why households in richer rural areas are willing to spend more on school fees: rates of return to education may be higher in richer

TABLE 4.13 *Regression analysis of household expenditure on school fees: rural sample: 1988 CASS Survey*

Independent variable	Notation	Coefficient
Household income per capita	HY	0.0119**
Provincial rural income per capita	PRY	0.0321**
Student aged 6–13	PS	18.89**
Student aged 14–19	MS	51.13**
Student aged 20+	HS	76.64**
Minority status	M_1	−6.69
Intercept		18.747**
$\bar{R}^2$		0.1236
F-value		234.6
Mean of dependent variable		40.1
No. of observations		9,944

Notes: 1. ** denotes statistical significance at the 1% level.
2. The dependent variable is household expenditure on school fees (*SF*).

rural areas, richer communities may demand and secure higher-quality schooling, and larger local subsidies may give a competitive advantage which, by providing opportunities for progression up the educational ladder, makes higher expenditure profitable.

The table also shows the marginal expenditure associated with an additional primary school, middle school and college student: 19, 51, and 77 yuan per annum respectively. These are our best estimates of rural school fees per pupil, as reported in the survey. The middle school fee of 51 yuan represents 1.9 per cent of the average income of rural households and 3.9 per cent of the average income of the lowest quarter. These do not represent great burdens. Moreover, the fact that we found a rise in household income per capita did not greatly raise middle school enrolment suggests that inability to pay school fees is not an important cause of rural teenagers dropping out of school.

The other component of the private cost of schooling is income forgone. As most rural teenagers not in school are engaged in household production activities, an income cannot be attributed to them individually, and the few who do receive income—workers in rural industry—may be unrepresentative. Moreover, even where income is attributable to these young workers, it need not measure the income forgone by the household on account of school attendance if other household members are underemployed.

Again, the survey provides some relevant evidence. Of the group aged

14–19, the proportion obtaining income (albeit a share of family income) is 81 per cent. This proportion rises monotonically over the age-range, from 23 per cent at age 13 to 94 per cent at age 19. It appears that income forgone through school attendance becomes increasingly important to the rural household over the middle school years. A study of 60 (rural) counties showed that 55 per cent of village pupils dropping out of primary school took up some form of work, mostly farm work; for those leaving lower-middle school the corresponding figure was 83 per cent (Yang and Han 1991: 48–9). It is more difficult for urban children to enter economic activities. Not surprisingly, therefore, the incidence of drop-out is sensitive to rural or urban location and, within rural areas, to the income level of a county (Table 4.14). The annual rate of drop-out is high from rural primary schools in poor areas and from rural middle schools generally.

We attempt to measure the opportunity cost of rural schooling in Table 4.15. The equation predicting rural household income shows the coefficients for different types of labour. An adult wage-earner makes the greatest contribution by far to household income. A non-waged working adult also adds a significant amount, but so too does a school drop-out aged 17–19 (who would be in upper-middle school). Drop-outs aged 11–13 (primary school) make a negligible contribution to household income, and those aged 14–16 (lower-middle school) an intermediate one. It would seem that the

TABLE 4.14 *Drop-out rates for rural and urban areas by educational level, 1989*

	Drop-out rate (%)	
	Rural	Urban
Lower-middle school		
Male	7.3	3.1
Female	6.8	2.0
Primary school		
Male	1.5	0.4
Female	1.8	0.4
Rich regions (male and female)	0.3	—
Poor regions (male and female)	4.3	—

Notes: 1. Drop-out is defined as leaving school before graduating from the cycle.
2. Rich regions are those counties within the sample with annual income per capita above 800 yuan and poor regions those below 300 yuan.

Source: Yang and Han 1991.

TABLE 4.15 *Regression analysis to estimate the household income forgone through schooling: rural sample: 1988 CASS Survey*

Independent variable	Notation	Coefficient
Intercept		2,338.85**
Wage earners aged 20+	W	2,226.33**
Non-waged working members aged 20+	N	325.63**
Drop-outs aged 11–13	N_1	21.16
Drop-outs aged 14–16	N_2	131.88
Drop-outs aged 17–19	N_3	278.81**
Current pupils aged 11–19	S	−51.62
$\bar{R}^2$		0.168
F-value		345.5
Standard error of estimate (%)		71.2
Mean of dependent variable		3,725.33
No. of observations		10,258

Notes: 1. ** denotes statistical significance at the 1% level.
      2. The dependent variable is rural household income in yuan p.a.

oldest drop-outs are hardly less valuable to the household than working adults: there is a serious opportunity cost involved in continuing to upper-middle school. However, the household income forgone prior to that stage is small: if the opportunity cost is high it must be on account of non-income-earning activities such as household chores. This evidence suggests that a demand constraint may well operate on upper-middle school enrolments.

Another possible reason for poor enrolment in middle schools in rural China is that their low quality reduces demand. The lack of funds keeps down teachers' salaries and this contributes to the inadequacy of teachers in rural areas. Urban public expenditure per pupil was on average 4.3 times higher than rural in primary schools, and 2.5 times higher in middle schools, during the period 1979–82 (Guan 1983). Further evidence of differential funding is obtained from a case study of primary schools in Gansu province in 1984 (World Bank 1988: 369, 412). The annual recurrent cost per pupil in urban public schools was 100 yuan; in rural schools it was 34 yuan.[2] The public subsidy per pupil was 89 yuan in urban and 11 yuan in rural schools. Whereas urban people had on average to fund at most 11 yuan, rural people (at the household or village level) had to pay 23 yuan per pupil. Thus rural people had to pay more for what was likely to be a much lower quality of schooling. The same case study noted that most urban primary teachers were public employees and most of their rural counterparts were locally hired. The typical village primary school teacher in Gansu was unqualified, received only 61 per cent of the average pay of public primary school teachers (25 per cent from public subsidy and 36 per cent as village contributions in cash or kind), taught more than one grade in a single class, and might engage also in farming. Another indicator of low quality was the fact that 19 per cent of rural children were over age, compared with 11 per cent of urban children in Gansu (World Bank 1988: 363, 413). Lower quality must limit rural pupils' human capital acquisition and diminish their chances in the meritocratic competition for places at technical schools and colleges, and this may reduce their demand.

The 1990 population census records the percentage of people of each age according to their highest level of education (PRC, SSB 1993). Figure 4.5 converts this into a percentage enrolment rate for the year in which they were at the median age for the relevant level of education.[3] There was an explosion of middle school enrolment during the Cultural Revolution, reflecting the egalitarian objectives of that time. The consequent deterioration in the quality of middle school education brought a reversal of policies when the Cultural Revolution came to an end. We see the effects in Figure 4.5.

The remarkable similarity of the movements in urban and rural areas suggests that the explanation is to be found in national rather than sector-specific policies or behaviour. Why was there a sharp fall in enrolment rates in both urban and rural China from 1977 to 1985? Between those years enrolment in lower-middle schools fell by 20 per cent and teachers by 9 per cent; and the equivalent figures for upper-middle schools were 59 and 40 per cent. The number of middle schools fell by more than half (by 54 per cent) (PRC, SSE 1989: 360–71).[4] The authorities were trying to improve the quality of secondary education by closing many of the schools opened dur-

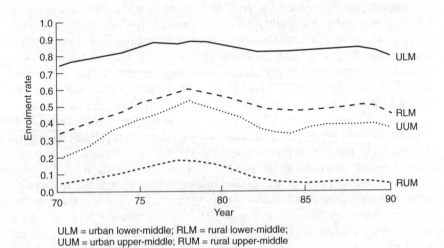

ULM = urban lower-middle; RLM = rural lower-middle;
UUM = urban upper-middle; RUM = rural upper-middle

FIG. 4.5 *Enrolment rates of lower- and upper-middle schools in urban and rural areas: from population census, 1990*

ing the Cultural Revolution and reducing the number of teachers, particularly unqualified teachers. They did so by reducing financial support and shifting the financial burden downwards. Upper-middle school places were rationed by means of competition in primary and lower-middle school examinations. It is very likely, therefore, that the secondary system became supply-constrained. The introduction of the household responsibility system over the same period (1978–85) increased the opportunity cost of school attendance for peasant households. It is possible, therefore, that the fall in rural middle school enrolments was due to a fall in demand. However, that would not explain why urban enrolments behaved so similarly. Combining this with the previous evidence, it seems that rural education was partly supply- and partly demand-constrained.

4.7 CONCLUSION

In China, one's birthplace is crucial in determining one's life chances. It governs both economic and educational opportunities. The greatest spatial distinction is the rural–urban divide. Other than age, the most important factor influencing a person's educational attainment is whether he lives in a rural or an urban area. The standardized mean difference in favour of urban-dwellers is no less than 4.6 years, and it has not diminished over the decades. The reasons are to be found in the separate administrative and funding arrangements for rural and urban education and also in terms of opportunity costs and perceived economic returns. Provincial differences are greater in the rural than the urban areas. The rural educational attainment of a province is strongly positively related to its income per capita, reflecting the decentralized funding of rural public expenditures. There is no such urban relationship owing to the more centralized funding arrangements, but educational provision appears to improve with size of city.

As in many countries, family background is found to play a powerful role in educational attainment. Even in the Chinese system of educational rationing based on meritocratic criteria—in which education generally cannot be bought privately—educated parents can improve the educational opportunities of their children, for instance through their absorption of attitudes and acquisition of human capital in the home. We found that the educational attainment of parents does indeed assist the education of their children, and that there are often increasing marginal returns to parental education. In the rural areas mothers are more important than fathers and the education of both parents has a greater influence on the education of daughters than of sons: female education appears to be more discretionary than male. The greater educational attainment of urban people implies that their children have an advantage over rural children in the competition for places in the upper rungs of the educational ladder.

Ethnic and gender discrimination in education are not apparent in urban China but appear to live on in rural China. The educational difference between men and women is negligible for urban-dwellers under 30. By contrast, rural women are generally at an educational disadvantage, for which there is a plausible economic explanation in terms of opportunity costs and future returns to parents. Minority status people remain at an educational disadvantage in the rural areas despite the policies of affirmative action.

The private demand for education in urban China is generally high. This result appears surprising in view of the compressed urban wage structure: the income gain from additional schooling has been small in absolute terms, in relation to other income determinants, and in relation to other poor countries. However, education may also be sought because of the security, attractiveness, and status of the careers that it offers. Urban education appears to be now fairly universal at the lower rungs, and to be supply-constrained at the upper rungs of the educational ladder.

Over half of the rural population aged 14–19 had dropped out of school. Attendance did not appear to be very sensitive to income per capita either at the household or at the province level. However, potential household income per capita—including the income forgone by attending school—was more powerful. Rural middle school fees were generally not high in relation to household incomes but both opportunity cost and dropping out rose sharply over the age range 14–19. The large fall in middle school enrolment since the introduction of the rural reforms is to be explained mainly by supply considerations but there may also be a demand element.

Rural China is being transformed through rural industrialization, which now accounts for over 100 million workers (Knight and Song 1993*b*: 174–5). Wood (1994), in his explanation of the manufacturing export success of East Asian countries, argued that even labour-intensive industrialization requires at least basic education. Knight and Song (1993*b*, 180–9) found that the returns to education are substantial among rural industry employees in China. It is probable that future private and social returns to post-primary education in rural China are underestimated by both people and government, too much influenced by the past and the present.

The most important policy issue is to devise means of expanding the educational opportunities of rural people. For this purpose it can be important to know whether the system is supply-constrained or demand-constrained: our evidence suggests that both forms of constraint operate on secondary school enrolments in rural China. However, both constraints can be loosened by additional public funding. For instance, demand can be increased by reducing school fees or by spending to improve the quality of education. Government should introduce policies which reduce the inequality of public funding as between rural and urban areas and, within rural areas, redistribute funds towards the poorer areas.

NOTES

This chapter is written by John Knight and Li Shi, and follows closely their paper 'Educational attainment and the rural–urban divide in China' (Knight and Li 1996). The authors are grateful to Li Shi for generously allowing us to use the material for which he was jointly responsible.

1. As shown by a Chow-test and the significance of many of the interaction terms when urban residence is interacted with all other explanatory variables in an equation restricted to the urban sample provinces.
2. A weighted average of rural public schools and the, much more common, village schools.
3. E.g. the enrolment rate for primary school is derived from the percentages of people whose highest level of education completed was primary school or above. The median age is assumed to be 20 for college, 16 for upper-, and 13 for lower-middle school, and 9 for primary school.
4. No breakdown into urban and rural is available for teachers and schools, nor into lower and upper for schools.

REFERENCES

Behrman, Jere, and Wolfe, Barbara (1984). 'Who is schooled in developing countries? The role of income, parental schooling, sex and family size', *Economics of Education Review*, 3 (3): 231–45.

Birdsall, Nancy (1985). 'Public inputs and child schooling in Brazil', *Journal of Development Economics*, 18 (1): 67–86.

——and Sabot, Richard H. (1994). 'Vicious circles: human capital, growth and equity in East Asia', Washington, DC: World Bank, processed.

Fang Fuxi, Chen Suansuan, and Xi Huiyuan (1990). 'Survey on studying burden of middle school students in Haidian District, Beijing', *Education Research*, July, Beijing: Institute of Education (in Chinese).

Griffin, Keith, and Zhao Renwei (eds.) (1993). *The Distribution of Income in China*, London: Macmillan Press.

Guan Rongkai (1983). 'Analysis of budget for primary and middle education in Anxin and Chengde counties, Hebei Province', *Education Research*, July, Beijing: Institute of Education (in Chinese).

Hao Keming, Tan Songhua, and Zhang Li (1992). 'The socio-economic environment for introducing universal education in rural China and its development trends', *Social Sciences in China*, 13 (2): 35–49.

Haveman, Robert H., and Wolfe, Barbara L. (1984). 'Schooling and economic well-being: the role of non-market effects', *Journal of Human Resources*, 19 (3): 377–407.

Khan, Azizur Rahman, Griffin, Keith, Riskin, Carl, and Zhao Renwei (1993). 'Household income and its distribution in China', in Griffin and Zhao (1993).

Knight, John, and Li Shi (1993). 'The determinants of educational attainment in China' in Griffin and Zhao (1993).

Knight, John, and Li Shi (1996). 'Educational attainment and the rural–urban divide in China', *Oxford Bulletin of Economics and Statistics*, 58 (1): 81–115.

——and Song, Lina (1993a). 'The spatial contribution to income inequality in rural China', *Cambridge Journal of Economics*, 17 (2): 195–214.

——(1993b). 'Workers in China's rural industry', in Griffin and Zhao (1993).

——(1993c). 'Why urban wages differ in China', in Griffin and Zhao (1993).

—— and Sabot, Richard H. (1990). *Education, Productivity and Inequality. The East African Natural Experiment*, Washington, DC: World Bank and Oxford University Press.

Peoples' Republic of China, State Statistical Bureau (PRC, SSB) (1987). *Statistical Data of National Income 1949–1986*, Beijing: China Statistical Press (in Chinese).

—— —— (PRC, SSB) (1988). *China Population Statistics Yearbook 1988*, Beijing (in Chinese).

Peoples' Republic of China, State Committee of Education (PRC, SCE) (1989). *Statistical Yearbook of Education in China 1988*, Beijing (in Chinese).

—— —— (PRC, SSB) (1993). *Tabulation on the 1990 Population Census of the Peoples' Republic of China*, 2, Beijing (in Chinese).

Psacharopoulos, George, and Woodhall, Maureen (1985). *Education for Development. An Analysis of Investment Choices*, Washington, DC: World Bank and Oxford University Press.

Wood, Adrian (1994). *North-South Trade, Employment and Inequality*, Oxford: Clarendon Press.

World Bank (1984). *World Development Report 1984*, Washington, DC: World Bank.

—— (1988). *China. Growth and Development in Gansu Province*, Washington, DC: World Bank.

—— (1991). *World Development Report 1991*, Washington, DC: World Bank.

—— (1993). *The East Asian Miracle. Economic Growth and Public Policy*, Washington, DC: World Bank and Oxford University Press.

Yang Nianlu and Han Min (1991). 'Studies on dropout and repetition of students in primary schools and lower-middle schools', *Education Research*, March, Beijing: Institute of Education (in Chinese).

Yang Xianjun (1988). 'Survey of planned destinations of middle school students in Guangzhou and Xian cities', *Education Research*, January, Beijing: Institute of Education (in Chinese).

5

Health

The fulfilment of such basic needs as freedom from illness, malnutrition, and premature death may well be correlated with income but this relationship is unlikely to be close. The capability of people to live long and healthy lives is an important element of welfare but it is not well measured by the income they receive.

Many of the major health hazards found in developing countries with high mortality rates now have inexpensive solutions (Cornia 1989: 165-7). For instance, birth-related problems can be tackled by mean of pregnancy-management programmes, digestive tract infections respond to rehydration therapy, immunization provides protection against half a dozen communicable diseases, and an essential drug programme, covering fifteen to twenty basic products, can provide primary health care for various infectious, respiratory and insect-borne diseases. These policies, together with safe water supply programmes and nutritional interventions, mean that it is within the power of the governments even of poor countries to reduce mortality rates. Higher incomes permit households to be healthier and governments to finance better health services but we would also expect the political aim and will of the government to be an important determinant of premature death rates.

China may well be a case in point. Since liberation in 1949 China has made great strides in reducing mortality rates. The crude death rate fell from 1.80 per cent in 1950 to 0.95 per cent in 1965, to 0.68 per cent in 1985, and to 0.66 per cent in 1993 (PRC, SSB 1986: 72, PRC, SSB 1994: 59). China's relative success may be associated with the emphasis placed on preventive health measures and on improving the health environment, e.g. by means vaccination and sanitation policies, and with egalitarian concerns to alleviate poverty. The distribution of deaths by causes in China in the period 1973-5 has been compared with those for a model low-income country and a model high-income country (World Bank 1983, iii: 27). The comparison shows that China was in the process of 'epidemiological transition', in which mortality from infectious, respiratory, and parasitic diseases is much reduced and the proportion of deaths due to cancer and circulatory diseases is much increased. The pattern of mortality in China was midway between those for typical low- and high-income countries: infectious, respiratory, and parasitic diseases accounted for 26 per cent of deaths in China and for 44 and 11 per cent of deaths in low- and high-income countries respectively, whereas the proportions for cancer and circulatory diseases combined were 36, 19, and 47 per cent respectively.

These average figures may conceal a health divide between rural and urban China. Rural–urban differences in income, sanitation, environment, and administrative and funding arrangements make it likely that health-care provision will also differ. Because the rural and urban health systems are so distinct, we contrast them under the following headings: institutions, provision, finance, and outcomes.

5.1 THE INSTITUTIONAL DIVIDE

Health care has evolved in quite separate ways in rural and urban China. The institutions, organization, and administration of health services are also subject to a rural–urban divide. We examine the rural and urban institutions separately.

In 1949 rural China lacked an effective health-care system. The health services were largely curative and in the hands of traditional practitioners. The new government gave priority to preventive over curative care, and organized campaigns against particular diseases including immunization against half a dozen common diseases. With the formation of the communes, the number of commune (township) health centres increased rapidly. In 1965 Mao criticized health policy for favouring the urban areas and called for a rapid change in priorities (Shanghai-IDS 1993: 13). In the ensuing years emphasis was given to the 'barefoot doctor' programme, which brought health care of a sort to almost all brigades (administrative villages). By 1970, 1.2 million barefoot doctors had been trained, and 3.6 million brigade health aides. Barefoot doctors were part-time farmers who received a share of collective income like other brigade members. The commune structure also assisted the development of cooperative medical schemes, sharing health risks among brigade members. The rural health service had three tiers, corresponding to the county, the commune, and the brigade; the same three tiers (county, township, and village) exist today.

The dissolution of the communes after 1978 had serious implications for rural health care. Townships and villages no longer had the resources or the political directives to fund health care on a cooperative basis. Except where revenue was available from township and village enterprises, cooperative health schemes collapsed: the proportion of villages covered fell from 82 per cent in 1978 to 5 per cent in 1986 (Shanghai-IDS 1993: 32). The bare-foot doctors had to rely more heavily on user charges and sales of medicines. The number of village health workers declined although—through a programme of training and certification—their quality improved. In 1988 there were 732,000 certified village doctors in China's 734,000 villages, and 1,714,000 village health workers altogether (ibid.: 34). At the township level, health centres, and at the county level, hospitals, became more dependent on user charges; and preventive programmes were commonly no longer fully subsidized.

The decentralization of rural health-care funding in the period of economic reform increased inequalities in health services between rich and poor rural areas. Almost three-quarters of the funds for rural health services came from user charges, but these were less important in relatively prosperous areas possessing township and village industry.

In urban China the emphasis from the start was on state-supported health care. Two major employment-related health schemes were established in 1951. These were the public service medical scheme and the state labour insurance scheme. Together they cover all state employees, totalling nearly 100 million members in 1987. In addition, many collective enterprises and institutions organize health-care schemes for their employees. Thus almost all urban workers—excepting only workers in the small private and self-employment sectors—are covered by health insurance schemes, many of them free of charge.

The public service medical scheme provides virtually free health services to public service employees and retirees. Members are entitled to care at designated facilities which are paid by the scheme on a user-charge basis. Their dependants may also be partly subsidized. In 1987 membership of the scheme totalled 23 million. The state labour insurance scheme covers employees and retirees of state enterprises and is funded from enterprise welfare funds. The scheme meets all costs of members on a user-charge basis and half the costs of their dependants. In 1987 the membership totalled 72 million and dependants 60 million. Many urban collective enterprises provide collective labour insurance for their workers. The various schemes offer different levels of reimbursement of health-care costs, up to three-quarters for members. Partial support may also be offered to the dependants of members. Workers in urban collectives numbered 36 million in 1987, although not all would have been covered.

5.2 HEALTH-CARE PROVISION AND ACCESS

The provision of health care is very unequally distributed between urban and rural China. Adequate indicators of provision are hard to come by as it is a matter of quality as well as quantity. The quality of medical services varies with the concentration of population. High-quality and specialized hospitals are generally located in the cities, whereas low-quality county-level hospitals are located in county towns, township health centres in township headquarters, and village clinics in the villages. The same ordering is to be found in the availability of hospital beds per 1,000 people (Table 5.1). These disparities might represent either political rank and

TABLE 5.1 *Hospital beds per 1,000 people by popula-tion concentration and by political rank, 1986*

	Hospital beds per 1,000 people
34 big cities	6.42
All cities	4.48
Counties	1.54
Townships	0.88

Notes: 1. The thirty-four big cities include the three province-level municipalities, all provincial capital cities and cities with a population over 10 million.
2. Most rural hospitals are county hospitals, located in the county towns. These are included in the counties figure but not in the townships figure.

Source: PRC, MOPH 1987: 493–4.

TABLE 5.2 *Hospital beds and qualified medical doctors per 1,000 people, cities and counties, 1949–95*

	Hospital beds per 1,000 people		Qualified medical doctors per 1,000 people	
	Cities	Counties	Cities	Counties
1949	0.63	0.05	0.70	0.66
1957	2.08	0.14	1.30	0.76
1965	3.78	0.51	2.22	0.82
1978	4.85	1.41	2.99	0.73
1986	4.48	1.54	3.25	0.84
1995	5.66	1.26	3.86	0.85

Note: In order to ensure comparability, the 1995 figures are extrapolated on the basis of the percentage changes in beds, doctors and people since 1986.

Source: PRC, MOPH 1987: 493; PRC, SSB 1996: 69, 715.

power or economies of scale in the face of transport costs and difficulties; both are likely to be relevant.

Two measures of access to high-quality health care are the number of hospital beds and the number of qualified medical doctors, both expressed per 1,000 people. Information is available for cities and for counties (includ-ing county towns). This is shown in Table 5.2 for selected years of the period 1949–95. There was a sharp urban–rural contrast in the provision

TABLE 5.3 *The use of curative care services per 1,000 people in urban and rural China, 1985*

	Urban	Rural	Urban (rural = 100)
Visits per fortnight	147	97	150
Hospital admissions per year	51	32	160
Inpatient length of stay, day per year	1,340	477	280

Source: PRC, MOPH 1986, cited by Yu 1992: 52.

of hospital beds throughout. Urban provision was more than four times greater than rural provision in 1995. Having been minimal in both urban and rural China in 1949, the availability of qualified medical doctors improved greatly in urban areas thereafter, but there was no progress in rural areas. In 1995 urban availability was over four times as high as rural.

Curative health services are more intensively used in urban than in rural China, as Table 5.3 shows. Whether in terms of visits to a health-care provider, hospital admissions, or length of inpatient stay, urban use exceeds rural use. The number of salaried health workers per 1,000 people in 1977 and 1986 is shown in Table 5.4. Urban and rural China differed not only in the quality of service—the greatest disparity being in senior health staff— but also in the quantity. In 1986 the urban areas had on average 6.73 salaried health workers per 1,000 people whereas the rural areas averaged 2.14. It is plausible that the confinement to salaried health workers understates rural provision. However, the evidence suggests that the inclusion of unsalaried rural health workers might add only 0.67 per 1,000 rural people.[1]

The location of provision could give a misleading picture of access. For instance, the higher-quality and more plentiful hospitals and other medical facilities that are found in cities could be made available to country as well as city people. However, three factors diminish the access of rural people to urban hospitals: transport problems associated with distance, administrative exclusion, and user charges.

First, transport costs and difficulties hinder rural people, especially when they are ill or when they live in remote areas. Unless they have relatives in the city, peasants who are referred to an urban hospital must find and pay for accommodation if they have to wait for admission. Secondly, particularly in the pre-reform period, medical treatment in the cities was rationed. Whereas all urban residents were registered with a hospital, rural people had no such entitlement. Even if they were referred to an urban hospital, they were likely to receive lower priority than urban-dwellers. A peasant might need to rely on the intermediation of an urban resident or enter a grey market. Thirdly, the economic reforms have made urban medical

TABLE 5.4 *Salaried health workers per 1,000 people in urban and rural China, 1977 and 1986*

	1977		1986	
	Urban	Rural	Urban	Rural
Doctors and assistant doctors of traditional medicines	0.30	0.24	0.47	0.27
Pharmacists of traditional medicine	0.16	0.08	0.12	0.05
Senior health staff	1.32	0.18	2.02	0.29
Middle local health staff	3.07	0.68	2.85	0.81
Lower health staff	1.53	0.45	1.27	0.72
Total health workers	6.37	1.63	6.73	2.14
Total health workers (thousand)	1,063	1,278	1,774	1,733
Total population (million)	167	783	264	811

Notes: 1. Senior staff are either Western or traditional Chinese medicine qualified doctors, public health doctors, pharmacists, and high-level technicians; middle-level staff are assistant doctors, nurses, midwives, and technicians; lower-level staff are village doctors, village midwives, and health aides.
  2. The figures include all workers paid wholly or partly by government or collectives.

Sources: World Bank 1989, annexe table H-14; PRC, SSB 1991: table 3.1.

services more marketable: hospitals are required to meet many of their costs from user charges. However, this has had the effect of rationing the rural sick by price instead of by the rule. Whereas most urban people are covered by public service, state labour, or collective labour insurance schemes, only a small minority of rural people are insured against the heavy costs involved in hospital treatment.

We can gain an impression of the quality of rural medical care from a national survey of 90,000 village doctors in 1990 (De Geyndt, Zhao, and Liu 1992): 73 per cent had no more than lower-middle school education, and 56 per cent reported receiving no more than one year of training; 81 per cent were part-time doctors, only a third regarding health care as their major economic activity; 53 per cent of the sample were aged 40 or over, and these were likely to have been barefoot doctors in the 1970s. Their clinical knowledge and skills were limited: 84 per cent themselves wanted to receive additional training. Yet they were often the first and the last source of medical care available to villagers.

The quantity and quality of rural health care is described in a 1987 study of twenty counties in sixteen provinces (Shanghai-IDS 1993). Almost 100 households in each of 160 villages in fifty-two townships were covered: there were questionnaires at the household, village, township, and county levels.

TABLE 5.5 *Rural health-care provision and access: rural health-care survey, 1987*

County analysis	
Hospital beds per 1,000 people	1.8
Licensed health workers per 1.000 people	3.3
Immunization rate (%)	95.5
Household analysis	
No. of visits to a health provider per annum	3.1
People who did not seek treatment among those who reported an episode of illness (%)	23
Proportion of people who were referred by a doctor to a hospital but not admitted (%)	25
Admission rate to a hospital per 1,000 people of which:	35
township health centres/district hospital	21
county hospital	9
upper level hospital	5
Hospital days per 1,000 people	358

Notes: The survey results are generally reported separately for rich, intermediate, and poor groups of counties. These are aggreagated here by the number of counties (county analysis) or villages (household analysis).
Source: Shanghai-IDS 1993.

Table 5.5 presents some survey evidence on provision and access. There were fewer than two hospital beds (at county level or below), and only 3.3 trained health workers, per 1,000 people, but the immunization rate (of children under 7 years against six basic diseases) was almost universal. A quarter of those who reported an episode of illness did not seek treatment, and a quarter of those who were referred by a doctor to a hospital did not seek admission. Although thirty-five people per 1,000 were admitted to a hospital, they generally went to a township health centre or equivalent; only five reached a hospital above county level. There were on average 3.1 visits to a health provider per annum. It appears that everyone has access to health care of sort. Of more concern was the quality of that health care and the needs of seriously ill poor rural people.

5.3 HEALTH-CARE FINANCES

The sources and channels of health financing in China are varied and complex. They include both direct and indirect government spending, different types of insurance scheme, and expenditure by enterprises, communities, and individuals. The government has no systematic estimate of total health expenditure, and the data are not available for such an estimate. The

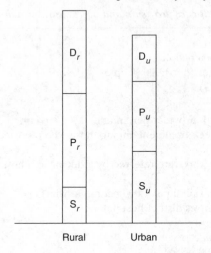

FIG. 5.1 *Health-care needs and their fulfilment*

difficulties are compounded by our concern to distinguish urban and rural revenues and expenditures.

The qualitative account above of health care in China nevertheless suggests certain broad hypotheses, best described in Figure 5.1. The two columns represent per capita health-care needs and their fulfilment in the rural and urban areas. The health-care needs of an average rural and average urban person, N_r and N_u respectively, are measured vertically by the lengths of the columns. S indicates the contribution towards the fulfilment of need made by the public subsidy, and P the contribution made from private funding. $E = S + P$ shows the total expenditure on health care, and the residual deficit, D, shows that part of need which is not met.

One hypothesis is that total need, $N = D + P + S$, is greater in rural than in urban China, reflecting the inferior health status of rural people. Urban health expenditure nevertheless exceeds rural, so that unmet need is smaller in urban areas. Moreover, sources of funding differ, with urban people being more heavily subsidized and rural people paying more. In summary, and as the figure illustrates, we expect:

$N_r > N_u$

$E_r < E_u$

$D_r > D_u$

$S_r < S_u$

$P_r > P_u.$

TABLE 5.6 *Health-care expenditure and funding in rural China: rural health care survey, 1987*

Expenditure

Average medical care fee per visit (yuan):

outpatient visit to:	county hospital	6.4
	township health centre	5.6
	village health station	2.1
inpatient admission to:	county hospital	164.6
	township health centre	82.8
inpatient per day at:	county hospital	13.6
	township health centre	10.6

Total fees per person per year (yuan):

outpatient care	12.0
inpatient care	3.3
total medical care	15.3
Total expenditure on health services per person per year (yuan)	20.4
Household income per person per year (yuan)	671.0

As a proportion of household income (%):

medical care fees	2.3
total expenditure on health care	3.0

Funding

Proportion of total expenditure on health services funded by (%):

public funds (village, township, county, and above)	29
fees (self-payment or local insurances)	71

Proportion of households financing health care by means of (%):

self-payment	65
local medical insurance	31
state medical insurance	2
other	2

Inpatient days per 1,000 people, financed by:

self-payment	243
local insurance	477

Proportion referred to hospital who did not seek care (%), financed by:

self-payment	21
local insurance	7

Note: Data based on the latter source had generally to be aggregated across rich, intermediate, and poor counties using the weights implicitly provided.

Sources: Gu *et al.* 1993; Shanghai-IDS 1993.

Table 5.6 sets out information on health-care expenditure and its funding, derived from the rural health care survey of 1987. The cost of outpatient visits for medical treatment was low but inpatient treatment, especially in county hospitals, was costly in relation to rural income per capita. This would have affected the minority with serious health problems: average fees for medical care represented only 2.3 per cent of household income per capita. User charges, whether paid by the individual or through local insurance, accounted for nearly three-quarters of funding. Public subsidies were relatively minor, averaging little more than 5 yuan per capita. Clearly, $S_r < P_r$. Two-thirds of households paid for their own health care, and less than one-third were covered by local medical insurance schemes. However, local insurance was important to the quality of health care. The insured spent twice as long in hospital as the uninsured and, of those referred to a hospital, 21 per cent of people paying for themselves did not seek care, as opposed to 7 per cent of those with local insurance.

Some township, village, and private (TVP) enterprises provide collective labour insurance to their workers, involving partial payment of health-care expenses for members and possibly their dependants. If all TVP workers were covered, rural membership would have numbered 93 million in 1987 and expenditure would have been 9 yuan per member (World Bank 1989: annexe table I-3). It is likely, however, that many, if not most, rural enterprise workers were not insured, in which case expenditure per member would have exceeded 9 yuan. The schemes offered the most subsidized health care (apart from that of the few state employees) in rural China.

The CASS 1988 national household survey provided information on private health-care expenditure (Table 5.7). Household spending per person on health care was roughly the same in rural and urban areas. In terms of Figure 5.1, $P_r = P_u$. Moreover, for those households reporting a birth, private expenditure on antenatal care and childbirth was nearly twice as high in the rural areas. Whereas there would rarely be a subsidy in rural China, the average payment by the work unit reported in urban China (107.9 yuan) ensured that, with regard to maternity services, $S_r < S_u$ and $E_r < E_u$.

The 1988 national household survey permits an analysis of the determinants of urban household medical expenditure. Where:

TABLE 5.7 *Private expenditure on health care in rural and urban China: 1988 CASS survey*

Yuan p.a.	Rural	Urban
Private expenditure on health care	14.1	14.6
Private expenditure per birth on prenatal care and childbirth	76.5	42.6

Notes: 1. The numbers of rural and urban households in the sample were 10,258 and 9,009 respectively.
2. In the rural case private expenditure on health care explicitly includes contributions to local insurance schemes.

P = private medical expenditure by an urban household

M = number of household members in paying category i,

we estimated P as a function of each M_i (Table 5.8). The coefficients on M_i represent the expenditures per additional household member in that paying category, i.e. the marginal health expenditures. An additional member covered by public medical care (M_c) slightly reduced household expenditure, possibly because it gave other members access to free medicines. Part-payers (M_p) added 9 yuan per member and full-payers (M_t) 20 yuan, with other members (M_o) adding 17 yuan. However, members covered by public medical care formed the majority (55 per cent) whereas those paying their full medical costs constituted only 17 per cent of the total.

Table 5.9 shows that in 1987 some 130 million urban workers were covered by medical insurance schemes. In addition, many of their dependants received partial support. In 1987 the subsidy per member averaged 84 yuan in the public service, 172 yuan in state enterprises, and 86 yuan in urban collectives (higher if not all collective workers were covered). The average for public service employees concealed wide variation: senior cadres generally have access to much better facilities than do other public servants. In both the public service and the state enterprises the real cost per worker exploded during the 1980s, rising at 9 and 16 per cent per annum respectively. This was attributed mainly to the lack of incentives for economizing on the part of providers and patients and to weak financial controls (Shanghai-IDS 1993: 59).

TABLE 5.8 *Regression analysis: the determinants of urban household medical expenditure: 1988 CASS survey*

Independent variable	Notation	Mean value	Coefficient
Members covered by public medical care	M_c	1.88	−2.618
Members paying part of medical costs	M_p	0.69	8.928**
Members paying all of medical costs	M_t	0.58	19.521**
Members with other forms of medical care	M_o	0.28	16.530**
Intercept			32.838**
Adj. R^2		0.01	
F-value		26.16	
Dependent variable	P	49.96	
No. of observations	N	9,009	

Notes: 1. ** denotes that the coefficient is significant at the 1% level.

2. The dependent variable is medical expenditure by urban households, in yuan p.a.

TABLE 5.9 *Coverage and expenditure per capita on medical insurance schemes in urban China, 1980 and 1987*

	1980	1987	Annual real growth rate 1980–7
Membership (millions)			
Public service	15.8	22.5	6.0
Labour insurance, state enterprises	64.4	71.6	1.5
Labour insurance, urban collectives	24.3	36.4	6.0
Expenditure per member (yuan)			
Public service	42	84	8.5
Labour insurance, state enterprises	50	172	15.5
Labour insurance, urban collectives	25	86	15.5

Notes: 1. The data for the public service insurance scheme are for 1986, not 1987.
2. The real rates of growth of expenditure are obtained by correcting the 1987 figures by the deflator implicit in the source tables.

Source: World Bank 1989, annexe tables I-1, 2, and 3.

The final identifiable source of health-care funding is the public subsidy coming from central and local governments for health-care activities, programmes, and salaries (excluding insurance schemes). In 1987 this amounted to 5.4 yuan per person (World Bank 1989: table I-1). The problem is to divide this into rural and urban expenditure. The public funds at county and township level available to the 1987 sample of counties averaged 4.8 yuan per person (Shanghai-IDS 1993: table 6.7). If this figure was accurate for rural China as a whole, the residual urban figure would have been 7.3 yuan per person.

The various estimates of urban and rural expenditure are brought together in summary form (Table 5.10). The table depends on various sources and requires numerous assumptions: it merely indicates broad orders of magnitude. It is clear that health expenditure per person is lower in rural China ($E_r < E_u$). This is largely because of the extent of urban subsidies ($S_r < S_u$). Depending on the source, household expenditure per person is either roughly the same or higher in rural areas ($P_r \geq P_u$).

5.4 HEALTH OUTCOMES

5.4.1 The rural–urban divide in health status

One of the best available guides to the health status of a population, and thus to its health-care needs, is life expectancy or its correlate, the

TABLE 5.10 *Urban and rural expenditure per capita on health care, about 1987* (*yuan p.a.*)

Source of funding	In the notation of Fig. 5.1	Urban	Rural
Private	P	14.6[a]	—
Private and local insurance	P		14.1[a]/20.4[b]
Insurance schemes	S	62.2[c]	—
Public subsidy	S	7.3[b,c]	4.8[b,c]
Total	E	8.4.1	18.9/25.2

Note: Insurance schemes are regarded as private payments in rural areas (being locally funded by the beneficiaries) and public subsidies in urban areas (being non-contributory).

Sources: [a] CASS national household survey; [b] 1987 Rural Health-care Survey; [c] World Bank 1989.

mortality rate. A broken series on the mortality rate in urban and rural China is available for the Communist period (Figure 5.2). The terrible effects of the great famine of 1959–61, especially in rural China, are evident from the figure. The rural mortality rate was consistently above the urban rate throughout the period, although the gap was narrower after the mid-1970s.

The most outstanding feature of the figure is not the rural–urban differential but the remarkable decline in both the rural and urban mortality rates during the first three decades after liberation. In relation to GNP per capita, China's low mortality rate represented an extreme outlier in a cross-country analysis for 1988 (Knight and Song 1993: 81). Any comparison of health status in urban and rural China should recognize that China as a whole does well by comparison with other low-income countries, especially in preventive health care.

We examined three main reasons for the sharp decline in mortality, although a precise decomposition of their contributions was not possible (Knight and Song 1993). One was the rise in levels of income per capita over that period. However, on the basis of the observed relationship across the counties of rural China (reported in Table 5.13 below), income growth would explain no more than a third of the decline in the rural mortality rate. It is plausible, and consistent with our estimates, that mortality is particularly sensitive to income at low income levels. The alleviation of rural poverty—via land reform, the communal pooling of risks, and social relief programmes—may therefore have magnified the effect of income. The emphasis placed on preventive health care in the 1950s and on mass curative care in the 1960s must have been important, for instance in explaining the sharp fall in mortality from preventable diseases. The introduction of

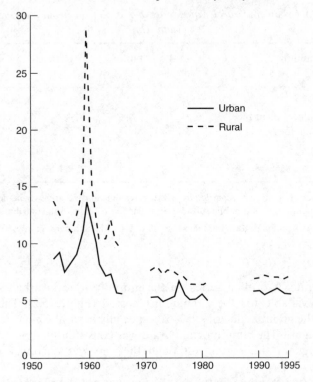

FIG. 5.2 *Mortality rate per 1,000 people, rural and urban*

communal health insurance for urban people in the 1950s and for rural people in the late 1960s and early 1970s clearly also played a part.

'In the long run we are all dead.' Better guides to health status than the overall mortality rate are the infant (years 0–1), child (here defined as years 1–4), and premature (here years 5–64) mortality rates. They are available from the 1990 national census for city, town, and county areas. These categories do not correspond to the urban–rural division. The cities (accounting for 30 per cent of the national population) include the population of the rural areas under the cities' jurisdiction: the 'non-agricultural' population as a proportion of the total was 43 per cent in cities, 21 per cent in towns, and 4 per cent in counties. Thus a comparison of cities with towns and counties is likely to blur and to understate the urban–rural differences in mortality rates.

Table 5.11 shows the county mortality rate to be the highest in each case, and the city rate the lowest. The infant rate was 60 per cent higher in the counties than in the cities, the child rate 81 per cent higher, and the premature rate 22 per cent higher. Various health status indicators are available for 1987 both for urban and rural China and for four categories of rural

TABLE 5.11 *Age-specific mortality rates per 1,000 people, rural and urban China, 1989*

Ages:	Infant 0–1	Child 1–4	Premature 5–64	Percentage of population
China	22.46	2.10	4.31	100.0
County	27.13	2.60	4.68	46.8
Town	18.76	1.75	4.19	23.6
City	16.92	1.44	3.85	29.6
County (city = 100)	1.60	1.81	1.22	—

Source: PRC, SSB 1993, vol. 4: 32–55.

TABLE 5.12 *Indicators of health status, urban and rural areas, and rural areas by level of development, 1987*

	Infant mortality rate		Life expectancy		Mortality rate tuberculosis	
	per 1000 births	rural = 100	years	rural = 100	per 100,000	rural = 100
Urban	20.0	43	71.5	107	419	60
Rural	46.5	100	66.6	100	694	100
Rural: area 1	29.9	64	69.4	104	486	70
area 2	38.8	83	68.2	102	540	78
area 3	52.1	112	65.0	98	825	119
area 4	96.2	207	59.0	89	1083	156

Note: Rural areas are classified according to the level of development of the economy and social services. Area 1, the most developed, accounts for 22% of counties, area 2 for 32%, area 3 for 36%, and area 4, the least developed, for 10%.

Source: Rao *et al.* 1989, cited by Yu 1992: 57.

area classified according to level of development (Table 5.12). Not only is the rural infant mortality rate more than double the urban but it is three times higher in the poorest rural area than in the richest. Urban life expectancy is five years longer than rural, but life expectancy in the richest rural area is ten years longer than in the poorest. Similarly, the gap in mortality rates from tuberculosis is large between urban and rural China but even larger within rural China. Rural health status is inferior to urban even for the richest areas, but it is far worse for the poorest. These differences are large enough to warrant further investigation of the role of income.

5.4.2 *The relationship between income and health*

How can the rural–urban gap in mortality rates be accounted for? Is the
explanation to be found in the underlying health status or in the provision
of health care? In terms of Figure 5.1, is the gap due to a difference in
the length of the columns ($N_r > N_u$) or to a difference in expenditures
($E_r < E_u$)? Either could produce a difference in residual unmet needs
($R_r > R_u$). And if the former explanation is correct, is the inferior underlying health status of rural people to be explained by their lower income,
i.e. by rural poverty?

These questions cannot be examined directly but an analysis of the determinants of health status within rural China is illuminating. A national survey of the causes of death was undertaken in 1976, involving identification
of some 20 million deaths in the previous three years and retrospective
diagnosis of their causes (Chen *et al.* 1990). The study was made in sixty-
five rural counties spread throughout China, and provided information on
standardized mortality rates. The researchers tried to describe how people
live as well as how they die: there were biological variables, food composite
and diet variables, lifestyle variables, and economic, social, ecological,
geographic, and demographic characteristics of counties. Mortality rates
were found to vary widely from one part of the country to another. This
provided an opportunity for investigating the correlates of disease and
hypotheses about the causes.

We have made use of the survey in order to examine, in an exploratory
way, the relationships between premature death and certain socio-economic
variables (Knight and Song 1993). We concentrate here on one basic relationship—that between income per capita and mortality. We would expect
to find a negative relationship between income levels and age-specific mortality rates prior to old age. Households and communities with more income
can feed and live better and purchase more health care. Only in the case
of diseases associated with prosperous lifestyles would we expect to find a
positive relationship between income and premature death.

In examining the causes of mortality it is necessary to distinguish between
exogenous and endogenous variables (Schultz 1984; Behrman and
Deolalikar 1988). Endogeneity is likely to arise when variables are not predetermined but are chosen by households or communities given their circumstances and constraints. Health-care inputs into the health production
function are normally endogenously chosen. The underlying determinants
of health are well represented in the data but the health-care inputs are not.
Households or communities in poor health may receive additional, unobserved, curative health care. In that case, the coefficients on some included
variables tend to be closer to zero in our equations than they would be in
simultaneously determined equations that controlled for treatment. Insofar
as additional income generates additional but unobserved health-care

inputs, we cannot explore all the mechanisms by which income reduces the mortality rate. Even though we lack choice variables, some of our regressors may nevertheless be endogenous. The underlying healthiness of a community can influence not only its mortality rate but also its ability to earn income. Poverty may contribute to poor health, and poor health may contribute to poverty. It is possible, therefore, that the coefficient on income will be biased in equations predicting mortality.

We estimated regression equations for three age-specific mortality rates:

M_i = infant (<1 year) mortality rate

M_y = child (<15 years) mortality rate

M = premature (<65 years) mortality rate.

A variety of economic, geographic, lifestyle, nutrition and diet, and sanitation variables were included as explanatory variables in order to isolate as far as possible the independent influence of income. Those variables which were not statistically significant were eliminated from the equation, except that the income coefficient was always retained. The logarithm of mortality was generally superior to mortality itself. Table 5.13 presents the best-fitting results in each case. It also shows the coefficient on the income variable when that alone is included in the equation, in order to pick up effects of income working indirectly through other variables.

The least satisfactory equation is that predicting infant mortality. Only 21 per cent of the variance in $\ln M_i$ can be explained by the two significant explanatory variables, income and adult height. The coefficient on $\ln Y$ implies an income elasticity of infant mortality of −0.31, i.e. a doubling of income per capita reduces the infant mortality rate by 31 per cent. An increase in the mean height (159 cm) of the adult population (aged 45–54) by one standard deviation (2.6 cm) reduces the infant mortality rate by 26 per cent. We take height to represent the general long-run standard of nutrition in the local community.

Child mortality is the only case in which $\ln Y$ is not significantly negative. No less than 60 per cent of the variance in the dependent variable can be explained by the significant explanatory variables. Adult height is again extremely important in reducing child mortality. On average, eggs are eaten thirty-eight times a year but the standard deviation among counties is high (thirty-one times). The significant negative coefficient implies that a halving of egg consumption, to nineteen times a year, would raise child mortality by 12 per cent. The variables representing sources of drinking water have significant coefficients. Some 73 per cent of the population obtain their drinking water from wells as opposed to surface sources. If the remaining 27 per cent could switch to well sources, the child mortality rate would fall by some 15 per cent.

No less than 53 per cent of the variance in $\ln M$ can be explained by the

TABLE 5.13 *Regression analysis: the determinants of age-specific mortality rates: 1973–75 rural mortality survey*

Independent variables	Notation	Coefficients		
		Infant (<1 year) $\ln M_i$	Child (<15 years) $\ln M_y$	Premature (<65 years) $\ln M$
Intercept		21.789**	34.140**	13.729**
Income per capita, in logs	$\ln Y$	−0.305**	0.036	−0.261**
Percentage of college graduates in population	E_u		−1.012*	
Percentage literacy rate in population aged over 12	E_i			0.007**
Height (cm).	H	−0.102**	−0.216**	−0.040**
Weight (kg).	W		0.101**	
Percentage who have smoked manufactured cigarettes daily for more than 6 months	C_s			−0.003**
Eggs (times p.a.)	E_g		−0.006**	
Percentage drinking shallow well water	W_{sw}		−0.006**	−0.002**
Percentage drinking deep well water	W_{dw}		−0.005**	−0.003**
Mean value of dependent variable		3.633	4.415	6.106
Adjusted R^2		0.212	0.576	0.529
F-value		7.326	10.138	9.789
Percentage standard error of estimate		62	39	17
No. of observations		47	47	47
Coefficient on $\ln Y$ in equation with only intercept and $\ln Y$		−0.353**	−0.399**	−0.205**

Notes: 1. ** denotes significance at the rate of 5% and * at the 10% level.
2. The dependent variables are the infant, child, and premature mortality rates. These are cumulative and are expressed per 1,000 people.
3. As the percentages W_{sw}, W_{dw}, and W_s add up to 100% in each county, only two are included, W_s (surface water) being excluded from the equation.

Sources: Chen *et al.* 1990.

five significant independent variables. A doubling of county income per capita would reduce the premature mortality rate by 26 per cent, and an additional standard deviation in height would reduce it by 10 per cent. If surface sources of water were replaced by well sources, the mortality rate would fall by 7 per cent. Smokers, expressed as a percentage of the population, also have a statistically significant effect. A reduction in the mean proportion (33 per cent) by one standard deviation (to 18 per cent) would reduce the premature mortality rate by 5 per cent.

It is possible that the inclusion of income-related characteristics among the explanatory variables biases downwards the measured effect of income on mortality. The final row of Table 5.13 therefore shows the income elasticities derived from equations containing only intercepts and income terms. The strength of the negative relationship does indeed increase in the case of infant mortality, and the relationship becomes significantly negative for child mortality. However, in the case of premature mortality the coefficient, although remaining significantly negative, is slightly reduced in absolute terms.

Since we have disease-specific premature mortality rates, we can explore the determinants of death from specific causes. In particular we seek to distinguish the diseases of poverty, common before the epidemiological transition, from the diseases of prosperity, common after the transition has been made. The former group is likely to include infectious and respiratory diseases and the latter group heart disease, stroke, and cancer. The latter diseases account for about 40 per cent of premature deaths in the mortality survey. We expect the income elasticity of disease-specific premature mortality to vary according to the nature of the disease.

Table 5.14 shows the coefficient on the income variable ($\ln Y$) in equations using it alone to estimate disease-specific premature mortality rates ($\ln M_i$). The income elasticity in the case of stroke and cancer is negative but low and not significant. However, it is positive for lung cancer, having a significant value of 0.43 for men (who smoke more than women). Lung cancer is the disease that best fits the description of a disease of prosperity. Mortality is significantly reduced as income increases in the case of tuberculosis, digestive diseases, pregnancy and birth diseases, and some types of heart condition, including hypertensive and rheumatic heart diseases.

Income generally has a statistically significant and quantitatively important negative effect on mortality. The strength of the estimated relationship is impressive. How is it to be explained? The true relationship may be weaker than the coefficient suggests. Causation can run both ways: income may itself be reduced by ill-health. If income is low and mortality high when health is poor, income is negatively correlated with the error term in the equation and the algebraic value of the coefficient on income is biased downwards. Nevertheless, there are plausible explanations for the observed inverse relationship. At the time of the mortality survey, most rural people were members of health insurance schemes provided by their communes. The quantity and the quality of health care, both preventive and curative, would depend partly on the income of the commune and partly—through user fees—on the income of members. Rural health-care units were required to mobilize local resources. Consequently, 'the more affluent communities

TABLE 5.14 *The relationship between income and disease-specific mortality rates: 1973–5 rural mortality survey*

Disease	Coefficient on $\ln Y$ in equation predicting $\ln M_j$
Cancer	−0.114
Female lung cancer	0.201
Male lung cancer	0.429**
Tuberculosis	−0.275*
Other infectious diseases	−0.313
Pneumonia diseases	−0.291
Digestive diseases	−0.507***
Respiratory diseases	0.126
Pregnancy and birth	−0.512**
Stroke	−0.109
Heart disease:	
myocardial infarction and coronary disease	−0.258
hypertension	−0.531**
hypertension, myocardial infarction, and coronary disease	−0.393**
rheumatic disease	−0.492**
other	0.394**

Note: *** indicates statistical significance at the 1%, ** at the 5%, and * at the 10% level.

Source: Knight and Song 1993: table 5.

can afford to subsidize health-care costs, invest more to increase the quantity and raise the quality of their personnel, and enjoy easier access to better health care' (World Bank 1983, iii: 50.). Income might also have influenced mortality rates through its effects on nutrition and sanitation insofar as these were not adequately represented by our available proxies.

Two main sources can help us to explain the inverse relationship between income and mortality in rural China. One is the rural health-care survey of 1987. The counties were divided into three categories on the basis of income per person: rich, intermediate, and poor. Table 5.15 presents some relevant results for the survey. The three categories differed greatly in village income per person, dependence on agriculture, and the extent of TVP production (rows 4–6). The health status of people was worse in the poor counties according to all four of our measures (rows 7–10). The fact that the main distinction is between the poor group and the other two suggests a non-linearity in the relationship of health status to income: illness thrives in conditions of extreme poverty.

Turning to health facilities, we see that access to and use of hospitals was best in the rich and worst in the poor counties (rows 11–14). Residents of

TABLE 5.15 *Results from the rural health-care survey, 1987, by income level of counties*

Row	Table source		Rich counties	Intermediate counties	Poor counties
		1. Sample size			
1	4.2	No. of counties	6	7	7
2	4.8	No. of townships	13	21	18
3	4.13	No. of villages	45	62	53
		2. Economic characteristics of villages			
4	4.10	Average income per person (yuan)	918	565	328
5	4.10	Agricultural income as proportion of total income (%)	21	62	69
6	4.10	Average enterprise production per person (yuan)	3,446	336	129
		3. Health status of people			
7	5.2a	People reporting subjective ill-health in last two weeks (%)	7.7	6.3	9.4
8	5.2a	People reporting significant limitation of activity in last two weeks (%)	2.1	1.8	3.1
9	5.5	People reporting at least one visit to a health provider in last two weeks (%)	5.7	4.8	7.5
10	5.5	No. of visits to a health provider per annum	2.8	2.4	4.3
		4. Health-care provision and access			
11	4.3	Hospital beds per 1,000 people in county	2.2	1.8	1.4
12	5.22	Admission rate to a hospital per 1,000 people	60	28	24
13	5.15	Hospital days per 1,000 people	640	234	175
14	5.15	Hospital days per 1,000 people, children aged 0–4	963	355	143
15	5.9	People who did not seek treatment among those who reported an episode of illness (%)	26	24	21

TABLE 5.15 *Continued*

Row	Table source		Rich counties	Intermediate counties	Poor counties
16	5.10	Reasons given for not seeking treatment: proportion reporting expense (%)	14	34	48
17	5.18	People referred to hospital but not seeking admission (%)	6	23	42
18	5.20	Reasons for not seeking admission: proportion reporting expense (%)	36	51	63
19	6.7	Private expenditure on health care per person (fees and insurance) (yuan)	17.8		11.4
20	4.4	Village health workers per 1,000 people in county	1.1	1.3	1.4
21	4.6	Immunization rate in county (%)	96	93	95
		5. Cooperative health care schemes (CHCS)			
22	4.13	Villages with a CHCS as a proportion of total (%)	67	35	25
		Average enterprise product per person (yuan), in villages:			
23	6.10	with a CHCS	3,209	226	81
24	6.10	without a CHCS	1,808	103	40
		Hospital days per 1,000 people, in villages			
25	5.15	with a CHCS	697	288	209
26	5.15	without a CHSC	535	213	143

Source: Shanghai-IDS 1993.

poor counties were less likely to seek admission if referred to a hospital, and more likely to cite expense as their reason for inaction (rows 16–18). However, poor villagers suffered no disadvantage in the number of health workers available, and in their rates of immunization against the basic diseases (rows 20–1). Part of the difference in health care was due to a much greater prevalence of cooperative health-care schemes in the rich counties (row 21), such schemes being closely related to village industry as a source of funds (rows 22–3). People with local insurance made greater use of health-care facilities, for instance in their use of hospitals (rows 24–5).

The evidence of the survey is consistent with the view that health status depends partly on poverty irrespective of health care. For instance, people in poor counties reported more subjective ill-health, visited a health provider more often, and sought treatment if ill just as often. Nevertheless, in the provision of health-care facilities and in access to them, the residents of poor counties were often at a disadvantage: their health may have been further impaired through lack of treatment.

The rural sample of the CASS 1988 national survey of household incomes in China provides an opportunity to examine expenditure on health care by rural households in relation to income. Table 5.16 presents equations explaining expenditure on health care. Three explanatory variables are used, two as proxies for household need: the number of household members (H) and the number of visits to a hospital or clinic (V). The latter would be a poor proxy for need if income were a determinant of the decision to visit a hospital or clinic. However, over 80 per cent of a sample of rural people claimed to have seen a doctor when they were ill, and the coefficient of ln Y in the equation predicting ln V (the first column), although significantly positive, is only 0.07. Thus when household income doubles, visits to the hospital or clinic increase on average by only 7 per cent. We treat V as an indicator of ill-health that is largely independent of income, and therefore include it in the equations predicting expenditures on health care. The variable representing willingness to pay for health care is the net income reported by households (Y). All the dependent variables and income are presented in logarithmic form.

The coefficient on H is in each case significantly positive: the larger the household, the greater is its expenditure on health care. Similarly, the coefficient on V is everywhere positive and significantly so: *ceteris paribus*, the more hospital visits household members have to make, the more does the household spend on health care. The income elasticity of demand for health care is significantly positive in each case. The coefficient in the equation predicting total medical expenditure (E) is 0.35. Expenditure on prenatal care and childbirth (E_m) is also positively related to income, the coefficient being 0.23. Although the equations using levels rather than logs generally fit less well, the coefficient on income is uniformly and significantly positive. However, the implied marginal propensity to spend

TABLE 5.16 *Regression equations to explain expenditure on health-care by rural households: 1988 CASS survey*

Independent variables	Notation	Coefficients		
		No. of visits to hospital $\ln V$	Total medical expenditure $\ln E$	Expenditure on prenatal care and childbirth $\ln E_m$
Intercept		0.821**	0.516**	1.866**
Net household income	$\ln Y$	0.067**	0.351**	0.227**
Number of household members	H	0.058**	0.026**	0.022**
No. of visits to hospital	V		0.040**	0.001**
Mean of dependent variable		1.635	3.690	3.735
Mean of dependent variable in levels		8.01	87.38	77.77
Adj. R^2		0.015	0.148	0.021
F-value		50.58	371.7	8.83
Standard error of the estimate (%)		94.0	115.4	110.7
No. of observations		6,475	6,412	1,126
Marginal propensity to spend in equation using levels instead of logs: Net household income	Y	0.0001*	0.010*	0.008**

Notes: 1. * indicates statistical significance at the 10% and ** at the 1% level.
2. The dependent variables are $\ln V$, $\ln E$, and $\ln E_m$.

out of income is low: a mere 1 per cent of additional income is devoted to health care. The income elasticities proved robust to alternative specifications of the health-care expenditure equation.

The most surprising result of this exercise is that the income elasticity of demand for health care, although significantly positive, is significantly below unity: as income rises, a smaller proportion of household income is spent on health care. We can illustrate this by showing how E rises with Y, holding the other explanatory variables constant at their mean values. As income rises from 1,000 yuan to the mean, 2,886, and to 5,000 yuan, so total medical expenditure rises from 30 to 43 and to 52 yuan in turn, representing 3.0, 1.5, and 1.0 per cent of income respectively. Some doubt might be cast on the estimates: if poor households were less healthy and had greater health-care needs, and if the inclusion of H and V as explanatory variables failed to standardize adequately for the differences in the needs of rich and poor households, the estimated income elasticity would be biased downwards. Nevertheless, it appears that differences in medical expenditures cannot explain why mortality is strongly responsive to income level.

There are two possible reasons for the sensitivity of mortality to income in rural China. One is that poor people, although having reasonable access to treatment for minor illness, are at a particular disadvantage in the treatment of life-threatening illness. This is likely to require sophisticated facilities in county or above-county hospitals, with the attendant costs of access, hospitalization, and treatment. The other reason is that income level may have an important direct effect on the need for health care and hence on mortality. For instance, extreme poverty often means contaminated environments and malnutrition lowers the body's defence against infection. Income may thus have its effect on mortality through such variables as nutrition, housing, and the village environment.

Both of these explanations for intra-rural variation are likely to be no less important in explaining the urban–rural difference in premature mortality rates. Comparing urban and rural areas, not only is there a large difference in health care but also in access to high-quality, life-saving medical treatment, in household income per capita, and in the quality of the residential environment. Disparities in the quality and the length of life, as governed by differential health status and health care, are important dimensions of the divide between urban and rural China.

5.5 CONCLUSION

Premature death and its inverse, life expectancy, together with its correlate, health status, are important determinants of the quality of life. The standard of living has various dimensions. One dimension, measured income, was shown to be an important influence on another, the ability to live a long, healthy life. The complementarity between them is another example of vicious and virtuous circles at work in the process of economic development.

Their great difference in mean incomes contributes to a considerable difference in the underlying healthiness of people in urban and rural China. Rural health needs are greater than urban, but this is not reflected in greater health care. The institutional divide creates a gap between urban and rural provision of and access to health services. The rural population is at a disadvantage in both the quantity and the quality of health care. Moreover,

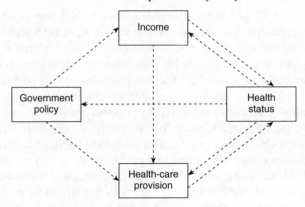

Fɪɢ. 5.3 *The interaction between health, health care, income and government policy*

urban services are much more heavily subsidized, so that rural people have to pay no less than urban people for health care. The unfulfilled health needs of rural-dwellers are far greater, and this worsens their already inferior health status. A fairer distribution of health-care resources would be assisted by more unified institutional arrangements, so making the extent of inequality more transparent.

Some of the relationships examined in this chapter are presented schematically in Figure 5.3. The relationships are indicated by arrows. By comparison with urban China, rural China has lower income and receives lower government policy priority, both of which reduce rural health-care provision. Lower income and lower health-care provision in turn worsen health status. Inferior health status increases the need for health care but there is only a partial response. It also reduces income, so contributing to a vicious circle.

Two caveats should be borne in mind. First, the diverse and complex health-care systems in China are not readily amenable to economic analysis. Accurate accounts of health care and health outcomes require more, specifically designed, surveys and a greater government concern to quantify the extent of public subsidies. Secondly, our emphasis on the rural–urban comparison diverts attention from China's good record, even in rural areas, by comparison with most poor countries. It is probably the high quality of health care in urban China that is the real international outlier.

NOTE

1. Since the total number of village health workers recorded in 1986 was 1,785,000 (World Bank 1989: annexe table H-12), corresponding to the 1,240,000 middle- and lower-level salaried staff (annexe table H-14), the number of unsalaried rural health workers might be the residual 545,000.

REFERENCES

Behrman, Jere R., and Deolalikar, Anil B. (1988). 'Health and nutrition', in Hollis Chenery and T. N. Srinivasan (eds.), *Handbook of Development Economics*, Amsterdam: North-Holland: 631–711.

Chen Junshi, Campbell, T. Colin, Li Junyao, and Peto, Richard (1990). *Diet, Life Style and Mortality in China. A Study of the Characteristics of 65 Chinese Counties*, Oxford: Oxford University Press.

Cornia, Giovanni Andrea (1989). 'Investing in human resources: health, nutrition and development for the 1990s', *Journal of Development Planning*. 19: 159–88.

De Geyndt, Willy, Zhao Xiyan, and Lui Shunli (1992). *From Barefoot Doctor to Village Doctor in Rural China*, World Bank Technical Paper 187, Washington, DC: World Bank.

Gu Xingyuan, Bloom, Gerald, Tang Shenglan, Zhu Yingya, Zhou Shouqi, and Chen Xingbao (1993). 'Financing health care in rural China: preliminary report of a nationwide study', *Social Science Medicine*, 36 (4): 385–91.

Knight, John, and Lina Song (1993). 'The length of life and the standard of living: economic influences on premature death in China', *Journal of Development Studies,* 30 (1): 58–91.

People's Republic of China, Ministry of Public Health (PRC, MOPH) (1986). *Health Services in Rural Areas*, Beijing (in Chinese).

——— (PRC, MOPH) (1987). *China Health Yearbook, 1987.* Beijing: Peoples' Health Publication House (in Chinese).

—— State Statistical Bureau (PRC, SSB) (1987). *Statistical Yearbook of China 1986*, Beijing.

——— (PRC, SSB) (1991). *Statistical Yearbook of China 1991*, Beijing.

——— (PRC, SSB) (1993). *Tabulations on the 1990 Population Census of the Peoples' Republic of China* (four volumes), Beijing: Population Census Office under the State Council and Department of Population Statistics (in Chinese).

——— (PRC, SSB) (1994). *Statistical Yearbook of China 1994*, Beijing.

——— (PRC, SSB) (1996). *Statistical Yearbook of China 1996*, Beijing.

Rao Keqin *et al.* (1989). 'Research on the classification of Chinese health status', *Journal of Chinese Health Statistics*, 2.6 (in Chinese).

Shanghai-IDS Health Finance Group (1993). 'Financing Rural Health Services in China: Adapting to Economic Reform', Research Report, Apr.

Schultz, T. Paul (1984). 'Studying the impact of household economic and community variables on child mortality', *Population and Development Review*, supplement to vol. 10: 215–36.

World Bank (1983). *China, Socialist Economic Development* (three vols.), Washington, DC: World Bank.

—— (1989). 'China Long-Term Issues in Options for the Health Sector. Annexes' (draft), Washington, DC: World Bank.

—— (1992). *China. Long Term Issues and Options in the Health Transition*, World Bank Country Study, Washington, DC: World Bank.

Yu Dezhi (1992). 'Changes in health care financing and health status: the case of China in the 1980s', Innocenti Occasional Papers, Economic Policy Series, 34, Florence: Unicef International Child Care Development Centre.

6

Housing

Housing is one dimension of the standard of living in which it is possible that rural people enjoy an advantage over urban people. Housing in most societies performs three main functions: it provides shelter, it is a form of wealth, and it denotes social status. In providing shelter it meets a human need no less basic than that met by food. In rural China housing performs all three functions, particularly in recent years. In urban China, because of the way in which it is owned and allocated, housing has mainly provided shelter.

6.1 THE INSTITUTIONAL DIVIDE

The division of China into rural and urban compartments is nowhere clearer than in housing policy. Households with rural *hukous* are allocated land both for farming and for housing by rural local governments. Their rights to these houses are secure but they do not amount to full private ownership. Land normally belongs to the village or locality, and each household has access to land sufficient for one dwelling. Only households of the village have rights to land. For many years migration was severely restricted and even now in-migrants are normally temporary and accommodated by their employers. The inalienability of housing land and the lack of permanent inter-village migration mean that there is no rural housing market. Rural housing is self-organized subject to these constraints: rural people must finance and build their own houses.

From the late 1950s onwards the Chinese government nationalized much of the urban housing stock and stopped new urban private housebuilding. Former rentiers were initially allowed to live in part of their properties and to receive small rents, but during the Cultural Revolution ownership was fully transferred to the State and the private market disappeared. Very few owner-occupied houses remained, and even these were pared down in size. Only in the late 1980s were the original owners of state-managed rental housing allowed to reclaim their properties.

Urban households have houses allocated to them by the State or its agents such as enterprises and local governments. State work units are expected to house their employees and municipalities are expected to house other urban households. Rents are nominal and thus urban housing is highly subsidized; rents are said to fall short even of maintenance costs. Until the mid-1990s there were only very small private rental and private ownership sectors. Urban housing, therefore, is organized for workers and not by them. Whereas rural people are fairly secure, the allocation of urban housing, mainly by their employers, puts urban people in a position of potential dependence and vulnerability.

The causes of the rural–urban divide in housing administration may lie in the following considerations. The poverty of most rural community organizations and the lack of state intervention at the village level places the burden of housebuilding on peasant households. The allocation of housing land by the village community is an extension of the system of allocating farming land. The arrangements for urban housing, by contrast, may originate in the ideological disapproval of private house ownership, in the desire to control and restrict non-productive investment, in the paternalistic and controlling role chosen for employing enterprises, which were anyway the main source of surplus for investment under the planning system, and in the economies of scale and organizational requirements of large-scale, high-density urban residential investment.

A crude indication that rural housing is in one respect superior to urban housing is given in Table 6.1, showing the living area per capita of both rural and urban households, based on national sample surveys. It should not be concluded from the table that rural housing is superior to urban housing, however, as quality may be valued more highly than quantity.

Rural households enjoyed twice as much living space per capita as urban households over the period 1978–95, and the ratio rose, from 2.3 in 1978 to 2.6 in 1995. Moreover, rural living space more than doubled over the seventeen years, being almost $21\,m^2$ per capita in 1995. Urban living space rose rapidly as well, from 3.6 to $8.1\,m^2$ over that period. The greater living space in rural areas no doubt reflects the greater availability of land. Its rapid growth represents rising incomes, the result of the rural economic reforms, and is a reflection of growing demand. Urban living space was probably supply-constrained, reflecting housing shortage. Its rapid growth is to be explained by the rising norms for permitted and allocated living space and the heavy investment in urban housing during the period of economic reform.

There is another indication that urban housing has been supply-constrained rather than demand-constrained. The rapid growth in urban real incomes in the 1980s produced a remarkable increase in the ownership of consumer durables. This is illustrated in Table 6.2. By contrast, rural households, even though having significantly lower incomes than their urban counterparts, accumulated relatively more wealth. Rural people had an incentive to save in order to build houses; this the urban people lacked. A national household income and expenditure survey conducted by the Chinese Academy of Social Sciences in 1986 illustrates the consequent

TABLE 6.1 *Living area per capita of rural and urban households, 1978–1995*

	Living area per capita (m^2)		
	Rural	Urban	Rural/urban
1978	8.1	3.6	2.3
1979	8.1	3.7	2.2
1980	9.4	3.9	2.4
1981	10.2	4.1	2.5
1982	10.7	4.4	2.4
1983	11.6	4.6	2.5
1984	13.6	4.9	2.8
1985	14.7	5.2	2.8
1986	15.3	6.0	2.6
1987	16.0	6.1	2.6
1988	16.6	6.3	2.6
1989	17.2	6.6	2.6
1990	17.8	6.7	2.7
1991	18.5	6.9	2.7
1992	18.9	7.1	2.7
1993	20.7	7.5	2.8
1994	20.2	7.8	2.6
1995	21.0	8.1	2.6
1995 (1978 = 100)	259	225	115

Sources: PRC, SSB 1990: 324; 1994: 288; 1996: 321.

TABLE 6.2 *Urban households: percentage owning selected consumer durables, 1981–95*

	1981	1982	1983	1984	1985	1986	1987	1988	1989	1990	1991	1992	1993	1994	1995
Washing machines	6	16	29	40	48	60	67	73	76	78	81	83	86	87	89
Refrigerators	0	1	2	3	7	13	20	28	36	42	49	53	57	62	66
Colour televisions	1	1	3	5	17	27	35	44	51	59	68	75	79	86	90

Sources: World Bank 1992: table 1.12; PRC, SSB 1994: table 9–10; 1996: table 9–7.

difference (Table 6.3). Sixty-one per cent of rural wealth took the form of housing, whereas no urban wealth took that form. Moreover, a 1987–8 survey of farmer households in four rural counties indicated that over half the farmers had invested in housing improvement or expansion since 1983; for these households housing expenditure exceeded annual income and also productive investment (Feder *et al.* 1990). Thus, the difference in housing

TABLE 6.3 *Income and wealth of rural and urban households, 1986*

	Rural	Urban
Household size (persons)	4.98	3.38
Annual income per household	2,145	3.360
Wealth per household	4,244	4,922
of which: financial assets	747	2,168
value of durables and tools	888	2,754
value of housing	2,609	0
Wealth/income ratio	1.98	1.46

Source: World Bank 1992: table 1.13.

Note: The survey comprised 3,860 urban and 3,640 rural households.

arrangements as between the urban and the rural areas has important implications for household saving and wealth.

Over the years the Ministry of Construction has improved its norms for urban house construction standards: from 34 to 38 m^2 in 1972–7 to 56 m^2 in 1990 (World Bank 1992: 10). Investment in urban housing was very limited during the planning period. In 1949 the stock was 520 million m^2. Gross additions between 1950 and 1978 were 530 million m^2 and between 1979 and 1989 1,200 million m^2. By 1989 the stock stood at 3,010 million m^2 (part of the increase represented private housing in newly incorporated urban areas). No less than 46 per cent of the urban housing stock at the end of 1988 was of 1980s' vintage (ibid. 5–6). This newer vintage involved improved housing standards.

6.2 URBAN HOUSING

Housing in urban China is often overcrowded. In their sociological study of urban China in the pre-reform period, Whyte and Parish (1984: 80–1, 340–3) paint a vivid picture of the distress and conflicts caused by overcrowding and the need to share bathing, toilet, and cooking facilities. However, slum conditions are rare. Brick and concrete structures predominate, and there are few of the wood and tin shanty towns that are common sights in other poor countries. Thus there is a lower limit to the quality of housing for permanent urban residents. However, there was—at least until recent years—also an upper limit, in that better housing was seen as a luxury that would detract from the State's investment and development goals.

Table 6.4 presents some characteristics of urban households in the 1988 CASS national household survey, according to the type of housing they occupied. No less than 84 per cent of the sample were living in public

TABLE 6.4 *Some characteristics of urban households by housing type: 1988 CASS survey*

	Public housing	Rented accommodation	Private housing		
			Inherited	Built	Bought
No. of households (per cent of all households)	84	2	7	7	0.4
Household income (yuan p.a.) total	3,696	3,822	2,945	3,260	4,856
per worker	1,858	2,109	1,618	1,596	2,160
No. of household members	3.51	3.40	3.49	3.80	3.82
Size of accommodation (m^2)	38.9	30.9	47.6	67.4	62.5
Percentage of household heads employed by the State	87	67	66	65	71

housing, 2 per cent were in privately rented accommodation, and 14 per cent were in their own homes, whether inherited, built, or bought (7, 7, and 0.4 per cent respectively). Of those households living in public housing, 87 per cent had household heads who were employed in the public sector. In the case of the remaining 13 per cent it is possible that members other than the household head were state employees, so giving the household access to public housing. Income and income per worker were highest for households which had bought their own home or who were renting accommodation. Although it was in privately owned houses—whether inherited, built, or bought—that the size of accommodation was largest, the size was smallest in privately rented accommodation.

6.2.1 The quantity and quality of urban housing

How do urban housing conditions vary according to household income? Data are available from the national urban household survey of the State Statistical Bureau (SSB) in 1986 (PRC, SSB 1989), separately for cities and towns (Table 6.5). Households were grouped into income fifths. Living space per capita rose slightly through the quintiles but the main distinction was between the top fifth and the rest. For instance, a much higher percentage of the top-fifth households occupied more than $10\,m^2$ per capita. With regard to quality indicators, the percentages with piped water and with

TABLE 6.5 *Housing conditions of households in cities and county towns: household fifths classified by income level, 1986*

| | Average | Cities | | | | | | Average | Towns | | | | | |
| | | Fifth | | | | | | | Fifth | | | | | |
		lowest	second	third	fourth	top			lowest	second	third	fourth	top
Living space per capita (m²)	6.8	6.1	6.6	6.3	6.8	8.7		8.5	7.1	8.0	8.0	9.0	11.1
Percentage distribution:													
−4m²	30.8	39.3	35.0	32.3	28.1	19.1		16.5	26.3	20.0	17.0	13.4	5.7
4–6m²	22.1	23.9	24.5	24.2	22.2	15.2		20.4	21.2	23.9	22.4	20.9	13.6
6–8m²	16.1	13.2	15.7	16.8	17.8	17.0		18.5	16.6	18.8	19.4	20.1	17.5
8–10m²	9.5	7.3	7.8	9.6	9.9	12.6		14.8	10.9	13.1	15.2	16.7	18.2
10 + m²	11.3	8.1	7.4	8.0	11.5	21.8		23.1	16.1	17.3	19.6	23.4	39.0
Percentage distribution with:													
piped water for exclusive use	44.5	29.4	39.0	44.8	53.2	56.2		58.8	51.4	57.6	59.7	61.2	63.7
no sanitary facilities	71.9	81.4	74.2	71.0	68.6	64.4		47.6	54.0	50.6	46.9	46.4	39.9
kitchen for exclusive use	71.2	60.0	68.4	72.1	76.3	79.0		66.2	64.7	68.1	67.6	64.8	66.0
public housing	68.8	52.7	67.5	71.5	75.4	76.9		80.6	74.7	80.9	82.0	82.1	83.4

Source: World Bank 1992: tables 1.10 and 1.11, citing SSB, PRC 1989. However, the English-language version of the latter, available to us, does not contain these data.

sanitary facilities rose monotonically through the income groups. The same is true for occupation of public housing: contrary to Western practice, public housing is in no sense provided particularly for poor people.

In order to isolate the influence of household income and other relevant characteristics on house size, a regression analysis was conducted on the 1988 CASS urban household sample, with house size (H), measured in square metres, or size in logged form (h) as the dependent variable (Table 6.6). Consider each variable in turn. Size is positively and significantly related to income, although the effect is slight. The relevant concepts of income are household income (Y) and household income per capita (Y_p), and their logs (y, y_p). Equation 1 shows a marginal propensity of house size to increase with income of 0.0011 and equation 2 a corresponding elasticity of 0.070. We can see in another way that the effect of income is small by varying income from one standard deviation below the mean to one standard deviation above (from 1,894 to 5,868 yuan per annum). Based on eq. 1, house size rises by only $4.19\,m^2$, *ceteris paribus*, i.e. by 10 per cent of the mean $(41.60\,m^2)$. The response of house size to income is somewhat greater when both are expressed in per capita terms. In equations (not shown) omitting the number of household members and using H_p and Y_p, h_p and y_p, the coefficients are 0.0013* and 0.181* respectively.[1] It is possible that some of the independent variables, such as province, are acting as proxies for income. When only income and number of household members are retained as explanatory variables, the marginal propensity rises to 0.0016* but the elasticity is down to 0.139* (equations not shown). We conclude that house size is not as responsive to income as it would be if there were a housing market.

House size increases with the number of household members but the effect is less than proportionate. The decline in house size per capita, based on eq. 1, is from $21.9\,m^2$ for one member, to $12.2\,m^2$ for three members, to $8.8\,m^2$ for five members. The substitution of a continuous variable representing number of household members for the N_i dummy variables in eq. 2 yields a coefficient of 0.103** (equation not shown). This implies that house size increases by 10 per cent with each additional household member. The system of allocating urban living space makes only rather limited allowance for size of family.

Compared with public housing, size is significantly smaller in the case of rented accommodation and significantly larger in the case of private ownership. It is largest for homes built by the owner, the case most likely to involve scope for choice and thus most likely to reflect demand rather than supply. However, the group of owner-builders is too small and potentially too biased a subsample to serve as an accurate guide to market demand. The influence of conurbation size and congestion on house size is shown by the negative coefficient for Beijing.

Among the most favoured economic sectors are commercial services

TABLE 6.6 *House-size function analysis of urban households: 1988 CASS survey*

Independent variables		Coefficients	
		H	*h*
Intercept		27.615**	2.736**
Household characteristics			
Household income	Y	0.0011**	0.070**
No. of household members = 1	N_1	−18.459**	−0.517**
= 2	N_2	−3.347**	−0.076**
= 4	N_4	2.978**	0.094**
= 5 or over	N_5	7.896**	0.185**
Rented accommodation	How_2	−8.746**	−0.313**
Private: inherited	How_3	10.553**	0.143**
self-built	How_4	27.460**	0.411**
purchased	How_5	19.460**	0.339**
Beijing	P_1	−7.334**	−0.294**
Shanxi	P_4	1.236	0.006
Liaoning	P_6	−10.936**	−0.348**
Anhui	P_{12}	0.702	0.010
Henan	P_{16}	2.136*	0.045*
Hubei	P_{17}	4.809**	0.081**
Guangdong	P_{19}	7.743**	0.117**
Yunnan	P_{23}	3.904**	0.051**
Gansu	P_{26}	1.656	0.027
Household head characteristics			
Female	S_2	0.886	0.032
Age −20	A_1	5.594*	0.198**
21–5	A_2	6.276**	0.196**
31–5	A_4	−3.030**	−0.075**
36–40	A_5	−0.210	0.010
41–5	A_6	1.744	0.058**
46–50	A_7	6.166**	0.172**
51–5	A_8	7.694**	0.215**
56–60	A_9	9.663**	0.265**
61–5	A_{10}	13.360**	0.324**
66+	A_{11}	15.772**	0.342**
Community college	E_2	−1.194	−0.041
Technical school	E_3	−2.215*	−0.056**
High school	E_4	−1.222	−0.032
Middle school	E_5	−1.865*	−0.054**
Primary school graduate	E_6	−2.965**	−0.061**
Three years or more of primary school	E_7	−2.724**	−0.069
Fewer than three years of primary school	E_8	1.926	0.006
Communist Party member	Cp_1	2.437**	0.056**

Table 6.6 *Continued*

Independent variables		Coefficients	
		H	h
Owner of private or individual enterprise	Oc_1	−3.046	−0.061
Owner and manager of private or individual enterprise	Oc_2	−0.068	0.120
Professional	Oc_3	0.285	0.031
Responsible official of government	Oc_4	6.404**	0.153**
Factory director or manager	Oc_5	5.304**	0.139**
Office worker	Oc_6	1.535**	0.055**
Contract worker	J_2	−0.602	0.064
Working in private business	J_3	−0.994	−0.057
Other	J_4	4.581	0.136
Collective ownership	Ow_c	−0.337	−0.024
Private ownership	Ow_p	6.778	0.122
Sino-foreign joint venture	Ow_f	4.189	−0.189
Other ownership type	Ow_o	−8.341*	0.145*
Agriculture and other primary	Es_1	9.875**	0.170
Mining	Es_2	1.199	0.061
Geological prospecting	Es_4	4.179	0.064
Construction	Es_5	1.706	0.047
Transport, communication, post, and telecommunications	Es_6	1.916*	0.050
Trade, restaurants, catering, material supplying, and marketing	Es_7	3.904**	0.099
Real estate and public utilities	Es_8	7.039**	0.134
Personal services	Es_9	−1.481	−0.001
Health, sports, and social welfare	Es_{10}	4.526**	0.104
Education, culture, and arts	Es_{11}	2.759**	0.066
Scientific and technical services	Es_{12}	3.874**	0.117
Finance, insurance	Es_{13}	7.712**	0.176
Party, government, and social organ	Es_{14}	8.323**	0.185
Other	Es_{15}	12.268**	0.228
Unclassified	Es_{16}	9.837	0.292*
F-value		51.936	61.734
Adj. R^2		0.282	0.319
No. of observations		8404	8404
Mean of dependent variable		41.605	3.604

Notes: 1. * denotes significance at the 5% level and ** at the 1% level.
2. The omitted categories among the dummy variables are; N_3 (three household members), How_1 (public housing), P_{10} (Jiangsu), S_1 (male), A_3 (age 26–30), E_1 (college graduate), Cp_2 (not Communist Party member), Oc_7 (labourer), J_1 (permanent employee), Ow_3 (state ownership), and Es_3 (manufacturing).
3. The dependent variables are urban house size measured in m^2 (H) and its logarithm (h).

TABLE 6.7 *House size, house size per capita, and number of household members, by age-group: urban sample, 1988 CASS survey*

	Age-group		
	–30	31–45	46+
House size	37.2	37.3	46.9
House size per capita	11.8	10.8	14.1
No. of household members	3.14	3.46	3.32

(Es_7), real estate and public utilities (Es_8), finance and insurance (Es_{13}), and party, government, and social organs (Es_{14}). These are likely to be sectors in which enterprises possess the financial or political power needed to provide good housing to their employees. Education of the household head plays little role in determining house size—probably less than in most countries. The main distinction is between college graduates and those having less education: college graduates are allocated more space. Similarly, government officials and enterprise managers are better accommodated. Communist Party membership is also beneficial. These characteristics can be regarded as proxies for status, seniority, and power. However, their combined effect is not huge: being a college instead of a middle school graduate, a government official instead of a labourer, and moreover a Communist Party member, together add only 36 per cent to mean house size, *ceteris paribus*.

Size bears an unexpected non-linear relationship to age. It is significantly higher for household heads under 26 than for those in the omitted age-group 26–30 (A_3), and significantly higher also for those aged over 45, with size now rising almost monotonically with age. We argued above that there are powerful vintage effects in housing quality. These might provide the explanation for the non-linear relationship between size and age of household head. If the younger cohorts are allocated the 1980s' housing, they stand to benefit. If the seniority at work implied by age gives preference in the allocation of housing, that might explain the rise in size with age beyond 40. The number of household members provides a clue to the smaller house size, *ceteris paribus*, of the middle age-groups (Table 6.7). The middle group have the same house size as the young group, but their larger families depress their house size per capita. The old group have the largest house size and house size per capita.

Table 6.8 presents a rent function for urban households, with Re = rent in yuan per annum or $re = \ln Re$ as the dependent variables. The mean value of the rent is remarkably low: only 1.3 per cent of household income. Although only a small part of the variance can be explained (adj. $R^2 = 0.16$), a number of coefficients are significant. In particular, private rented accommodation involves a much higher rent than does public housing (the omitted house type), and there are large differences among provinces. Compared with Guangdong (P_{19}), which sets the highest rents, Shanxi (P_4) and Anhui (P_{12}) set the lowest. Location in the far suburbs of a city (Lo_4) reduces the rent, as we would expect in a market economy. Both house size and income per capita raise the rents significantly but the coefficients imply that the effects are economically negligible. Rent is at such a nominal, non-market-clearing level that it cannot be well explained by the normal demand and supply considerations.

TABLE 6.8 *Rent function analysis of urban households: 1988 CASS survey*

Independent variables		Coefficients	
		Re	*re*
Intercept		29.244**	3.336**
Household income per capita	Y_p	0.004	0.00005**
House size (m^2)	H	0.489**	0.010**
Non-central part of city	Lo_2	−0.499	−0.044*
Suburb of city	Lo_3	−1.660	−0.023
Far suburb of city	Lo_4	−16.137**	−0.358**
Private ownership, inherited	Ht_2	−4.413	−0.289**
Rented private accommodation	Ht_3	96.704**	0.866**
Private ownership, self-built	Ht_4	−11.853	−0.649**
Private ownership, purchased	Ht_5	−11.502	−0.607
Beijing	P_1	−2.676	−0.070
Shanxi	P_4	−16.642**	−0.481**
Anhui	P_{12}	−15.513**	−0.404**
Henan	P_{16}	−1.822	−0.488**
Hubei	P_{17}	−12.205**	−0.364**
Guangdong	P_{19}	9.235	−0.062
Yunnan	P_{23}	−11.107*	−0.418**
Gansu	P_{26}	3.237	−0.101**
Six other provinces	P_0	−22.661	−0.718*
Member of Communist Party	Cp_1	−0.456	0.066**
F-value		11.338	73.323
Adj. R^2		0.026	0.156
No. of observations		7,427	7,427
Mean of dependent variable		47.955	3.6252

Notes: 1. * denotes significance at the 5% and ** at the 1% level.
2. The omitted categories are: central part of city (Lo_1), public housing (Ht_1), Jiangsu (P_{10}), and not a member of the Communist party (Cp_2).
3. The dependent variables are rent p.a. in yuan (*Re*) and *re* (= ln *Re*).

Finally, we present a housing standards function for urban households (Table 6.9). In the absence of market rents as a proxy for value of housing, we constructed a housing standards index, being the sum of the points arbitrarily given for various housing characteristics as set out in Table 6.10. The

TABLE 6.9 *Housing-standards function analysis of urban households: 1988 CASS survey*

Independent variables		Coefficients
Intercept		16.766**
Household characteristics		
Household income	Y	0.0002**
Rented accommodation	How_2	−4.221**
Private accommodation: inherited	How_3	1.158**
self-built	How_4	6.042**
purchased	How_5	5.446**
One household member	N_1	12.081**
Two household members	N_2	5.828**
Four household members	N_4	−1.474**
Five or more household members	N_5	−2.866**
Household head characteristics		
Female head	S_2	0.418
Community college graduate	E_2	−0.493
Technical school graduate	E_3	−1.119**
High-school graduate	E_4	−0.992**
Middle school graduate	E_5	−1.116**
Primary school graduate	E_6	−1.665**
Three or more years of primary school	E_7	−2.984**
Fewer than three years of primary school	E_8	−2.202**
Age 16–20	A_1	2.365*
21–5	A_2	2.406**
31–5	A_4	0.139
36–40	A_5	−0.768**
41–5	A_6	−0.036
46–50	A_7	−1.517**
51–5	A_8	−0.138
56–60	A_9	−1.784**
61–5	A_{10}	0.090
66–70	A_{11}	0.840
Collective ownership	Owc	−0.499
Private ownership	Owp	0.332
Joint venture or foreign firm	Owf	3.116
Other ownership	Ow_0	−2.026*
Owner of private business	Oc_1	−1.792
Owner and manager of private business	Oc_2	−2.333

Table 6.9 *Continued*

Independent variables		Coefficients
Professional	Oc_3	−0.133
Responsible official	Oc_4	1.380**
Factory manager or director	Oc_5	1.631**
Office worker	Oc_6	0.272
Agriculture and other primary	Es_1	1.952
Mining	Es_2	0.319
Geological prospecting	Es_4	1.215
Construction	Es_5	0.624
Transport and communication	Es_6	1.184**
Trade, catering, commerce	Es_7	1.084**
Real estate and public utilities	Es_8	1.244
Personal services	Es_9	0.656
Health, sports, and social welfare	Es_{10}	2.285**
Education, culture, and arts	Es_{11}	0.793*
Scientific and technical services	Es_{12}	1.704**
Finance and insurance	Es_{13}	2.164**
Party, government, and social organs	Es_{14}	1.942**
Other	Es_{15}	1.437
Not easily classified	Es_{16}	1.563**
Communist Party member	Cp_1	1.141
F-value		35.537
Adj. R^2		0.172
Mean of dependent variable		16.296
No. of observations		8,797

Notes: 1. * denotes significance at the 1% and ** at the 5% level.
      2. The omitted categories among the dummy variables are as for Table 6.6.

index contains both a quantity component and several quality components: there is a highly significant positive relationship between quantity and quality. The mean index score is 16.30 and the standard deviation 8.74. Of course, a scoring system that placed greater weight on basic needs would produce a higher score with lower standard deviation—a consideration relevant to any comparison with rural housing.

More household members means a lower standard of housing. The effect of income on the index is positive but negligible. Being in privately rented accommodation reduces the standard. The effect of the age of the household head is interesting, and different from the effect on quantity alone. The index is higher, *ceteris paribus*, for ages below the omitted category ($A_3 = 26$–30) and generally lower for ages above it. This is consistent with young people being allocated the new, higher-quality accommodation. The

TABLE 6.10 *Scoring system for the index of housing standards: urban sample, 1988 CASS survey*

Characteristic	Category	Score	Mean value or proportion
Running water	none	0	0.00
	shared	1	0.20
	own tap	2	0.80
Sanitary facilities	none	0	0.36
	shared	1	0.17
	toilet, no bath	2	0.38
	toilet, bath	3	0.08
Heating	none	0	0.57
	other	1	0.26
	central	2	0.17
Air-conditioning	none	0	0.99
	yes	1	0.01
Kitchen	none	0	0.13
	shared	1	0.06
	own kitchen	2	0.81
Electricity	none	0	0.004
	yes	1	0.996
Telephone	none	0	0.97
	yes	1	0.03
House size	area per capita	m^2	11.81

more educated, and officials and managers, do well, as do Communist Party members. It is noteworthy that work units in the manufacturing sector provide housing of a lower standard than do those in other sectors.

As the dispersion of the index indicates, housing standards in urban China are by no means even. How is accommodation allocated? During the pre-reform period allocation was based in principle on household numbers, with recognition of economies of scale. The norm was for two persons to be assigned to a one-room unit, three to five persons to a two-room unit, and six to eight persons to a three-room unit (Zhou and Logan 1996: 399). However, because there was insufficient housing to meet the norms, allocation was also based on other criteria. These include the power of employers: across work units the quantity and quality of housing rise with the importance and profitability of the work unit. Within the work unit, in principle the allocation is made by housing committees on the basis of housing scores using clear criteria of need and desert that are known to workers. These include occupation, seniority, and rank: at one time work units' norms were 42–5 m^2 for workers, 45–50 m^2 for lower-level cadres, 60–70 m^2 for division-level cadres, and 80–90 m^2 for high-level cadres (ibid. 399, 406).

However, the allocation is sometimes politicized and personalized: political loyalty and connections can be influential.

We found little evidence from the 1988 survey to suggest that the allocation rewards efficiency or promotes equity (Tables 6.6 and 6.9). Indeed, it has been claimed that 'the most overwhelming tendency may be to promote the capricious redistribution of income through housing due to the random happenstance of such factors as work unit availability of housing, historical circumstances of individuals, and use of influence to obtain housing by individuals not particularly meritorious of it on productivity grounds' (World Bank 1992: 81). A combination of scarcity and inequality in power over allocation contributes to inequality of access to housing, which in turn produces observable inequalities of comfort and status in urban China.

Not only quantity but also quality is related to vintage of housing. Partly by definition, larger houses are more likely to have kitchens and toilets, and maintenance practices contribute to the premature deterioration of the older stock (World Bank 1992: 15). The strong positive correlation between quality and quantity is illustrated in Table 6.11, drawn from the 1988 urban sample. Households are placed into three groups according to the size of their housing area, and the percentage of households with various facilities is shown. Larger houses are much more likely to have running water, a toilet, and their own kitchen.

The incidence of new house-building and the criteria for allocating new housing become crucial in these circumstances. The enormous windfalls that accrue to households awarded new housing generate public dissatisfaction

TABLE 6.11 *The relationship between quality and quantity of housing, urban sample: percentage of households with various facilities, by size of housing area, 1988 CASS survey*

Percentage of households with:	Housing area of household (m²)		
	small ≤20	medium >20, ≤40	large >40
Running water provided	45	80	92
Sanitary facilities:			
none	53	38	29
shared	36	19	10
toilet, no bath	11	40	45
toilet and bath	1	3	15
Kitchen:			
none	36	13	5
shared	21	6	1
own kitchen	43	81	94

with the system and create pressures to increase urban house building. Only 10 per cent of a sample of households in Tianjin expressed satisfaction with their housing (World Bank 1992: 21). It is plausible that urban households, in demanding better housing, could in recent years exert pressure on enterprises and governments to use resources for that purpose (ibid. 18). Thus, although supply-constrained, urban housing has become partly demand-driven.

Both the official annual household surveys and the 1988 CASS household survey confine their urban samples to permanent urban residents. Their housing data therefore do not include the housing of temporary residents, in particular the rural–urban migrants whose numbers have increased considerably in recent years. The housing which is available to them is generally of inferior standard, both in quantity and quality. Many are poorly accommodated by their employers and others often rent cramped living space in slums with poor facilities. They are prepared to endure bad accommodation—normally inferior to their rural housing—because of the other advantages of urban life and work and because hardship is easier to accept if it is temporary.

6.2.2 Urban housing subsidies

The demand for bigger and better urban housing stems partly from the rise in urban real incomes in recent years and partly from the heavy subsidization of urban housing. Two attempts to measure urban housing subsidies will be described. One is based on Wang (1990), as reported in World Bank (1992: 38–41). The housing subsidy is defined as the rational rent (R) minus the actual rent (Re). R is assumed to equal 3.16 yuan per m^2 of rentable space and is derived from assumed average housing asset values of 241 yuan per m^2 of constructed space. The importance of the housing subsidy, calculated on this basis, is shown in Table 6.12. The implication of these estimates is that the housing subsidy grew remarkably between 1978 and 1988, by 29

TABLE 6.12 *Size of urban housing subsidy, 1978–88*

	Living space per capita (m^2)	Housing subsidy (yuan)		
		per m^2	per worker	total (billion)
1978	4.20	0.65	49.6	4.7
1982	5.61	1.23	107.0	12.2
1985	7.46	1.95	236.3	29.2
1988	8.80	3.03	428.9	58.4

Source: World Bank 1992: 39, citing Wang 1990.

per cent per annum: from 6.7 per cent to 15.6 per cent of urban worker income; from 1.3 per cent to 4.2 per cent of GNP.

The other estimate of the urban housing subsidy is based on the 1988 survey (Khan *et al*. 1993). For households occupying public housing, the replacement value of the dwelling unit was calculated by applying the provincial average cost of house-building to the reported area of the accommodation and making some allowance for differences in quality based on reported sanitation facilities. The rental value was assumed to be 8 per cent of the replacement cost. Actual rent paid was subtracted from the rental value to arrive at the net subsidy. On that basis the annual urban housing subsidy was estimated to average 334 yuan per capita, no less than 18 per cent of urban disposable income per capita (ibid. 49). This could represent as much as 8.0 per cent of national income in 1988.[2]

In the 1990s the privatization of urban housing was declared a policy objective (Tolley 1991: 1). The creation of a market for urban housing might be expected to shift the basis for its allocation from positional power to purchasing power. In turn a housing market should involve greater class-based residential segmentation—with only high-income households being able to afford the new housing built by real estate developers and having good locations and facilities. However, it is possible for partial housing market reforms to be absorbed into the existing framework of institutional allocation.

That is precisely how the, still limited, housing reforms evolved. An active urban land market developed, in which land-use rights are transferred. However, existing institutions and power relationships remain important. Local governments and state-owned enterprises are important players in the market—even in the game of land speculation. Lack of information in the incipient market, institutional interventions, and bargaining relationships mean that land prices differ widely. Positional power and the ambiguity of property rights mean that private fortunes can be, and are, made. The emerging housing market is only a quasi-market, as there are multiple prices, largely on account of the numerous state interventions and restrictions. The variation in prices occurs in both the rental and the ownership markets.

Many of the new houses built in the 1990s were privately built by real estate developers but the buyers were generally employers rather than households. An estimate for cities in thirteen provinces in 1995 placed the monthly subsidized rent at 0.8 yuan, the rent in publicly supported housing development projects at 8.8 yuan, and the open market rent at 14.3 yuan per m^2 on average. The housing subsidy actually rose in recent years, from 18 per cent of the average state sector wage in 1990 to 31 per cent in 1995 (Wang 1997: tables 3, 5).

There was a growing discrepancy within the urban economy between state sector employees, who generally received a housing subsidy, and the increasing numbers in the non-state sector who, having to find their own accommodation, did not. This arbitrary division encouraged the practice of 'one family, two systems', by which one member works in the state sector to secure housing and other welfare benefits for the family and the other works in the non-state sector at a higher wage.

The policy of selling houses to their occupants spread rapidly in the 1990s. This posed a problem: how can people be persuaded to buy their houses if housing is being provided almost free of charge? It appears that urban households were induced to buy by the prospect of future rent increases and the large element of subsidy in the purchase prices. Estimated selling prices for the same sample of cities in thirteen provinces were 680 yuan per m^2 for publicly owned housing, 1,070 yuan in publicly supported housing development projects, and 1,740 yuan in the open market (Wang 1997: table 4). Enterprises and governments were effectively capitalizing the future rental subsidies. The fact that they garnered the proceeds provided an incentive for them to implement the policy of privatizing houses.

The issues facing policy-makers can be illustrated in Figures 6.1 and 6.2. The market demand curve D relates the quantity (q) of housing demanded to its price (the rent r). The market supply curve S is an upward-sloping function of r. The bureaucratically determined supply (q_1) is given by the vertical supply curve S'. The short-run market price (r_m) would be shown by the intersection of D and S' at point a. Given the low actual rent for housing (r_a), however, there is excess demand equal to the length of $q_1 q_4$.

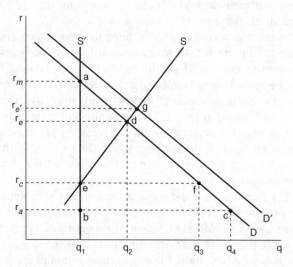

FIG. 6.1 *The transition to an urban housing market: excess market demand*

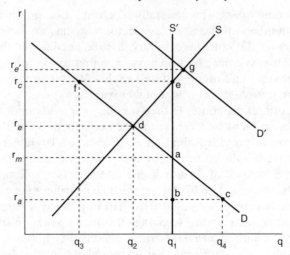

F IG. 6.2 *The transition to an urban housing market: excess market supply*

In a free market the long-run equilibrium market price (r_e) would be determined by the intersection of D and S at point d.

Assume that rents are raised to cover the full cost of housing, denoted
by r_c. In Figure 6.1 that would reduce excess demand to the length q_1q_3.
However, a consequential policy of increasing the urban wage bill to compensate for the loss of housing subsidy (the rectangle r_cebr_a) would shift the
demand curve outwards to (say) D'. In the long run this would involve a
new equilibrium market rent r_e'.

Figure 6.1 illustrates a case of excess demand even when urban-dwellers
pay full-cost rents. Figure 6.2, drawn equivalently in all other respects, illustrates an alternative case in which the current excess demand for housing
(q_1q_4) would become excess supply (q_1q_3) if full-cost rents were charged.
Accordingly, the housing stock contracts over time as current supply
exceeds the new demand at price r_c. If compensation is paid for the loss of
the housing subsidy (the rectangle r_cebr_a), excess supply need not appear.
For instance, given the new demand curve D', then $r_e' > r_c$. With or without
compensation, the long run equilibrium market price (r_e' or r_e) would exceed
the short-run market price (r_m).

Which of the two figures is the more appropriate for urban China? Zax
(1993) attempted to measure the unrestricted demand for urban housing,
using the 1988 CASS survey. He compared two housing types: households
in state-owned houses (the predominant type) and those which had built
their own houses (the type most likely to reflect demand for housing). He
estimated a probit equation to explain choice of housing type, and two
house size regression equations (ibid., table 4). More wage income, more

education, Communist Party membership, and an older household head made it likelier that the household would occupy a state-owned rather than an own-built house. These same factors increased the living area of state-owned accommodation. House size was much more sensitive to the number of household members in the own-built than in the state-owned sector: the coefficient was three times as large. However, the unobservable characteristics of households played a crucial role, as shown by the high correlations between the error terms of the probit and OLS equations. Households whose unobserved characteristics made them particularly likely to choose own-built (or state-owned) housing also had larger own-built (or state-owned) houses than could be predicted from their observed characteristics.

The mean living space in own-built houses was $68\,m^2$ and in state-owned houses $39\,m^2$. This suggests a huge pent-up demand for urban housing space. However, we must ask: what size would households in state-owned houses demand if they were permitted free choice? Zax's simulations (1993: table 5) attempted to answer this question. Drawing households at random, i.e. ignoring unobserved characteristics, the predicted size of own-built houses would be smaller even than those in the state sector, whereas households possessing the unobserved characteristics of the own-built sector would demand much larger houses. As the nature of these unobserved characteristics is crucial, we must ask: how did a select few households have access to building land? It is possible that many of the own-built houses are located in small towns or former rural areas now reclassified as urban. In that case it may have been the availability of free or cheap land that caused owners to build large houses. Alternatively, personal connections and influence may explain both the tenure and the size. In either case the own-built sector cannot provide an accurate measure of general demand for urban living space.

A World Bank report, illustrating from a 1989 case study, argued that the majority of urban households would be unable to afford the debt servicing required for the purchase at full cost of their houses, nor could they afford to pay the full-cost rent (World Bank 1992: 32–45, 117–25). Housing would then absorb too high a proportion of their income. This suggests that, without compensation, the demand for urban housing would fall drastically as prices rose. However, that inference would be misleading, for three reasons. First, most of the voluntary purchases by households have been heavily subsidized. Secondly, the free market for both housing and housing services remains too narrow and imperfect to serve as a reliable guide. Thirdly, the discontent resulting from the raising of rents without compensatory raising of wages would pose a potential threat to social and political stability. It is not yet clear whether the quantity and quality of housing in urban China is under- or over-provided by comparison with a free market outcome.

6.3 RURAL HOUSING

The mean size of rural houses was $95\,m^2$ and the coefficient of variation in size 54 per cent. Table 6.13 explains rural house size h (the logarithm of area in m^2) in terms of household and location characteristics. No less than 18 per cent of the variance in size can be explained by the equation (and 24 per cent when province dummy variables are included).

Consider first the characteristics of the household head. It makes no difference whether the head is male or female but Communist Party membership raises household size significantly. Education appears to be irrelevant. The age dummy variables are almost all highly significant. House size falls monotonically with age to age-group 26–30 (the omitted group), thereafter rising monotonically to 51–5, then declining monotonically. Unlike urban houses, rural houses are not allocated: the age pattern cannot reflect allocation rules. Sample selection bias, or accommodation passed down by parents, might explain the large size for the small number of young household heads. The rise after 30 cannot simply be explained by need or by demand, since we are standardizing both for household size and for income. It might represent a wealth effect, i.e. households accumulate savings before they build, or an irreversibility effect, i.e. houses are not shrunk as family need diminishes.

Our hypothesis is that the private nature of rural housing permits greater responsiveness to household needs. Thus, for instance, house size might respond more to household numbers in rural than in urban areas. Table 6.14 shows that rural house size per capita decreases as the number of household members increases. This could of course reflect the scope for economies of scale in house space. However, the table also shows that house size expands proportionately somewhat less rapidly with household numbers in rural than in urban areas. A possible explanation is that the need for additional space for additional people is much more acute in the much smaller urban houses.

A better indicator of responsiveness to demand is the coefficient on the logarithm of income (0.233). It implies that a doubling of income raises house size by 23 per cent. This contrasts with the lower corresponding coefficient in urban areas (0.070). These coefficients may understate the influence of income if other independent variables are acting as proxies for income. When all other variables except household size are dropped from the equations, the rural and urban coefficients indeed increase to 0.256 and 0.139 respectively.

Finally, location and type of household activity play a role. Hilly locations increase size but mountainous ones decrease it; both coefficients are statistically significant. To be located in a non-suburb, i.e. a genuinely rural area, reduces house size by no less than 12 per cent. If a household has an urban residence *hukou* or contains a local cadre, it has a larger house on average.

TABLE 6.13 *Regression analysis of rural house size: rural sample: 1988 CASS survey*

Independent variables		Coefficients
Intercept		2.595**
Ln of income	y	0.233**
1 household member	H_1	−0.490**
2 " "	H_2	−0.273**
3 " "	H_3	−0.099**
4 " "	H_4	−0.042**
6 + " "	H_6	0.102**
College or above	E_1	0.037
Professional school	E_2	−0.087
Upper-middle school	E_3	0.004
Primary school, 4–6 years	E_5	0.002
Primary school, 1–3 years	E_7	0.094**
No education	E_8	−0.042*
Age –20	A_1	0.196**
21–5	A_2	0.069*
31–5	A_4	0.022
36–40	A_5	0.073**
41–5	A_6	0.126**
46–50	A_7	0.166**
51–5	A_8	0.186**
56–60	A_9	0.166**
61–5	A_{10}	0.148**
66+	A_{11}	0.066
Hilly		0.024*
Mountainous		−0.043**
Poor area		−0.024
Non-suburb		−0.129**
Five-guarantee household		−0.001
Wage-earner household		0.005
Urban resident household		0.082**
Local cadre household		0.046*
Household head female		−0.006
" " with wage income		−0.027
" " not Party member		−0.060**
F-value		71.169
Adj. R^2		0.184
Mean of dependent variable		4.401
No. of observations		10,267

Notes: 1. The dependent variable is the logarithm of house size in m² (h).
       2. The omitted categories in the dummy variable analysis are five household members, lower-middle school, age 26–30, plain area, non-poor area, suburb, not a five-guarantee household, rural resident household, not a local cadre household, and household head being male, not a wage-earner, and a Party member.

TABLE 6.14 *House size and house size per capita by size of household: urban and rural samples, 1988 CASS survey*

No. of household members	House size (m^2)		House size per capita (m^2)	
	Urban	Rural	Urban	Rural
1	21.9	49.9	21.9	49.9
2	34.1	62.0	17.6	31.0
3	36.7	73.8	12.2	24.6
4	40.4	78.2	19.9	19.4
5	44.2	81.5	8.8	16.3
6		90.3		15.0

Note: The estimates are based on the urban and rural equations predicting the logarithm of house size (h), setting other explanatory variables to their mean values. The estimates presented are geometric means.

When a set of province dummy variables was introduced into the equation, they showed wide interprovince variations in house size. The hypothesis was that provinces with high rural income per capita would have large rural houses. However, a simple regression analysis of income per capita on standardized house size yielded a negligible and non-significant coefficient. Factors other than income per capita must be important in explaining why rural Beijing has a large negative coefficient (implying that house size is 8 per cent lower than in the omitted province, Jiangsu) whereas rural Shanghai has a positive coefficient (+36 per cent), poor Yunnan is positive (+17 per cent), and rich Jilin is negative (–6 per cent).

Two measures of the quality of rural housing are available—original value per square metre (V) and estimated value per square metre (E). Both are presented in the regression analysis predicting quality in Table 6.15. Location is important: being in a hilly or a mountainous area (probably proxies for lower income), an officially designated poor area, and a non-suburb area all reduce the quality of housing by more than 20 per cent. A five-guarantee household (a sign of poverty) has less than two-thirds the quality of house, and a local cadre household has 10 per cent higher quality than a peasant household. Curiously, female-headed households have higher-quality houses. However, the age of the household head is irrelevant, and education has an effect only in the case of the least educated, whose quality of housing is lower. Value per square metre decreases as household size increases, possibly reflecting economies of scale. The coefficient on income implies an income elasticity for house quality of 0.31 (original value) or 0.39 (estimated value). When only income and household size are included as explanatory variables, these elasticities rise to 0.35 and 0.43

TABLE 6.15 *Regression analysis of the quality of rural housing: rural sample, 1988 CASS survey*

Independent variables		Coefficients	
		$\ln V$ $(= v)$	$\ln E$ $(= e)$
Intercept		1.309**	0.796**
L_n of income	y	0.307**	0.393**
1 household member	H_1	0.240*	0.350**
2 " "	H_2	0.084	0.125*
3 " "	H_3	0.137**	0.170**
4 " "	H_4	0.048*	0.064**
5 " "	H_6	−0.071**	−0.106**
College or above	E_1	−0.048	0.042
Professional school	E_2	0.003	−0.004
Upper-middle school	E_3	−0.004	−0.016
Primary school, 4–6 years	E_6	−0.029	−0.021
Primary school, 1–3 years	E_7	−0.174**	−0.126*
No education	E_8	−0.111**	0.128**
Age −20	A_1	−0.047	−0.046
21–5	A_2	−0.069	−0.072
31–5	A_4	0.054	0.058
36–40	A_5	0.027	0.040
41–5	A_6	0.001	0.003
46–50	A_7	0.030	0.034
51–5	A_8	0.013	−0.000
56–60	A_9	−0.021	−0.045
61–5	A_{10}	0.069	0.049
66–70	A_{11}	0.065	0.088
Hilly		−0.351**	−0.280**
Mountainous		−0.382**	−0.231**
Poor area		−0.240**	−0.235**
Non-suburb		−0.295**	−0.219**
Five-guarantee household		−0.463**	−0.440*
Wage-earner household		0.057	0.032
Urban residual household		−0.024	0.148**
Local cadre household		0.122**	0.091**
Household head female		0.103**	0.112**
" " with wage income		−0.009	0.003
" " Party member		−0.002	0.001
F-value		64.65	49.77
Adj. R^2		0.187	0.150
Mean of dependent variable		3.288	3.602
No. of observations		9,151	9,151

Notes: 1. * denotes statistical significance at the 5% and ** at the 1% level.
2. The dependent variables are the logarithm of V, the original value of the house per m^2, denoted by v, and the logarithm of E, the estimated value of the house per m^2, denoted by e.
3. The omitted categories in the dummy variable analysis are as for Table 6.13.

respectively (equations not shown). The coefficient in a single variable regression equation implied that a 10 per cent rise in income per capita from the mean would raise province house value per square metre by 5.6 per cent. From this, as from the previous results, we obtain a picture of housing quality being sensitive to economic variables, both in absolute terms and by comparison with house size. It would seem that increases in income cause rural households to improve the quality of their housing rather than the quantity.

Table 6.16 attempts to explain the estimated value of rural houses in terms of household income, assets, and members. The value of the average household's house is equal to 116 per cent of its income. Reported household financial assets increase house value significantly but not substantially, and productive assets and land have positive but non-significant coefficients. Income is the crucial variable: the marginal propensity to spend on housing, i.e. to add to its value, is 0.84. Oddly, the coefficient on the number of household members is significantly negative, although household size does not alter house value substantially. The implication is that house value is even more responsive—positively—to income per capita than to income per household. It is notable that, on average, indebtedness in respect of housing (90.3 yuan) was only 2 per cent of household income and 2 per cent of house value. No more than 7 per cent of rural households had incurred housing debt: for them the average debt was 1,464 yuan. House building and improvement are funded very largely from accumulated savings.

All but one of the indicators of urban housing standards in the 1988 survey are lacking for the rural sample. The exception is whether a house

TABLE 6.16 *Regression analysis of the estimated value of rural housing: rural sample,*
1988 CASS survey

Independent variables		Mean values	Coefficients
Intercept			1,723.722**
Household savings (yuan)	S	418.2	0.151**
Cultivated land (mu)	L	11.7	0.709
Value of productive fixed assets	A	1,078.7	0.0003
No. of household members	H	5.0	−94.821**
Household income (yuan p.a.)	Y	4,035.8	0.837**
F-value			508.678
Adj. R^2			0.217
Mean of dependent variable		4,698.0	
No. of observations		9,164	

Note: The dependent variable is the estimated mean value of the house of the rural household.

has electricity. It is impressive that 86 per cent of the rural sample had access to electricity. However, they were not evenly spread. We see in Table 6.16 that the houses without electricity were disproportionately located in mountainous terrains, in officially designated poor areas, and in poor provinces. Twenty-seven per cent of household heads without access to electricity had little or no education, compared to 15 per cent of those with electricity. The average household income per capita was 24 per cent higher in houses with electricity. This is further evidence that the quality of rural housing is sensitive to income, although it is probably the income of the locality, rather than the income of the household, that matters in the case of electricity.

6.4 CONCLUSION

Both institutionally and substantively, rural and urban housing in China are very different. With their land confiscated, economic activities curtailed, and financial assets insecure, until the end of the Cultural Revolution the peasants had only one form of asset: their houses. Even during the reform period housing was the most important source of security for rural families. As rural differentiation occurred, so housing came to serve all three purposes of shelter, wealth, and status. By contrast, the public ownership of housing in the urban areas meant that housing could not serve as a form of wealth-holding.

The size of urban housing is considerably smaller than in the rural areas: the average amount of space in urban houses was only 11.8 m^2 per capita

TABLE 6.17 *Rural households with and without electricity: rural sample, 1988 CASS survey*

	With electricity	Without electricity
Percentage of households:		
with no education or primary 1–3	15	27
in mountainous terrain	18	36
in officially poor area	15	45
with a Communist Party member	15	11
in Henan	4	14
in Guizhou	2	9
in Yunnan	3	9
Mean value per household		
income per capita	862.0	693.8
No. of cases	7,912	1,243

in 1988. Unfortunately, the 1988 survey did not permit an empirical comparison of quality. However, it is probable that on average the quality of urban housing is much higher. Rural people have to build and improve their own houses; moreover, they do so from their own savings without the help of mortgages as houses are not alienable. By contrast, urban households pay only nominal rents and thus enjoy a heavy subsidy of their housing.

Neither the size nor the quality of urban housing is sensitive to income; nor is either sensitive to the size of household. By contrast, characteristics representing status, seniority, and power have an influence on both quantity and quality, reflecting the criteria for allocating urban housing. There is a U-shaped relationship between house size and age of household head; the more interesting because it transcends institutional arrangements, being found also in the countryside. House size is more sensitive to income in rural than in urban areas, but rural housing quality is particularly sensitive to income. Location within the countryside is also important; both quantity and quality are inferior in the poor, mountainous, non-suburb areas. The rural income per capita of a province, by contrast, appears to affect the quality but not the size of rural houses. Generally, the analysis suggests that the quantity, and particularly the quality, of housing are more sensitive to income and ability to pay in rural than in urban China.

The urban housing reforms of the 1990s have not eliminated the urban advantage over rural areas in public provision and support for housing. The urban rental subsidy rose as a proportion of the urban wage over the period 1990–5, and housing sales involved generous capitalization of future subsidies, i.e. implicit capital gains. The reforms have, however, increased the extent of segmentation and unfairness within the cities. The partial marketization of urban housing, being based on unchanging institutional foundations, maintained rural–urban inequalities and enlarged intra-urban inequalities in housing.

In summary, rural people have in their houses a form of wealth-holding and a source of security, and they have relative freedom to choose the quantity and quality of their accommodation, provided that they can pay for it. There is no housing market in rural China but in their housing decisions people behave as if one existed. Housing offers urban people limited freedom and security and cramped living conditions, but their accommodation is probably of a higher quality and it is practically free of charge. With houses being allocated to them and households having little choice, housing outcomes in urban China have been far removed from market outcomes. The bureaucratic allocation system gives rise to delays, queues, and complaints. There are too many dimensions, with their implicit valuation problems, to decide whether urban or rural people are better off in terms of housing.

NOTES

1. * denotes that a coefficient is significant at the 5% and ** at the 1% level.
2. Given that national income per capita was 1,066 yuan and urban population was 25.8% of total population (PRC, SSB 1991: 32, 79).

REFERENCES

Feder, Gershon, Lau, Lawrence, Lin, Justin, and Luo Xiaopeng (1989). 'Agricultural credit and farm performance in China', *Journal of Comparative Economics*, 13: 508–26.

Khan, Azizur Rahman, Griffin, Keith, Riskin, Carl, and Zhao Renwei (1993). 'Household income and its distribution', in Keith Griffin and Zhao Renwei (eds.), *The Distribution of Income in China*, London: Macmillan.

Peoples' Republic of China, State Statistical Bureau (PRC, SSB) (1989). *A Survey of Income and Expenditure of Urban Households in China, 1986*, Beijing: China Statistical Information and Consultancy Service Centre.

——— (1990). *Statistical Yearbook of China, 1990*: Beijing (in Chinese).

——— (1991). *Statistical Yearbook of China 1991*: Beijing (in Chinese).

——— (1994). *Statistical Yearbook of China 1994*: Beijing.

——— (1996). *Statistical Yearbook of China 1996*: Beijing.

Tolley, George S. (1991). 'Urban housing reform in China. An economic analysis', World Bank Discussion Paper 123: Washington, DC.

Wang Lina (1997). 'Housing price and income distribution in China', Beijing: Institute of Economics, Chinese Academy of Social Sciences, July, processed.

Wang Yukun (1990). 'The size of housing subsidies in China', paper prepared for the World Bank Housing Reforms in Socialist Economies Policy and Research Seminar, Washington, DC, processed.

Whyte, Martin King, and Parish, William L. (1984). *Urban Life in Contemporary China*, Chicago: University of Chicago Press.

World Bank (1992). *China. Implementation of Options for Urban Housing Reform*, World Bank Country Study Washington, DC.

Zax, Jeffrey S. (1993). 'Latent demand for urban housing in the Peoples' Republic of China', Discussion Papers in Economics, 93–21, Dept. of Economics, University of Colorado at Boulder.

Zhou Min, and Logan, John R. (1996). 'Market transition and the commodification of housing in urban China', *International Journal of Urban and Regional Research*, 20 (3): 399–420.

PART IV

THE MOVEMENT OF FACTORS

7

Rural–Urban Transfer of Capital

We turn our attention to the transfer of factors of production between rural and urban China. Chapters 8 and 9 deal with the movement of labour, and this chapter the movement of capital. The net transfer of capital from the rural sector (T_r) can be defined in various equivalent ways, made identical by national accounting conventions: saving minus investment $(S_r - I_r)$, output minus expenditure $(Y_r - E_r)$, and exports minus imports $(X_r - M_r)$, i.e. the rural trade surplus. Thus:

$$T_r \equiv S_r - I_r \equiv Y_r - E_r \equiv X_r - M_r. \tag{7.1}$$

The basic hypothesis is that T_r is large and positive. Our objective is not only to measure this intersectoral resource flow but also to explain it. We examine the institutional mechanisms by which capital has been transferred in the absence of a well-functioning capital market.

It has long been argued that, by lowering agriculture's terms of trade with industry, governments, particularly those of socialist countries in the early stages of economic development, are able to extract a surplus from agriculture for industrialization. This issue was prominent in the famous industrialization debate in the Soviet Union during the 1920s, when Preobrazhensky (1926) was the most prominent advocate of this strategy. The old debate has recently been subjected to theoretical analysis (for instance, Sah and Stiglitz 1984, 1986, and 1992; Blomqvist 1986; Carter 1986; Li and Tsui 1990). Section 7.1 follows that theoretical literature but differs from it in using the techniques of trade theory and offer curve analysis. It draws on Knight (1995).

Did the Chinese government introduce a policy of 'price-scissors' and thereby effect a transfer of capital from the rural to the urban sector? In Section 7.2 we use our theoretical framework to address this question. Section 7.3 investigates the direction, extent, and form of the intersectoral resource transfer. Section 7.4 examines government expenditure priorities as between the rural and the urban sector, concentrating on investment and on subsidies. The underlying objective of the chapter is to tackle the question: who, ultimately, paid for industrialization in China? The concluding Section 7.5 attempts an answer.

7.1 THE THEORY OF PRICE-SCISSORS AND INTERSECTORAL RESOURCE TRANSFERS

Figure 7.1 represents the standard offer curve diagram of international trade theory, with two sectors—agriculture producing food (measured on the vertical axis) and industry producing manufactures (measured on the horizontal axis). The terms agricultural and rural are used interchangeably, as are the terms industrial and urban. The indifference map of rural people has as its origin O_A and that of urban people O_I. The rural sector is assumed throughout to produce a fixed quantity of food OO_A, and the urban sector a fixed quantity of manufactures OO_I. Provided that food and leisure are interchangeable at a constant exchange rate, the vertical axis, OO_A, can be thought of as comprising food for sale, food for self-consumption, and leisure. The offer curve of the rural sector, derived from its indifference map, is OC_A and that of the urban sector OC_I. OC_A and OC_I are assumed to have the normal shapes, i.e. the elasticity of the offer curve (the ratio of the proportionate change in imports to the proportionate change in exports) is initially positive but it declines and possibly becomes negative. For instance, OC_A is initially upward-sloping but it becomes flatter and, provided the demand for imports becomes price-inelastic, eventually bends backwards.

   With free markets the stable equilibrium trade is shown by the intersection of the offer curves at point a. The rural sector chooses to sell O_z of

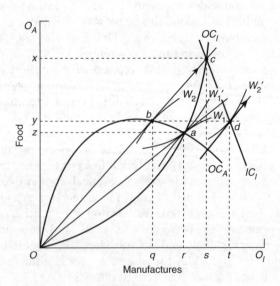

FIG. 7.1 *The Preobrazhensky case*

food for O_r of manufactures, and the urban sector chooses to buy O_z of food for O_r of manufactures. Trade is balanced and the terms of trade are shown by the ray O_a. Given O_a, the rural sector is on its highest feasible indifference curve, W_1; similarly, the urban sector is on its highest feasible indifference curve, W_1'.

Now assume that government imposes terms of trade that are less favourable to agriculture, shown by the ray Oc. Agriculture chooses point b, offering to sell Oy of food for Oq of manufactures. However, industry chooses point c, offering to buy Ox of food for Os of manufactures. There is excess demand for food, xy, and excess supply of manufactures, qs—imbalances which cannot be eliminated by means of price adjustments. How does the economy respond? There are various possibilities. We consider each in turn, and we also consider ways by which government can effect an intersectoral transfer of resources other than through the terms of trade.

7.1.1 A tax on urban workers

Sah and Stiglitz (1984) analyse the mechanism which they regard as the policy instrument advocated by Preobrazhensky in the 1920s. The government is assumed to control both the price of the urban good and the wage received by urban workers. By reducing the wage relative to the price, government can effectively tax urban workers and increase the surplus available for investment. Government is assumed to eliminate the excess demand for food by reducing the industrial wage relative to the industrial price level. As their real income falls so, given freedom to allocate their consumption optimally, urban workers move down their income consumption curve IC_I. Provided that both food and manufactures are normal goods, IC_I slopes downwards to the right. Excess demand for food is eliminated when urban workers' consumption point is at d, and their welfare level is W_2', in Figure 7.1. Rural consumption of manufactures is Oq, urban consumption is O_It, and the residual manufactures, qt, are the surplus appropriated by government for capital accumulation. Rural welfare falls from indifference curve W_1 to W_2. The capital accumulation is assumed to raise future, not current, welfare.

We conclude, as do Sah and Stiglitz (1984), that Preobrazhensky's 'first proposition' is indeed correct: by lowering agriculture's terms of trade, government is able to increase the investible surplus of the economy. They go on to refute Preobrazhensky's 'second proposition', which is that a reduction of agriculture's terms of trade does not require a fall in the welfare of urban workers. Sah and Stiglitz claim that the welfare of urban workers must decline, a result on which they place some stress (ibid. 129, 136). Figure 7.2 illustrates this result. To assist Preobrazhensky's case, assume that the offer curve OC_I is backward-bending. However,

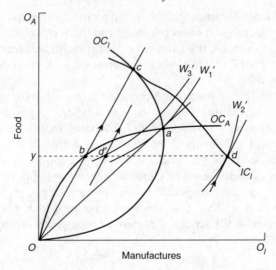

FIG. 7.2 *The Preobrazhensky case: the effect on urban welfare*

because of the negative substitution effect, the income-consumption curve IC_l, passing through c, is to the right of OC_l below c. Thus a reduction in urban workers' incomes to eliminate the excess demand for food (at d) again results in a fall in welfare (to W_2'): the slope of industry's offer curve is not crucial.

If urban welfare is to be raised by the intervention designed to improve its terms of trade and extract an investible surplus, both goods must be rationed to the urban sector. Assume that government rations urban workers to the amount of marketed food available (Oy) and to the amount of manufactures available once the rural (yb) and the government (bd') demand have been met. Government reduces the income of urban workers so that they can just buy the consumption bundle at point d' and thus enjoy welfare level W_3'. Contrary to the case analysed by Sah and Stiglitz (1984: 127), urban workers cannot allocate their income optimally but, again contrary to Sah and Stiglitz, they can be made better off by the government intervention ($W_3' > W_1'$).

7.1.2 *Political coercion and constraints*

In Figure 7.3 the situation is again one of a price-scissors and excess demand for food, with rural-dwellers choosing point b and urban-dwellers point c. Assume that, instead of reducing the urban wage, the government overcomes the shortage of food by imposing quota targets on agriculture. The government is assumed to enforce a food marketing target of Ox. Rural

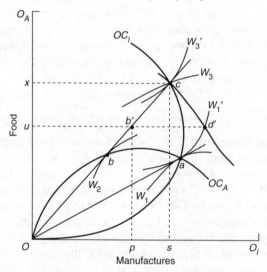

FIG. 7.3 *The Preobrazhensky case: coercion and political constraints*

people must accept position c and corresponding welfare level W_3, which is lower than W_1 at a and even lower than W_2 at b. Agriculture thus meets industry's demand for food, Ox, and receives in return Os of manufactures. Trade is balanced at the prices of food and manufactures imposed by government. The welfare of urban people has been raised ($W_3' > W_1'$) and that of rural people lowered.

The coercion of rural production can be viewed as facilitating the extraction of an investible surplus. It does this by enabling government to tax urban people without causing their welfare to fall below the non-intervention level. The need to maintain minimum living standards for urban workers is often seen as a political requirement (Preobrazhensky 1926; Lipton 1977). Assuming, for example, that the urban welfare constraint is W_1' in Figure 7.3, it would be possible for government both to lower the wage in industry relative to the price of manufactures and to coerce food marketing so that an investible surplus is extracted despite the constraint. Point b' ($O_A u$ of food and Op of manufactures) represents the consumption of rural people, point d' the consumption of urban people, and $b'd'$ the surplus extracted by government and spent on manufactured capital goods.

A second form of political constraint can be postulated—the existence of a minimum level of peasant food consumption. To keep Figure 7.3 simple, we again use points b' and d' but give them a quite different meaning. $O_A u$ now represents the minimum rural food consumption, implying that the maximum food-marketing quota is Ou. Rural people consume at point

b', urban people at point d', and $b'd'$ is the surplus extracted. If this is the chosen policy, rather than one involving some lesser marketing quota or no quota at all, it must be because government would prefer to secure a higher welfare level than W_1' for urban people even if it means less surplus extraction, but is constrained by rural subsistence needs.

7.1.3 Investible surplus with unaltered terms of trade

Consider a government wishing to extract an investible surplus from agriculture without altering the terms of trade. One alternative intervention is the direct taxation of agriculture. A direct tax equal to Ow drives rural people along their income-consumption curve IC_A to consumption point g and welfare level W_4 in Figure 7.4. Since urban people remain at point a, there are excess supplies of food gh and of manufactures ha, available for the State to spend the tax revenue on and use for capital accumulation.

Another method of surplus extraction is for the State to ration the quantity of manufactures supplied to peasants: assume that it makes only Op available. Rural producers then have an incentive to reduce their sales of food to Ot and thus consume at point i, that is to sell no more than is needed to buy the manufactures available. It is interesting to note that supply response is perverse in this rationing case. A rise in the food price would reduce, and a fall would increase, food sales over a range of prices: rural producers simply adjust their sales so as to finance the fixed expenditure on manufactures.

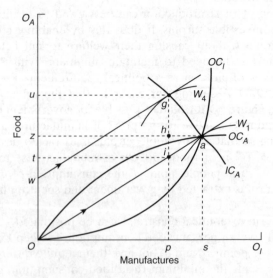

FIG. 7.4 *The effect of a direct tax on the rural sector*

The effect of rationing manufactures to peasants is thus to create an excess demand for food, equal to tz in Figure 7.4. If in response the government imposes a food-marketing target of Oz, it compels rural people to consume at point h. The forced saving of the agricultural sector, equal to ps of manufactures, is available for government use. The State accumulates capital goods and the rural sector of necessity acquires money balances—a capital inflow in lieu of imported manufactures.

7.1.4 Intersectoral resource transfers

Consider the implications of our analysis for intersectoral resource transfers. We begin with Figure 7.5. With flexible prices, rural–urban trade is balanced at the equilibrium point a. This is on a contract curve, CC, representing the locus of points of tangency of rural and urban indifference curves. Provided that the offer curves intersect only once, no more than one of the tangents passes through the origin O. Retaining the market-clearing assumption—so that the sum of rural and urban demands equals the supply of each good—introduce independent saving and investment decisions. Consider an expenditure equilibrium on the contract curve, say at point f, generating a relative price given by the tangent at f, which cuts the vertical axis at point u and the horizontal axis at point v.

The intersectoral resource transfer can be thought of as the difference between expenditure and income in each sector. Because the expenditure of the rural sector, uO_A, falls short of its income, OO_A, it runs a trade surplus, uO. Correspondingly, the high expenditure of the urban sector, vO_I,

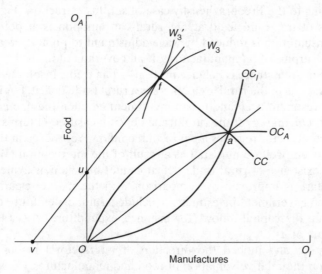

FIG. 7.5 *Intersectoral resource transfer without government intervention*

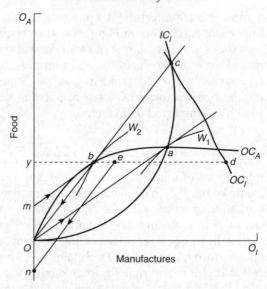

FIG. 7.6 *Intersectoral resource transfer: the Preobrazhensky case with valuation at actual and free market prices*

generates a trade deficit, vO. This urban trade deficit represents the net transfer of resources from the rural to the urban sector, measured in terms of manufactures. It is a resource transfer that results not from government intervention but from individual saving and investment decisions.

Reverting to the Preobrazhensky case of surplus extraction (Figure 7.6), the terms of trade are fixed at Oc, rural consumption is at point b and urban consumption is reduced by wage adjustment to point d, creating the investible surplus of bd manufactures. If all government investment occurs in the urban areas, there is balance in rural–urban trade. Insofar as the government invests in the rural areas, there is a rural trade deficit. For instance, if rural investment is eb and urban investment ed, then the line en, drawn parallel to Ob, marks off the rural trade deficit measured in terms of food, On. The rural sector receives a net resource inflow. Yet we see in the figure that its current welfare must fall as a result of the intervention ($W_2 < W_1$). Thus the existence of rural trade deficit cannot be taken as evidence that rural welfare is improved by comparison with the market-clearing case. Even when government investment is included, rural expenditure need not rise despite the capital inflow (for instance, expenditure at e is less than expenditure at a).

The extent and indeed the direction of intersectoral resource flows depends on the relative valuation of food and manufactures. Consider the case in which all government investment is urban. Rural expenditure is at

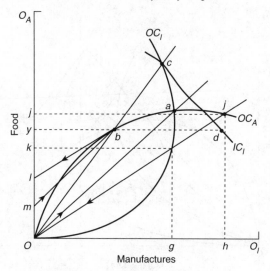

F<small>IG</small>. 7.7 *Intersectoral resource transfer: the Preobrazhensky case with valuation at world prices*

point *b* and, at the prevailing imposed prices, there is balance in trade. Yet the rural good is undervalued compared with non-intervention prices. The application of market-clearing prices is shown by the line *mb*, drawn parallel to *Oa*. The rural sector is accordingly seen to run a trade surplus, equal to *Om* when expressed in terms of food. Insofar as free market prices reflect social values, there is a net transfer of resources, as valued by society, from the rural to the urban areas, despite the observed balance in trade.

An equivalent argument would apply if the economy traded externally at world prices. Using Figure 7.7, which corresponds precisely to Figure 7.6, assume that *Oi* is the world price ray—even more favourable to agriculture than the closed economy price ray, *Oa*. At world prices there would be excess demand for manufactures equal to *gh*, and excess supply of food, *jk*, both of which could be simultaneously met through balanced external trade. The application of the world price ray, *Oi*, as reflecting social opportunity costs, would in this case further increase the social value of rural net exports. Although internal trade is apparently balanced (rural expenditure is at point *b*), at world prices the rural sector has an internal trade surplus of *Ol* expressed in terms of food.

7.1.5 The effect of industrialization

Since the reason for surplus extraction is often to promote rapid industrialization, it is relevant to consider the effect of achieving this objective. The box becomes elongated, as indicated by O'_i in Figure 7.8. The effect is to

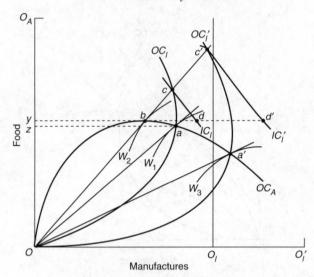

FIG. 7.8 *The effect of industrialization*

shift outwards the offer curve of the urban sector, to OC_i'. The market-clearing terms of trade move in agriculture's favour, as shown by the ray Oa'. Rural people benefit from industrialization because the increased demand for food raises its relative price: their consumption rises from point a to point a'.

We revert to the case in which government extracts an investible surplus by worsening agriculture's terms of trade. In Figure 7.8 the imposed price ratio is shown by the ray Oc and the investible surplus by bd. If, with industrial expansion, the terms of trade remain Oc, there is an increase in the excess demand for food and in the excess supply of manufactures. A further reduction in the urban wage in relation to industrial prices provides greater scope for surplus extraction: the investible surplus increases from bd to bd'. With product market-clearing, industrialization would normally help peasants as well as urban workers: the increase in industrial production from OO_i to OO_i' raises rural welfare from W_1 to W_3. Government failure to allow agriculture's terms of trade to improve means that rural people, with their current welfare remaining at W_2, are effectively financing the additional investment made possible by industrialization.

7.2 PRICE-SCISSORS IN CHINA

We again divide China's economic history under Communism into two policy regimes: the period of centralized planning from the early 1950s until

1978, and the period of greater decentralization, combining plan and market, since 1978. Official statistics record rapid economic growth and impressive industrialization. Recorded real GNP increased on average by 6.0 per cent per annum between 1952 and 1978. Industrial production grew by 11.3 per cent per annum, and the share of industry in GNP rose from 20 to 44 per cent.[1] The corresponding annual growth rates between 1978 and 1995 were 9.8 per cent and 12.0 per cent respectively. The share of industry did not rise further after 1978 because its relative growth was offset by a relative price decline. An important reason for the rapid economic growth was the high proportion of GDP devoted to investment: on average, 26 per cent in the first period and 36 per cent in the second. How did China, starting in conditions of extreme poverty and even in 1994 recording GNP per capita of only $530 (World Bank 1996: 188), manage to accumulate capital and industrialize so rapidly?

7.2.1 The rural–urban terms of trade

It is widely accepted that the Chinese price structure has implicitly taxed agriculture, in that farm producer prices were set low in relation to the prices of manufactures (in the English language literature see, for instance, Lardy (1983), Riskin (1987), Zhao and Wiemer (1991), and Sheng (1993a)). The State was in a position to do this because, under the planning system, it held a monopoly of trade and determined both agricultural and industrial prices. Moreover, the low food prices permitted the State to set low nominal wages, so enabling it to obtain high profits from industry. The profits, in turn, were used for state investment, particularly investment for industrialization. State control over the movement of labour and capital prevented the price distortion from having unwanted allocative effects.

The standard interpretation of Chinese industrialization thus corresponds closely to the Preobrazhensky case as explained in Section 7.1. For instance, the Chinese government, by imposing terms of trade equal to Oc and depressing urban incomes to welfare level W_2' in Figure 7.1, could induce rural people to opt for consumption point b and urban people for point d, so generating an investible surplus of manufactures equal to bd.

'Procurement planning' in agriculture, introduced in the 1950s, required the peasants to deliver target supplies of food to the State at prices determined by the State. The establishment of the communes can be seen, *inter alia*, as an institutional response to the need to force these deliveries (Perkins 1966: 57, 95). Producer prices were held fairly constant throughout the ensuing two decades. Although great emphasis was placed on food grain production, grain consumption per capita actually fell between 1957 and 1978 (Lardy 1983: 159). The inefficiency of the agricultural sector resulted in the effective rationing of many foodstuffs, i.e. demand exceeded supply. Thus the government attempted to resolve the contradiction between the low food prices needed for accumulation and the high prices needed for food production by a combination of compulsory purchases from producers and rationing of consumers. The emergence of pricing policy after the death of Mao can be seen as a response to the inadequacy of that policy. The development of a free market for food other than the subsidized urban rations ended effective rationing and introduced dual prices.

The beneficiary of high saving and investment in China was the industrial sector. During the planning period, between 1952 and 1978, real output in industry grew more rapidly than in agriculture by 8.1 per cent per annum. During the reform period, 1978–95, the corresponding figure was 5.9 per cent. The analysis of Figure 7.8 illustrates how such unbalanced growth in supply can cause a fall in the market-clearing price of manufactures relative to food. Unless the state-imposed terms of trade move correspondingly, there is growing scope for surplus extraction. Given constant surplus extraction, therefore, we expect rapid industrialization to be accompanied by improving terms of trade for agriculture. Indeed, the official index of the terms of trade between agricultural and industrial goods shows a consistent improvement from the inception of planning onwards, and particularly after the rural reforms began in 1978. For instance, with 1950 as 100, relative agricultural prices were 172 in 1968, 198 in 1978, 300 in 1991, and 380 in 1995 (Table 7.1).

The improvement in the official index of agriculture's terms of trade nevertheless raises questions about the relevance of the Preobrazhensky model. In an econometric analysis in which their dependent variable was real capital formation per worker in industry and one of their independent variables the ratio of agricultural to industrial prices, Li and Tsui (1990) found that its coefficient was significantly positive, contrary to their theoretical prediction. However, the fact that the dependent variable also rose over time has other possible explanations which might conceal a negative Preobrazhensky effect. As we argue in Section 7.2.3, the rapid growth of labour productivity in industry made it possible for both the agricultural terms of trade to improve and industrial profits per worker to increase.

There is another reason for doubting whether the trend improvement in the terms of trade series vitiates the application of the Preobrazhensky model to the Chinese economy. The series itself is regarded with scepticism. Lardy (1983: 111) and Riskin (1987: 244–8) argued that the price of industrial goods sold in the rural areas was unrepresentative, being based on a narrow range of consumer goods relevant to the early period and not reflecting the growing importance of high-priced industrial inputs into agricultural production. The simultaneous existence of numerous prices during the reform period makes it difficult to construct accurate indexes of

TABLE 7.1 *Price indices: agricultural and industrial products and their terms of trade,*
1951–95 (1950 = 100)

	Purchase price of farm and sideline products (1)	Retail price of industrial products in rural areas (2)	Their terms of trade (3) = (1)/(2)
1951	119.6	110.2	108.5
1952	121.6	109.7	110.8
1953	132.5	108.2	122.5
1954	136.7	110.3	123.9
1955	135.1	111.9	120.7
1956	139.2	110.8	125.6
1957	146.2	112.1	130.4
1958	149.4	111.4	134.1
1959	152.1	112.4	135.3
1960	157.4	115.5	136.3
1961	201.4	121.2	166.2
1962	200.1	126.6	158.1
1963	194.4	125.3	155.1
1964	189.5	122.9	154.2
1965	187.9	118.4	158.7
1966	195.8	115.0	170.3
1967	195.5	114.1	171.3
1968	195.2	113.8	171.5
1969	194.9	112.1	173.9
1970	195.1	111.9	174.4
1971	198.3	110.2	179.9
1972	201.1	109.6	183.5
1973	202.8	109.6	185.0
1974	204.5	109.6	186.6
1975	208.7	109.6	190.4
1976	209.7	109.7	191.2
1977	209.2	109.8	190.5
1978	217.4	109.8	198.0
1979	265.5	109.9	241.6
1980	284.4	110.8	256.7
1981	301.2	111.9	269.2
1982	307.8	113.7	270.7
1983	321.3	114.8	279.9
1984	334.2	118.4	282.3
1985	362.9	122.2	297.0
1986	386.1	126.1	306.2
1987	432.4	132.2	327.1
1988	531.9	152.3	349.2
1989	611.7	180.8	338.3
1990	595.8	189.1	315.1
1991	583.8	194.8	299.7
1992	603.9	200.9	300.6
1993	684.6	224.6	304.8
1994	957.8	263.2	363.9
1995	1148.3	301.9	380.4

Sources: PRC, SSB 1991: 230; 1996: 255.

agricultural and industrial prices. Zhao and Wiemer (1991) argued that the official price index of industrial goods in rural areas over the 1980s (although by then more broadly defined) understated the true increase because farmers had to switch their sources of inputs from supplies at state prices to supplies at (much higher) market prices.

In what ways did the terms of trade improve for the peasants during the reform period? From 1978 onwards government encouraged the revival of food markets and diminished the importance of quota, or contract, procurement: in 1978 the quota represented 79 per cent of State grain procurement and in 1989, 50 per cent (Table 7.2). State above-quota, or negotiated, purchase of grains grew correspondingly in importance, as did marketed grain not sold to the State. Whereas no grain went to market in 1978, the proportion was 17 per cent in 1989 (Table 7.2). Considering the three main grains (rice, wheat, and corn) the quota price (from 1985, the contract price) remained constant over the decade 1979–89, except for a 35 per cent increase when the contract system was introduced (Sicular 1992: 34–6). As the market price was substantially above the contract price, the mixed average price rose as markets became more important. However, the tax implicit in mandatory procurement became increasingly transparent as alternative outlets (negotiated state purchases and free markets) expanded, so creating peasant discontent. The terms of trade fluctuated around a constant trend after the mid-1980s, but began to rise sharply from 1993, as government finally brought its contract purchase prices towards market prices (see Table 7.1).

7.2.2 The social value of agricultural production

China's economy was initially relatively closed: imports accounted for under 3 per cent of GDP on average during the planning period, rising to 10 per cent in the 1980s, and 18 per cent in the 1990s. Only recently did world prices become relevant to the determination of domestic prices. World prices can be taken as the appropriate criterion for the social valuation of production by a government willing to pursue the gains from trade. In the absence of trade, market prices are a better guide to social values than state-imposed prices. Consider the evidence on the relationships among state prices, market prices, and world prices of food.

Riskin (1987: 245) reported that in the mid-1970s the ratio of the price of various manufactured consumer goods in relation to the price of rice was far higher in Guangzhou (Canton) than in nearby Hong Kong, the home of unfettered world prices. The data are presented in Table 7.3. The average ratio for the six commodities was 5.8 times higher in Guangzhou than in Hong Kong.

Even in 1987, after the agricultural terms of trade had improved greatly, producer prices of the major crops were well below international prices. A

TABLE 7.2 *Producer sales of grain to the free market and to the State, 1977–89*

	Marketed grain (million tonnes)					Percentage of total		
	Total	To free market	To State			To free market	To State at quota or contract price	To State at above-quota or negotiated price
			Total	At planned quota or contract price	At above-quota or negotiated price			
1977	47.67	0.00	47.67	37.75	9.92	0	79	21
1978	50.73	0.00	50.73	37.75	12.98	0	74	26
1979	60.10	2.53	57.57	35.00	22.57	4	58	38
1980	61.29	4.22	57.07	34.33	22.74	7	56	37
1981	68.46	5.22	63.24	30.38	32.86	8	44	48
1982	78.06	5.97	72.09	30.32	41.77	8	39	54
1983	102.49	5.75	96.74			6		
1984	117.25	9.77	107.48			8		
1985	107.63	17.01	90.62	75.00	15.62	16	70	14
1986	115.16	19.01	96.15	60.75	35.40	17	53	31
1987	120.92	21.72	99.20	50.00	49.20	18	41	41
1988	119.95			50.00			42	
1989	121.38	20.98	100.40	50.00	50.40	17	41	42

Source: Sicular 1992: table 3.

TABLE 7.3 *The terms of trade between rice and selected industrial goods in Guangzhou and Hong Kong, mid-1970s*

Industrial good	Place of manufacture	Kg. of rice required to buy one unit in		Ratio: Guangzhou /Hong Kong (3) = (1)/(2)
		Guangzhou (1)	Hong Kong (2)	
Portable radio	Guangzhou	14.0	6.0	2.3
Thermos flask	Guangzhou	15.5	3.5	4.4
Sewing machine	Shanghai	616.5	124.0	5.0
Bicycle	Shanghai	582.0	110.5	5.3
Camera	Shanghai	462.5	59.0	7.8
Alarm clock	Shanghai	75.5	7.5	10.1

Note: The rice was husked and polished rice, and the industrial goods were identical brands sold in both Guangzhou and Hong Kong.

Source: Riskin 1987: table 10.11, citing Liu 1980: 5–6.

World Bank study of the major grain crops at current average yields for the 'northern' region (of six) in China compared the profitability of crops at actual producer prices and at border prices. The ratio of 1987 border prices to mixed average farm gate procurement prices of rice, wheat, and corn were 3.9, 2.2, and 1.0 respectively. At actual prices the ratios of net revenue to cost per unit were 0.8, 1.3, and 1.7 respectively; and at border prices 3.0, 2.6, and 1.7. The gross underpricing of rice and wheat made them barely worth producing, at least in that part of China (World Bank 1991: 101–2).

The US Department of Agriculture made a study of producer subsidy equivalents (PSEs) for twenty-two agricultural commodities and various countries in 1986–7. It found China's PSE to be numerically greater than – 20 per cent, this being the extreme, open-ended, category (World Bank 1991: 111–12). Thus the average producer prices of agricultural goods were below the relevant international prices by more than 20 per cent. By 1988 the rural free market prices of the major grains were reported to be not much below their export and import unit values. However, the World Bank view was that the yuan was considerably overvalued: when the official price of the yuan was replaced by a shadow price (assumed to be 43 per cent lower), all grains were well below their border prices even in the free market (World Bank 1990*b*: 18–19, 31).

Table 7.4 shows the producer prices of three major grains in relation to their market prices over the period for which free markets existed and data are available. The market price greatly exceeded the quota price and its successor, the contract price, throughout the years 1977–89; it even exceeded

TABLE 7.4 *Producer prices: the ratio of free market prices to state procurement prices of grains, 1977–89*

| | Ratio of market price to: | | | | | | | | |
| | Quota price | | | Above-quota price | | | Contract price | | |
	Rice	Wheat	Corn	Rice	Wheat	Corn	Rice	Wheat	Corn
1977	3.45	2.66	2.23	2.65	2.47	1.72			
1978	3.01	2.73	1.83	2.31	2.10	1.41			
1979	2.42	2.02	1.28	1.61	1.35	0.85			
1980	2.36	1.95	1.28	1.57	1.30	0.85			
1981	2.36	1.95	1.28	1.57	1.26	0.76			
1982	2.36	1.95	1.28	1.57	1.21	0.76			
1983									
1984	1.50	1.50	1.50	1.00	1.00	1.00			
1985									
1986									
1987									
1988								2.75	1.46	1.47
1989								4.40	1.96	2.05

Note: Some regional variation in contract prices was introduced in 1986; the mid-point of the range is used to calculate the ratio.

Sources: Sicular 1992: 33–4; 1993: 58, 62, 67.

the above-quota price of both rice and wheat. Even as late as 1989 the ratio of market to contract price was as large as 4.40 for rice, 1.96 for wheat, and 2.05 for corn. In that year sales at state contract prices represented 41 per cent of total sales by producers (Table 7.2).

We lack the evidence to make a precise estimate of the extent to which the State depressed the prices of peasant output below the levels that would have prevailed without state intervention. However, the various pointers suggest that the ratio of market prices, and of world prices, to imposed prices of the main foodstuffs exceeded two to one during the planning period, and that the ratio continued to be high throughout the 1980s.

7.2.3 *The sources of funds for industrialization*

We turn to the sources of funds for industrialization. Table 7.5 shows capital accumulation and profits both in the economy as a whole and in industry. The best available measure of capital accumulation—gross investment in fixed assets (column 2)—rose progressively from 15 per cent of national income in the years 1953–7 to as much as 25 per cent in the 1980s. In

TABLE 7.5 Investment and profits in the economy and the industrial sector, 1953–90

	Rmb100 million			Per cent of national income			Government income from enterprises		Industrial sector				
	Capital accumulation		Investment in capital construction	Capital accumulation		Investment in capital construction	Rmb100 million	Per cent of accumulation of fixed assets	State-owned industrial enterprises				Investment in capital construction Rmb100 million
									Rmb100 million		Per cent of investment in capital construction		
	Total	Fixed assets		Total	Fixed assets				Profits	Profits plus taxes	Profits	Profits plus taxes	
	1	2	3	4	5	6	7	8	9	10	11	12	13
1953–7	998	622	588	25	15	15	567	91	280	391	112	156	250
1958–62	1,732	1,295	1,206	32	24	22	1,172	91	839	1,205	115	166	728
1963–5	811	589	422	23	17	12	650	110	504	738	240	351	210
1966–70	2,047	1,372	976	25	17	12	1,384	101	1,095	1,691	202	312	542
1971–5	3,644	2,650	1,734	32	23	15	2,139	81	1,739	2,731	178	279	978
1976–80	4,993	3,782	2,324	33	25	15	2,241	59	2,539	3,733	206	303	1,232
1981–5	7,982	6,323	3,410	31	25	18	1,211	19	3,263	5,415	211	350	1,547
1986–90	20,034	14,284	7,349	35	25	13	278	2	3,500	7,906	92	208	3,803

Sources: PRC, SSB 1986 and 1991.

the planning period, government income from enterprises, i.e. profits accruing to the State as owner (column 8), either exceeded investment in fixed assets or fell slightly short of it. Thereafter the relative importance of government income from enterprises declined until in the years 1986–90 it represented only 2 per cent of investment in fixed assets, reflecting the decentralization of management, enterprise retention of profits, and widespread loss-making. In the industrial sector, investment in capital construction has generally fallen well short of profits, and even more so of profits plus taxes (columns 11 and 12). From 1963 onwards, industrial profits plus taxes were more than double investment in state-owned industrial enterprises. Thus the industrial sector more than provided the saving needed for industrialization. This is of course consistent with the price-scissors theory: the favourable terms of trade for industry permitted high profits and high investment in that sector.

The improvement in the rural terms of trade is confirmed in Table 7.6, which shows net product per worker in agriculture and industry at both current and constant prices, and also their implicit relative prices. At constant prices, net product per worker grew far more rapidly in industry (4.0 per cent per annum, on average, between 1957 and 1990) than in agriculture (1.2 per cent). However, the improved terms of trade meant that, at current prices, productivity growth in agriculture slightly exceeded that in industry, both in the planning period and in the reform period. In 1952 the ratio of productivity in industry to that in agriculture was 9.1 to 1. By 1975, the ratio had fallen to 6.6 at current prices but had risen to 12.2 at 1952 prices. These trends continued during the reform period: by 1990, the ratios were 4.7 and 18.9 respectively.

Table 7.6 also shows that the nominal wage in industry grew less rapidly (by 3.9 per cent per annum on average between 1957 and 1990) than did productivity per worker at current prices (4.6 per cent). In terms of its own product price, the industrial wage rose by 3.3 per cent per annum over that period; deflated by urban retail prices, it rose by only 1.1 per cent per annum. With the wage lagging productivity, the nominal surplus per worker in industry grew by no less than 5.0 per cent per annum. It was already 141 per cent of the wage in 1957, and as much as 198 per cent in 1990. In real terms, also, the industrial surplus per worker grew exponentially (by 3.7 per cent per annum on average), so permitting rapid capital accumulation in industry. It was thus the fast growth of industrial labour productivity, itself assisted by capital accumulation, that outweighed the effect of worsening terms of trade and permitted capital accumulation in industry. Industrial wages did not grow so rapidly as to appropriate all the benefits of rising productivity per worker.

The rise in product per worker is of course not necessarily attributable to labour: causal relationships between output and various inputs require investigation by means of production functions and total factor

TABLE 7.6 *Agricultural and industrial product per worker, industrial wage, and surplus per worker, at current and constant prices, 1952–90*

| | Net product per worker | | | | Implicit price ratio of agriculture to industry 1957 = 100 | Ratio of net product per worker in industry to that in agriculture | | Average wage per worker in industry | | Surplus per worker in industry | |
| | Current prices yuan p.a. | | Constant prices 1957 = 100 | | | Current prices | 1952 prices | Yuan p.a. | Constant retail prices 1957 = 100 | Yuan p.a. | Constant product prices 1957 = 100 |
	Industry	Agriculture	Industry	Agriculture							
1952	1803	199	103.9	84.0	95	9.1	9.1	446	77	1357	107
1957	1536	221	100.0	100.0	100	7.0	7.3	637	100	899	100
1965	1711	291	110.9	93.2	140	5.9	8.7	652	93	1059	93
1970	1949	296	147.4	89.0	175	6.6	12.2	609	88	1340	138
1975	2156	338	168.0	115.6	188	6.4	12.7	613	87	1543	164
1980	2687	454	206.3	100.0	242	5.9	15.1	803	101	1884	197
1985	3788	799	272.0	138.0	289	3.4	14.5	1213	124	2575	252
1990	6817	1463	369.8	150.2	366	4.7	18.9	2284	141	4533	335
Average annual growth rate											
1957–80	2.5	3.2	3.3	0.0	3.9	—	—	1.0	0.0	3.3	3.0
1980–90	9.8	12.4	6.0	4.2	4.2	—	—	11.0	3.4	9.1	5.5
1957–90	4.6	5.9	4.0	1.2	4.0	—	—	3.9	1.1	5.0	3.7

Source: PRC, SSB 1991.

productivity analysis, of the sort conducted by Jefferson, Rawski, and Zheng (1990). At 1980 prices, the capital/labour ratio in industry was found to rise by 3.3 per cent per annum over the 1980s (ibid.: table 4), so contributing to the rise in output per worker both directly and indirectly via embodied technical progress. The authors found the contribution of labour to industrial output growth over the 1980s to be relatively small by comparison with those of capital, intermediate goods, and technical progress (ibid.: table 7). Thus even acceptance of the normative principle of reward according to contribution would not justify wage increases in line with productivity increases.

From the standpoint of positive economics, given labour mobility and market competition there is no reason why industrial workers should benefit from productivity increases unless the marginal product of labour is raised not only in industry but also throughout the economy. The important empirical question is whether industrial workers possess the bargaining power—explicit or implicit—to appropriate the rise in industrial product per worker. In this respect an interesting distinction can be made between the planning period and the reform period (Table 7.6). Industrial labour productivity growth was considerably higher in the latter than in the former period. This was partly offset by the accelerated growth of industrial wages (examined in Chapter 2, Section 2.2). Urban workers became better able to appropriate part of the productivity gains with the introduction and expansion of enterprise-level performance-related bonuses and other payments during the 1980s. Nevertheless, the real surplus per worker rose consistently—except for the calamity of the Great Leap Forward—averaging annual growth of 3.0 per cent over the planning period and 5.5 per cent over the reform period.

7.3 MEASURING THE INTERSECTORAL RESOURCE TRANSFER

It was argued that the Preobrazhensky model does not require a net resource flow, as conventionally measured, from rural to urban areas (Figure 7.6). Given the assumptions of the model, a reduction in the price of food decreases the value of rural exports and so constrains rural imports: trade balance is maintained. However, if part of the investible surplus is invested in agriculture, there is a rural trade deficit. Trade imbalance can also result from discrepant saving and investment decisions. How have resources moved between industry and agriculture in China? It is very difficult, with the existing data, accurately to measure the net capital flow between industry and agriculture.

Four estimates of the intersectoral resource transfer are presented in Table 7.7, columns 1 and 2 showing the trade surplus of the agricultural sector and columns 3 and 4 that of the rural sector. In each case one esti-

TABLE 7.7 *Intersectoral resource transfers between the agricultural and the non-agricultural sectors and the rural and the urban sectors, 1952–90*

	Trade surplus				National income
	Agricultural sector		Rural sector		
	1	2	3	4	5
Annual average (100 million yuan)					
1952–9	4	−12	−7	2	871
1960–9	−16	−37	−17	−26	1,280
1970–9	−108	−153	−75	−97	2,474
1980–5	−278	−292	−105	−21	4,883
1980–90	—	−294	—	112	5,652

Notes: 1. Col. 1 is taken from Nakagane (1989, table 1, col. 9) ('trade surplus of the agricultural sector in the narrow sense'). It is estimated as $T_a = X_a − M_a$, where X_a = total purchases of farm and sideline products, and M_a = imports of the agricultural sector in the narrow sense. M_a = rural retail sales of social commodities − rural sales of catering trade − material consumption non-agricultural workers − intrasectoral material consumption by the state farm population.
  2. Col. 2 estimates $T_a = Y_a − E_a$, defining Y_a as income of peasants from selling (farm) products and E_a as rural retail sales of social commodities − rural retail sales to the non-agricultural population. Retail sales to the non-agricultural population is derived by multiplying rural retail sales per worker by the number of non-agricultural workers.
  3. Col. 3 is taken from Nakagane (1989, table 3, col. 4). It is derived as the trade surplus of the rural non-agricultural sector (table 3, col. 3) + the trade surplus of agriculture in the narrow sense (table 1, col. 9) − material consumption of non-agricultural workers in the commune sector (table 1, col. 5).
  4. Col. 4 estimates $T_r = Y_r − E_r$, where Y_r = income of peasants from selling products + service income of peasants, with the addition of new (or newly separated) sources of rural income (peasants' net income from collective business, from economic union and from industrial and manufacturing activities) when these were reported (1984–). E_r is total retail sales of social commodities, i.e. the difference between E_r (col. 4) and E_a (col. 2) is that rural retail sales to the non-agricultural population are included in E_r.

mate (columns 1 and 3) is that made by Nakagane (1989) and the other (columns 2 and 4) by ourselves. The agricultural and the rural sectors are distinguished despite their near-identity during the planning period because after 1978 they increasingly diverged. By 1990, as much as 16 per cent of non-agricultural value added was produced in the rural areas, and 17 per cent of industrial value added. By definition, it appeared, there was no urban agriculture. Nevertheless, no less than 10 per cent of national income was not produced in the traditional location (PRC, SSB 1991: 32, 322, 376). The estimates suffer from both conceptual and empirical inadequacies. The precise methods of calculation are explained in the notes to the table: the text is confined to basic concepts, limitations and results.

There are two ways of estimating the trade balance of a sector. One is to measure the trade surplus directly from exports and imports ($T = X - M$) and the other is to measure it as the difference between sector income and final expenditure ($T = Y - E$). Nakagane measured the trade surplus of agriculture as $T_a = X_a - M_a$, using purchases of farm products as his proxy for X_a and rural retail sales less deductions for intra-sector trade and for expenditure by the non-agricultural rural population as the proxy for M_a. We measured $S_a = Y_a - E_a$, where Y_a is the income of peasants and E_a is rural retail sales minus retail sales to the non-agricultural population. In the case of T_r, the rural trade surplus, Nakagane measured T_r as $T_a + T_{nr}$, where T_{nr} is the trade surplus of the non-agricultural rural sector. We estimated T_r as $Y_r - E_r$, where Y_r is the income of peasants from agricultural and non-agricultural activities and E_r is rural retail sales.

The main difficulty with the $X - M$ method lies in distinguishing sector production which is exported from that which is consumed internally, and in distinguishing expenditure on imports and on sector production. The main difficulty with the $Y - E$ method lies in distinguishing final and intermediate expenditure: the Y and E concepts should correspond. The data, taken mainly from PRC, SSB (1991) and earlier editions, are often inadequately defined and their method of collection unexplained. The estimates should therefore be taken merely as indicating broad tendencies.

In the 1950s and 1960s the difference between the rural and the agricultural sector trade balances was negligible. Moreover, the size of the trade balance, although consistently negative in the 1960s, was small in relation to national income. The agricultural and rural trade deficit grew in the 1970s. For instance, the deficit of the agricultural sector averaged 14 per cent of recorded value added in agriculture. In the 1980s a discrepancy arose between the agricultural and rural sectors. The agricultural trade deficit grew, representing 11 per cent of agricultural value added. The rural trade deficit fell in the early 1980s and became a trade surplus in the late 1980s. This change from a resource inflow into the rural sector to a resource outflow reflects the growth of rural industry in the 1980s, much of whose product was exported to the urban sector.

The evidence of Table 7.7 suggests that, during the period of centralized planning, the rapid industrialization of China's economy was not financed by means of a transfer of capital from agriculture. The trade balance of both the agricultural and the rural sector was negligible or negative throughout. The saving required for industrial investment must have been generated within the industrial sector itself. However, this is precisely the outcome that would be expected had a policy of price-scissors been in operation. The adverse terms of trade imposed by government on agriculture permitted industrial enterprises to pay wages that were low in relation to industrial prices and thus to generate surpluses.

What would have been the direction and size of the intersectoral resource transfer had the products of the agricultural sector been valued at market rather than imposed prices? In order to estimate the internal terms of trade in the absence of state intervention, we need to know what prices would have been in free markets. If they exist, the actual market prices are a possible guide, although they are potentially misleading in that residual markets represent disequilibrium rather than equilibrium outcomes. International (border) prices are relevant in a small open economy, but China's size and relative isolation for many years render their use suspect. In practice, neither of these measures is available on a systematic basis. Nevertheless, our review of the available evidence in Section 7.2.2 suggests that the ratio of free market, and world market, prices to producer prices of agricultural commodities was substantial for much of the Communist period. The ratio could well have exceeded two to one during the planning period, and it was only gradually eroded in the process of economic reform.

A simulation analysis was conducted to show the effect on the intersectoral resource flow of assuming that market prices were the relevant measuring rod. In Table 7.8 either X_r or Y_r was used in the estimation of the net resource flow ($T_r = X_r - M_r = Y_r - E_r$). Our simulation method was to multiply X_r or Y_r by 1.5, 2.0, and 2.5 in turn. The simulations thus answer the question: what would the trade balance of the agricultural or rural sector be if its prices were raised by 50, 100, or 150 per cent? The exercise accounts for only the direct effects and not for the indirect, general equilibrium effects of such a price change. In Figure 7.6, showing the Preobrazhensky case with valuation at both actual and free market prices, the simulation corresponds to measuring the trade balance as the surplus *Om* rather than zero.

The results of the simulation exercise are set out in Table 7.8. In every case (all four measures, all five periods, and all three assumed market values) the trade balance of the peasantry is now positive: at market prices the net resource flow is outward. Moreover, the size of the surplus may be large. Averaging over measures and periods, even the simulation based on prices being raised by 50 per cent implies a trade surplus equal to 10 per cent of reported national income. The corresponding figures for the 100 and 150 per cent simulations are 21 and 33 per cent.

There is a lively but inconclusive empirical literature on intersectoral resource flows in China. The various estimates based on actual prices suggest that the net flow over the four decades of Communist rule was generally into, and not out of, agriculture (Ishikawa 1988; Nakagane 1989; Sheng 1993a, b). Apparently unpersuaded that agriculture's terms of trade were artificially held down, Ishikawa (1988), Nakagane (1989), and Karshenas

TABLE 7.8 *Simulation analysis: intersectoral resource transfers, 1952–90, assuming market price to exceed procurement price by 50, 100, or 150 per cent*

Sector	Table 7.7 column number	Percentage price increase	Trade surplus, annual average (100 million yuan)				
			1952–9	1960–9	1970–9	1980–5	1980–90
Agriculture	1	50	109	125	132	447	
		100	214	266	371	1,096	
		150	321	407	611	1,804	
	2	50	94	104	86	386	492
		100	200	244	326	1,065	1,118
		150	305	385	566	1,743	1,743
Rural	3	50	99	123	165	504	
		100	205	264	405	1,182	
		150	311	405	645	1,861	
	4	50	107	115	143	658	749
		100	213	256	382	1,336	1,375
		150	319	396	623	2,015	2,001
National income			871	1,280	2,474	4,883	5,652

(1993) inferred that agriculture did not finance China's industrialization. By contrast, Sheng (1993*a*,*b*), using surrogate market prices, found that the price-scissors created a net resource outflow from agriculture, and the literature in Chinese (summarized in Sheng 1993*a*: 103–7), using prices based on the labour theory of value, has generally obtained the same result. However, neither of the above methods for placing a social value on output is persuasive. Our own analysis shows that the sign and size of the net resource flow are sensitive to assumptions about the undistorted terms of trade. Moreover, on the valuation assumptions which we find plausible, the evidence suggests that there has been a substantial net capital flow from the rural to the urban sector both in the planning and the reform periods.

7.4 GOVERNMENT EXPENDITURE PRIORITIES

The allocation of public expenditure between rural and urban areas by the various tiers of the Chinese government is extremely complex and opaque. We have conducted some analysis in the cases of education (Chapter 4), health care (Chapter 5), and housing (Chapter 6). Here we concentrate on two aspects of public expenditure which help to reveal government priorities on the use of the investible surplus: sectoral investment allocation and consumer subsidies.

7.4.1 *The allocation of investment*

We examine the priority that the Chinese government placed on the agricultural sector, and on the rural sector, in its investment and general expenditure policies. The State has played only a minor investment role in rural China. During the planning period most investment was carried out by collective units (the communes, brigades, and production teams), and during the reform period by households and local authorities (townships and villages). The policy of local self-reliance for rural China generally required local communities to improve their own infrastructures. Table 7.9 shows the pattern of rural investment in two years of the reform period, 1985 and 1993. Three things stand out: the trivial share of the State in the total; the greater importance of non-agricultural than agricultural investment for both collectives and individuals, reflecting their relative profitability; and the growing importance of collectives (township- and village-owned enterprises) as rural industrialization proceeded.

TABLE 7.9 *The pattern of investment in fixed assets in rural China, 1985 and 1993*

	State	Collective-owned	Individual	Total
		(Hundred million yuan)		
1985				
Total	1,681	328	535	2,544
Agricultural	44	21	72	137
Rural	44	199	478	721
Rural (per cent of row)	6	28	66	100
Loans to agriculture	36			
Loans to rural non-agriculture	53			
1993				
Total	7,658	2,231	1,476	11,365
Agricultural	64	127	166	357
Rural	64	1,631	1,138	2,833
Rural (per cent of row)	2	58	40	100
Loans to agriculture	313			
Loans to rural non-agriculture	552			

Notes: 1. State investment is not divided between rural and urban. To complete the table, the plausible assumption is made that state non-agricultural investment in rural China is negligible.
2. There are minor discrepancies between the two sources.

Sources: PRC, SSB 1994: 139, 145; RDI, CASS 1994: 50.

In the absence of rural capital markets, local communities were greatly dependent on their own savings for investment. There is econometric evidence that local agricultural prosperity was important for funding non-agricultural investment in the early years of reform, but that local rural industry itself increasingly became the source of surplus for further industrialization (Knight and Song 1993: 197–205). This dependence on own success, together with learning-by-doing and economies of scale and of agglomeration, set in train processes of cumulative causation which increased rural inequality. These processes were observable even at the level of the individual village, at least partly on account of the need to rely on funds from within the village (Knight and Li 1997). Except among provinces during the planning period, the institutional mechanisms for spatial redistribution of public revenue to unsuccessful rural areas were weak (Knight and Song 1993: 205–9).

Throughout the Communist period the priority that the State accorded to urban industrialization meant that little of its investment was available for agriculture or for rural areas. The State was neither the initiator nor the agent of rural production, as it was of urban production, although even its loans to agriculture were relatively minor (Table 7.9). Nevertheless, the higher tiers of government had a potentially important role in those aspects of agriculture with powerful externalities: water conservation, technology, and extension.

Table 7.10 shows how state budgetary expenditure was allocated to agriculture over the Communist period (government agricultural expenditure and investment as a percentage of total expenditure and investment, and also in real terms per head of rural population). One peak state investment period was in the early years of the communes, when government was keen to show their benefits by investing in commune infrastructure such as electricity and water conservation. The communes themselves made efforts to mobilize surplus labour for local public works (Nolan 1988: 56). Accordingly, the proportion of cultivated land under irrigation rose from 24 per cent in 1957 to 32 per cent in 1965, and to 45 per cent in 1978 (Lin 1994: 37). There was another burst of state agricultural investment at the start of the rural reforms. However, the effect of decollectivization and its success was to reduce the investment efforts of both lower and higher tiers of government over the 1980s. It was a common complaint that rural infrastructure suffered (World Bank 1990c: 10; Lin 1994: 63–6). Government reacted belatedly, and as a result the share of agriculture in state investment improved in the 1990s (RDI, CASS 1994: 40–1). In real terms state agricultural investment per head of rural population declined during the reform period, reviving somewhat only recently. All this is apparent in Table 7.10.

The most telling statistic is that, at the time of the 1990 population census, agriculture supported 60 per cent of Chinese households but received

TABLE 7.10 *Government expenditure to support agriculture, in relation to total government expenditure and in real terms, 1952–94*

	Government expenditure on agriculture as a percentage of total government expenditure			Agricultural tax as a percentage of expenditure on agriculture	Government real expenditure on agriculture per head of rural population (1976–80 = 100)	Government real capital construction in agriculture per head of rural population (1976–80 = 100)
	Capital construction	All expenditure	All expenditure net of agricultural tax			
1952–5	6.9	5.4	−7.6	240	16	19
1956–60	4.1	10.9	4.1	63	57	89
1961–5	16.9	14.4	8.0	44	53	50
1966–70	10.1	9.2	3.2	65	42	52
1971–5	11.1	10.2	6.4	37	65	83
1976–80	12.8	13.2	10.5	21	100	100
1981–5	8.4	9.5	7.1	25	81	56
1986–90	9.4	8.4	5.9	29	94	59
1991–4	15.4	9.7	6.4	33	114	73

Sources: PRC, SSB 1991: 183, 187, 189, 192, 199; PRC, SSB 1996: 69, 223, 228–9, 233.

only 9 per cent of the state budget. Even this exaggerates the State's net budgetary contribution to agriculture. Deduction of the direct tax on farm output, the 'agricultural tax', shows a substantially smaller net expenditure, especially in the planning period (Table 7.10). For instance, the agricultural tax exceeded state expenditure on agriculture in the period 1952–5, was 65 per cent of it in 1966–70, and 33 per cent in 1991–4.

7.4.2 Urban consumer subsidies

Over the reform period, as marketization occurred, the State faced a growing conflict between the needs to provide rural incentives and to avoid urban discontent. Somehow it had to offer the peasants carrots instead of sticks but without taking the carrots from the workers. This conflict provides us with a test of government priorities as between rural and urban people.

It is instructive at this point to return to the theory of Section 7.1, in particular Figures 7.1–7.3. According to the standard price-scissors analysis, the removal of government intervention and the restoration of the market-determined terms of trade should improve the welfare of urban-dwellers despite the relative increase in the price of food. This is illustrated in Figure 7.1 by the rise in urban welfare, from indifference curve W_2' at point d to W_1' at point a. However, we argued that urban-dwellers can be protected from the adverse welfare effects of the price-scissors. For instance, Figure 7.2 was used to show that, although urban rationing leads to suboptimal allocation of urban income, it reduces the need to compress the urban wage in order to eliminate excess demand for food. Similarly, it was argued with respect to Figure 7.3 that the compulsory procurement of food reduces the welfare of rural people but makes possible the extraction of an investible surplus without necessarily reducing urban welfare. The economic reforms commenced in 1978 from a situation of compulsory procurement and rationed distribution of food. It is likely, therefore, that the subsequent gradual movement towards the marketization of food threatened to worsen the welfare of urban-dwellers rather than to improve it.

Throughout the planning period prices in the limited urban free markets were well above the state prices of food sold to urban-dwellers. During the reform period state retail prices converged towards market prices. The free market price of food in general was 69 per cent above the state price in 1978, 28 per cent above in 1985, and 4 per cent above in 1992 (Table 7.11). The difference was greatest, and slowest to wither, in the case of basic foodstuffs. For instance, the market retail price of grain was double the state retail price in 1990, and still 19 per cent above it in 1992 (Table 7.11).

We see in Table 7.12 that the mixed average retail price of grain exceeded the mixed average producer price during the planning period, but that the reverse was the case over the reform years. For instance, the retail

TABLE 7.11 *Consumer prices: state and free market prices of agricultural goods sold to consumers, and their ratio, 1962–90*

	State price (1965 = 100)	Free market price (1965 = 100)	Free market price (state price = 100)	Free market price of grain (state price = 100)
1962	50.5	97.3	270.0	
1965	100.0	100.0	140.0	
1970	101.6	102.8	142.0	
1978	106.0	127.0	169.0	
1985	181.0	165.5	128.0	
1990	367.3	283.4	107.7	200.0
1992	387.4	287.5	103.6	118.6

Notes: 1. Consistency requires that these goods be the farm products (including grain, vegetable oils, vegetables, meat, fish, fruit, etc.) listed in Table 7.13.
2. The *Statistical Yearbooks* ceased publishing these series in 1993.

Source: PRC, SSB 1993: table 7.14.

TABLE 7.12 *Producer and consumer prices: the mixed average purchase and retail prices of grain, 1952–93*

	Mixed average price per tonne		
	Purchase (yuan)	Retail	
		(yuan)	(as percentage of purchase)
1952	138.4	197.8	143
1957	162.0	220.0	136
1965	229.2	237.4	104
1978	263.4	294.8	89
1985	416.1	383.3	93
1990	716.0	528.1	74
1993	825.3	740.5	90
1995	1560.5	1335.1	86

Note: The prices are weighted averages of both state and market prices; details of the calculation are not provided by the sources.

Sources: PRC, SSB 1993: 243–4; 1994: 245; 1995: 239; 1996: 261, 269.

price fell short of the producer price by 11 per cent in 1978, by as much as 26 per cent in 1990, and by 14 per cent in 1995. After 1978 the State supplied urban residents with staple foods at retail prices well below its procurement prices.

The resultant shortfall in proceeds had to be met from public funds. Table 7.13 shows the size of the consequent urban consumer food subsidies. Our measure of these subsidies is the total value of price subsidies on grain, cotton, and edible oil. This excludes 'other price subsidies', some of which are on consumer goods such as meat. In 1980, 1985, 1990, and 1995 'other price subsidies' added an extra 15, 32, 42, and 59 per cent respectively (PRC, SSB 1996: 243). Using our conservative estimate, we see that price subsidies grew from 1.0 per cent of government expenditure in 1978 to a peak of 12.9 per cent in 1983. Thereafter they declined slowly over the 1980s, to

TABLE 7.13 *Government price subsidies on grain, cotton, and edible oil: at 1978 prices, and as a percentage of government expenditure and of GDP, 1978–95*

	Price subsidies		
	100 million yuan, at 1978 prices	As percentage of:	
		Government expenditure	GDP
1978	11.1	1.0	0.3
1979	53.1	4.3	1.3
1980	95.7	8.4	2.3
1981	129.5	12.5	3.0
1982	142.2	12.7	3.0
1983	163.6	12.9	3.1
1984	173.1	11.9	2.9
1985	155.0	9.9	2.2
1986	126.3	7.7	1.7
1987	138.7	8.6	1.6
1988	129.1	8.2	1.4
1989	152.7	9.3	1.6
1990	147.6	8.7	1.4
1991	137.9	7.9	1.2
1992	107.5	6.0	0.8
1993	93.9	4.8	0.6
1994	70.6	3.5	0.4
1995	70.8	3.4	0.4

Note: The value of the subsidies is deflated by the implicit GDP deflator.

Sources: PRC, SSB 1991: 27; 1996: 42, 223, 243.

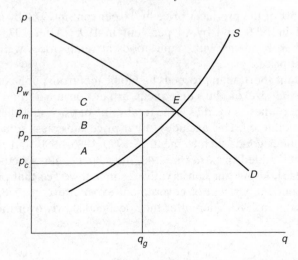

FIG. 7.9 *The transfer from peasant producers to urban consumers*

8.7 per cent of government expenditure in 1990, and more rapidly over the
1990s, to 3.4 per cent in 1995. At their peak, the price subsidies represented 3.1 per cent of GDP. A World Bank report (1991: 146) based its estimates
of consumer food subsidies (over a more limited period) on government
internal figures of losses on the distribution of staple and non-staple foods.
On that basis the subsidies appeared considerably higher: in the peak year,
1983, they were 18.3 per cent of government expenditure and 4.1 per cent
of GDP.

These subsidies have represented an enormous transfer from the agricultural to the non-agricultural population. Moreover, they understate the
extent of the transfer. Figure 7.9 clarifies. Assume that the government
procures q_g of food from farmers to distribute as the urban ration. Market
demand and supply are shown as the curves D and S, and the free market
price as p_m. Assume that the government intervention leaves D and S unaf-
fected, and that p_m is thus the price at which non-quota food is sold. The
producer price received from government is p_p, and the urban consumer
price paid to government is p_c. The rectangle A represents the consumer
subsidy, being the revenue burden on government. However, the rectangle
B is also part of the transfer (from producer surplus to consumer surplus)
as p_m is the loss borne by producers on account of their enforced sales to
government. Indeed, if the price that would prevail with free trade is the
world price, p_w, there is a further loss to producers, represented by the areas
C and E, as p_w is then the effective opportunity cost. The area $C + E$ is
positive on the assumption, plausible for China, that $p_w > p_m$.

A World Bank report (1990*a*: 18) estimated the financial cost to government of grain and vegetable oil subsidies in 1988 as 26 billion yuan (corresponding to rectangle *A*), and the net loss of farm revenue on mandatory grain sales as 23 billion yuan (rectangle *B*), producing a total economic cost of the transfer no less than 48 billion yuan. This transfer was equivalent to 215 yuan per urban recipient, or 18 per cent of urban income per capita in 1988; and it was equivalent to 39 per cent of rural income per capita in that year. Most remarkable is the fact that total budgetary expenditure on agriculture in 1988 was under 22 billion yuan (PRC, SSB 1993: 193). Thus what the State took out of agriculture by paying lower procurement prices than market prices was more than double what the State put into agriculture.

Not only did the redistribution of income resulting from food subsidies increase inequality between rural and urban areas but it also increased inequality within urban areas. In 1990 the urban population numbered 302 million (PRC, SSB 1991: 61) but the population classified as 'non-agricultural' numbered 236 million (PRC, EBCAY 1991: 159). As some of these 'non-agricultural' people were cadres working in the rural areas, more than 66 million (22 per cent) of the urban population were classified as 'agricultural'. They did not possess urban registration *hukous* and therefore did not qualify for subsidized food rations. The urban residents discriminated against in this way were either temporary migrants who had been long enough in town to be counted as urban in the census of population or residents of small or recently reclassified urban areas.

The implication of these subsidies, and of the way in which they grew in the wake of increases in producer prices, is that government perceived urban-*hukou* holders to be a group whose welfare had to be protected. Government concern may have been with the political instability that might arise from social discontent among urban-dwellers, or with the inflationary consequences of real wage resistance by workers, or with the production consequences of disaffected morale among workers. Whatever the motive, government revealed clearly its underlying social welfare function.

7.5 CONCLUSION

The phenomena of price-scissors and intersectoral resource transfers are amenable to analysis using offer curves from international trade theory. An important point to emerge from the theoretical analysis is that, in examining the sectoral funding of investment, it can be misleading to look at the actual trade balance between the rural and the urban sectors. The hand that wields the price-scissors can effect an invisible transfer from the rural sector. Indeed, the relative invisibility of the transfer and the opaqueness of the burden add political attractiveness. The extent of the sacrifice for capital accumulation is ultimately represented by consumption and welfare levels. Our analysis showed that, if its terms of trade are worsened through intervention, a net capital inflow into agriculture is actually consistent with agriculture's shouldering much of the burden of sacrifice. The theoretical framework could be readily and usefully applied to the Chinese economy. It was extended to incorporate such Chinese features as compulsory deliveries of food, consumer rationing, political constraints, and the dynamic effects of industrialization.

The rural–urban terms of trade appeared to move consistently in favour of rural China over the forty-five years of our study. The main reason for this trend was rapid industrialization, which raised industrial output relative to agricultural output. Assisted by low food prices and low wages, the industrial sector generated the surplus required for capital accumulation. The rapid growth of labour productivity raised the investible surplus per worker in industry, the relative decline in industrial prices notwithstanding. This occurred during the planning period, when wages were static. However, it was also true of the reform period, despite the rent-sharing between enterprises and their workers which propelled real wages upwards.

Whether the price-scissors policy continued to operate depends on whether the market equilibrium terms of trade improved as rapidly as the actual terms of trade. The evidence relating producer prices to market prices and world prices of food suggests that the peasants received much less than the social value of their output. It is plausible that the ratio of social values to producer prices of food exceeded two to one during the planning period, and that this continued to be the case for staple grains until the 1990s.

At actual prices, the direction of intersectoral resource transfer was towards the peasants for much of the Communist period. However, our simulation analysis suggests that, over the plausible range of social values for their product, the net transfer was not only away from the peasants but also large. Rural saving exceeded investment, i.e. there was a net capital outflow from rural to urban China. The price-scissors policy generated an investible surplus, which was invested largely in the urban sector. The State accorded priority to urban industrialization whereas it required rural communities to be self-sufficient: state investment in agriculture was negligible. Thus it was the peasants who paid for industrialization in China.

Part of the investible surplus was diverted to the support of urban workers and their 'iron rice bowls'. The urban wage exceeded the rural supply price even during the planning period. The government's concern to protect the living standards of urban workers is clearly revealed by the increase in food subsidies in response to the growth of producer price incentives during the reform period. The budgetary expenditure on urban food subsidies actually came to exceed budgetary expenditure on agriculture. Clearly it was not only future generations that gained from the price scissors: urban-dwellers also benefited. Thus the Chinese experience does not correspond precisely to the Preobrazhensky model of industrialization. However, the fact that urban income was at least twice as high as rural income throughout both the planning and the reform periods is not primarily to be explained by the lack of free product markets. The lack of an equilibrating labour market was crucial: had the State permitted labour mobility and wage competition, urban workers could not have fared as well as they did. It is to intersectoral labour issues—the movement, reward, and regulation of rural labour—that we turn in Chapters 8 and 9.

NOTE

1. Unless otherwise stated, these and other statistics are derived from PRC, SSB 1996 or earlier editions. Industry is broadly defined to include all secondary sector activity other than construction (PRC, SSB 1996: 42).

REFERENCES

Blomqvist, Ake G. (1986). 'The economics of price scissors: comment', *American Economic Review*, 76 (5): 1188–91.

Carter, Michael P. (1986). 'The economics of price scissors: comment', *American Economic Review*, 76 (5): 1192–4.

Ishikawa, S. (1988). 'Patterns and processes of intersectoral resource flows: comparison of cases in Asia', in G. Ranis and T. P. Schultz (eds.), *The State of Development Economics*, Oxford: Blackwell.

Jefferson, Gary H., Rawski, Thomas G., and Zheng Yuxin (1990). 'Growth, Efficiency and Convergence in China's State and Collective Industry', Socialist Economies Reform Unit, Research Paper Series 1, Washington, DC: World Bank.

Karshenas, M. (1993). 'Intersectoral resource flows and development: lessons of past experience', in A. Singh and H. Tabatabai (eds.), *Economic Crisis in Third World Agriculture*, Cambridge: Cambridge University Press.

Knight, John (1995). 'Price scissors and intersectoral resource transfers: who paid for industrialization in China?', *Oxford Economic Papers*, 47 (1): 117–35.

——and Song, Lina (1993). 'The spatial contribution to income inequality in rural China', *Cambridge Journal of Economics*, 17 (2): 149–72.

——and Li Shi (1997). 'Cumulative causation and inequality among villages in China', *Oxford Development Studies*, 25 (2): 149–72.

Lardy, Nicholas (1983). *Agriculture in China's Modern Economic Development*, Cambridge: Cambridge University Press.

Li, Dominic, and Tsui, Kai T. (1990). 'The generalised efficiency wage hypothesis and the scissors problem', *Canadian Journal of Economics*, 23 (1): 144–58.

Lin, Justin Yifu (1994). 'Chinese agriculture: institutional changes and performance', in T. N. Srinivasan (ed.), *Agriculture and Trade in China and India*, San Francisco: International Centre for Economic Growth.

Lipton, Michael (1977). *Why Poor People Stay Poor: Urban Bias in World Development*, Cambridge, Mass.: Harvard University Press.

Liu Jungchao (1980). 'A note on China's pricing policies', paper presented to a workshop of the Department of Economics, State University of New York, Binghampton.

Nakagane, Katsuji (1989). 'Intersectoral resource flows in China revisited. Who provided industrialization funds?', *The Developing Economies*, 27 (2): 146–73.

Nolan, Peter (1988). *The Political Economy of Collective Farms*, Cambridge: Polity Press.

People's Republic of China, Editorial Board of the China Agricultural Yearbook (PRC, EBCAY) (1991). *China Agricultural Yearbook 1991*, Beijing: Agricultural Publishing House.

——State Statistical Bureau (PRC, SSB) (1986). *Statistical Yearbook of China 1986*, Oxford: Oxford University Press.

————(1991). *Statistical Yearbook of China 1991*, Beijing.

————(1993). *China Statistical Yearbook 1993*, Beijing.

————(1994). *China Statistical Yearbook 1994*, Beijing.

————(1995). *China Statistical Yearbook 1995*, Beijing.

————(1996). *China Statistical Yearbook 1996*, Beijing.

Perkins, Dwight H. (1966). *Market Control and Planning in Communist China*, Cambridge, Mass.: Harvard University Press.

Preobrazhensky, Evgeny (1926). *The New Economics*, trans. 1965, Oxford: Clarendon Press.

Riskin, Carl (1987). *China's Political Economy. The Quest for Development since 1949*, Oxford: Oxford University Press.

Rural Development Institute, Chinese Academy of Social Sciences (RDI, CASS). *Green Report. Annual Report on Economic Development of Rural China in 1993 and the Development Trends in 1994*, Beijing: China Social Sciences Publishing House.

Sah, Raaj Kumar, and Stiglitz, Joseph E. (1984). 'The economics of price scissors', *American Economic Review*, 74 (1): 125–38.

————(1986). 'The economics of price scissors: reply', *American Economic Review*, 76 (5): 1195–9.

————(1992). *Peasants Versus City-dwellers. Taxation and the Burden of Economic Development*, Oxford: Clarendon Press.

Sheng Yuming (1993a). *Intersectoral Resource Flows and China's Economic Development*, London: Macmillan.

——(1993b). 'The capital sources of China's industrialization', *The Developing Economies*, 31: 173–207.

Sicular, Terry (1989). 'China: food pricing under socialism', in Terry Sicular (ed.), *Food Price Policy in Asia. A Comparative Study*, Ithaca: Cornell University Press.

——(1992). 'What's wrong with China's agricultural price policies', *Journal of Asian Economics*, 3 (1): 29–56.

——(1993). 'Ten years of reform: progress and setbacks in agricultural planning and pricing', in Y. Y. Kueh and Robert F. Ash (eds.), *Economic Trends in Chinese Agriculture*, Oxford: Clarendon Press.

World Bank, China Department (1990a). 'Consumer food subsidies', Working Paper 2 of the Grain Sector Review, Washington, DC.

——(1990b). 'Grain marketing, price policy and foreign trade', Working Paper 7 of the Grain Sector Review, Washington, DC.

——(1990*c*). 'Investment in agriculture', Working Paper 8 of the Grain Sector Review, Washington, DC.

——(1991). *China. Options for Reform in the Grain Sector*, World Bank Country Study, Washington, DC.

——(1996). *World Development Report 1996*, Washington, DC: World Bank.

Zhao Xinghan, and Wiemer, Calla (1991). 'Closing the price scissors gap: reform and the interface between agriculture and industry', typescript.

8

Rural–Urban Migration of Labour: Macroeconomics

We have shown in Chapter 3 that China is characterized by an urban–rural income differential that is large by international standards. It is appropriate, therefore, that China's migration experience be examined against this international yardstick. We begin, in Section 8.1, by providing a theoretical framework for the analysis. Section 8.2 sets out the history of China's migration policy and experience, and explains the institutional controls over migration. The chapter goes on, in the remaining sections, to present a macroeconomic overview of the phenomenon in China. However, this broad approach limits the depth of the analysis. Chapter 9, by contrast, analyses a particular case study in depth and develops precise tests of hypotheses. However, its findings may not be generalizable to China as a whole. The strength of each of these complementary chapters is the weakness of the other.

Research on migration involves severe methodological problems. A census of population is likely to provide the best general picture of migration. However, there is a limit to the amount of information on migration that can be obtained from a census. Most applied research on migration has to be based on sample surveys. These can be either rural or urban surveys. The former examines migration from the origin, obtaining only indirect information on the destination, whereas the latter examines migration to the destination, only incidently learning about the origin. A rural household survey can provide a representative sample of migrants, making possible the comparison of migrants and non-migrants in order to examine the causes of migration, and can show the effects of migration on the rural household. However, such a survey is likely to lack detailed knowledge of migrants because many are absent from the homestead. An urban survey of migrants can collect detailed information on the migration process. However, we cannot tell from it how the migrants differ, in their characteristics and treatment, from other urban workers unless it is a general urban labour force survey. The different types of survey complement each other. In Section 8.3 we examine first urban-based and then rural-based surveys relating to migration. Section 8.4 poses the topical question: how many rural–urban migrants are there in China? The concluding Section 8.5 draws together the evidence and presents a general picture of migration in China.

8.1 A THEORETICAL FRAMEWORK

In free labour markets where the movement of labour is unrestricted and wages are determined competitively, we would expect migration to tend to equalize the returns to labour among rural areas and between rural and urban areas. In many developing countries this does not occur. The main symptom of this failure is a very considerable difference between rural and urban incomes. The income difference seems to be impervious to market forces.

This is generally explained in terms of one or more of the following arguments. First, employers find it profitable to raise wages above the competitive level. Examples of this argument are the 'efficiency wage' theory and the 'labour turnover' theory. According to the former, an increase in the wage raises the quality of recruits, improves morale, or reduces incentives to shirk, and according to the latter it cuts labour turnover and so reduces training costs. Secondly, employees are well organized and have the power to bargain with employers for higher wages. Thirdly, a broader version of this argument is the explanation in terms of 'urban bias'. The claim is that urban workers, and urban people generally, possess disproportionate political power and influence, and that this biases government policies in their favour. Urban incomes are raised and protected and urban infrastructure and services receive priority over rural.

Where an urban–rural income difference exists and cannot be closed, it acts as a magnet to migrants from the rural areas. The influx of migrants does not depress the wage; instead it generates urban unemployment. This phenomenon has led to the formulation of probabilistic migration models. Migrants are attracted by the prospect of securing wage employment. However, as migration occurs, urban unemployment and underemployment in the self-employment sector rise and the chances of securing wage employment fall. Net migration stops when migrants become indifferent as to whether to go or to stay. The equilibrating variable in this model is thus not the wage but urban unemployment.

A high urban wage is likely to generate high urban unemployment and poverty among the rural–urban migrants. Poor people may have escaped from rural poverty, but in some cases they have merely entered urban poverty. Cities are often ringed with slums. The squatters suffer from poor housing, inadequate infrastructure and services, low incomes, high unemployment in both its open and disguised forms, and the attendant social problems. Many governments attempt to oppose excessive urbanization of this sort but they are often both prisoners of urban bias and unwilling or unable to prevent the inflow of migrants. The economic and social problems which excessive rural–urban migration can cause have attracted much attention from development economists, and there is a large literature on the subject.

The temporary migration of household members should be studied in the context of the household—its resources, objectives, and constraints. The appropriate theoretical approach is to analyse the household costs and benefits of migration. Even if there is a net benefit from migration, the household may be constrained from migrating by lack of access or opportunities. Both household and individual characteristics may be relevant because they can influence whether a household has an incentive to send out a migrant, which household member it will send out, whether an individual has an incentive to migrate, and whether the household, or the individual, has an opportunity to migrate.

Consider first the benefits of migration. These are twofold: income gain and risk reduction. The additional income accruing to the migrant, part of which will be transferred to other household members, must be weighed against the opportunity cost in the form of household income forgone. The marginal product of household labour within the village is therefore directly relevant. Setting aside issues of intra-household income distribution, the net benefit is in principle quantifiable by means of household income function analysis. Absolute income gain is not necessarily the criterion for migration. In rural China there is frequently a strong community life within the village. It is therefore possible that people make income comparisons within their village reference groups, which generate feelings of relative deprivation or satisfaction. Relative incomes within the village may be more important than absolute income in explaining migration. In that case migration may be higher for the poorer within the village but not for the poorer villages, and higher in villages with greater inequality. Even though a migrant may be even more deprived in relation to the host area than to his village, he may feel less deprived on account of the migration because he continues to relate to the village.

Migration can reduce household risk whenever incomes from different sources are not perfectly co-variate. Migration may involve high short-term risk during the process of job search but, if the migrant finds employment, his subsequent risk is likely to be low and his income fluctuations weakly correlated with those of village income. The poorer the household the greater the harm from loss of income: the degree of risk-aversion is likely to decline as household income rises. Poorer households may therefore have a greater incentive to send out a migrant either if they face higher economic rents in migrant employment, or if they are more risk-averse than richer households. On the other hand, poorer households, being more risk-averse, may be unwilling to bear the initial risk of migration. The extent of risk and the benefits of reducing it are not easily quantified, and the risk hypothesis is accordingly difficult to test. Normally successful migration both raises income and lowers risk. However, if migration were found actually to lower household income, this would suggest that it served a risk-averting function.

The costs of migration include not only the indirect, opportunity costs but also the direct costs—including travel costs, payments for permits from the origin and destination authorities, and the cost of job search. These last costs can be substantially reduced if the job can be lined up before departure or on arrival. Hence the importance of contacts—relatives and friends—in easing the migrant's path to a job. Setting out from the village is a hazardous venture: for many it is a venture shrouded in ignorance, hearsay, curiosity, and optimism. Informational and support networks are important in reducing the risk that the venture will fail. The existence of migrants within the household or the village, whether absent or returned, makes migration less costly and less risky. Migration begets further migration on account of this diffusion process, and networks of migrants tend to cluster geographically.

Even if households or individuals have a strong incentive for migration, they may be prevented by lack of opportunities. If the labour market is not competitive and does not clear, a surplus of job-seeking migrants does not depress their wage. Employment is then rationed by employers according to their recruitment criteria. There is accordingly a risk that migration will fail. Constraints on the household or the individual can be brought within a cost-benefit framework using the concept of 'expected value'. If migrants are risk-neutral, the value of the benefit can be equated with the benefit of a sure job multiplied by the probability of obtaining it. This is a concept that underlies the probabilistic models of rural–urban migration: migration occurs, and urban unemployment and hence the probability of employment adjusts, until an equilibrium is reached. In equilibrium the expected value of the urban wage is equal to the rural supply price.

A distinction is drawn in the literature between the high-wage formal sector and the low-income informal sector providing either wage-employment or self-employment in the urban areas. The former is difficult to enter whereas the latter contains a free-entry segment. Migration can depress labour income in the free-entry segment to a level even below the rural supply price, if that offers the psychological benefit of improving the probability of a high-wage job. The equilibrium size of the informal sector will vary according to the institutions and recruitment practices of the labour market.

When faced with uncertainty migrants attempt to reduce the risks that they bear, and would indeed be prepared to pay for some form of 'insurance'. Hence the emergence of self-employed labour recruiters, of urban enterprises themselves going to recruit in the rural areas, and of rural labour organizations. Hence also the importance of informal contacts, which can provide informational and support networks.

These theoretical strands can be found in the extensive literature on rural–urban migration in developing countries. For instance, Todaro (1969), Sabot (1982), and many others have developed probabilistic models of migration, Banerjee (1986) has stressed the role of migrant contacts and networks, and Stark (1991) has analysed the effects of risk and relative deprivation on migration. We now have an analytical framework for our empirical examination of rural–urban migration in China.

8.2 THE INVISIBLE GREAT WALL

China has gone through different phases of rural–urban migration. Rapid industrialization occurred in the early years of Communist Party rule. It required the rapid growth of the urban labour force. This was made possible by rural–urban migration, as peasants responded to the call to assist in reconstruction and industrialization. For instance, between 1949 and 1957 the urban population increased by 56 per cent, from 10.6 to 15.4 per cent of the total population (Table 8.1). The net inflow of migrants from rural to

TABLE 8.1 *Urban population and net migration into the urban areas of China, 1949–93*

Period	Event	Urban population		Net rural–urban migration	
		Million	As per cent of total	Million	Million p.a.
1949		58	10.6		
1949–57	Rapid industrialization			30	3.3
1957		99	15.4		
1958–60	Great Leap Forward			25	8.3
1960		131	19.7		
1961–5	Strict controls and rustication			−26	−5.2
1965		130	17.9		
1966–77	Cultural Revolution			2	0.1
1977		167	17.6		
1978–83	Rural reform			46	7.7
1983		241	23.5		
1984–93	General economic reform			83	8.3
1993		334	28.1		
1949–77	Planning era			31	1.1
1978–93	Reform era			129	8.0
1949–93	Communist rule			160	3.6

Source: Gu and Li 1995: table 17; PRC, SSB 1986: 71; 1995: p. 59.

urban China cannot be directly observed. It must be derived as the residual difference between the growth of urban population, on the one hand,
and the part that is due to natural increase and rural–urban reclassification,
on the other. We rely on the estimates of Gu and Li (1995). On that basis,
30 million of the 41 million increase during the period 1949–57 represented net migration (Table 8.1).

This was also the period in which the instruments of control over the
movement of population were put in place. The collectivization of agriculture, culminating in the establishment of the communes, gave the State
power over rural people and their movement. The *hukou* system of household registration provided a means of preventing permanent change of residence, and the system of rationing grains, housing, and other necessities was
a means of restricting temporary migration. In the mid-1950s the State
became concerned about the tide of migrants and made various attempts
to stem it, including the introduction of centralized hiring of peasants, its
method of rationing basic necessities, and the enactment of a series of laws
to restrict movement (Goldstein and Goldstein 1990: 64–5).

Controls were loosened during the Great Leap Forward (1958–60) as
government accelerated industrialization and famine drove peasants from
the land. Some 25 million peasants moved to the towns and cities over these
three years (Table 8.1). It was not until the collapse of the Great Leap
Forward that the controls were reasserted in response to urban unemployment and food shortages. By then the urban population had reached 131
million. In the ensuing five years the inmigrants were sent back to their villages and strict curbs on migration were enforced. The urban population
fell slightly, as the effect of rustication outweighed that of urban natural
increase (Table 8.1).

The Cultural Revolution (1966–76) saw an exchange of urban and rural
labour. Urban youth and cadres—perhaps 17 million of them (Shen and
Tong 1992: 190)—were rusticated to the countryside. Peasants were draft-
ed into factories, partly in the cities and partly in new areas to which strate-
gic industries were moved as a precaution against war. Net migration was
estimated to be negligible over the decade (Table 8.1).

The rural reforms of 1978–84 involved the disbanding of the communes
and the introduction of the household responsibility system, so reducing
official intervention in the lives of peasants. The relaxation of controls,
the greater availability of food, the creation of urban grain markets, and
the return of young people from the countryside together brought a sharp
net inflow into the urban areas. Moreover, rural industrialization created
new towns populated by former peasants, and the accelerated rate of economic growth made residual urban jobs available for migrants. The loosening of registration controls rendered the measurement of migration less
accurate. Many migrants created jobs for themselves in the previously
repressed urban informal sector—as street-traders, shoe-repairers,

carpenters, household-helpers, etc.—making it difficult to identify them both at the place of work and at the place of accommodation. Nevertheless, net rural–urban migration over the five years 1978–83 is put at 46 million (Table 8.1).

The economic reforms were extended to urban China in the mid-1980s. The accelerated growth of the urban economy, the relaxation of rules on peasant settlement in towns and small cities, and the general loosening of social controls reduced the constraints on migration. Net rural–urban migration is estimated at no less than 83 million over the decade 1984–93, a period in which urban population grew by 92 million (Table 8.1).

Over the forty-five-year period 1949–93 net rural–urban migration was some 160 million, accounting for 58 per cent of the urban population growth. Whereas the corresponding figures for the planning era (1949–77) were 31 million and 28 per cent, for the subsequent reform era they were 129 million and 77 per cent respectively. Rural–urban migration has become an important phenomenon.

Throughout the period of Communist Party rule the differential in living standards between rural and urban areas has provided rural people with a great incentive to migrate townwards. Government has been concerned to stem the potential tide of rural migrants, and it has done so with varying degrees of vigour and success. The State has possessed a variety of instruments for controlling migration: the household registration (*hukou*) system, urban rationing of basic necessities, and laws regulating movement. By these means it built an 'invisible Great Wall' against rural–urban migrants, a wall that has become more permeable over time.

There are two forms of migration in China, which must be clearly distinguished. There is *hukou* migration, which is permanent, and non-*hukou* migration, which is temporary. In fact only the former is referred to as 'migration' (*qianyi*): the latter is called 'floating' (*liudong*). Consider each in turn.

Permanent migration is controlled through the registration system. Under a law of 1958 each Chinese person is registered as being resident in a particular place. Any change of registration requires official approval. This registration (*hukou*) system is implemented by public security bureaux that fall under the administration of local governments—cities and townships (formally communes). A change of *hukou* confers legal rights to be resident in the new locality and to share the resources of the community. In the case of the village, this involves rights to land for farming and housing. In the case of the city, it involves rights to a package of benefits, including state-subsidized food and housing and access to a permanent job. Although *hukou* migration is subject to strict control through central government policy, it is also influenced by local government concerns. Since possession of a *hukou* gives entitlement to local resources, there is an incentive for local governments to exclude outsiders from their resources. The *hukou* system, especially in the pre-reform era, functions as a *de facto* internal passport mechanism.

Entitlement to an urban *hukou* comes primarily through urban birth. *Hukou* migration for work can occur through job assignment or recruitment. Generally, if rural people acquire higher education, they can obtain an urban *hukou* through job assignment. Similarly, officers retiring from the military services (*zhuanye*) have an opportunity to obtain urban rights. Peasants can acquire urban *hukous* if their farmland is taken over for urban use, or if they are recruited by state enterprises to unpopular jobs such as road-worker or miner. Marriage between a rural and an urban person would not generally enable the former to acquire an urban *hukou*. Permanent movements between rural localities or from a large city to a small one are more easily permitted than movements from rural to urban areas and particularly to large and medium-sized cities.

The procedures for *hukou* transfers to a city are as follows. Each year a city government decides how many outsiders should be accepted by the city. Entry quotas are allocated to departments (the personnel bureau for 'cadres' and the labour bureau for 'workers'). A city enterprise can employ people from outside the city only if they are assigned by one of the bureaux or if it is allocated a quota. A *hukou* migrant has to find a willing employer who must apply to the local government on his behalf. Personal connections (*guanxi*) may be important. The successful applicant receives two certificates: one from the local public security bureau (*hukou zhun ruo zheng*) and another from the employer (*danwei jieshou zhangming*), allocating him to the city and the work unit. The previous *hukou* is simultaneously withdrawn. He must register at a neighbourhood office of the public security bureau, providing personal details. When the rationing of basic necessities was important, the ration was based on this registration and the reported personal characteristics.

In recent years the *hukou* system has been preserved but its effectiveness has declined. Without the need to provide subsidized food, city governments are somewhat less concerned to restrict *hukou* migration. It has become possible to buy an urban *hukou* in most of the towns and small cities at a high, revenue-raising price. However, the restrictions on the transfer of residential registration continue to be rigidly enforced in the case of permanent movement from the rural areas to the big cities.

We turn to temporary migration, i.e. movement without *hukou* transfer. During the planning period grain and some other necessities were distributed within an urban locality entirely through a system of ration coupons. Rural people could hardly survive for long in a city without rations. It was illegal to trade coupons although black markets did exist. Prior to the early 1980s, non-*hukou* migration was therefore extremely difficult. During the first stages of the reform, when a 'dual-track' price system operated, rationed food was distributed at low prices, as before, and higher prices prevailed in free food markets. Rural people could now obtain grain in the city, but only at the high, market prices. The coupon system was abolished in 1993, although it reappeared in some cities in 1994 in response to food price inflation. It had become easier for the non-*hukou* migrants to live in the city. Moreover, with free markets for food, peasants could buy grain to meet their production quotas, i.e. to pay their taxes in the form of compulsory grain sales to state agencies, so that they could more easily leave their farms.

The burgeoning inflow of rural–urban migrants in the 1990s threatened urban residents with economic competition—for jobs and for resources—and with social problems, such as disorder and crime. City governments have increasingly attempted to protect their citizens against these threats. They pursue active policies to regulate the inflow of migrants.

City labour bureaux are known to classify jobs into urban *hukou* jobs and jobs open to migrants but with urban workers receiving preference. To implement their policies city labour bureaux impose quotas on the number of migrants that each enterprise can employ; these are enforced by inspection teams. The restrictions are sensitive to the state of the city labour market, being tightened if unemployment rises. City governments make price as well as quantity interventions. Enterprises must pay for their quotas. Similarly, enterprises receive subsidies, in the form of tax relief, if they recruit redundant workers (*xia gang* employees, who need no longer attend work but continue to be paid low wages by the relinquishing enterprise).

These institutions are designed to ensure that rural migrants are allowed in to meet residual needs for labour, filling the jobs that urban residents do not want. The controls on migration insulate the urban labour market from the rural labour market, and segment the urban labour market between regular employees (with urban *hukous*) and temporary or casual employees (mostly with rural *hukous*).

Those migrants who cannot get urban *hukous* remain second-class citizens in the urban areas. They cannot enter 'permanent' jobs, with the associated welfare benefits, including medical insurance, retirement pension, and housing. Any welfare benefits they receive from their employers are a privilege and not a right. Their children may not be able to attend school in the city because they do not have the necessary neighbourhood *hukou;* if they are admitted, they are required to pay high fees. Most importantly, the migrants generally live in cramped and poor accommodation, often provided by their employers, and would find it very difficult to get accommodation for their families.

8.3 SURVEY EVIDENCE

We consider the evidence on migration that can be gleaned first from urban-based and then from rural-based surveys. Only one national urban-based survey of migrants into urban areas is known to us. This is a sample survey of migrants conducted in 74 cities and towns throughout China in 1986 (PRI, CASS 1988): 25,500 households were sampled, containing 100,300 people. The sample was stratified by city size, there being 43 cities (15 very large, 6 large, 12 medium and 10 small) and 31 towns, covering 16 provinces. Almost all of the results were presented separately for each city size, rather than for urban China, but the sample was found to be representative of people in cities and towns respectively for China as a whole (ibid. 331).

The majority of urban people in China were either born locally or arrived prior to 1949. However, 38 per cent of the permanent urban residents of the sampled households had arrived in their town or city after 1949; they were designated the in-migrants (Table 8.2). Inmigration increased during the period of economic reform: 15 per cent of permanent urban residents had arrived in the period since 1978, and 4 per cent had arrived in the previous two years. In addition to the permanent urban residents, permanent out-migrants (whose permanent residence was now elsewhere) represented 6 per cent of the permanent residents. There were also temporary residents (without local *hukous*) living in the sampled households of permanent residents; these numbered under 4 per cent of permanent residents, although they reached 9 per cent in dynamic Guangdong.

Unfortunately the survey tells us little about the extent and nature of temporary migration. The survey covered only those temporary migrants living in the sampled permanent urban households. It therefore excluded

TABLE 8.2 *Resident and migration status of household members: 74 cities and towns survey, 1986*

	Numbers	As per cent of permanent residents
1. *Permanent residents*		
Born in the city or town	62,165	62.0
In-migrants	38,102	38.0
Out-migrants	31,650	31.6
of which: long-term	7,606	7.6
short-term	24,044	24.0
Total permanent residents	100,267	100.0
2. *Not permanent residents*		
Temporary residents	3,628	3.6
Permanent out-migrants	6,177	6.2
3. *Total enumerated*	110,072	109.8

Notes: The dividing line between short- and long-term out-migration is one year.

Source: PRI, CASS 1998: 1, 109–13.

the many rural–urban migrant workers who live in hostels, hotels, dormitories, workshops, construction sites, and the like, and in accommodation outside the city boundaries. Nor were the sampled temporary residents likely to be representative of rural–urban migrant workers. Only 51 per cent had come from rural areas, 56 per cent had stayed for less than a month, and a mere 15 per cent had come for work-related reasons.

The survey is more informative about *hukou* migrants. A distinction can be made between cities and towns. Permanent in-migrants as a proportion of permanent residents were 37 per cent for cities and 45 per cent for towns. There is no clear pattern by city size but the figure is lowest (34 per cent) for very large cities. It appears that the *hukou* regulations were applied more tightly in the cities than in the towns, and most tightly in the very large cities.

Much of the *hukou* migration had taken place among urban areas. The proportion of urban migrants coming from the countryside was 41 per cent in the case of cities and 58 per cent in the case of towns (PRI, CASS 1988: 114–16). This means that rural–urban migrants accounted for only 17 per cent of permanent urban residents. Only a minority of the permanent moves (44 per cent) were work-related; almost as many (42 per cent) could be regarded as marriage- or family-related (ibid. 338). Most of the rural–urban migrant workers were university graduates, demobilized soldiers, or peasants who had lost their land to urban development. The permanent migrants generally considered that their move had been beneficial. No fewer than 71 per cent reported that their income had improved as a result of the move, 65 per cent their housing conditions, 65 per cent their career, 67 per cent their opportunities for education, 75 per cent their cultural life, and 77 per cent their living environment (ibid. 131–6). These results would probably be strengthened if we could isolate the rural–urban migrants. The rural people who had been able to secure urban registration were indeed fortunate.

Gu and Li (1995) reported a survey of migrants in Hubei province. They contrasted permanent migrants, who had moved their *hukou* registration, and temporary migrants, who had not (Table 8.3). The table shows that the permanent migrants were better-educated, reflecting the difficulty of poorly qualified people changing their places of registration. Only a quarter of permanent migrants had been registered in agricultural households, i.e. as peasants, before they migrated, whereas 90 per cent of temporary migrants held agricultural *hukous*. Similarly, very few of the temporary migrants (22 per cent) were from the urban areas. Whereas 74 per cent of permanent migrants worked in state-owned or collective enterprises, only 26 per cent of temporary migrants did so, the remainder working in private and individual enterprises. For both categories, the motives for migration extended beyond income to conditions, welfare, and security.

We examine two rural-based surveys, both conducted by the Rural

TABLE 8.3 *Characteristics of permanent and temporary migrants, Hubei province,*
1988

	Permanent migrants	Temporary migrants
Education		
upper-middle school or above	58	8
lower-middle school or below	42	92
Hukou before migration		
agricultural	25	90
non-agricultural	75	10
Origin: from		
city	26	6
town	30	16
village	44	78
Employment: ownership of enterprise		
state-owned	19	6
collective	55	20
private and other	26	74
Motive to migrate (workers)		
higher income	24	32
better conditions	25	26
better welfare	21	18
greater stability	14	18
other	15	5
Total	100	100

Note: Each figure is expressed as a percentage of its column total.
Source: Gu and Li 1995: 57–8.

Development Institute of the Chinese Academy of Social Sciences.[1] One
related to 1986 and the other to 1993; both are well representative of rural
China. We begin with the labour force survey of 1986 (RDI, CASS 1989).
This covered fifty-nine counties in eleven provinces, and over 1,000
natural villages with a total population of 432,000.

There are three main ways in which peasant households can attempt to
improve their incomes. One is to increase farm production, the second is
to transfer to non-farm activities in the village, and the third is to seek
income and employment outside the village. In recent years rural incomes
have increased rapidly in China as a result of all three strategies. In 1986
village labour was allocated as follows: 61 per cent in farm and 24 per
cent in local non-farm activities, and 15 per cent away from the village
(Table 8.4). However, 7,800 in-migrants partly offset the 27,000 migrants
from the village.

TABLE 8.4 *The allocation of labour, 1986 village survey*

	No.	Percentage of rural labour force
On the farm	107,873	60.6
In non-farm activities	43,223	24.3
Out-migrants	26,993	15.2
of which: in agriculture and fishing	2,179	1.2
In-migrants	7,793	4.4
of which: in agriculture and fishing	531	0.3
Total village-based labour	178,089	100.0

Source: RDI, CASS 1989: 16–18.

The survey documents the change in the village economy over the period 1978–86, i.e. the eight years after the inception of the rural economic reforms (Table 8.5). This provides the context for explaining migration behaviour. It is appropriate to deflate values by the rural retail price index. In real terms, the gross social output of the sample of villages rose fourfold and net income per capita threefold. Most remarkable was the restructuring of village production: primary production accounted for 85 per cent of the total in 1978 but for only 43 per cent in 1986. In that year agriculture represented no more than 25 per cent and industry no less than 43 per cent of gross social output. The population of these villages was up by less than a tenth, reflecting the introduction of the one-child-family policy, but the labour force was up by a third. The ratio of village labour to land thus rose. However, the rapid increase in non-agriculture employment relieved pressure on the land: primary sector workers fell in number. Economic progress was also assisted by the doubling of fixed assets, so raising the ratios of capital to labour and to land. There was a 15 per cent rise in the cultivated area per agricultural worker and a 62 per cent rise in the number of agricultural machines per agricultural worker. The 85 per cent increase in farm output cannot be explained by increased agricultural yields: grain production and yield were up by no more than 10 per cent. Rather, it was due to diversification away from grains, e.g. to oil-bearing crops, fishing, and other sideline activities, and to an improvement in the terms of trade (as measured by the ratio of product prices to the rural retail price index).

Table 8.6 documents the change in the village non-farm economy over the period 1978–86. It shows a phenomenal growth of non-agricultural output since the inception of the economic reforms which enabled the villages to respond to economic opportunities from a disequilibrium situation. Non-farm employment increased fourfold and real wages by half. The profits of non-farm enterprises provided local government revenues, in turn raising

TABLE 8.5 *Change in the village economy, 1978–86*

	1978	1978 (1986 prices)	1986	1986 (1978 = 100) (constant prices)
Gross social output (10,000 yuan)				
Primary	7,170	9,279	19,546	211
of which: agriculture	4,754	6,152	11,381	185
Secondary and tertiary	1,238	1,602	25,475	1,590
of which: industry	973	1,259	19,325	1,535
Total	8,407	10,880	45,020	414
Net income per person	115	149	475	319
Population (000)	375		410	109
Labour force (000)				
Primary	131		115	88
Secondary and tertiary	10		74	740
Total	141		189	134
Fixed assets				
total (10,000 yuan)	3,696	4,783	10,392	217
per worker	26.2	33.9	55.0	162
per mu of land	0.904	1.169	2.551	218

Note: 1978 values are converted to 1986 prices using the rural price index (PRC, SSB 1991: 243). Between 1978 and 1986 this index rose by 29.4%.

Source: RDI, CASS 1989: 5–6, 14, 19–21.

the quality of village services such as education and health. It is clear that most of the trebling in the village income per capita came about through local diversification, i.e. a transfer into non-farm village activities. How much was due to migration? Unfortunately the survey does not report remittances, and the measure of net income per capita is derived from gross social output in the village, not from the income of village members. Our only guide to the importance of out-migration for village income is the allocation of the village labour force: in 1986, 15 per cent were working away from the village whereas 24 per cent were in local non-farm activities.

Many peasant households seek to diversify their portfolio of activities but few become specialist migrant households. Nor do individuals necessarily specialize. Of the local non-farm workers—those who 'leave the land, stay in the village'—57 per cent had transferred their activity for the whole year and 43 per cent were seasonal. By contrast, only 21 per cent of the migrants—those who 'leave the land, leave the village'—were away from the village throughout the year and 79 per cent were seasonal. The most

TABLE 8.6 *Change in village non-farm economy, 1978–86*

	1978	1978 (1986 prices)	1986	1986 (1978 = 100) (constant prices)
1. Enterprises				
No. of enterprises	322		2,665	828
No. of employees	9,370		37,363	399
Gross output	1,498	1,939	23,545	1,214
Profit	257	333	3,607	1,083
Tax and fees to township government	161	208	2,380	1,144
Average income per employee	489	633	942	149
2. Household enterprises				
No. of household units	33		3,539	10,724
No. of workers	229		20,631	9,009
Gross output	56	72	8,777	12,190
Profit	7	9	1,218	13,533
Tax to township government	1	1.3	403	31,000
Rural enterprise income used for the community	152	197	653	331
Non-farm fixed assets	661	855	5,582	653

Note: As for Table 8.5.

Source: RDI, CASS 1989: 10–14.

common form of seasonal migration (56 per cent of the total) was for 3–6 months.

Table 8.7 makes it possible to compare the characteristics of three groups: the village labour force as a whole, non-farm workers, and migrants from the village. We see that men are more prone to change sector or location than are women. No less than 60 per cent of migrants were aged under 36. Precisely a third of the village labour force had more than primary schooling. This contrasts with 39 per cent for non-farm workers, 28 per cent for migrants, and 42 per cent for in-migrants. The sampled villages tended to export less-educated workers (35 per cent of whom were illiterate) and to import more-educated workers. Many of the in-migrants had artisanal skills. The more educated villagers had a better chance of securing local non-farm employment, illiterates being at a particular disadvantage in this respect. No less than 45 per cent of the non-agricultural workers were employed in industry and 18 per cent in construction. Very few of the migrants from the village entered agriculture, it being the most common for them to enter construction (32 per cent worked in that sector).

TABLE 8.7 *Characteristics of migrants by type of migration: 1986 village survey*

	Percentage of column total		
	Non-farm workers	Migrants from the village	All village-based labour
Male	74	78	53
Female	26	22	47
Age: –17	2	3	—
18–35	53	60	—
36–45	60	30	—
46–55	10	6	—
55+	2	1	—
Education: college and technical	0.1	0.1	0.2
upper-middle school	10	7	8
lower-middle school	29	21	25
primary school	41	37	38
illiterate	20	35	28
Agriculture	—	2	56
Other primary	—	6	8
Industry	45	17	20
Construction	18	32	4
Transport	8	6	3
Commerce	6	4	1
Catering	5	4	2
Other	18	29	5

Notes: Village-based labour comprises farm workers, non-farm workers, and migrants from the village. In-migrants are not included.

Source: RDI, CASS 1989: 16–19.

Table 8.8 shows the destinations of the migrants: 49 per cent remained in the rural areas and 51 per cent went to the urban areas. One-third of whole-year migration was to other villages and two-thirds to towns and cities. Similarly, seasonality was associated with proximity, it being most common for migration to rural areas within the province and least common to big cities. Almost two-thirds of migrants made their own arrangements to migrate and just over a third were organized by a collective.

In summary, in 1978 the rural economy of China had been in severe dis-equilibrium, effectively confining village labour to farmwork, mainly grain production. The relaxation of restrictions made possible both local non-farm and migration activities. During the early period of rural reform, the remarkable improvement in the village economies alleviated poverty and reduced surplus labour. Migration from the villages therefore probably

TABLE 8.8 *Destination of migrants: 1986 village survey*

	Percentage of column total			Seasonal as a percentage of total
	All migrants	Whole year	Seasonal	
Rural	49	35	52	85
of which: same county	21	14	22	86
other county, same province	24	15	27	87
other province	4	6	3	67
Urban	51	65	48	74
of which: rural town	5	6	5	77
county town	12	15	11	74
city	29	29	30	79
big city	4	12	2	34
abroad	6	3	0	3
Total	100	100	100	79

Source: RDI, CASS 1989: 17.

played a secondary role. Nevertheless, the incentive for migration remained strong despite the rapid rural industrialization, and could increasingly be acted upon. The 1986 survey suggests the following patterns of labour allocation. Better-educated, male workers, from both inside and outside the village, tend to enter village industry, the in-migrants often bringing particular skills. Less-educated, male workers are more prone to migrate from the village, largely on a seasonal basis, and to enter non-farm employment not requiring much skill. Women, by implication, are more likely to remain on the farm. Much migration into and out of the village is within the county and there is relatively little migration across provincial boundaries. Roughly half of the migrants go to other rural areas and half to urban areas; of the latter, two-thirds go to cities and one-third to towns.

A second rural survey, relating to 1993, was conducted by the Rural Development Institute specifically to gather information on migration and migrant incomes. It used a national sample of the Agricultural Bank of China, covering twenty-six provinces and 440 counties. The information to be gleaned from the brief questionnaire is set out in Table 8.9. The 13,000 households averaged 4.75 members, 2.60 labourers, and 0.26 migrants. Migrants were defined as household members who lived and worked outside the village for more than thirty days in 1993. The implication is that 10 per cent of rural labour force participants were migrants. Nearly a quarter of households (23.1 per cent) had at least one migrant, 18.9 per cent

TABLE 8.9 *Characteristics of rural households and migrants: 1993 migration survey*

	Mean value or percentage
Information on households	
Households (no.)	13,102
Household members (per household)	4.75
Household workers (per household)	2.60
Household migrants (per household)	0.26
Household with migrants (%)	23.10
Household income (yuan p.a.)	6,857
Migrant remittances as a proportion of household income (%)	7.49
Information on migrants	
Sex: male	81.9
female	18.1
Age (years)	30.0
Education completed: illiterate	3.6
semi-literate	3.4
primary	24.0
lower-middle	54.1
upper-middle	14.8
college	0.1
Destination: urban	81.0
rural	19.1
Sector of employment: agriculture	4.2
industry	21.6
construction	32.9
transport	10.3
commerce	31.0
Duration of migration (days)	206.3
Duration of migration (months): 1–3	18.6
4–6	29.2
7–9	19.1
10–12	33.1
Total income of migrant (yuan p.a.)	3,061
Remittances of migrant (yuan p.a.)	1,963
Remittances as a proportion of migrant income (%)	64.1

Notes: 1. All the data relate to the calendar year 1993.
    2. A mean is presented in the case of continuous variables and a percentage in the case of categorical variables.
    3. The omitted provinces are Heilongjiang, Shanghai, Guangdong, and Tibet.

Source: RDI, CASS: personal communication.

having one, 3.6 per cent having two, and 0.6 per cent having three migrants. By 1993 labour migration had become an important phenomenon in rural China.

We see from the table that 82 per cent of the migrants were male, their mean age was 30, and no less than 54 per cent of them had lower-middle school education. Eighty-one per cent migrated to urban areas and 19 per cent to rural areas. However, only 30 per cent left their province. Inter-province migration is both economically more costly and bureaucratically more difficult. The most important sectors of migrant employment were construction (33 per cent) and commerce (31 per cent).

The migrants were away from the village for an average of 206 days during 1993 (56 per cent of the time), although the standard deviation was high (102 days). The number of short-term (1–3 months) migrants was fairly low (19 per cent) and the number of non-seasonal (9–12 months) migrants somewhat higher (33 per cent). Among the latter were migrants who had been away since before 1993. A regression analysis with the total income of migrants as the dependent variable produced a highly significant coefficient on the explanatory variable 'days away from the household'. Each day away adds 11.65 yuan to migrant income: this is the best estimate of the daily wage of migrants in 1993.

The total income of migrants averaged 3,061 yuan over the year, of which 1,963 yuan was remitted home. It is clear from the high proportion of income remitted (64 per cent) that the typical migrant retains very close ties with the rural household and remains part of it. The average rural income per household, including migrant remittances, was 6,857 yuan. Migrant remittances represented 7.4 per cent of rural household income overall, and a much higher proportion—roughly a third—of income in the households containing migrants.

By 1993 migration had become an important source of employment for a quarter of rural households, and an even more important source of income for them. The 1993 migrants were better educated, less seasonal, and more urban-oriented than their 1986 predecessors. It is also plausible—although we lack the necessary evidence—that some migrants with rural *hukous* were becoming more attached to urban work and life, moving repeatedly between town and village.

8.4 HOW MANY RURAL–URBAN MIGRANTS?

At a recent conference on rural migration in China, a variety of figures for the number of rural–urban floating migrants were cited, ranging from 30 million to 150 million.[2] These discrepancies are partly due to the lack of good data and analysis. However, there are also conceptual difficulties.

To arrive at a precise figure, location, duration, and activity have to be specified. A rural migrant might be defined as someone who works 'outside', be it outside the village or the township or the county. It would be sensible, for instance, to exclude daily commuters. A distinction should be made between rural–urban and other sorts of migrant (rural–rural, urban–urban, urban–rural), and this requires definitions of rural and urban areas. What is the minimum period to count as migration: a week, a month, a year? We need to distinguish between work-related migrants and those who migrate for other reasons, for instance to visit relatives. The difference between stocks and flows of migrants should be recognized. A stock of migrants is the number on any particular date, whereas a flow is the number who migrate during a particular period, say a year. If the average length of time in the city is six months, then the number of migrant-years of work is half the number of workers who migrate; twice as many people are classified as migrants (the flow) as there are migrants on any day (the stock).

These conceptual and definitional problems help to explain the variety of estimates of rural–urban migrants in China. The problem is compounded by the lack of a single 'correct' concept. The choice of concepts, and thus of definitions, should depend upon the research questions being asked.

It is natural to begin with the census. The 1990 national census of population provides some but limited information on rural–urban migration. Migrants are defined as persons who moved their residence from one county or city to another county or city between 1 July 1985 and 1 July 1990. Residence in 1985 is defined as usual place of residence. Current residence in 1990 is broader than *hukou* registration. It includes also persons who were resident in the county or city and whose registration was unsettled or who had been away from their *hukou* place for over a year. This definition therefore included all such persons who were at least 5 years old, and not just those who moved in order to work. However, it excluded non-*hukou* migrants who had been away from their *hukou* place for less than a year, and *hukou* migrants who had moved more than five years previously.

We see from Table 8.10 that there were 34 million migrants on the census definition, of whom 43 per cent had moved for work-related reasons. On the one hand, this is likely to be a considerable underestimate of the total number of floating migrants (as it excludes those who had come in the previous twelve months), and the number of permanent migrants (as it excludes those who had come more than five years previously). On the other hand, rural–urban migrants constituted only half of the total (17 million). A third of the migrants had moved between urban areas and another seventh between rural areas. The reported rural–urban migrants represented 2.3 per cent of the population aged at least 5 in 1990.

A better indication of the importance of temporary migrants is to be obtained from a survey of the floating population of various Chinese cities

TABLE 8.10 *Migration by rural or urban origin and destination, 1985–90: 1990 census of population*

Origin	Destination (million)			Destination (per cent of total migrants)		
	Urban	Rural	Total	Urban	Rural	Total
Urban	11.47	1.32	12.79	33.6	3.9	37.5
Rural	16.72	4.58	21.30	49.0	13.4	62.5
Total	28.19	5.90	34.09	82.7	17.3	100.0
Total, work-related			14.66			43.0

Notes: 1. Migration is as defined in the text.
2. This summary information has been completed from the extremely detailed information of a 180-page table.

Source: PRC, SSB 1993: vol. 1, table 1.22; vol. 4, table 11.1.

in 1988 (Li and Hu 1991). The floating population represented 23 per cent of the permanent population of twenty-five cities (ibid.: table 22). The figure was 24 per cent for Beijing but as high as 42 per cent for Guangzhou. Numbers had consistently risen over the 1980s. For instance, the 1980 proportions had been 9 per cent overall, 7 per cent in Beijing, and 18 per cent in Guangzhou (ibid.: table 27).

These figures relate to large cities and may not apply to smaller cities and towns. However, an extrapolation would be illustrative. The twenty-five cities covered by the survey had a total population of 66 million in 1988, of which 12 million (18 per cent) were floating population. If the same ratio had applied to the urban areas in general, with their population of 287 million, the floating population would have been 52 million.

Not all of the floating population nor all of the permanent urban population are in the labour force. In fact only 58 per cent of the temporary migrants (in eleven of the surveyed cities) had come for economic reasons (Li and Hu 1991: table 1). However, in 1988 almost the same proportion (56 per cent) of people in permanent urban households were employed (PRC, SSB 1995: 262). Thus migrants represented roughly the same proportion of the urban labour force as of the urban population. Some of the floating population had come from other cities or towns. Only 59 per cent (in the seven cities for which data are available) were from the rural areas or from the rural suburbs of their host cities (Li and Hu 1991: table 6). Combining these figures from disparate sources, we infer that rural–urban temporary migrant labour amounted to 14 per cent of the permanent labour force (12 per cent of the total labour force) in the survey cities in 1988.

TABLE 8.11 *Temporary migration from rural areas, 1980, 1984, and 1988*

	1980	1984	1988
Migration flow (million)			
to all areas	35	59	98
to urban areas	26	41	61
Average duration of migration (per cent of year)	56	56	59
Migration stock (million)			
to all areas	20	33	58
to urban areas	15	23	36

Source: World Bank 1991: table 1, compiled from a variety of sources.

A World Bank study (1991), based on all the empirical information available at that time, arrived at estimates of temporary migration of rural people in China. These were not hard estimates but involved numerous assumptions. The number of temporary rural migrants rose rapidly over the 1980s—from 35 million in 1980 to 98 million in 1988 (Table 8.11). Of the 1988 migrants, 61 million migrated to the urban areas. The average duration of migration then averaged 59 per cent of a year. The stock of rural–urban migrants in that year was therefore 36 million, having risen from 15 million in 1980 (Table 8.11).

The 1993 national rural household survey conducted by the Rural Development Institute and discussed in Section 8.3 can be used to estimate the number of rural–urban migrants (Table 8.12). No fewer than 10.6 per cent of the rural labour force went outside the township for work for at least a month in 1993. Only 79 per cent of this number were rural–urban migrants, i.e. 8.4 per cent of the rural labour force. These figures represent the flow of migrants during the year. On average each migrant worked outside for 205 days. The figures can be converted into a stock—the number of migrants working outside the township on any date—from the average duration of migrant work (56 per cent of the year). On that basis 6.0 per cent of the rural workers were away from the township, and 4.7 per cent were in the urban areas, at any time.

The sample should be well representative of rural China as it covered 13,000 households drawn from 440 counties in twenty-six provinces. We extrapolate to China as a whole by multiplying the ratio of migrants to persons in the sample by the total rural population of China in 1993 (852 million). The results are also shown in Table 8.12. On that basis the number of rural people going to work outside their township during 1993 was 50 million, and the number working in the urban areas 39 million. The corresponding stock—the number of rural migrants at any time—would have been 28 and 22 million respectively. These may well be the best estimates

TABLE 8.12 *Estimate of the number of rural–urban migrants in China in 1993*

	Rural sample			Rural China No. (million)
	No.	Per cent of labour force	Per cent of population	
Persons	67,268			852
Labour force	37,076			443
Migrants				
total flow	3,931	10.6	5.8	49.8
rural-urban flow	3,086	8.3	4.6	39.1
total stock	2,208	6.0	3.3	28.0
rural-urban stock	1,733	4.7	2.6	22.0

Notes: 1. Migrants are defined as those who left the township to work for at least a month in 1993.
  2. The national figures are estimated by applying the ratio of migrants to rural people in the sample to the national rural population.
  3. The migrant stock, i.e. the number away from the township at any time, is estimated by multiplying the number of migrants by the ratio of mean days worked outside (206) to 365.

Sources: RDI, CASS 1994: 110–11; PRC, SSB 1995: 59, 278.

available of the recent size of the 'floating' population, i.e. temporary rural–urban migrants.

8.5 CONCLUSION

The rigid control of rural–urban migration was a cornerstone of the policies which created and maintained the rural–urban divide in China. Without it, the income disparity between urban and rural China would have served as a magnet to rural people wanting to better themselves, and it would not have survived. The 'invisible Great Wall' has become more permeable during the period of economic reform. However, it remains very difficult for rural-born people to acquire rights to permanent urban residence. Moreover, central and local governments attempt to control the flow of temporary rural–urban migrants so as to meet the needs of the urban economy while avoiding urban unemployment and giving preference to urban residents.

There is very little survey evidence as yet published on rural migrants temporarily working in the urban areas. There is rather more information based on rural household surveys, although it is largely of a descriptive nature. The evidence suggests that rural people have diversified away from farming into both local and migrant non-farm activities. It appears that, by 1993, migrant remittances accounted for over 7 per cent of rural household income, and for about a third of the income of migrant households. The average duration of absence away from home was under seven months. Migrant ties with their rural households thus remained strong. It is extremely difficult to quantify the number of rural migrants working in the urban areas. However, our estimates suggest that in 1993 about 10 per cent of rural workers migrated, and that the total flow to the urban areas was about 40 million.

It has not been possible with the available evidence to test hypotheses about migration of the sort set out in the theoretical section above (Section 8.1). Accordingly, we decided to conduct our own survey in a particular prefecture comprising both urban and rural areas, in order to gather the micro-level data necessary for hypothesis-testing. We report our analysis in Chapter 9.

NOTES

1. We are grateful to the Rural Development Institute for allowing us access to the surveys and to Dr Liu Jianjin for his collaboration in their analysis.
2. The International Conference on the Flow of Rural Labour in China, organized by the Research Centre for Rural Economy, Ministry of Agriculture, and the Ford Foundation, was held in Beijing, 24–7 June 1996.

REFERENCES

Banerjee, Biswajit (1986). *Rural to Urban Migration and the Urban Labour Market*, Bombay: Himalaya Publishing House.

Goldstein, Sidney, and Goldstein, Alice (1990). 'China', in Charles B. Nam, William J. Serow, and David F. Sly (eds.), *International Handbook on Internal Migration*, Westport, Conn.: Greenwood Press.

Gu Shengzu, and Li Zhen (1995). 'The impact of reform on structural change in the Chinese economy. The case of Hubei Province', Duisburg Working Papers on East Asian Economic Studies 24, Duisburg.

Li Mengbai, and Hu Xing (1991). *The Impact of the Floating Population on the Development of Big Cities in China*. Beijing: Institute of Urban and Rural Construction (in Chinese).

People's Republic of China, State Statistical Bureau (PRC, SSB) (1986). *Statistical Yearbook of China 1986*, Oxford: Oxford University Press.

———(1991). *China Statistical Yearbook 1991*, Beijing: State Statistical Bureau.

———(1993). *Tabulation on the 1990 Population Census of the Peoples' Republic of China*, 4 vols., Beijing: China Statistical Publishing House.

———(1995). *China Statistical Yearbook 1995*, Beijing: China Statistical Publishing House.

Population Research Institute, Chinese Academy of Social Sciences (PRI, CASS)

(1988). *China. Migration in 74 Cities and Towns. Sampling Survey Data, 1986*, Beijing: Population Research Institute (in Chinese).

Rural Development Institute, Chinese Academy of Social Sciences (RDI, CASS) (1989). *Survey Materials of the Chinese Village Labour Force, 1978–1986*, ed. by Yu De Chang, Beijing: State Statistical Bureau (in Chinese).

Sabot, Richard (ed.) (1982). *Migration and the Labor Market in Developing Countries*, Boulder, Colo.: Westview Press.

Shen Yimin, and Tong Chengzhu (1992). *Population Migration in China—Historical and Contemporary Perspectives*, Beijing: China Statistical Publication House.

Stark, Oded (1991). *The Migration of Labor*, Cambridge, Mass.: Blackwell.

Todaro, Michael (1969). 'A model of labour migration and urban unemployment in less developed countries', *American Economic Review*, 59 (2): 138–48.

World Bank (1991). 'China's Floating Population and the Labor Market Reforms', preliminary draft, word-processed, December, Washington, DC: World Bank.

9

Rural–Urban Migration of Labour: Microeconomics

The empirical analysis of the previous chapter, although nationally representative, was based on surveys that provide only limited or descriptive information. We therefore decided to conduct our own surveys in a particular city and its surrounding rural areas. This had the great advantage that we could delve more deeply into the causes, processes, and consequences of migration, but it suffered the potential disadvantage that its results might not have general applicability. We chose Handan municipality in Hebei province, a city which, with its surrounding counties, is well representative of a large part of inland China.

In Section 9.1 we describe the two surveys on which our microeconomic analysis will be based. In Section 9.2 we examine the causes of migration in two ways: by analysing the characteristics of migrants relative to non-migrants and by reporting attitudinal responses. In Section 9.3 we analyse the relationships between migrant income and other sources of household income, exploring the notions of substitutes and complements and of risk-spreading portfolios. Section 9.4 examines the processes of migration: the roles of the family in migration decisions, of information flows, and of urban contacts. Section 9.5 considers some of the consequences of migration, including the contribution that it makes to rural incomes and to the alleviation of poverty.

9.1 THE SURVEYS AND THE DATA

The surveys were conducted in Handan, a municipality comprising a city and surrounding counties in the southern part of Hebei Province, over 400 km from Beijing. The survey of rural–urban migrants was conducted in Handan itself, a city of nearly a million people, and the survey of rural households was conducted in two (rural) counties falling under the authority of the municipality, Handan county and Wuan city. Handan city and its surrounding areas are fairly typical of a large part of central China. The city has a good deal of heavy industry and the surrounding rural areas have medium density of population and average agricultural resources. These counties are not particularly poor nor remote, and the province contains poorer rural areas more distant from Handan and other cities. The surveys were planned and supervised, and the questionnaires and sampling procedures designed, by the authors. We are confident that the information which we gathered is reliable and appropriate for the purposes of this chapter.

The Handan survey of rural–urban migrants (RUM) was conducted in October 1992. The survey covers individual migrants, both those who have arrived in the city and those who remain in the county but have decided to migrate and are on the Handan job waiting list. Because it selects migrants, the sample does not permit a comparison of migrants and non-migrants or of their households, nor of the circumstances which cause some people to migrate and others to remain. However, the dataset does allow us to examine the rural–urban migrants, their attitudes, the conditions which caused them to go to the city, and the processes by which they migrated.

The flow of migrants into the city is a recent phenomenon which was not planned nor expected by the city government. Migrants have not been systematically monitored, registered, or organized. Migrants are scattered throughout the city and there is no single official department in charge of them. Although longer-term migrants are required to register at a police station, many seasonal and even longer-term migrants do not bother and can easily avoid police registration. Urban household surveys are not necessarily the best approach as they are likely to underrepresent migrants, many of whom live in makeshift housing, in streets, station sheds, workshops, or in peasant homes around the city. The *ad hoc* solution was to take a purposive but random sample of 737 migrants (workers without an urban *hukou*) concentrated in two activities. Some 552 migrants were sampled from thirteen enterprises in the city known to employ temporary migrants as well as permanent urban-dwellers. Another 185 were sampled at labour bureaux in the (rural) counties, where they had registered as job-seekers on the waiting list for employment in Handan.

The Handan rural household survey (RHH) was conducted in August 1993. The sample comprises 1,000 households in seven administrative villages (previously brigades) within two counties under Handan municipality. A stratified random sample of villages was chosen. The two main criteria in selecting the villages were distance from cities and income level. As could be expected, income level was closely related to either or both the extent of village industry and the endowment of agricultural resources. It was decided to sample from a limited number of villages because of the role that a village itself—its resources, organization, and social networks— might play in migration. The mean number of households sampled per village (140) was sufficiently large for reliable inferences to be drawn about villages. When selecting households within an administrative village we randomly chose a natural village (formerly production team) and sampled all its households, in order to avoid the bias that might enter through the casual replacement of unwilling households. The household questionnaires were supplemented with information gathered about each village.

The RHH survey, by distinguishing migrant and non-migrant workers, and households with and without migrants, can help to explain the determinants of migration. It can throw light on the processes and facilitating factors, and measure some of the economic costs and benefits. It is also possible to analyse the relationships between migration and poverty or its alleviation. The survey is confined to out-migrants from the villages as in-migrants lived separately from the sampled village households.

9.2 THE DETERMINANTS OF MIGRATION

Migration can be an individual decision or a household decision. In either case, both the individual and the household are relevant to the decision. For instance, an individual may decide whether to migrate but the decision may depend on the characteristics of the household and on the activities of other household members. Where migration is a household decision the identity of the chosen migrant may depend on individual characteristics. Similarly, the household head may take the decision bearing in mind the characteristics both of the household and of the potential migrant. The objective function can be governed by, but is in principle independent of, the decision process. Irrespective of how the decision is made, the welfare both of the migrant and of other household members is likely to be taken into account.

Accordingly, we adopt two approaches, both by means of binary logit analysis. In examining individual migration our dependent variable is the dichotomous variable indicating whether the worker is a migrant or a non-migrant. In analysing migration within the household, the dependent variable is whether the household does or does not contain a migrant worker. In both approaches it is desirable also to analyse the role of the environment in which the people live—best captured here by the characteristics of the village.

The analysis is based on the RHH survey, containing as it does both migrants and non-migrants. Labour migration is defined as work by a household member aged 16 or over outside the (rural) township (formerly commune), whether in a rural or an urban area, for at least one month during 1992. Eleven per cent of the 2,458 workers recorded in the survey were migrants, and 23 per cent of the 1,000 households reported having migrants. Eighty-three per cent of the migrants went to urban areas and 17 per cent to rural areas, although only 2 per cent worked in the farming sector. Over half (54 per cent) of the rural–urban migrants were away for ten or more months of 1992. The average distance migrated was not far (30 kilometres) but too far for commuting. Two-thirds (68 per cent) of the migrants worked within their own county.[1] The mean age of migrants was 34 years, 88 per cent were male, 57 per cent were household heads, and 71 per cent were

TABLE 9.1 *Mean characteristics of migrant and non-migrant workers*

	Migrants	Non-migrants
Mean age (years)	34	37
Male (%)	88	45
Household head (%)	57	37
Married (%)	71	76
No education (%)	4	14
Primary school (%)	28	34
Lower-middle school (%)	51	41
Upper-middle school (%)	12	9
Post-secondary school (%)	6	2
Communist Party member (%)	10	5
No. of observations	274	2,184

Source: RHH, 1993.

married. Two-thirds (68 per cent) had got beyond primary school. Table 9.1 shows mean values of these and other characteristics of both migrant and non-migrant workers. The migrants are on average younger than the non-migrants, and higher proportions of them are male, household heads, and Communist Party members; and they are distinctly better educated.

The type of migration which we can examine by means of the survey is temporary (otherwise the migrant would not be registered as part of the household) and not involving the entire household (otherwise the household could not be interviewed). Migration can have economic motives—income gain or income risk reduction—or social motives. However, the explanatory variables in our logit estimations can have both economic and social interpretations. For instance, the rural–urban income differential facing migrants might vary with age, and thus yield predictions about the age composition of migrants. However, age may be a proxy for such attributes as adventurousness and risk-taking. Similarly, men and women may have different economic incentives to migrate based on the income differentials that they face, or their different propensities to migrate might reflect their different social roles. Education might raise the economic benefits of migration or it might broaden horizons and boost confidence. Personal experiences such as army service and travel might overcome informational constraints or mould tastes. The variables most likely to have an unambiguous interpretation are economic variables such as income and wealth.

We examine first the migration of individual workers. The explanatory

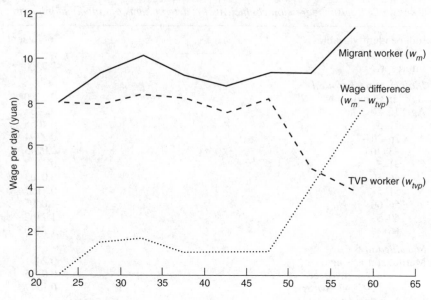

FIG. 9.1 *Daily wage of migrant and TVP workers, by age-group*

variables can be classified as biological (predetermined characteristics such as age and sex), social (educational, marital, and health status), and personal life-experience (army service, cadre service, Party membership, and travel experience). The results of a logistic regression (the dependent variable being migrant = 1) are shown in Table 9.2.

The biological variables are important and alone explain over 80 per cent of the baseline chi-square. There is significantly more migration of workers under 26 and significantly less of workers over 55: the probability of a worker aged 21–5 migrating is 9 per cent and of a worker aged 56–60, 2 per cent, *ceteris paribus* (Table 9.3). The reason cannot be found in terms of income gain. Migrant earnings are significantly higher, *ceteris paribus*, in the age-range 26–55 than in the range 16–25 (Table 9.4). Figure 9.1 shows the age profiles of the daily wages, of migrants (w_m) and of township, village, and private (TVP) enterprise employees (w_{tvp}) in the RHH sample.[2] The experience of migrants is rewarded in their wages: the gap ($w_m - w_{tvp}$) rises consistently with age. Economically rational rural workers should be more willing to migrate when they are older. The explanation for the observed converse relationship may lie in the fewer domestic responsibilities and the greater sense of adventure, modernity, and adaptability of young people.

The coefficient on female gender is significantly negative: the probability for men is 10 per cent and for women 6 per cent. The 11 per cent of

TABLE 9.2 *Logistic regression coefficients for determinants of individual migration*

Independent variables	Coefficient
Intercept	−2.7300***
Biological background	
Gender: female	−2.2290***
Age: 16–20	0.5437
21–5	0.4055
26–30	0.2794
36–40	0.0245
41–5	0.3417
46–50	0.0703
51–5	0.3157
56–60	−1.0005*
60–5	−1.2162
66+	−1.3360*
Social features	
Marital status: single	0.2401
divorced	0.0275
widow(er)	0.1777
Health status: normal	0.2443
weak	−0.6052
often sick	−0.8828
disabled	−1.0983
Education: college or above	1.5185**
professional high school	1.0144***
upper-middle school	−0.0696
4–6 years primary school	−0.0999
1–3 years primary school	0.2109
no education	−0.0008
Life experience	
Never served in army	−0.5668**
Never a local cadre	0.6498**
Not Communist Party member	0.4297
Has travelled to:	
very large city	0.1006
capital city of province	0.3145*
provincial-level city	0.2636
county town	0.2930
small town	0.4368**
other rural areas	−0.2570
Handan city	−0.0860
−2 log likelihood	1,682.69
No. of observations	2,377

Notes: 1. ***denotes statistical significance at the 1%, **at the 5%, and *at the 10% level.
2. Omitted dummy categories are: age 31–5, married, male, healthy, lower-middle school, has served in the army, has been a cadre, Party member.
3. The dependent variable is whether the individual is a migrant.

Source: RHH, 1993.

TABLE 9.3 *The propensity to migrate: probability estimates based on Table 9.2*

Characteristics	Probability (%)
Biological background	
gender: male	9.9
female	6.0
age: 16–20	9.7
21–5	8.6
26–30	5.9
31–5	7.7
36–40	6.0
41–5	8.2
46–50	6.3
51–5	7.9
56–60	2.3
61–5	1.8
66+	1.6
Social features	
marital status: married	6.1
single	7.6
divorced	6.2
widow(er)	7.2
health status: healthy	6.3
normal	7.9
weak	3.5
often sick	2.7
disabled	2.2
education: college or above	23.3
professional high school	15.5
upper-middle school	5.8
lower-middle school	6.2
4–6 years primary school	5.7
1–3 years primary school	7.6
no education	6.2
Life experience	
served in army	10.0
never served in army	5.9
was a local cadre	3.6
never a local cadre	6.7
Communist Party member	4.4
not Communist Party member	6.6
travel experience: travelled to:	
very large city —yes	6.8
—no	6.2

TABLE 9.3 *Continued*

Characteristics	Probability (%)
provincial capital —yes	7.7
—no	5.8
provincial city —yes	7.0
—no	5.5
county town —yes	6.6
—no	5.0
small town —yes	7.2
—no	4.8
other rural areas —yes	6.0
—no	7.6
Handan city —yes	6.2
—no	6.8

Note: The probabilities are calculated by giving all variables their mean values other than the variable being examined. When the probability is estimated by standardizing on all mean values the estimated probability is 6.3%. The actual proportion of migrants in the sample is 11.4%.

Source: RHH, 1993.

migrants who were female tended to be not the first but the additional migrants of their households. Over half (52 per cent) of the female migrants to Handan in the RUM survey had other family members working in Handan (compared with 30 per cent in the case of men). The urban labour market was less welcoming to women than to men: the monthly income of female migrants was 22 per cent lower than that of male migrants, *ceteris paribus* (Table 9.4).

Turning to social characteristics, we note that the coefficients on marital status are not significant (Table 9.2). Especially when the sorts of job open to rural–urban migrants require physical effort, their health status will be important. Those workers who were 'weak', 'often sick', or 'disabled' had lower probabilities of migration (2.2–3.5 per cent) than healthy or non-disabled workers (6.3–7.9 per cent).

With respect to educational level, there is a clear distinction between those with college or professional high-school education and those with less education (Table 9.2). The coefficients of the former are highly significant, their probabilities of migration being 23 and 16 per cent respectively, whereas the propensity to migrate among other categories falls in the range 5.7–7.6 per cent. The returns to college education for migrants are clear from Table 9.4, but there is no pattern among the other educational categories. For instance, a professional high-school graduate receives 19 per

TABLE 9.4 *Earnings function analysis of out-migrants*

Independent variables	Coefficients
Intercept	5.526***
Female	−0.251***
Not household head	−0.015
Age 21–5	−0.042
26–30	0.195*
31–5	0.315***
36–40	0.299**
41–5	0.226**
46–50	0.263**
51–5	0.119
56–60	0.259
61+	−1.089***
Education: professional high school	−0.209
upper-middle school	−0.193
lower-middle school	−0.206
4–6 years primary school	−0.283*
1–3 years primary school	−0.204
no education	−0.142
Not Communist Party member	0.051
Married	−0.047
F-value	4.856
$\bar{R}^2$	0.213
No. of observations	270

Notes: 1. *** denotes statistical significance at the 1%, ** at
the 5%, and *at the 10% level.
2. The omitted dummy variables are male, household
head, age 16–20, college education, Communist
Party member, not married.
3. The dependent variable is the logarithm of income
per month in yuan.

Source: RHH, 1993.

cent less than a college graduate and a primary school graduate receives
25 per cent less. Since many migrants are employed in temporary,
unskilled, unpleasant jobs, the limited influence of education on pay is
not surprising. When the occupation terms were added to the equation
(not shown), none of the coefficients was significantly different from the
omitted term, non-farm labourer. Table 9.5 shows that occupational
skills are very little rewarded in the temporary jobs that migrants normally
occupy.

TABLE 9.5 *Migrants by occupation: percentage distribution and mean wages*

	Percentage of total	Mean wage (yuan per month)
Cadre or managerial staff	11	286
Professional or technician	16	249
Office clerk	4	230
Service or supporting worker	12	206
Manual worker in non-farm sector	32	238
Skilled manual worker in non-farm sector	13	254
Manual worker in farm sector	9	251
Individual trader	2	208
Total	100	241

Note: The total number of migrants is 276.

Source: RHH, 1993.

Personal life experience can have a bearing on migration. Army service broadens the horizons and social skills of young migrants. The coefficient of army service is positive and almost doubles the probability of migration, from 6 to 10 per cent. Travel experience, whether to the capital city of a province or to a small urban town, significantly increases the propensity to migrate. This result could reflect personal qualities or represent the mind-broadening and information-gathering effects of travel. Service as a local cadre has a significantly negative effect, reducing the probability of migration to less than 4 per cent. Local cadres have the knowledge and contacts for local income opportunities.

We turn to the analysis of migration based on the household. We mean by this the migration of at least one household member. Seventy-seven per cent of households had no labour migrants, 19 per cent had one migrant, and only 4 per cent had two or more. The logistic regression estimates with dependent variable 'household has a migrant' are shown in Table 9.6.

No less than 57 per cent of the migrants were household heads. It is not surprising, therefore, that the characteristics of household heads are important in the logit equation. Three specifications are presented in the table: we concentrate on eq. (1) but the differences are generally only minor. Households with young (<26 years) or old (46–60 years) household heads are more prone to send out migrants—often the head in the former case and a child of the head in the latter. Table 9.7 shows the probabilities of the household having a migrant, changing one variable at a time while holding all others at their mean values. We see how the probability varies from 21 per cent (household head aged 16–20) to 6 per cent (36–40) to 19 per cent

TABLE 9.6 *Logistic regression coefficients for determinants of migration from households*

Independent variables	Coefficients		
	Eq. (1)	Eq. (2)	Eq.(3)
Intercept	−6.955***	−7.537***	−2.978***
Female-headed household	0.835***	0.559*	0.149
Age of household head: 16–20	0.641	0.683	1.405
21–5	0.210	0.163	0.307
31–5	−0.334	−0.237	−0.082
36–40	−0.808**	−0.779**	−0.548*
41–5	−0.526	−0.385	−0.012
46–50	0.343	0.388	0.617*
51–5	0.498	0.439	0.427
56–60	0.087	0.102	0.209
61–5	−0.709	−0.506	−0.584
66+	−1.008	−0.819	−0.837
Household head: never a soldier	−0.715**	−0.807**	−0.766**
never a cadre	0.672*	0.803*	0.729**
not a Party member	0.657*	0.721*	0.603*
No. of labourers: 2	0.193	0.469	0.059
3	0.560	0.845**	0.183
4	0.975*	1.413***	0.885**
5	1.684**	2.044***	1.106*
Household members	0.476***	0.468***	0.650***
Land (in mu)	−0.044	−0.047	−0.122***
Mean years of education per worker	0.069**	0.092***	0.022
Two-generation household	0.533	0.654	0.438
Three-generation household	0.585	0.575	0.600
Household with non-kin	−0.329	−0.139	0.035
Partly owned business	1.423***	1.119***	0.679*
Wholly owned business	0.027	−0.341	−0.411
No contact in urban area	−0.167	−0.217	−0.409**
Wealth (000 yuan)	0.033***	0.026**	−0.004
Agricultural income (000 yuan)	−0.190*		
Business income (000 yuan)	−0.890***		
TVP income (000 yuan)	−0.250**		
Income transfer, private (000 yuan)	−1.100***		
Income transfer, official (000 yuan)	−0.580*		
Income relief (000 yuan)	−1.670		
Non-migrant income (000 yuan)		−0.400***	−0.470**
Village: 1	3.313***	3.574***	
2	3.886***	3.535***	
3	2.090***	2.300***	
4	3.277***	3.402***	
5	2.446***	2.619***	
7	5.090***	5.149***	
Percentage of cases predicted correctly	84	82	81
−2 log likelihood: chi-square for covariations	357.178***	314.634***	185.461***
No. of observations	997	997	997

Notes: 1. *** denotes statistical significance at the 1%, ** at the 5%, and * at the 10% level.
2. Omitted dummy categories are: male-headed household, age 26–30, has been a soldier, has been a cadre, Party member, one labourer, one-generation household, household without non-kin, no partly owned business, no wholly owned business, contact in urban area, village 6.
3. The dependent variable is whether the household has a migrant.

Source: RHH, 1993.

TABLE 9.7 *The propensity to migrate: probability estimates based on Table 9.6*

Characteristics	Probability (%)
Household-head characteristics	
Male	18.9
Female	9.2
Age: 16–20	21.0
36–40	5.9
51–5	18.7
Has been a soldier	17.0
Never a soldier	9.1
Has been a cadre	6.0
Never a cadre	11.0
A Party member	6.1
Not a Party member	11.2
Household characteristics	
Mean years of education of household workers: 0	6.6
6	9.7
12	14.0
Has a partly owned business	30.1
No partly owned business	9.6
Contact in urban area	11.0
No contact in urban area	9.5
Land (mu): 3	11.0
6	9.8
9	8.7
Household workers: 2	9.2
4	18.1
Household members: 4	11.0
6	24.3
Wealth: mean	10.2
mean + one standard deviation	14.9
Income: mean	12.8
mean + one standard deviation	3.9
Village: 1	17.0
2	26.6
3	5.7
4	16.5
5	7.9
6	0.7
7	54.8

Note: The probabilities are calculated by giving all variables their mean value other than the variable being examined. When the probability is estimated by standardizing on all mean values the estimated probability is 10.2%. The actual proportion of migrant households in the sample is 23.2%. The calculations are based on eq. (1) in Table 9.6 except for the income simulations, which are based on eq. (2).

Source: RHH, 1993.

(51–5). However, none of the 'age of household head' terms is significant. Female-headed households produce significantly more migrants than male, the probabilities being 19 and 9 per cent respectively, whereas women were shown to be significantly less likely to migrate in the individual migration equations. The explanation for the apparently discrepant results is that only 10 per cent of female migrants are household heads and 78 per cent of the migrants in female-headed households are from the generation below. Forty-nine per cent of the households headed by married women and having a migrant do not have a husband registered in the household. The registration of the husband elsewhere could be an inducement to migration of a household member. We find that access to local economic opportunities and resources, as represented by the household head's service as a local cadre or by his Party membership, significantly reduces the incentive to produce a migrant.

The probability of migration rises with the number of household members, *ceteris paribus*. This suggests that migration can be induced by the need for income. Table 9.6 also shows that migration is increased significantly if the household has shares in a non-farm business, but not if the household has sole ownership. Given the severe capital-market imperfections, households with shares may migrate to raise the resources to acquire sole ownership, whereas those with sole ownership may be tied to the village by their business. The coefficient of average years of education per worker in the household is significantly positive. Primary schooling (a rise from 0 to 6 years of education) raises the probability of migration from 7 to 10 per cent, and secondary schooling (6–12 years) raises it further to 14 per cent. This result appears more powerful than the relation for individual migrants, for whom only college or professional high-school education had a significant effect. It suggests that education may play an attitudinal rather than a human capital role.

We paid greatest attention to the most obviously economic characteristics of households: labour, land, farm production, and household income and wealth. The number of household labourers has a powerful effect on the propensity to migrate: the relationship is positive, generally significant, and monotonic. For instance, the probability of sending out a migrant rises from 9 per cent when there are two workers to 18 per cent when there are four. By contrast, the availability of more land slightly reduces the household's propensity to migrate.

The coefficient on household wealth was (in two of the three equations) positive and significant: if wealth was raised from the mean by one standard deviation, the probability of migrating rose from 10 to 15 per cent. By contrast, household non-migrant income (farm income plus wages from local rural industry plus business income) had a consistently negative and significant coefficient. When the income variable was raised from the mean by one standard deviation, the probability of migration fell from 13 to 4 per cent. Non-migrant income was also separated into six components: all six had negative coefficients, five of them significant.

How are the positive coefficient on wealth and the negative coefficient on income to be reconciled and explained? Households with lower income, *ceteris paribus*, face a larger urban–rural income disparity and therefore they have a greater incentive to migrate. By contrast, wealth—although part of permanent income—has no effect on the income gain to be derived from migration. Insofar as migration is undertaken to overcome a credit constraint, the possession of wealth, if not illiquid, discourages migration. Insofar as wealth provides the funds for travel and job search and reduces the household's aversion to risk-taking, wealth encourages migration. Our finding that wealth raises the propensity to migrate is probably to be explained in these terms. In particular, wealth may give households the confidence that a migration failure will not prove disastrous for them.

The village coefficients are all large, positive, and significant relative to the omitted category, village 6, which is the most prosperous village. Whereas the propensity to migrate in village 6 is 1 per cent, in village 7, where migration is a way of life, it is no less than 55 per cent. In village 2, the poorest village, the propensity to migrate is 27 per cent. Are these village effects symptoms or causes? They might simply be acting as proxies for correlated variables such as education, wealth, and income. They might, however, be important in themselves. Those villages with a richer history of migration should have stronger social networks on which potential migrants can draw, and some villages might have institutions, such as labour recruiters or labour teams, which organize and encourage migration. Both social networks and migrant organizations can reduce some of the transaction costs and risks involved in labour migration.

A comparison of eqs. (2) and (3) in Table 9.6 shows that the elimination of the village dummy variables reduces the positive coefficients on education and on wealth, and makes the income coefficient more negative. As the villages with smaller standardized migration probabilities tend to be better educated, wealthier, and to have higher income (the negative correlations shown in Table 9.8) it is possible that the introduction of village effects exaggerates the roles of education and wealth in raising the propensity to migrate and understates the discouraging effect of income. It is no less possible, however, that village institutions play an independent role. Table 9.8 shows that villages whose migrants have more migration experience display significantly higher propensities to migrate, *ceteris paribus* ($r = 0.86$). Moreover, village 7, the village with the highest coefficient, is known to have a village-owned labour contract company which sends out construction teams.

In order to gauge the economic gain from migration we need to measure the supply price of rural workers, based on their opportunity cost. This can be related either to the marginal product of labour (representing the

TABLE 9.8 *The role of the village in migration*

| | Village | | | | | | | Correlation with probability (r) |
	1	2	3	4	5	6	7	
Standardized probability of migration	17.0	26.6	5.7	16.5	7.9	0.7	54.8	
Mean migration experience of migrants (months)	62.9	70.3	66.2	27.9	74.8	21.4	160.1	0.86***
Mean education of household (years)	6.0	5.5	5.7	6.3	7.8	8.1	6.5	-0.34
Mean wealth of household (000 yuan)	4.22	1.88	16.87	11.08	6.35	23.15	12.10	-0.33
Mean non-migrant income of household (000 yuan)	3.80	1.37	3.31	2.23	1.81	4.08	1.53	-0.63

Note: ***denotes statistical significance at the 1% level.
Source: RHH, 1993.

TABLE 9.9 *Regression analysis: household farm production function*

Independent variable	Mean	Coefficient
Intercept		414.50***
Intermediate inputs (yuan)	340.62	1.02***
Hours of labour p.a.	312.29	0.52***
Farming land (mu)	5.69	70.25***
$\bar{R}^2$		0.15
F-value		54.00
Mean of dependent variable (yuan)		1,326.10
No. of observations		913

Notes: 1. *** denotes statistical significance at the 1% level.
2. The dependent variable is household net farm income.

Source: RHH, 1993.

opportunity cost of migration to the household) or to the average income per capita (proxying the loss of income for the migrant). The former is relevant if the migration decision involves household income maximization, and the latter if it involves individual income maximization.

We attempted to estimate the marginal product of labour in agriculture by means of a household farm production function (Table 9.9). The equation implies that an additional hour of labour raises farm production on average by 0.52 yuan. To explore the relationship between labour supply to farming and to migration, we regressed farm labour inputs on land, number of household workers, and number of migrants (Table 9.10). The equation implies that the annual labour input on the farm is raised 22 hours by an additional mu of farming land and 59 hours by an additional household worker, and is lowered 84 hours by an additional worker migrating out. The out-migration of one worker therefore reduces net farm income by only 44 yuan. Moreover, if that worker does not migrate, he will work 59 hours on the farm and thus bring 31 yuan more to household farming income. Either of these concepts may be relevant to the marginal product of labour on the farm: 31 or 44 yuan per annum.

The rural supply price should be compared with the marginal income to be gained from migration. Migrant remittances were regressed on land and the number of migrants (Table 9.11). Shortage of land encourages remittances but the crucial factor is the number of migrants: the marginal product of labour (income to the household) from migration is 1,501 yuan per annum. This figure is vastly greater than the marginal product of labour on

TABLE 9.10 *Regression analysis: household farm labour hours*

Independent variable	Mean	Coefficient
Intercept		76.30***
Farming land (mu)	5.72	22.24***
No. of labourers	2.26	59.74***
No. of migrants	0.28	−84.02***
$\bar{R}^2$		0.19
F-value		67.77
Mean of dependent variable (hours)		315.07
No. of observations		879

Notes: 1. *** denotes statistical significance at the 1% level.
2. The dependent variable is the number of hours that the household spends on the farm over the year.

Source: RHH, 1993.

TABLE 9.11 *Regression analysis: migrant remittances to village households*

Independent variable	Mean	Coefficient
Intercept		328.33***
Farming land (mu)	5.47	−29.74***
No. of migrants	0.27	1,501.27***
$\bar{R}^2$		0.46
F-value		417.91
Mean of dependent variable (yuan)		580.34
No. of observations		996

Notes: 1. *** denotes statistical significance at the 1% level.
2. The dependent variable is annual migrant remittances to the household in yuan, both goods and cash.

Source: RHH, 1993.

the farm. It is on a par with household mean non-migrant income per non-migrant worker—1,403 yuan per annum—which might serve as an indication of average product per worker in the village. But it is distinctly higher than average income per person (639 yuan) which is the more appropriate concept for the supply price of a maximizing individual.

The implication of these results is that the average household has a great economic incentive to reduce or even abandon farming and to send out migrants. This is backed up further by the evidence of surplus labour on the farm. Farms average 5.8 mu in size, and on average 312 working days are put in. The average number of workers per household is 2.11, which implies a labour supply of 633 working days if each worker is available for 300 days a year. There is a strong incentive to diversify away from agriculture either into local non-agricultural activities or through migration.

It is to be expected that the large rural–urban income difference will produce a strong income motive for rural–urban migration. We can examine this hypothesis by considering the attitudinal responses of the 554 rural–urban migrants in the Handan RUM survey and of the 1,000 rural household heads in the Handan RHH survey (Table 9.12). The fact that the responses of the two groups are so similar increases confidence in the reliability of the results. §1 suggests that economic motives are indeed important in temporary migration. The most frequently cited main reasons for migrating were land shortage, income gain, and skill acquisition. All three imply an income motive.

Although the migration observed was of individuals leaving their households of registration temporarily, it is notable that respondents had their long-term sights on the city. If they found a satisfying job, nearly four-fifths of the migrants would want to stay in it as long as possible, and only a small number were target workers (§2). While over a third of the migrants had a family member with them in the city (§3), 90 per cent of those without one wanted family members to join them, although frequently 'not yet' (§4). The most important conditions were that the respondent should first have a well-paid and long-term job and suitable accommodation (§5). More than half of the rural household heads, in answering a more hypothetical question, would want to move their family to the urban areas. Over two-thirds of respondents would like to get urban residence registration (§6). Moreover, more than half of those who did not wish to acquire an urban *hukou* gave as their reason the high charge made for transferring their registration (§7). When household heads in the RHH survey were asked the purchase price of an urban *hukou*, 51 per cent of respondents said 5,000 yuan precisely. The mean value was 3,912 yuan, i.e. 136 per cent of a migrant's annual wage. The sale of urban *hukous* has become a source of local government revenue.

This evidence that many rural people wanted to migrate on a long-term basis indicates the continuing disequilibrium nature of the Chinese labour market. A major reason for the disequilibrium is the disadvantage of rural people without urban *hukous* in competing with permanent urban residents for jobs and resources—as reflected in the market value of such *hukous*. Interestingly, the benefits of urban living were seen to be broader than income: the more frequently cited reasons were a convenient life, better

TABLE 9.12 *Attitudinal responses of rural–urban migrants and rural household heads*

§	Percentage of those responding	
	Rural–urban migrants	Rural household heads
1 *Main reason for migrating*		
shortage of land	34	7
more income obtainable	22	30
to learn skills	28	24
2 *If a satisfying job is found, duration of the work*		
as long as possible	78	73
learn skills and leave	13	16
save money and leave	8	12
3 *Family member or members here*	38	—
4 *Want family to join you*		
yes	54	59
yes, but not yet	36	—
no	10	41
5 *Conditions required to move your family**		
you have a long-term well-paid job	41	35
you have suitable accommodation for them	22	22
6 *Want an urban hukou*	70	49
7 *Main reason for not wanting an urban hukou*		
transfer charge too high	53	53
hard to get urban housing	9	8
wants to keep farming land	9	14
8 *Reasons for wanting an urban hukou**		
better education	28	20
convenient life	25	24
higher status	14	15
more income	13	16
9 *Main criterion for next job*		
higher income	51	57
better status	12	8
better working conditions	11	11
long-term contract	8	6

Notes: * relates to the first three reasons given.
— denotes that the question was not asked.

Source: RUM, 1992 (col. 1); RHH, 1993 (col. 2).

education, and higher status (§8). Income was the most important criterion for a job (§9) but the job was seen as only part of the urban package.

9.3 MIGRATION: SUBSTITUTE OR COMPLEMENT?

Table 9.13 shows the distribution of household labour inputs among various economic activities, both for all households in the RHH survey and for each quarter classified by household income per capita. Nearly two-thirds (64 per cent) of labour time is spent farming, local enterprise employment and migration are equally important (13–14 per cent), and non-farm business is least time-consuming (9 per cent). The penultimate column shows the total working days available per household (assumed equal to the number of household workers ×300). A comparison of this with total days worked yields a surplus labour rate (surplus days as a percentage of days available), shown in the final column. The surplus labour rate is high for all quarters but it falls from 33 per cent for the poorest to 23 per cent for the richest quarter. The high surplus labour rate suggests that the length of time that most households work is not voluntarily chosen, i.e. that farmwork is limited by availability of land and work in other activities by lack of opportunities.

Table 9.14 shows the implicit income per day from each of these activities. The considerable income variation across activities suggests that households should have strong preferences among them. For the sample as a whole, business income is the highest, followed by migration, local enterprise employment, and finally farming. Whereas daily income from migration is stable across quarters, daily income from other activities rises with income per capita. Thus the incentive to prefer migration diminishes as income per capita rises. For the poorest quarter of households, migration is the highest-paying activity; for the richest quarter it is on a par with farming. The amount of time spent in farming declines monotonically as income per capita rises; all the non-farm activities expand but in particular enterprise employment.

The difference in mean income between the richest and the poorest quarters is decomposed in Table 9.15. The majority of the difference (54 per cent) is due to differences in the level and composition of labour inputs. Why do the poorer households not work more days, and why do they not substitute away from their low-income activities, in particular farming, in favour of their high-income activities?

There are two possible explanations. The first is that poor households are poor because they have limited income-generating opportunities. Such households may be constrained by limited land and by the limited non-farmwork they can get. Farmwork is a residual activity, pursued only up to the point at which the marginal product of labour on the farm justifies the

TABLE 9.13 *The distribution of household labour among agricultural and non-agricultural activities, days and percentages, by income per capita quarter*

Quarter of households ordered by income per capita	Agriculture	Non-agriculture			Total time worked	Total time available	Surplus labour rate
		Business	Enterprise employment	Migration		days	percentage
	labour days (percentages)						
Poorest quarter	301	28	38	36	404	603	(33)
	(75)	(7)	(9)	(9)	(100)		
Second quarter	321	38	40	52	452	642	(30)
	(71)	(8)	(9)	(12)	(100)		
Third quarter	264	43	59	71	438	634	(31)
	(60)	(10)	(13)	(16)	(100)		
Richest quarter	265	53	112	71	501	655	(23)
	(52)	(11)	(22)	(14)	(100)		
All households	288	41	62	58	449	634	(29)
	(64)	(9)	(14)	(13)	(100)		

Source: RHH, 1993.

TABLE 9.14 *Income per day from various economic activities of households, by income per capita quarter*

Quarter of households ordered by income per capita	Income per day (yuan)				
	Farm work	Non-farm work			Total
		Business	Enterprise employment	Migration	
Poorest quarter	3.82	6.22	5.51	8.13	4.15
Second quarter	4.68	7.80	5.94	8.14	5.74
Third quarter	7.53	8.46	7.32	8.79	8.81
Richest quarter	9.06	17.08	7.23	9.67	12.65
Total	6.28	10.47	6.79	8.70	7.94

Source: RHH, 1993.

TABLE 9.15 *Decomposition of the difference in mean incomes between the highest and lowest household income quarters*

	yuan p.a.	percentage
Mean income of households in:		
highest quarter	6,338	
lowest quarter	1,677	
difference	4,661	100
Due to differences in:		
total hours		18
composition of activities		36
pay per activity day		46

Source: RHH, 1993.

marginal effort. Opportunities for local employment are rationed on account of limited resources or demand, and opportunities for migration are rationed on account of limited information or contacts. The second explanation is that households are unconstrained and are able to choose the level and composition of their labour inputs. They might, for instance, choose to retain farmwork, despite its lower income per day, as a risk-spreading form of insurance. Similarly, they might choose to limit their

TABLE 9.16 *Availability of non-farm jobs and deterrents to job search*

	Percentage of respondents
Have you ever looked for a non-farm job?	
yes	64
no	36
Main reason why not:	
no urban contacts	42
no funds to set up own business	23
no skills	27
no local TVPs	7

Source: RHH, 1993.

migration work, despite the higher reward per unit of labour, because of the risks, separation, and inconvenience that it involves. On this view, household differences in income are due to household differences in tastes.

Consider the survey evidence for or against these rival interpretations. A pointer against the voluntary choice explanation is suggested by Table 9.16: 36 per cent of rural household heads had never looked for a non-farm job; more than 40 per cent of these gave as their main reason their lack of urban contacts, and lack of business funds and lack of skills accounted for a further quarter each. The same constraints may in practice have operated against those who were not deterred from looking for non-farm jobs.

A pointer to the constrained choice explanation is the extent of surplus labour among rural households (Table 9.13). Moreover, the surplus labour rate depends on the degree of household diversification of activities. Table 9.17 shows that 22 per cent of households have income only from farming, and a further 50 per cent have income from farm and local non-farm sources. The next most common categories are households with income from both farm and migration (17 per cent) and households having all three income sources (10 per cent). The surplus labour rate is highest for households with only farm income (38 per cent) and lowest for households with all three income sources, those with two sources being intermediate. Income per capita is also seen to rise with the degree of diversification. Table 9.18 presents the results of a regression analysis of the number of days worked by households. Standardizing for the number of workers in the household and for their household resources, the number of household activities is an important determinant of days worked. By comparison with farmwork only, two activities add 165–240 days and three activities 355 days, the mean number of days worked being 444.

These results suggest that underemployed households which diversify their economic activities can become less underemployed and derive more

TABLE 9.17 *Proportion of households with various types of income source*

	Proportion of households (%)	Mean number of workers	Mean number of days worked	Surplus labour rate (%)	Income per capita (yuan per annum)
One source only					
farm	22	1.80	342.6	37.5	585
local non-farm	1	2.25	482.5	29.9	2,677
migrant	0	2.50	647.5	12.1	2,000
total	23	1.82	350.2	37.0	657
Two sources only					
farm + local non-farm	50	2.16	451.2	29.6	898
farm + migrant	17	2.32	480.3	28.3	969
local non-farm + migrant	0	1.00	352.5	17.7	—
total	67	2.19	458.4	29.0	952
All three sources	10	2.26	562.6	24.0	1,129

Notes: 1. 993 households were analysed.
2. The surplus labour rate is 100 $(A - W)/A$, where A = days available = no. of workers × 300, and W = days worked.

Source: RHH, 1993.

TABLE 9.18 *Regression analysis: the determinants of the number of days worked by households*

Independent variables	Coefficients
Intercept	63.162***
Labourers	85.650***
Land (mu)	18.656***
Productive assets (000 yuan)	1.848**
Household works in:	
local non-farm only	56.881
migration only	39.674
farm plus local non-farm	164.773***
farm plus migration	205.646***
non-farm plus migration	240.229***
all three activities	354.961***
$\bar{R}^2$	0.385
F-value	70.019***
Mean of dependent variable	443.843
No. of observations	995

Notes: 1. *** denotes statistical significance at the 1% and ** at the 5% level.
2. The omitted dummy variable category is 'farm only'. Households are classified according to whether they work any days in the activity.
3. The dependent variable is the number of days worked by the household.

Source: RHH, 1993.

income per capita. Given that diversification is largely at the expense of surplus labour, entry into local non-farm and migration activities by households is more plausibly a matter of opportunities than of preferences.

9.4 THE PROCESS OF MIGRATION

In a perfectly competitive labour market in which all agents have perfect information, entry to the market ensures a wage at the going rate. Only limited general information is required for a would-be migrant to participate in the labour market. All that is needed is knowledge of the market wage. Job-specific information is unnecessary and irrelevant. Transaction costs of market participation are negligible. The process of migration would have little intrinsic interest in such a market.

If the labour market is imperfect or market information is imperfect, transaction costs become positive and can be important. These transaction costs include the monetary and time costs of acquiring information, much of which comes under the heading of job search. In imperfectly competitive labour markets and with imperfect information, the existence of wage differences involves searching for preferred jobs. It is no longer sufficient to have general market information: job-specific information becomes important. The process of migration becomes worth studying as an illustration of how institutions evolve and individual behaviour adapts to the need to minimize the transaction costs involved in urban labour market participation.

Table 9.19 throws light on the process of migration among the 554 rural–urban migrants in the RUM survey who were already working in enterprises in Handan. The migrants tended to be young and to have middle school education (§1). More than two-thirds were male and most were unmarried. Only a fifth were household heads; three-quarters were the children of household heads. Most had previous migration experience: two-thirds had first migrated prior to 1992 and one-third prior to 1990 (§2).

More than half of the migrants had themselves taken the decision to migrate; parents had done so in a fifth of the cases and family in another sixth (§3). Where the migrant was the household head, the migrant generally took the decision. But three-quarters of households were headed by parents: here half of the migrants decided for themselves, and the other half relied on the household head or family consultation (§4).

This evidence does not necessarily mean that migrants are concerned with themselves rather than their households. To examine this issue we analyse the extent and uses of migrant remittances. We distinguish between households headed by the migrant and those headed by the migrant's parent. Although the migrants who are household heads concentrate more on housebuilding, there is no difference in the sum of housebuilding and family support: in each group these two uses together account for three-quarters of respondents (§5). Both uses can be seen as expenditure on the family rather than on the individual. Moreover, the facts that remittances average no less than three-quarters of migrant income and that there is no significant difference in the remittances of household heads and non-heads (Section 9.5 below) suggest that migrants are concerned to promote the interests of their rural households.

The majority of migrants had household members, relatives, or friends in the city: fewer than a third had no contacts at all (§6). The family were equally distributed among spouse, children, and parents. Almost two-thirds of migrants reported no other migrant in their rural household (§7). Nearly half the respondents claimed that more household members wished to migrate (§8). These results are suggestive of a process of chain migration in which one act of migration encourages another.

TABLE 9.19 *The process of migration: rural–urban migrants and rural out-migrants*

§		Percentage of those responding	
		Rural–urban migrants	Rural out-migrants
1	*Mean characteristics of migrants*		
	age (years)	(24.1)	(33.6)
	education (years)	(7.4)	(7.2)
	household members (number)	(5.1)	(4.2)
2	*Percentage of migrants*		
	married	38	71
	male	71	88
	registered in a non-suburb rural area	82	100
	middle school graduate	65	63
	household head	21	57
	child of household head	73	31
	migrated before 1992	66	81
	migrated before 1990	34	58
3	*Who made the decision to migrate?*		
	self	58	62
	parents	20	14
	family consultation	17	14
4	*If migrant is the household head*		
	self	79	77
	If parent is the household head		
	self	51	*
	parent	24	*
	family	21	*
5	*Main use of migrant income:*		
	if migrant is the household head		
	house-building	54	34
	family support	22	35
	if parent is the household head		
	house-building	40	*
	family support	33	*
6	*Urban contacts*		
	family	22	22
	relatives	31	17
	friends or fellow-villagers	17	5
	none	29	56
7	*Number of migrants in migrant household*		
	one	62	83
	two	23	8
	more than two	15	9
8	*More household members wish to migrate?*		
	yes	44	—
	no	56	—

Notes: * denotes that there were too few cases.
— denotes that the question was not asked.

Source: RUM, 1992 (col. 1); RHH, 1993 (col. 2).

Table 9.19 presents the same information for the 232 out-migrants from the village in the RHH sample. The main contrast is that the out-migrants tend to be older and to have migrated earlier than the rural–urban migrants; they are more often married and more often the head of the household. Other differences (e.g. fewer urban contacts and fewer co-migrants) may arise from the selective nature of the RUM sample of migrants to the city.

The costs of migration have the following components: travel costs, psychological costs, opportunity costs, search costs, and job costs. We examine the light that the RUM survey throws on each, using Table 9.20.

TABLE 9.20 *The costs of migration for rural–urban migrants*

§		Of those responding	
		mean value	percentage
(i) *Travel costs*			
1	Coach stop in township		62
2	Means of transport to the city:		
	coach		54
	foot or bike		24
	train		22
3	Migrant from:		
	Hebei Province		76
	Handan Prefecture		57
	Handan or Wuan counties		11
	more than 500 km. away		12
4	Cost of trip (yuan)	38	
5	Cash brought on the trip (yuan)	129	
(ii) *Psychological costs*			54
6	Prefers job with lower pay if closer to home		71
7	Why did you come to work in this city?		
	have family, relatives		43
	have friends, fellow-villagers		22
	easy to find jobs		7
	higher income		8
	closer to home		14
8	Main difficulty of living in the city		
	less support in time of need		48
(iii) *Opportunity costs (yuan p.a.)*			
9	Wage in current job	2,158	
10	Wage in local TVEs	1,249	
11	Non-migrant income per worker in household	475	

TABLE 9.20 *Continued*

§	Of those responding	
	mean value	percentage
(iv) Search costs		
12　How did you first hear of this place?		
network		70
of which: family, relatives		46
friends, villagers		24
media		13
official organs		7
chance		10
13　Received general information on the Handan		55
labour market before coming		
14　Source of this information		
network		81
of which: family, relatives		45
friends, villagers		36
media		7
official organs		6
chance		6
15　Do you have contacts in Handan?		
none		22
household members		24
relatives		34
friends		19
(v) Job costs		
16　Deposit paid to the employer (yuan)		
if information came from the media	129	
if information came from networks	48	

Source: RUM, 1992 (§§1–15); RHH, 1993 (§16).

(i) Travel costs

Nearly two-thirds of migrants had a long-distance coach stop in their township (§1) and more than half the sample had come by coach (§2). The mean distance from the village to the nearest city or county town was 40 km (79 *li*) but the mean distance to Handan was no less than 242 km (with a huge standard deviation). Three-quarters of the sample were from Hebei Province and three-fifths from the ten counties in Handan municipality, but only a tenth were from the counties—Handan and Wuan counties—that surround the two cities. There were some long-distance migrants, mainly from Sichuan and Yunnan; no less than 12 per cent had come over 500 km (§3).

The total cost of the trip to the city was not expensive, averaging 38 yuan (§4). An analysis regressing travel cost (c) on distance to Handan in *li* (d) produced:

$$c = 18.825*** + 0.040***d$$

($\bar{c} = 38.448$, $\bar{d} = 484.975$, $\bar{R}^2 = 0.402$, $N = 554$, and *** indicates significance at the 1 per cent level). Thus the marginal cost per 100 km (200 *li*) was 8 yuan. On average migrants had brought with them 129 yuan as cash for the trip (§5).

(ii) Psychological costs

Two-thirds of the sample were willing to sacrifice pay to be closer to home (§6). This suggests that there are psychological costs of separation, for which the migrants want compensation. An alternative explanation is that the compensation is required for the greater economic costs of longer distance. However, we have seen that the marginal travel cost of migrating a longer distance is low, and the average monthly migrant wage is 4.7 times the average journey cost of migration.

The role of family and friends in the choice of destination indicates the importance of informational and support networks in reducing the psychological or economic costs of migration (§7). However, it is difficult to separate the two: migrants may receive subsidies and job openings from their contacts as well as security and company. Half the respondents felt that the main difficulty of living in the city was the lack of people who could provide support in time of need (§8).

(iii) Opportunity costs

The opportunity cost of migration itself is the loss of household income during the process of migration and job search, and that of migrant employment is the loss of household income during the absence of the migrant while working. The RUM survey provides two measures of opportunity cost, non-migrant income per worker in the rural household (r) and wage income in the rural industries of the migrant's village or township (i).

What relationship do the variables r and i bear to w, the migrant's current wage? The great variability of w in the sample (the coefficient of variation was 75 per cent) suggests that different wages in uncompetitive markets might reflect different rural supply prices. However, the ratio of r to i to w in the RUM sample was no less than 1 to 2 to 4 (§9–11). On average, the wage from migrant employment far exceeded the income forgone. All migrants would have had an incentive to enter even the worst-paid jobs. It is not surprising, therefore, that a regression analysis uncovered no significant relationship between w and either r or i. Rather, the wages that

migrants receive might reflect the efficiency of their job search in segmented labour markets.

(iv) Search costs

The role of networks in the job search process is extremely powerful. There
are a number of pointers to this conclusion. Over two-thirds of the
rural–urban migrants had heard of Handan through their networks, within
which family and relatives were more important than friends and fellow-
villagers (§12). Together the media and official organs accounted for only
a fifth of cases. More than half of the sample had received general information on the Handan labour market before they came (§13). In four-fifths
of these cases the source was their social networks (§4). Asked 'why did you
choose to come to work here?', the migrants' first reason in two-thirds of
the cases was the presence of networks. More direct economic reasons—
job and wage opportunities—accounted for only a sixth of the replies (§7).
Only a fifth of the migrants had no contacts at all in Handan, whereas nearly three-fifths had family or relatives (§15).

Whether searching through his network of contacts or by other means, a
migrant can be expected to end the search process and accept a job paying
somewhere between the wage he feels he ought to be paid and the minimum wage he will accept. Indeed, this appeared to be the case in the RHH
sample: the mean expected wage was 279 yuan, the mean minimum acceptable wage was 225 yuan, and the mean current wage of migrants was 239
yuan per month.

(v) Job costs

Another type of transaction cost is the cost of building up trust. An employer incurs costs in hiring and training a worker, and needs to protect his
investment. One form of insurance is to require the recruit to pay a deposit,
to be forfeited if he performs or behaves badly. Another is to recruit via a
contact within the enterprise, so making the intermediary liable for the
recruit's inadequacy or withdrawal. A third solution is to require both a
deposit and a sponsor, with a trade-off according to the degree of liability
shouldered by the contact.

A second reason why recruits may be required to pay for their job is
to improve their incentives to identify with the enterprise. The practice
of having new workers lend to, or invest in, the business is well established
in China (Islam 1991: 697, 716). Finally, employers may require payment as a rationing device. If there is excess demand for jobs, they have
a scarcity value, and employers are able to sell the rents to their rent-
seeking recruits.

The deposit paid to the employer by migrants in the RHH sample

depended on the method of recruitment. It averaged 39 per cent of
the monthly wage if the job information came from social networks, and 75
per cent if it came from the media (§16). This difference suggests that
employers need less insurance if there is a sponsor who can be held
responsible for the worker. In that sense networks play the role of reducing transaction costs.

9.5 THE CONSEQUENCES OF MIGRATION

The consequences of migration are many and various. The Handan surveys
enable us to explore two in particular. First, to what extent do rural households benefit from migration of their members through the receipt of remittances? Secondly, how far does migration of labour alleviate poverty and
reduce income inequality in the rural areas?

The RHH survey contained data on migrant remittances, being the total
income transferred in cash or kind to the rural household during 1992. Of
the 232 households containing a migrant in the RHH survey, 206 received
remittances and only 26 did not. The average remittance was 1,984 yuan
per annum, representing 73 per cent of the average migrant income. That
migrants remit nearly three-quarters of their income suggests strongly that
they remain an integral part of the rural household and promote its interests. What determines the size of remittances that a household receives?
This can be expected to depend on the characteristics both of the recipient
household and of the remitting migrant.

We can treat the sample of migrants either as a censored or as a truncated dataset. It is a censored dataset in the sense that the non-remitters all
have a zero value of remittances. The OLS regression model, when applied
to remitters and non-remitters combined, fails to account for the qualitative difference between limit and non-limit observations; the coefficient
estimates are inconsistent. Use of the tobit model, by contrast, produces
maximum likelihood estimates that are consistent. The alternative approach
is to treat the dataset as truncated, i.e. to analyse only the subsample of
remitters, deleting the zero observations. However, the OLS regression
model again yields inconsistent estimates for the migrant sample. Once
more, maximum likelihood estimation overcomes the problem.

It is not necessarily the case that the MLE estimates are to be preferred:
that depends on the economic question being posed. If the purpose is to
know the true relationship for the migrant sample as a whole, the MLE
coefficients are appropriate. However, if our concern is with the subsample
of remitters only, the OLS coefficients should be used.[3]

Table 9.21 presents both OLS and MLE estimates for both the migrant
and the remitter samples. As it turns out, the choice of equation makes
little difference to the substantive conclusions. Women remit more than

TABLE 9.21 *The determinants of migrant remittances: OLS and MLE remittance functions (yuan p.a.)*

Independent variables	Coefficients			
	Migrants		Remitters	
	OLS Eq. (1)	MLE Eq. (2)	OLS Eq. (3)	MLE Eq. (4)
Scale		1,244.492		1,200.793
Intercept	322.136	−75.223	931.637**	325.362
Migrant female	312.695	414.008	91.371	248.624
Migrant's age	−8.688	14.204*	−12.423	15.519**
Migrant has no contact	−260.550	−214.331	−235.533	−214.576
Days of migration	1.317***	0.908**	1.192***	0.840*
Cost of migration (yuan)	1.417***	1.014*	1.180**	0.795*
Migrant's wage (yuan)	0.371***	0.297***	0.240***	0.202***
Household non-migrant income (yuan)	−0.128***	−0.120***	−0.130***	−0.125***
Household wealth (yuan)	0.026**	0.024***	0.043***	0.041***
No. of household members	112.590*	104.007*	103.189	78.626
$\bar{R}^2$	0.254		0.211	
F-value	8.874***		6.483***	
Log-likelihood		−1,982.538		−1,752.993
Mean of dependent variable	1,984.284	1,984.284	2,234.728	2,234.728
No. of observations	232	232	206	206

Notes: 1. *** denotes statistical significance at the 1%, ** at the 5%, and * at the 10% level.
2. The dependent variables are the remittance of the migrant (eqs. 1 and 2) and of the remitting migrant (eqs. 3 and 4).

Source: RHH, 1993.

men, although the difference is not statistically significant. This may reflect stronger ties of women to the rural household (married women remit more than unmarried women). Remittances rise significantly with age in the MLE estimates, possibly reflecting the degree of responsibility felt towards the rural household. Remittances tend to be higher the larger is the household. *Ceteris paribus*, household size can be taken as a measure of need. Remittances are smaller, although not significantly so, if the migrant has no contact at the point of destination: more may be needed for living expenses. Remittances do not depend on whether the migrant is a household head: the coefficient (not shown) is slightly negative and not at all significant. Heads and non-heads appear to be equally concerned with the welfare of their rural households.

Remittances rise significantly with the cost of migration: this cost may be serving as a proxy for the remoteness and poverty of the sending area. The total income of migrants depends on the wage rate and on the number of migrant days away from home. The coefficient of the wage rate (converted to an annual figure) is highly significant and implies a marginal propensity to remit of about 0.25 for migrants as a whole (eqs. (2) and (4)) and also for migrants who remit (eq. (3)). The number of days of migration is also significant. For instance, a migrant away all year would remit 230–360 yuan more than one away for three months. Household wealth and non-migrant income both have significant effects, the coefficient of the former being positive but that of the latter negative. Understandably, a fall of 100 yuan in non-migrant income increases remittances by about 12 yuan. Less obviously, a rise of 100 yuan in wealth (i.e. productive farm and non-farm assets plus savings) increases remittances by about 3 yuan. Many households with substantial productive assets run businesses. The positive relationship may reflect the need for households with more productive assets to pay off debts or overcome credit constraints on investment.

The standard deviation of remittances (1,497 yuan) was 75 per cent of the mean (1,984 yuan). Consider the potential contribution of the income variables to this variation, using eq. (2) of Table 9.21. What is the effect on the level of remittances of a rise in each variable by one standard deviation? For household non-migrant income, remittances fall by 368 yuan, for the migrant's wage rate, there is a rise of 67 yuan, and for migrant days away from home, the rise is 181 yuan. The income variables as a group are important in explaining the differences in remittances among migrants.

How important were migrant remittances in rural household incomes and what relationships did they bear to other sources of income? Table 9.22 refers to both the RUM and the RHH surveys. In the former survey information was gathered on the income, by source, of the migrant's household in 1991, and on whether the household contained a migrant in that year. In the latter survey the same information was obtained for 1992. The table shows the sources of income for migrant households (group 1), non-migrant households (group 2), and all households.

There is a distinct difference in the results of the two surveys. In the RUM survey, the migrant households actually obtained more farm income (Y_f) than the non-migrant households, so that their local incomes (Y_{nm}) were on a par. Migrant households then obtained additional income from migration (Y_m), raising their income (Y) to more than double that of non-migrant households. In the RHH survey, incomes from farming were the same for the two types of household, but local income from non-farming was 250 per cent higher for non-migrant households. Their advantage in local income (half as much again as migrant households earned) was more than offset by income from migration: non-migrant households received only three-quarters of the total income of migrant households. Incomes in the RHH

TABLE 9.22 *Sources of income of migrant, non-migrant, and all households*

	Notation	Households			
		With migrants	Without migrants	All	Without (with = 100)
RUM Survey, 1992					
Income from farming	Y_f	818	622	713	76
Income from non-farming	Y_{nf}	116	316	223	272
Local income	Y_{nm}	934	938	936	100
Migrant income	Y_m	1,303	0	605	0
Total factor income	Y	2,237	938	1,541	42
No. of observations		342	395	737	
RHH Survey, 1993					
Income from farming	Y_f	1,253	1,285	1,277	103
Income from non-farming	Y_{nf}	645	1,615	1,390	250
Local income	Y_{nm}	1,898	2,900	2,667	153
Migrant income	Y_m	1,984	0	460	0
Total factor income	Y	3,882	2,900	3,127	75
No. of observations		232	768	1,000	

Note: $Y = Y_{nm} + Y_m = Y_f + Y_{nf} + Y_m$.

Source: RUM, 1992; RHH, 1993.

survey were generally much higher than in the RUM survey, reflecting the relative prosperity of the survey areas in Handan and Wuan counties. What emerges from both surveys is that income from migration is very important to the migrant households, accounting for more than half of their income: migration raises household income substantially.

The crucial question is the counterfactual: what would the income of group 1 households be if they did not have migrants, i.e. what is the opportunity cost of migration? If we can estimate their opportunity cost we can predict the income of each group 1 household in the absence of migration. It is then possible to arrive at a measure of inter-household income distribution, and an assessment of poverty, with and without the migration actually observed. It is also possible, by using the logistic regression equation predicting migration (Table 9.6), to simulate the effect of increased opportunities for migration. Assuming that the proportion of households with migrants is doubled from 23 to 46 per cent, we can predict which additional households will have a migrant, and what their income will be. In that way a third comparator income distribution can be generated.

The RUM survey is not suitable for this purpose. The rural households in the RUM survey are not representative of rural households as they all contained a migrant in 1992: the non-migrant households in the RUM

TABLE 9.23 *Regression analysis: household local production function*

Independent variables	Means	Coefficients
Intercept		266.351
Farming land (mu)	5.474	107.834***
Farming assets (000 yuan)	1.177	61.475
Non-farming assets (000 yuan)	4.504	92.063***
Non-migrant labourers	1.840	405.954***
$\bar{R}^2$		0.072
F-value		20.369
Mean of dependent variable (yuan)		2,090.520
No. of observations		993

Notes: 1. ***denotes statistical significance at the 1% level.
2. The dependent variable is household local factor income.

Source: RHH, 1993.

survey were of course those that had not contained a migrant the previous year. It is possible that temporarily low income in 1991 induced some of these households to send out a migrant in 1992. Accordingly, the analysis is conducted on the RHH survey.

In order to calculate the opportunity cost of migration we estimate a household non-migration income equation, making Y_{nm} a function of various household characteristics (Table 9.23). Y_{nm} excludes transfers and migrant income, so representing local factor income. All three factors of production—land, capital, and labour—are important. We see that the marginal product of labour is 406 yuan per annum. We take that to be the opportunity cost of migration.

We have the following distributions of household income:

(i)   actual factor income ($Y = Y_{nm} + Y_m$);
(ii)   actual non-migrant factor income (Y_{nm});
(iii) migrant income contributed to the household, as measured by remittances (Y_m);
(iv)   the simulated income in the absence of migration ($\hat{Y}_1$);
(v)   the simulated income if the proportion of households having a migrant is doubled from 23 to 46 per cent ($\hat{Y}_2$).

The distribution $\hat{Y}_1$ is calculated as:

$$\hat{Y}_1 = Y_{nm} + O_c \cdot M,$$

where O_c is the opportunity cost of a migrant (406 yuan, derived from the coefficient on the number of non-migrant labourers in Table 9.23) and M is the number of migrants in a household. $\hat{Y}_2$ is calculated as:

TABLE 9.24 *Measures of income inequality for various actual and simulated income distributions*

Income concept	Notation	Gini coefficient
Actual income	Y	0.400
Non-migrant income	Y_{nm}	0.448
Migrant income	Y_m	0.824
Income in the absence of migration	$\hat{Y}_1$	0.426
Income with more extensive migration	$\hat{Y}_2$	0.347

Source: RHH, 1993.

$$\hat{Y}_2 = Y - O_c + Y_r$$

for all households which do not have a migrant but are predicted to do so if 46 per cent of households have a migrant, and $\hat{Y}_2 = Y$ otherwise. Y_r is the average remittance of a migrant (1,984 yuan). Thus a migration decision adds 1,578 yuan $(Y_r - O_c)$ to annual household income.

Table 9.24 shows the extent of income inequality among households, as measured by the Gini coefficient. The value of the Gini for actual income (0.400) is fairly high. There is extreme inequality of migrant income as most households have none (0.824). It might appear, therefore, that migration increases inequality. That is not necessarily the case, however: much depends on whether poor or rich households send out migrants. Moreover, we know that the coefficient on household non-migrant income in the household migration equation is significantly negative (Table 9.6): *ceteris paribus*, additional local income discourages migration. When the migrant households have their migrant income replaced by opportunity cost, the simulated income of households in the absence of migration has a Gini coefficient of 0.426. Thus the effect of migration is slightly to diminish income inequality: the Gini coefficient falls from 0.426 without migration to 0.400 with migration.

The second simulation assumes that the opportunities for migration improve dramatically, so that the number of households sending out migrants is doubled. The additional migrant households are selected as those most likely to produce a migrant on the basis of the logistic equation in Table 9.6. Each of the additional 23 per cent of households is assumed to send out one migrant and to forgo non-migrant income accordingly. The Gini coefficient falls from 0.400 to 0.347: again, migration is good for equality.

Not only does migration reduce rural income inequality but it also helps to reduce rural poverty. This we see by examining the proportion of households below possible poverty lines given the actual frequency distribution

TABLE 9.25 *The effects of migration on the incidence of poverty*

Income concept	Notation	The percentage of households with income below (yuan p.a.):				Mean income (yuan p.a.)
		400	1,000	2,000	3,000	
Income in the absence of migration	$\hat{Y}_1$	17.0	37.0	61.4	79.0	2,521
Actual income	Y	5.9	15.0	34.8	57.6	3,101
Income with more extensive migration	$\hat{Y}_2$	1.9	5.5	9.5	14.6	3,280

Source: RHH, 1993.

of household incomes and the two simulated frequencies (Table 9.25). An ending of migration reduces mean household income by 19 per cent, and raises the proportion of households with annual income below 1,000 yuan from 15 to 37 per cent. A doubling of migration raises the mean by 6 per cent, and reduces the proportion of households below 1,000 yuan to only 6 per cent.

Lipton (1982: 209–13) argued, on the basis of village studies from various developing countries, that remittances tend to be small compared with rural incomes, and that they tend to go disproportionately to the better-off households, i.e. migration worsens rural income inequality. Neither of these conclusions is true of the Handan rural household survey. In rural Handan, migration is on a sufficiently large scale and is sufficiently well rewarded to raise mean incomes substantially, and remittances provide disproportionate help to the poorer households.

9.6 CONCLUSION

The case study of Handan has enabled us to delve more deeply into the phenomenon of rural–urban migration than is normally possible, whether in China or in other countries. We were particularly helped by the pioneering juxtaposition of two research instruments, a rural origin survey and an urban destination survey. The particularities of this, or of any other, survey area make generalization a hazardous venture. Nevertheless, the powerful and readily explained regularities in the data have yielded many insights which are likely to have more general applicability.

Migration is a socio-economic phenomenon which is not necessarily to be explained simply in terms of economic variables. For instance, migrants

are more likely to be male, unmarried, and healthy. They are also disproportionately young although the economic incentive to migrate increases
with age. Life experiences are relevant: broadened horizons through previous army service or travel encourage labour migration, and access to local
economic opportunities through Party membership or experience as a local
cadre discourages it. College or professional high-school education encourages migration but education is little rewarded in the lowly jobs to which
these rural-based temporary migrants generally have access.

The larger the household's labour force, the more likely it is to send out
a migrant. More local income for the household decreases the propensity to migrate, probably by reducing the economic gain from migration.
By contrast, more household wealth increases it. Wealth may have this
effect by overcoming liquidity constraints on migration and reducing aversion to risk-taking. The powerful influence of the village on the propensity to migrate suggests that social networks are important in facilitating
migration.

Households have a strong economic incentive to diversify away from
farming: income could increase substantially if labour were transferred
from the farm to work away from the village. Indeed, the attitudinal evidence suggests that many rural people want to migrate on a long-term basis,
and that economic motives are important although not exclusive. The institutional impediments to permanent urban settlement maintain a state of
disequilibrium in the labour market.

There is considerable surplus labour in the rural households around
Handan, but there is less surplus labour in the households with higher
income per capita and in those which have diversified away from farming.
It appears that poorer households fail to work longer hours and to substitute away from low-income activities, in particular farming, because they
are constrained by limited opportunities. Both local non-farm employment
and migration may be rationed, the former by limited resources or demand
and the latter by limited information or contacts.

The process of migration is worth examining because of the various forms
of transaction cost which can influence the extent and form of migration.
Irrespective of who takes the migration decision, it appears that migrants
are motivated by the welfare of their rural households. The travel costs of
migration are generally low for migrants to Handan city. The role of
family and friends in the migration process indicates the importance
of informational and support networks in reducing the psychological and
economic costs of migration.

The extent of migrant remittances could be well explained by economic
variables. Remittances are sensitive to migrant incomes and to household
non-migrant incomes, the former positively and the latter negatively, as we
would expect. The fact that households with greater productive assets
receive more remittances suggests that households with businesses need to

repay debt or accumulate more funds. *Ceteris paribus*, households with more members—and therefore greater needs—receive larger remittances, whereas migrants who lack urban support—and therefore themselves have greater needs—send smaller remittances.

It is an important question whether migration from rural areas helps to alleviate poverty and to reduce income inequality. In some societies it is not the poor who migrate and migrant remittances actually make rural income distribution more unequal. Our simulation experiments showed that migration of labour from the villages of Handan is a powerful mechanism both for alleviating poverty and for reducing inequality. The effects of such migration are favourable on grounds both of efficiency (raising output and having low opportunity cost) and of equity (disproportionately helping poor households). There is a case for relaxing the institutional impediments to the migration of rural labour.

NOTES

1. This includes county towns such as Wuan city but not Handan city which is a province-level city.
2. The more appropriate comparison is between migrants and farm workers, but the individual contributions of the latter cannot be isolated.
3. Greene 1993: 682—98, sets out all these issues.

REFERENCES

Greene, William H. (1993). *Econometric Analysis*, 2nd edn., New York: Macmillan.
Islam, Rizwanul (1991). 'Growth of rural industries in post-reform China', *Development and Change*, 22 (4): 687–724.
Lipton, Michael (1982). 'Migration from rural areas of poor countries: the impact on rural productivity and income distribution', in Richard Sabot (ed.), *Migration and the Labor Market in Developing Countries*, Boulder, Colo.: Westview Press.

PART V
CONCLUSIONS

10

Precis, Policy, and Perspective

In this chapter we do three things. In Section 10.1 we summarize the conclusions of each chapter, and integrate them into an argument. Section 10.2 considers the policy implications of the analysis when government objectives are partly exogenous and partly endogenous to the interplay of economic forces. Finally, Section 10.3 places the Chinese experience within a broader empirical and theoretical context of rural–urban relationships.

10.1 PRECIS OF THE ARGUMENT

We have been concerned to analyse rural–urban economic relationships in China in both a normative and a positive sense: to evaluate and also to explain the difference in economic welfare between peasants and workers.

10.1.1 Rural–urban comparisons of economic welfare

The most important point to emerge from our comparison is that the ratio of urban to rural income per head is large in China. This has been the case throughout the period of Communist Party rule: the ratio has generally had a value of between 2 and 3. The ratio has not fallen with time or with economic development. For instance, having been 2.36 in 1978, it fell to a trough of 1.85 in 1983 and then rose almost continuously to 2.87 in 1995. Moreover, the official definitions of urban income understate the true value, mainly because they exclude various benefits-in-kind that are important in China, in particular subsidized urban housing. Thus, in 1988 the ratio derived from the official household sample survey was 2.19 whereas that derived from the CASS survey, using more appropriate definitions, was 2.42. The CASS survey revealed that the inequality of urban income is remarkably low by international standards (the Gini coefficient was 24 per cent in 1988). Rural inequality is considerably higher (34 per cent), much of it being spatial. The Gini coefficient for rural and urban China combined is higher than in either sector alone (38 per cent), i.e. the urban–rural income gap contributes to overall income inequality. The income differences between the rural and urban sectors cannot be dismissed as insignificant by comparison with other dimensions of income inequality in China.

The rural–urban divide is apparent not only in income but also in education, health care, and housing. The most important factor influencing a person's educational attainment, or enrolment, after his age, is whether he lives in a rural or an urban area. The standardized mean difference in educational attainment is no less than 4.6 years in favour of urban-dwellers. Moreover, it has not diminished with time or with economic development. There is evidence that schooling cost per pupil, public subsidy per pupil, and the average quality of teachers are all far higher in urban than in rural areas. Thus rural children have been, and remain, at a disadvantage in both the quantity and quality of their education. What marks out 'educational poverty' in rural China is living in a poor province, being old and female, and having minority status.

There is a considerable gap between urban and rural provision of and access to health services. The rural population is at a disadvantage in both the quantity and quality of health care. Moreover, urban services are much more heavily subsidized, so that rural people have to pay no less than urban people for health care. Yet the great difference in mean incomes contributes to the contrast in the underlying healthiness of people in urban and rural areas. This means that the unfulfilled health needs of rural-dwellers are far greater, which in turn worsens their already inferior health status. Using the extreme measure of unhealthiness, mortality, we found from the 1990 census of population that the rates for infants and children were 1.60 and 1.81 times higher in the countryside than in the cities, and the premature mortality rate 1.22 times higher.

Accommodation per capita is considerably larger in rural than in urban China: the ratio trended upwards from a low of 2.2 in 1979 to a high of 2.8 in 1993. Urban people live in cramped conditions, each person having only $5\,m^2$ even in the mid-1980s. However, it appears that the quality of urban housing is much higher than rural. Rural-dwellers have to build and improve their own houses, and must do so without the help of mortgages, whereas urban-dwellers pay only nominal rents and thus enjoy heavy subsidies of their housing. Rural housing has come to serve all three purposes of shelter, status, and wealth, whereas urban housing could not until very recently become a form of wealth-holding. Housing is an important source of security for the rural people, whereas urban people have rather less certain access to and security of housing. There are too many dimensions, with their valuation problems, to decide whether urban- or rural-dwellers are better off in terms of housing.

Even the addition of education, health, and housing to conventionally measured income yields too narrow a concept of 'well-being'. At various points in the book we have considered the relative degrees of freedom and of security that different people enjoy. The assessment is mixed, and anyway changing over time. Perhaps the greatest difference between rural and urban people is that they have different forms of security. Peasants have secure access to farming and housing land, whereas workers have their 'iron rice bowls', guaranteeing, at least until very recently, secure jobs, pensions, and other welfare benefits. Peasants face more variable incomes than workers. Peasants had more, and earlier, freedom to pursue their economic self-interests locally, but they were in the past prevented from migrating to the—generally preferred—cities, and they are still prevented from settling in the cities.

We conclude that there is a very substantial difference in the income (at the narrowest) and in the well-being (at the broadest) of rural and urban households in China. This disparity is temporally and spatially pervasive. Although both sectors, and particularly the rural sector, contain considerable inequality within them, the rural–urban divide is the outstanding characteristic of Chinese inequality.

10.1.2 Explaining the rural–urban divide

The Communist Party, when it came to power, proceeded to build an institutional framework in which the State, dominated by the Party, divided China into rural and urban compartments, separated in terms of administration, finance, and resources. The State either prevented or controlled the flow of funds and resources between the two sectors. Rural residents, forming the great majority of the Chinese population, were governed by the urban representatives of the State. During the period of economic reform the policies of decentralization and marketization contracted the role of the State and expanded the role of market forces. However, the institutional framework remained in place. The rural–urban divide was little dented, and income disparities were even greater in 1995 than they had been at the start of the reforms in 1978.

The ratio of urban to rural income per capita has been large throughout the period of Communist Party rule, generally having a value of between 2 and 3. In explaining this disparity, we recognized the overwhelming importance of politics. In the early years the new government was securely in power, having won over almost all the population. Ideological objectives were therefore a luxury which could be pursued with little hindrance. Later on, and particularly after the Cultural Revolution, the State became more sensitive to threats to political stability. The retention of power became an important influence on economic policy.

Economic factors frequently did not govern economic policies directly. Their influence, such as it was, appeared indirectly, by affecting the interests of various political actors and provoking political responses. We attempted to analyse economic outcomes by reference to the interests of various institutions and groups in society, and the pressures—normally implicit rather than explicit, passive rather than active—that they could exert on a government whose primary objective was to stay in power.

Underlying the urban bias often observable in state policies and institutions was state bias, to be explained in terms of the concerns and objectives of the Chinese leadership.

There appeared to be no simple relationship between poverty and political pressures. In the early years, almost everyone was poor and the low degree of inequality was generally accepted: pressures on government were weak. In later years, the relationship was complicated by the presence or the absence of relative deprivation and by institutional and organizational strength. What counted more than whether a social group was actually deprived was whether it felt deprived and, if so, whether members of the group could do anything about it, either individually or collectively.

The process of economic reform gave rise to clearer economic groups and perceptions of group interests. Change became possible, and some people could now become rich, but that raised the question in people's minds: who would become rich? The rural–urban divide was more apparent because the two sectors could now communicate and interact directly, whereas they had previously interacted only through the intermediation of the State. Conflicts of economic interest came into the open, revealed for instance by the discrepancies between the producer, market, and consumer ration prices of staple foods.

Consider the policies of government as they evolved. The first tasks of the Communists, when they came to power, were the elimination of the landlord class, land reform, and the introduction of centralized economic planning. During the period of centralized planning, the main economic policy objective was rapid urban industrialization. The terms of trade between agriculture and industry was an important policy variable to this end. Following the example of the USSR, the government depressed the terms of trade in order to provide cheap food in relation to manufactures, and thereby to secure high industrial profits for reinvestment. The hand that wielded the price scissors effected a transfer from the rural to the urban sector. The relative invisibility of the transfer and the opaqueness of the burden added political attractiveness. The price-scissors policy, the State's failure to solve the incentive problems posed by the communes, and ideological distractions all help to explain the relative stagnation of rural income per capita up to 1978.

It is plausible that the ratio of appropriate social values to producer prices of food exceeded 2 to 1 during the planning period, and that this continued to be the case for staple grains until the 1990s. Measured at actual prices, there appeared to be a net capital inflow into agriculture for much of the communist period whereas, measured at social values, there was a large net outflow. The peasants bore most of the sacrifice in consumption, and effectively paid for industrialization. The rapid growth of industry relative to agriculture helped to improve both the equilibrium and the actual terms of trade. The improvement in labour productivity increased the investible surplus per worker in industry, not only before but also after real wages began to rise.

Although the government espoused a 'rational, low-wage system' for urban workers during much of the planning period, real wages were set at a level which enabled urban households to enjoy a higher standard of living than their rural counterparts. The disparity was exacerbated by the job security and welfare benefits provided by urban (very largely, state) employers. Thus part of the investible surplus was diverted to the support of urban workers and their 'iron rice bowls'. Clearly it was not only future generations that gained from the price-scissors: urban-dwellers also benefited. There is a fine line between 'efficiency wage' and 'political pressure' explanations of the relatively high urban wage. Worker discontent, low morale, and threat to political stability are all aspects of the same latent power which residentially concentrated, interacting workers appeared to possess. The urban/rural income and consumption ratios remained high but fairly constant throughout the planning period. The exception was the sharp rise in the ratio during the famine that followed the Great Leap Forward, which hurt peasants more than workers.

The period of decollectivization, 1978–84, was one of rapid growth in peasant incomes. The changes reflected a shift in the concerns of the Chinese leadership from the ideological to the economic. The rural reforms were that rare economic event, a Pareto improvement with hardly any losers. It is interesting that the reforms went further and faster than was intended. A process of atomized peasant behaviour and cumulative causation pulled the leadership along behind. Urban real wages also rose in this period, reflecting the change in government objectives. Nevertheless, there was a sharp fall in the urban/rural income ratio.

In the mid-1980s government attention turned from rural to urban reform policies. The once-for-all nature of the gains from decollectivization and the policy reluctance to raise food prices produced agricultural stagnation for some years thereafter, ameliorated by rapid rural industrialization and an increase in temporary migration to the cities and towns. Government policy with regard to procurement, producer prices, and consumer prices of grain and other necessities provides a good test of the relative political influence of workers and peasants. The government's concern to protect the living standards of urban workers is clearly revealed by the increase in food subsidies in response to the increase in producer prices. The budgetary expenditure on urban food subsidies actively came to exceed budgetary expenditure on agriculture. The tardy and tortuous dismantling of the price-scissors policy suggests that the urban minority were politically more important to government than the rural majority.

Urban real wages rose sharply over the period of urban reform. This occurred despite the abundant supply of rural labour that was potentially available. It was made possible by the restriction of competition from rural labour and the decentralization of power to enterprises. Managers appeared willing—mainly for efficiency wage reasons—to share profits with their employees. The urban/rural income ratio accordingly grew steadily and rapidly in the decade after 1984.

We used microeconomic analysis to delve into the nature and determinants of the urban–rural income gap. Only a minor part of the gap can be explained in terms of differences in the productive characteristics of rural and urban workers. The great majority is due to differences in the income-generation process. Part of this, in turn, is the result of fiscal intervention. In net terms, government taxes peasants and subsidizes workers. The ratio of urban to rural income per capita in 1988 was 2.42. However, it would have been 1.48 had direct taxes and subsidies not been in place. Even this overstates the true ratio in the absence of fiscal intervention because it ignores the invisible price-scissors resource transfer, made politically attractive by its invisibility.

The urban–rural income gap is greater in poor than in rich provinces. Urban incomes are standardized at a high level by institutionalized wage determination whereas rural incomes reflect regional disparities in natural resources and economic opportunities. Both the prevalence of an urban–rural income gap in all provinces and its greater size in the poorer provinces suggest that rural–urban migration is not occurring adequately, and market forces are not operating effectively, to equalize urban and rural incomes.

The productive characteristics of urban workers are generally not well rewarded by their employers. Such urban wage differences as exist among provinces are less likely to reflect local market forces than informal profit-sharing between enterprises and their employees. The growing importance of bonuses in urban incomes appears to provide incentives at the enterprise rather than the individual level, and to segment the urban labour market by enterprise, area, and economic activity. The ratio of the mean wages of urban and rural employees is considerably smaller than that of mean household income per capita. The rural wage varies across provinces according to rural income per capita, indicating that market forces are part of the story. But not the whole story: the excess of the rural wage over the rural supply price is probably due to local government imitation of the state wage system, and rent-sharing and efficiency wage payments by collectively owned and private enterprises.

Much of the considerable inequality of rural income per capita is spatial in character, reflecting the vast size and diversity of the country. Spatial inequality existed even under the egalitarian policies of the pre-reform period, but both spatial and household inequalities have increased during the reform period. We found reasons to expect that processes of cumulative causation are at work, increasing inequality at the province, county, village, and household levels. In some areas rural industrialization has proceeded rapidly, labour shortages have emerged, and rural incomes have risen towards urban incomes. In other areas, rural development is limited, surplus labour is chronic, and the potential economic gain from rural–urban migration is very great. For these reasons it can be misleading to confine the analysis to *the* urban–rural income gap at the national level.

The reasons for the superior provision of education in urban areas is to be found mainly in the separate administrative and funding arrangements for rural and urban education, but partly also in terms of opportunity costs and perceived economic returns. Provincial differences are greater in the rural than in the urban areas. The rural educational attainment of a province is strongly related to its rural income per capita, reflecting the decentralized funding of rural public expenditures. There is no such urban relationship, owing to the more centralized funding arrangements, but educational provision appears to improve with size of city.

Ethnic and gender discrimination in education are not apparent in urban China but appear to live on in rural China. The educational difference between men and women is negligible for urban-dwellers under 30. By contrast, rural women are generally at an educational disadvantage, for which there is a plausible economic explanation in terms of opportunity costs and future returns to parents. Minority status people are at an educational disadvantage in the rural areas despite the policies of affirmative action.

The private demand for education in urban China is generally high. This result appears surprising in view of the compressed urban wage structure: the income gain from additional schooling has been small in absolute terms, in relation to other income determinants, and in relation to other poor countries. However, education appears to be now fairly universal at the lower rungs, and to be supply-constrained at the upper rungs of the educational ladder. Their greater quantity and quality of education implies that urban children have an advantage in the competition for those rationed places.

Over half of the rural population aged 14–19 had dropped out of school. Attendance did not appear to be very sensitive to income per capita either at the household or at the province level. However, potential household income per capita—including the income forgone by attending school—was more powerful. Rural middle school fees were generally not high in relation to household incomes, but both opportunity cost and dropping out rose sharply over the age range 14–19. The large fall in middle school enrolment since the introduction of the rural reforms is to be explained mainly by supply considerations but there may also be a demand element. The importance of parental education in providing educational opportunities for children serves to pass on the rural disadvantage from one generation to another.

China has a good health-care record, even in rural areas, by comparison with most poor countries. The emphasis placed on preventive medicine, especially during the commune period, bore dividends. It is probably the high quality of health care in urban China that is the real international outlier. There is a disparity in health-care inputs, which can be illustrated from the following urban/rural ratios. In 1985 the ratio for visits to curative care services was 1.50, in 1986 the figure for health-care workers per 1,000 people was 3.14, and in 1995 the ratio for hospital beds and qualified doctors per 1,000 people were 4.49 and 4.54 respectively.

This unfairness in the distribution of resources is the result of the institutional divide in health-care arrangements, which in turn stems from the separate administration of rural and urban areas. Urban residents have widespread access to state-supported health care. For instance, all state employees are covered by the public service medical scheme or the state labour insurance scheme. Only workers in the private and self-employment sector and rural–urban migrants are not covered by health insurance schemes. Many urban workers, at least until recently, enjoy free access, and many dependants receive partial support. The rural cooperative health schemes that operated during the commune period collapsed during the reform period. Especially in the poorer villages, which cannot afford collective insurance schemes, rural households face user charges for curative care and medicines. Other than for preventive care such as the vaccination of children, peasants' access to state-subsidized services is limited.

There is a rural–urban disparity not only in health-care inputs but also in health outcomes. It arises partly because health needs are less adequately met in rural areas, in terms of both the quantity and the quality of health care. The other reason is that the rural–urban income divide creates a difference in underlying healthiness. We found that mortality is sensitive to income level in rural China, reflecting variation both in access to health care and in proneness to illness. The complementarity between income and the ability to lead a long, healthy life is an example of vicious and virtuous circles at work in the process of economic development.

There has been a move towards the marketization and privatization of various social services in China, including education and health care. The criterion for access is increasingly ability to pay rather than residential status. In one sense, this trend is weakening the rural–urban divide. The access of rich rural people is improved and that of poor urban people is worsened. Nevertheless, the process is far from complete. Moreover, given the size of the urban/rural income ratio—which in the mid-1990s had reached a record level—a rationing by income rather than by residential status continues on average to have similar effects.

Rural and urban housing are very different in China, and that is because they are institutionally divided. The poverty of most community organizations and the policy of self-reliance, involving a lack of state intervention at the village level, places the burden of house building on peasant households. The allocation of housing land by the village community is an extension of the system of allocating farmland. The public ownership of urban housing, by contrast, may originate in the ideological disapproval of private housing ownership, in the desire to control and restrict non-productive investment, in the paternalistic and controlling role chosen for employing enterprises, which were anyway the main source of surplus for investment under the planning system, and the economies of scale and organizational requirements of large-scale, high-density urban residential investment.

Rural people have to build and improve their own houses; moreover, they do so from their own savings without the help of mortgages as their houses are not alienable. By contrast, urban households pay only nominal rents and thus enjoy a heavy subsidy. House size and, particularly, house quality are sensitive to household incomes in rural areas. Neither the size nor the quality of urban housing is sensitive to income; nor are they sensitive to the size of the household. By contrast, characteristics representing status, seniority, and power have an influence on both quantity and quality, reflecting the criteria for allocating urban housing.

During the commune period the rural sector was expected to be self-reliant. The peasants had to take care of themselves and not be a fiscal burden on government. During the reform period this policy was maintained: there was little fiscal transfer from the urban to the rural areas. West and Wong (1997: 306) report a huge difference in urban and rural revenue raised per capita in 1992 for both a rich (Shandong) and a poor province (Guizhou): the ratios were 6.0 and 7.4 respectively.[1] The disparity is very largely due to the industry-centred tax base. Urban-rural fiscal redistribution occurred through various channels, e.g. grants and earmarked subsidies. In Shandong, fiscal transfers reduced the ratio to 3.9; rural expenditure was raised above revenue by 28 per cent and urban lowered by 18 per cent. Of course, cities have greater infrastructural needs than rural places, but West and Wong (ibid. 307–8) show that health and education services were much superior in the urban areas of their case studies. Recall also the finding from the CASS national household survey that urban households received 39 per cent of their income in the form of subsidies whereas rural households paid a net tax of 2 per cent. The fiscal system displays a powerful urban bias.

The rigid control of rural–urban migration was a cornerstone of the policies which created and maintained the rural–urban divide in China. Without it, the income disparity would have served as a magnet to rural people wanting to better themselves, and it would not have survived. The 'invisible Great Wall' has become more permeable during the period of economic reform. However, it remains very difficult for rural-born people to acquire the right to permanent urban residence. Moreover, central and local governments attempt to control the flow of temporary rural–urban migrants. Their objective is to meet the needs of the urban economy while avoiding urban unemployment and giving preference to urban residents.

Peasant households responded to the new opportunities to raise their incomes by sending out migrants. By 1993 migrant remittances accounted for over 7 per cent of rural household income, and about a third of the income of migrant households. The average duration of absence away from home was under seven months. Migrant ties with their rural households thus remained strong. It is extremely difficult to quantify the number of rural migrants working in the urban areas: hence the wide range of 'guesstimates' that are reported. Our estimates suggest that in 1993 about 10 per cent of rural workers migrated, and that the total flow to the urban areas was about 40 million.

Our pioneering juxtaposition of two research instruments, a rural origin survey and an urban destination survey, provided helpful insights into the phenomenon of the rural–urban migration, albeit for a particular area of China. We found that migration is a socio-economic phenomenon which is not necessarily to be explained simply in terms of economic variables. For instance, migrants are more likely to be male, unmarried, and healthy. They are also disproportionately young although the economic incentive to migrate increases with age. Life experiences are relevant: broadened horizons through previous army service or travel encourage labour migration, and access to local economic opportunities through Party membership or experience as a local cadre discourage it. College or professional high-school education encourages migration but education is little rewarded in the lowly jobs to which these rural-based temporary migrants generally have access.

The larger the household's labour force, the more likely it is to send out a migrant. More local income for the household decreases the propensity to migrate, probably by reducing the economic gain from migration. By contrast, more household wealth increases it. Wealth may have this effect by overcoming liquidity constraints on migration and reducing aversion to risk-taking. The powerful influence of the village on the propensity to migrate suggests that social networks are important in facilitating migration.

Households have a strong economic incentive to diversify away from farming: income could increase substantially if labour were transferred from the farm to work away from the village. Indeed, the attitudinal evidence suggests that many rural people want to migrate on a long-term basis, and that economic motives are important although not exclusive. The institutional impediments to permanent urban settlement maintain a state of disequilibrium in the labour market.

There is considerable surplus labour in the rural households of our survey, but there is less surplus labour in the households with higher income per capita and in those which have diversified away from farming. It appears that poorer households do not work longer hours and do not substitute away from low-income activities, in particular farming, because they are constrained by limited opportunities. Both local non-farm employment and migration may be rationed, the former by limited resources or demand and the latter by limited information or contacts.

The process of migration is worth examining because of the various forms of transaction cost which can influence the extent and form of migration. Irrespective of who takes the migration decision, it appears that migrants are motivated by the welfare of their rural households. The travel costs of migration were found to be generally low. The role of family and friends in the migration process indicates the importance of informational and support networks in reducing the psychological and economic costs of migration.

The extent of migrant remittances could well be explained by economic variables. Remittances are sensitive to migrant incomes and to household non-migrant incomes, the former positively and the latter negatively, as we would expect. The fact that households with greater productive assets receive more remittances suggests that households with businesses need to repay debt or accumulate more funds. *Ceteris paribus*, households with more members—and therefore greater needs—receive larger remittances, whereas migrants who lack urban support—and therefore themselves have greater needs—send smaller remittances. The development of temporary rural–urban migration in recent years has provided an important, and for some even the main, source of income for rural households. It has served as a safety valve to the discontent and pressures emanating from the growing urban/rural income ratio since the mid-1980s.

10.2 IMPLICATIONS FOR POLICY

The policy implications of our analysis can be approached in two ways. One is to assume that government formulates its objectives exogenously, i.e. independently of the pressures arising from the economic interests of various groups in society. We might, for instance, assume that government possesses a given social welfare function which makes no distinction between rural and urban people *per se*, and that the poorer the person, the higher the value placed on additional income. By this criterion, various Chinese government policies can be regarded as errors, attributable to imperfect knowledge or control. We suggest what these are, and how they might be remedied.

The second approach is to recognize the endogeneity of government, i.e. that government is itself an economic agent, whose objectives are determined by the political economy. The social welfare function is in principle predictable from the relevant model, and government—more realistically, different segments and tiers of government—responds in predictable ways to dangers, threats, and pressures. Government may be self-interested, in that it is ultimately concerned with staying in power. On this view, the apparent policy errors are in fact chosen correctly in the pursuit of government objectives. For instance, there may be good political reasons to favour urban people over rural. The remedy therefore lies in changing these objectives. The issue becomes one of influencing the balance of pressures that mould government policy.

In reality, all governments, including the Chinese, warrant a combination of both approaches. It is nevertheless arguable that the Chinese government became less exogenous and more endogenous after the Cultural Revolution ended and as the economic reforms progressed. Conflicts of interest, previously hidden, became more open, and there was more scope for perceptions of relative deprivation. Fiscal decentralization led to a greater dispersion of power among the tiers and segments of government, so increasing the scope for policies reflecting different economic interests.

10.2.1 *Exogenous government*

The fact that urban food subsidies came to exceed state expenditure on agriculture was a stark indication that expenditure priorities needed attention. A high proportion of Chinese households, and an overwhelming proportion of poor Chinese households, are entirely or crucially dependent on agriculture for a living. There is a good case in equity for government to reorder its priorities in favour of the rural sector in general and of agriculture in particular.

The price-scissors policy was slowly withdrawn during the reform period as producer prices of staple food procured by the State were hesitantly moved in the direction of market prices. Consumer food subsidies rose correspondingly, so as to protect urban workers, and began to fall significantly only in the 1990s. The declining importance of food in urban expenditure and the rapid growth of real wages after the mid-1980s—when the urban reforms began in earnest—provided the State with an opportunity to allow both producer and consumer prices of staple foods to approach market prices. However, the opportunity was not seriously grasped until 1992. The remaining elements of enforced procurement of grain at less than undistorted market prices and of food subsidies to urban residents cannot be justified in terms either of efficiency or of equity. Central government should ensure that the lower tiers of government do not issue promissory notes to farmers instead of money. The leadership should do this not simply by banning promissory notes but by addressing the fiscal problems that force local governments into this practice.

Rural China is being transformed through rural industrialization. However, progress has been spatially very uneven, and there are signs that processes of cumulative causation are at work. Rural industrialization is the main source of the growing inequality within rural China. It is important that government at different levels should provide encouragement and incentives for the undeveloped rural areas to overcome the initial obstacles to industrialization.

We found evidence that rural workers employed in TVP enterprises tend to be better educated, and that the returns to education among TVP employees are substantial. It is probable that future private and social returns to post-primary education in rural areas are underestimated by both people and government, too much influenced by the past and the present. Given their absolute and relative educational disadvantage, it is important to devise means of expanding the educational opportunities of rural young people. Our evidence suggested that both supply-constraints and demand-constraints operate in secondary education, according to circumstances. However, both constraints can be loosened by additional public funding. For instance, demand can be increased by reducing school fees or by spending to improve the quality of education. Government should introduce policies which reduce the inequality of public funding between rural and urban areas and, within rural areas, redistribute funds towards the poorer areas. There appears to be a strong case for expanding professional high schools, which provide technical skills appropriate to rural industry and, unlike colleges, do not serve as a passport to the cities.

Health-care facilities are better in urban than in rural China, and the disparity in unfulfilled health needs is even greater. There is a case for a redistribution of medical resources towards the rural population. This would require a reduction in the state subsidies currently provided to urban-dwellers as part of their 'iron rice bowl'. A fairer distribution would be assisted by more unified institutional arrangements, so making the disparity more transparent. Transparency is important: accurate accounts of health care and health outcomes require more, specifically designed, surveys and a greater government concern to quantify the extent of public subsidies.

In the 1990s the State embarked on a policy of urban housing reform. The object was to sell public housing to its occupants, so ridding the State of its fiscal burden. However, housing rents would first have to be raised: why else would an urban household be willing to buy a house that it occupied at a nominal rent? In fact, the urban rental subsidy rose as a proportion of the urban wage over the period 1990–5, and housing sales involved generous capitalization of future subsidies, i.e. implicit capital gains. The reforms have, however, increased the extent of segmentation and unfairness within the cities. The partial marketization of urban housing, being based on unchanging institutional foundations, maintained rural–urban inequalities in housing. A more complete marketization of housing is required, in which urban households either pay market rents or purchase their houses at market prices.

There is an underlying issue which bears on all three aspects of social services that we have analysed—education, health, and housing. It is the net fiscal flow between rural and urban China. Inadequate funding and murky division of responsibilities for basic social services in rural China often put the burden on the users. Many villages have a heavy responsibility for social services, including supplementary finance for primary education and basic health care. Government sets targets but does not provide sufficient funding for their achievement. To meet these mandates, rural authorities are under pressure to levy additional fees. The poorer authorities often fail to do so: we found evidence that the provision of education and health care in rural areas is sensitive to local income levels.

As West (1997: 282) argues, the higher tiers of government need to decide on a minimum level of social services for all rural people, and to ensure that level of provision through fiscal transfers. To this end and by these means, county and township budgets should be strengthened to remove from villages the financial responsibility for the minimum services. This suggestion may appear to be idealistic and impractical in two respects. First, there are fiscal constraints on government as a whole. However, some progress could be made by reducing the rural–urban disparity in public subsidies. Secondly, the distribution of fiscal power and responsibility among the different elements of government reduces the ability of central government to impose uniform standards. Economic reform involved fiscal decentralization, so favouring areas with strong tax bases and weakening the extent of equalizing fiscal transfers. By contrast, given the growth in the ratio of urban to rural income per capita in recent years (from 1.88 in 1985 to 2.72 in 1995), equity required an increasing net fiscal transfer from urban to rural China. Part of the problem lies in the separate administration of rural and urban areas, making the relevant comparisons administratively more opaque and easier to gloss over.

Urban real wages rose rapidly during the period of urban economic reform, reflecting the growth of labour productivity in urban enterprises, the decentralization of powers to managers, managerial profit-sharing with employees, and the absence of a well-functioning urban labour market. Real wages are likely to go on rising rapidly, and the urban–rural income disparity is likely to widen, unless wages become more competitively determined. Of great importance to the creation of a flexible urban labour market is the wage competition which rural–urban migrants can bring to the incumbent urban workers.

Rural-urban migration can be viewed as a potentially powerful equilibrating mechanism to reduce the vast urban–rural income gap that persists in China. Although prevented for much of the planning period, such migration reached a considerable scale during the reform period, and now contributes substantially to rural household incomes. Permanent movement remains severely restricted, except to small or new towns, and temporary migrants are at a serious disadvantage, relative to urban residents, in the urban labour market. The rural sector as a whole could gain from a loosening of the controls on migration.

Migration also has implications for the distribution of rural income. It is important to know whether migration alleviates poverty and reduces inequality within the rural sector. In some societies it is not the poor who migrate, and migrant remittances actually make rural income distribution more unequal. Our simulation experiments showed that the migration of labour from the villages that we studied is a powerful mechanism for alleviating poverty and reducing inequality. The effects of such migration are favourable on grounds both of efficiency (raising output and having low opportunity cost) and of equity (disproportionately helping poor households). However, this conclusion need not hold throughout China. For instance, there may be poorer, more remote areas in which only the better-off households possess the resources and opportunities for migration.

There is a case for relaxing the institutional impediments to the voluntary migration of rural labour. Peasants differ from workers in that they have an alternative income source—from farming—to provide security. The policy of giving employment priority to urban workers can therefore be understood. The dangers of excess rural–urban migration should also be guarded against. Nevertheless, a more flexible and welcoming policy towards the urban employment of rural people would to some extent both reduce and offset the effects of the urban bias policies.

A government with the social welfare function posited above would share our vision for the future elimination of the rural–urban divide. In principle the more complete marketization of the economy should assist this process. The development of competitive labour and capital markets, and of markets for social services and staple foods should each play a role. Inequality would remain, and it could well increase in various dimensions, but it would no longer correspond so closely to residential status and *hukou* registration. It is nevertheless possible that institutional distinctions would maintain the rural–urban divide even in a competitive market economy. After all, the urban/rural income ratio rose steadily over the decade 1985–95, when the role of the plan was contracting and that of the market expanding. Institutions should therefore be made location-blind. For instance, rural–urban discrepancies in public subsidies should be eliminated, and pension schemes, social security provision, and health-care insurance and arrangements should be open to all who can afford the charges.

10.2.2 Endogenous government

We consider various ways in which the economic welfare of rural people could receive a greater weight in the social welfare function of the Chinese government. It may be possible for the political leadership, if it is concerned about urban bias within the machinery of government, to change perceptions and attitudes. For instance, the lack of relevant statistical information—sometimes reflecting the administrative divide—means that rural–urban inequalities are often insufficiently recognized and under-researched. Cadres need to understand rural life if the governors are not to be alienated from the governed. In rusticating educated urban youth during the Cultural Revolution, Mao Zedong appeared to recognize this point.

In the 1980s the State's power to govern the countryside was eroded. Decollectivization left village cadres with vaguely defined authority and limited resources. Village government was often ineffective, and villagers showed little interest in joining the Communist Party. The relationship between cadres and peasants was strained by financial mismanagement and the arbitrary imposition of taxes and levies. To cope with this crisis of legitimacy, the State had to rejuvenate grassroots institutions: it decided to encourage peasant participation.

Wang (1997) described the State's response. An amendment of the Chinese Constitution in 1982 gave legal recognition to village committees, and by 1985 there were over one million such committees throughout China. In 1988 the Ministry of Civil Affairs began to encourage elections of village committees, and by the mid-1990s 90 per cent of village committees were elected. Village representative assemblies emerged spontaneously over the 1980s, and by the mid-1990s more than half of China's villages had established such assemblies. This grassroots democracy helped to improve village governance, for instance by reducing mismanagement and improving village cohesion. The accountability of democratically elected cadres meant that they were more effective in meeting peasant demands. Being elected, they had more authority over the villagers, and they could better accomplish village tasks and enforce state directives.

The State tried by these means to strengthen its influence and support in rural China (Wang 1997: 1437–40). However, there remains an underlying conflict between the peasants and the State on account of its urban bias policies. The growth of grassroots democracy aroused political consciousness. It is an important question whether peasants will acquire the power to influence policy decisions not only at the village level but also at the township, county, province, and national levels of government. However, this might require the democratic election of township, county, and higher leaders as well.

White *et al.* (1996) argued that the development of 'civil society' is important in bringing about political change. On the basis of case studies in rural China, they found that 'social organizations' grew from nothing after 1978, partly because they became permitted and partly because the new economic opportunities provided incentives. The diversification of power over economic resources generated a consciousness of specific group interests. The social organizations include trade unions, womens' federations, occupational groups, and enterprise, trade, technical, and cultural associations. Many of these can be seen as intermediaries between government and people. In principle, they are able to articulate peasant interests and influence official policy.

In practice, the influence of rural social organizations is weak because of their frequent dependence on local governments or state agencies. Nor are they directly concerned with the central issue, i.e. peasant feelings of relative deprivation and of unfair treatment. White *et al.* (1996: 180–3) argued that the emergence of civil society was not as strong in the rural areas as in the urban areas. Rural actors are relatively scattered and hard to organize above the level of the village or small town, and their ability to do so is crucially dependent on the goodwill of government. There remains a degree of associational repression in rural China, i.e. the demand exceeds what the State is willing to supply or permit. This finds two main forms of expression. One is the continuing importance of informal connections and personal and kinship networks. Secondly, there have been outbursts of protest and violence, along with the appearance of spontaneous peasant associations. Local governments generally recognize that the discontent needs to be channelled in manageable ways, but fear that official peasant associations would become a vehicle of stronger protest. The authors concluded that associational repression is unsustainable: the political leadership should provide more scope for social organizations. With the strengthening of the peasant voice that would ensue, peasant interests might acquire a greater weight in government policy objectives.

Moore (1993) argued that, as South Korea and Taiwan developed, their governments switched from urban bias to rural bias policies. His main explanation was in terms of the changing structure of the economy which, for instance, reduced the need to extract a surplus from the agricultural sector and increased the political threat from rural–urban migration. Similarly, some of the changes taking place in the Chinese economy may assist the peasants. For instance, the price-scissors policy is becoming less important for the accumulation of capital. The diminishing share of food in urban household budgets makes urban real incomes less sensitive to the price of food. Rural people may be assisted by the greater awareness of their relative position that better education, more opportunities for temporary migration and travel, and improved communications can foster. The increased marketization of the economy may itself reduce the degree of urban bias in government policies insofar as it accords greater weight to market-based allocation of resources and income and less weight to location-based allocation.

To illustrate the various influences on policy-making, we consider the possible future evolution of government policy on rural–urban migration. The organization of government is relevant. The Ministry of Public Security is responsible for the administration of *hukou* migration, whereas the Ministry of Labour has responsibility for temporary labour migration. The Ministry of Labour itself, although having a hierarchical structure of authority, comprises various tiers whose interests reflect their constituencies.[2] The headquarters in Beijing is concerned to provide the regulatory framework to ensure orderly and controlled migration that will not threaten political stability. At the province level, labour-surplus provinces like Sichuan are keen to promote outflows of labour to other provinces, whereas labour-attractive provinces like Guangdong are keen to control their inflows. At the city level, ministry officials within the city government attempt to regulate and restrict migrant inflows, so as to ensure employment priority for their citizens. At the county level, employment bureaux officials in labour-surplus counties attempt to inform and organize potential migrants, and have a revenue incentive—through fees—to promote migration.

Will rural–urban migration increase in future years? The answer depends on various considerations. Of great importance is the size of the urban–rural income gap, which in turn depends on the extent of urban bias in future government policy. A second consideration is whether rural industry, having competed successfully and thrived in a situation of market disequilibrium, can continue to increase its market share, or whether it will be held back by lack of technology and of skilled labour and by the rising efficiency of urban industry. The latter in turn will depend on the pace of reform of the state-owned enterprises. Without continued rapid rural industrialization, the pressure to migrate will be greater. Thirdly, opportunities for migrants in the cities will depend on the extent to which surplus labour is eliminated from the state sector. An active policy of retrenchment of state employees, with the consequent danger of urban unemployment, would reduce the permitted urban inflow of rural migrants. Fourthly, even if the State severely limits the inflow of rural people into large, established cities, it may permit fairly unrestricted migration into expanding county towns and small, new cities. If, in the future, more urban development is channelled into county towns and small cities, this policy may indirectly loosen the constraints on rural–urban *hukou* migration.

The future of migration depends also on factors unrelated to the policies of the time. One question is whether migration, still limited in scale, might reach a 'take-off' stage, beyond which social networks, support systems, and migration patterns feed on themselves. Of crucial importance is the rate of growth of the urban economy, and consequently of urban employment, in relation to the rate of growth of the urban labour force. The latter should slow down as the one-child-family policy, introduced in about 1980, has an effect on the number of urban-born labour market entrants.

This discussion of policy-making on migration illustrates three points. First, many other government policies impinge on, and interact with, migration policies. Secondly, the Chinese government is not a single entity with a clear policy agenda. Rather, it is made up of various tiers and localities, each with responsibilities and powers over different aspects of migration.

Thirdly, the various governmental tiers and localities tend to represent the interests of their constituencies. Although it would be misleading to regard this form of representation as interest group politics, policy-making on migration appears to mimic interest group politics.

Another example of the need to view government as a number of inter-acting economic agents is provided by the difficulties experienced in attempting to reform the urban labour market. Such reform has been tardy because the problems are systemic and require system-wide action by var-ious tiers and segments of government. Labour market reform inevitabil-ity connects with other urban reforms, for instance, with regard to public finance, enterprise, bankruptcy, housing, social services, unemployment, training, and migration policies. A worker leaving a job has had to give up much more than the job. At least until very recently, he also lost the mini-welfare state provided by his 'iron rice bowl'. This made workers reluctant to quit, and employers reluctant to dismiss them. Attempts to achieve a more flexible labour market will involve severe hardship and accordingly meet resistance from urban workers unless these interrelated problems are solved together.

10.3 THE CHINESE EXPERIENCE IN PERSPECTIVE

The Chinese case can be viewed from two perspectives, the empirical and the theoretical. First, comparisons can be made with other countries, so as to establish whether the rural–urban divide in China is ordinary or extraordinary. Secondly, various models of rural–urban relationships can be examined for their relevance to the Chinese experience.

10.3.1 Comparisons with other countries

Many countries now conduct a periodic national household survey, but fewer report on the surveys in forms accessible to us, and still fewer make the crucial rural–urban distinction. Table 10.1 presents results for twelve countries on which we could obtain data. Only Zimbabwe and South Africa exceed China in their ratios of urban to rural income per capita. These two southern African countries have in the past been subject to powerful class and race bias in government policies, for which the rural–urban distinction serves as a proxy. Their rural households, reliant on farming and labour migration, possess very little land and resources, and have been powerless and neglected. China's successful neighbours, Taiwan and South Korea, report extremely low urban/rural ratios; indeed, in South Korea there appears to be no difference between urban and rural living standards. The ratios in Sri Lanka, Egypt, Iran, and Turkey are all well under 2. Thailand and the Philippines come closest to matching China, but in both countries the ratio is lower. In terms of size, resources, structure, and level of development, the economy of India is most similar to that of China. However, the Indian ratio of consumption per capita is only half the Chinese. This may be because in India markets operate more freely, factors of production can move unhindered, there is a wealthy landlord class, and there is a more democratic form of government.

All but one of our countries has a sizeable urban–rural income gap, although no doubt some gaps would not survive standardization for productive personal characteristics. China is not unique but it is unusual, at least by Asian standards. State institutions and government policies are responsible for China's artificially great rural–urban divide.

It is interesting to compare the Chinese policy on migration with that in two of the countries which appear in Table 10.1. We noted the extremely high urban/rural income ratio in South Africa. That country has a history

TABLE 10.1 *The ratio of urban to rural income, and consumption, per capita, selected countries, recent years*

Country	Year	Ratio of urban to rural:	
		Income per capita	Consumption per capita
China	1995	2.72	3.41
Taiwan	1995	1.32	1.43
South Korea	1994		1.03
India	1987–8		1.49
Iran	1991		1.82
Turkey	1994		1.71
Philippines	1991	2.26	2.17
Thailand	1990	2.23	2.66
Sri Lanka	1990–1	1.79	1.33
Egypt	1990–1		1.50
Zimbabwe	1990–1	3.57	
South Africa	1993	3.14	

Notes: 1. In South Korea the ratio is per household, not per capita; in Taiwan, Iran, and the Philippines the per capita figure is derived from the household figure and the average number of members per household.
2. In Taiwan, Thailand, South Africa, and Zimbabwe, aggregation into urban and rural categories was necessary, based on population weights.

Sources: PRC, SSB 1996: 280–2; Republic of China 1996: 168–9; Bank of Korea 1996: 260–1; Drèze and Sen 1995: table A3; Islamic Republic of Iran 1995: 12, 173–4; Republic of Turkey 1997: 631; Philippines National Statistical Coordination Board 1996: 1–14, 2–10; Thailand National Statistical Office 1994: 41, 51; Dept. of Census and Statistics, Sri Lanka 1993: 21; World Bank 1995: 8; Bartsch 1997: 17; Zimbabwe, Central Statistical Office 1994: tables 2.2, 3.1a, 3.3a; Project for Statistics on Living Standards and Development 1994: 321.

of extensive but controlled migration. The most important form of control has been a restriction on the urban settlement of rural people, enforced by a system of registration similar to the *hukou* system. Much labour migration has therefore been of a temporary nature, with workers leaving their families behind in the rural areas. In parts of the country from which migration is extensive, this has led to the disruption of rural social and economic life. Rural industrialization has been encouraged but with little success. The huge urban–rural income disparity provides powerful incentives for migration. With the ending of effective controls on migration in recent years, particularly since the transfer to democracy, rapid urbanization has occurred. Whereas unemployment was previously a disguised rural phenomenon, it has increasingly taken both an open and disguised form in the cities. This poses a threat to social stability. With the advent of democracy there should in time be greater emphasis on poverty alleviation, but in the meantime the withdrawal of labour controls has mainly had the effect of transferring poverty from the rural to the urban areas.

India has similarly developed a system of temporary rural–urban migration, although problems of landlessness have also contributed to permanent urbanization. We noted that the urban–rural consumption disparity in India is small compared with China. Often the rural-based and the urban-based branches of the family retain close links and provide two-way support. Urban self-employment is quantitatively very important in India. Many migrants enter the informal sector and never transfer into formal sector employment. The labour market facing Indian peasants appears to be only weakly segmented.

Comparing it to South Africa and India, China displays interesting similarities and differences. China is characterized by a successful rural industrial sector, offering peasants local non-farm opportunities which might otherwise require migration. China shares with South Africa a large urban–rural income disparity, but its restrictions on permanent and temporary migration have so far avoided the current South African problem of high unemployment and informal sector underemployment in the cities. In India the relative freedom of movement, the large urban informal sector, and the sheer weight of market forces have avoided the severe labour market segmentation that exists in China. By comparison, the choices facing Chinese peasants are therefore more constrained.

Rural-urban income inequalities are not only to be found in poor countries of the late twentieth century: they are a more general phenomenon. For instance, in *The Wealth of Nations*, Adam Smith (1776: ch. 10) argued that 'the inhabitants of a town, being collected into one place, can easily combine together' to prevent free competition, whereas 'the inhabitants of the country, dispersed in different places, cannot.' Throughout Europe, townspeople 'incorporated' themselves, that is they regulated to restrict entry to industries, trades, and occupations so as to increase their profits and wages, whereas rural people did not. The latter 'have not only never been incorporated, but the corporation spirit never has prevailed among them.' The effect was to 'break down that natural equality which would otherwise take place in the commerce which is carried on between (town and country).' 'Stock and labour naturally seek the most advantageous employment. They naturally, therefore, resort as much as they can to the town, and desert the country' (ibid. 113–14). The forms, mechanisms, and degree of rural–urban division may vary from one nation or one era to another, but there are underlying reasons why it is often to be found.

10.3.2 *Models of rural–urban relationships*

Consider the relevance to the Chinese case of four possible models of the relationship between the rural and urban sectors of a developing economy. These are the Lewis model, the price-scissors model, the urban bias model, and the state bias model. Any interpretation of government policy, or of changes in policy, invites the criticism that the beneficiaries of the policy are too readily assumed to have been responsible for it. It is difficult to adduce direct evidence of the influences that govern policy, but all too easy to infer them. We recognize this methodological problem. Nevertheless, the four models provide a framework for a plausible and consistent account of policymaking.

As Puttterman (1992*a*, *b*) argues, economic reform did not simply accelerate the transfer of labour from the agricultural or rural to the industrial or urban sector, in line with the Lewis model. Rather, it led to the growth of a third sector—non-urban, non-State, non-agricultural—the rural industrial sector. The relationship of the new sector to the two existing sectors is both complementary and competitive. It was promoted by agricultural development and it in turn promoted agricultural development. Although it diverts resources from agriculture, the opportunity cost of rural labour is low. There is an elastic supply of labour to rural industry, but rural households stepping into industry often keep a foot in agriculture. Rural industry has competed with urban industry, particularly for raw materials in the early stages of the reform process, and for markets in the later stages. It differs from state-owned industry in having a commercial, hard budget character. It contributed to the falling profitability of state enterprises, which occurred as a result of the price reform and the opening up of competition.

The new sector developed in the rural rather than the urban areas largely because of the institutional divide between rural and urban China that the State had created. Only in the rural areas could economic agents respond to the supernormal profits available in light industry. Moreover, the policy of rural fiscal self-reliance created a strong incentive for rural authorities to promote the industrialization of their localities. In this sense

the institutional divide generated a degree of 'rural bias', in contradistinc-
tion to the more familiar urban bias in state policies. The fact that the most
dynamic industrial growth in recent years took place in the rural sector
should in itself have reduced the urban/rural income ratio. However, as this
development was more than offset by other changes, the ratio actually rose
after the mid-1980s.

The evolution of policy and the economy can be illustrated in Figure 10.1.
The circles represent the rural and urban sectors, with their relative areas
proportional to population in 1970 and 1990. The upper part of the figure
shows the situation in the pre-reform period, with the rural (R) and urban
(U) sectors separate and coinciding with the agricultural (A) and industrial (I) sectors. The lower part shows the situation after the development
of the third sector, rural industry (I_r). This is located within R. However, the
figure shows a degree of overlap between the rural and urban areas, representing a semi-industrialized, semi-urban, 'grey area'. This contains people who are generally not accorded urban privileges but some of whom are
reported by the census of population as living in newly classified urban locations. Part of rural industry (I_{ur}) is to be found in the grey area and part
(I_r) in the purely rural area. Our argument is that the rural–urban divide
has become more porous and less tidy in recent years. The rural–urban

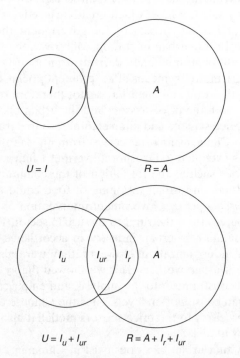

FIG. 10.1 *The blurring of the rural–urban divide*

distinction is being blurred, and it is no longer equivalent to the agriculture–industry distinction. The main reason for this is rural industrialization—itself a product of the institutional divide—and the socio-economic changes that it brought about. Although it was trivial at the start of the economic reforms, and slight even in 1988, the overlap between the rural and urban frequency distributions of household income per capita has gradually increased. Some rural people in some parts of China are now better off than most urban people.

The Lewis model of the transfer from agriculture to industry is indeed relevant to China. The model depicts well the process that operated within the rural sector after 1978. The basic elements of the model are present in rural China: an elastic supply of labour from agriculture to industry, and the industrialization which was achieved through the reinvestment of profits within the industrial sector. The model requires qualification only in the level of the rural industry wage rate—above the supply price of rural labour—and in the spatial immobility of rural labour.

The Lewis model is a rather less appropriate description of the relationship between the rural and the urban sector. For the planning period the distinction between rural and urban corresponded to that between agriculture and industry. There was rapid industrialization, which involved the transfer of labour from the rural to the urban sector. However, government set the industrial wage at a level which greatly exceeded the supply price of rural labour, and it was necessary for government therefore also to restrict and control rural–urban migration. Moreover, the funds for industrial investment, although nominally derived from industrial profits, were extracted from agriculture by means of government pricing policy. The relationship between the rural and the urban sector therefore requires a model that incorporates both the price-scissors and the urban bias policies.

The theory of price-scissors and intersectoral resource transfers could be readily applied to China, using offer curves from international trade theory. The theory was extended to incorporate various Chinese features. Some government policies such as the formation of the communes, compulsory procurement of food, and urban rationing of food could be seen to flow from the price-scissors policy. Government intervention on prices effected a transfer of resources from the rural to the urban sector. These were used for capital accumulation in urban industry, in accordance with the price-scissors model of industrialization. However, they were also used to raise the consumption of urban workers. This we showed theoretically by incorporating political constraints into the analysis, and empirically by comparing rural and urban consumption levels. Thus the Chinese experience does not correspond precisely to the price-scissors model: it also requires a role for the urban-bias model.

It is very likely that urban bias does exist in China, in two senses. First, government allocates fewer resources to the rural sector than it would if it were concerned only with raising economic efficiency, as determined by shadow prices. Secondly, rural-dwellers receive less priority than they would if the government social welfare function made no distinction between rural and urban residence *per se*, and placed a greater value on additional income, the poorer the person. As Lipton (1977: 13), writing of poor countries in general, put it: 'the rural sector contains most of the poverty, and most of the low-cost sources of potential advance; but the urban sector contains most of the articulateness, organization and power.' Bates (1993: 223) summarized the urban bias displayed by the State in socialist countries in the following terms. Socialist governments create large bureaucracies, forge strong ideological ties with urban labour, and are committed to industrialization and to public ownership; hence their concern to ensure low food prices and high industrial profits. Socialist governments accordingly adopt policies against the interests of their poorest citizens—the peasants. The Chinese case corresponds well to this general account.

Although the policies of the Chinese government can be accurately described as involving urban bias, the underlying reason for the policies is better described as state bias. The primary motivation was the preservation of government by the Chinese Communist Party. The failure to close, or even to diminish, the rural–urban gap in income and welfare stems from the need to stave off potential political threats to the regime. Even during the early years of economic reform, when the rural sector received priority, the motive was to restore political legitimacy with the peasants and to relax the most serious constraint on the growth of the economy. We do not claim that the State entirely understood or controlled economic events. Take, for instance, the issue of promissory notes instead of money to peasants for their produce in the late 1980s and early 1990s. This was clearly not a policy objective of central government—indeed, it tried in vain to outlaw the practice. However, it was the outcome of its other policies, such as that requiring local governments largely to raise their own revenue and the set of policies making investment in industry more profitable for local government than investment in agriculture.

The Chinese political process should not be viewed as the outcome of conflicting articulated pressures from various organized interest groups. The Communist Party is too dominant for that. Rather, the urban-bias policies reflect the latent political power of urban-dwellers. The government purchases an 'insurance policy' to ensure that urban workers will refrain from political protests which could challenge it, and that they will not threaten production and therefore state revenue.

It is apparent that no single model of rural–urban economic relationships is sufficient to describe the Chinese experience. In fact, all four models that we considered are relevant in at least some respect. They were therefore combined to produce an encompassing model 'with Chinese characteristics'.

NOTES

1. Comparing prefecture-level cities and non-urban counties.
2. This account is based on discussions which we held with ministry officials at the national, provincial, city, and county levels, on a tour organized for us by the ministry in 1995.

REFERENCES

Bank of Korea (1996). *Economic Statistics Yearbook 1996*. Seoul: Bank of Korea.

Bartsch, Ulrich (1997). 'Interpreting household budget surveys: estimates for poverty and income distribution in Egypt', Economic Research Forum Working Paper Series 97-14, Cairo: Economic Research Forum.

Bates, Robert H. (1993). 'Urban bias: a fresh look', *Journal of Development Studies*, 29 (4): 219–28.

Department of Census and Statistics, Sri Lanka (1993). *Household Income and Expenditure Survey 1990/91, Final Report*, Colombo.

Dréze, Jean, and Sen, Amartya (1995). *India. Economic Development and Social Opportunity*, Delhi: Oxford University Press.

Islamic Republic of Iran (1995). *A Statistical Reflection of the Islamic Republic of Iran*, Tehran.

Lipton, Michael (1977). *Why Poor People Stay Poor: Urban Bias in World Development*, Cambridge, Mass.: Harvard University Press.

Moore, Mick (1993). 'Economic structure and the politics of sectoral bias: East Asian and other cases', *Journal of Development Studies*, 29 (4): 79–128.

People's Republic of China, State Statistical Bureau (PRC, SSB) (1996). *Statistical Yearbook of China 1996*, Beijing: China Statistical Publishing House.

Philippines, National Statistical Coordination Board (1993). *1993 Philippines Yearbook*, Manila.

Project for Statistics on Living Standards and Development (1994). *South Africans Rich and Poor: Baseline Household Statistics*, Cape Town: South African Labour and Development Research Unit, University of Cape Town.

Putterman, Louis (1992*a*). 'Industrial boundaries, structural change, and economic reform in China', *Modern China*, 18 (1): 3–13.

——(1992*b*). 'Dualism and reform in China' *Economic Development and Cultural Change*, 40 (3): 467–93.

Republic of China (1996). *Statistical Yearbook of the Republic of China 1996*, Taipei: Director General of the Budget, Accounting and Statistics.

Republic of Turkey, State Institute of Statistics, Prime Ministry (1997). *Statistical Yearbook of Turkey*, Ankara: State Institute of Statistics.

Smith, Adam (1776). *The Wealth of Nations*, London: Everyman's Library (1910 edn.).

Thailand, National Statistical Office (1994). *Report on the 1990 Household Socio-Economic Survey. Whole Kingdom*, Bangkok: National Statistical Office.

Wang Xue (1997). 'Mutual empowerment of state and peasantry: grassroots democracy in rural China', *World Development*, 25 (8): 1431–42.

West, Loraine A. (1997). 'Provision of public services in rural PRC', in Christine P. W. Wong (ed.), *Financing Local Government in the Peoples' Republic of China*, Hong Kong: Asian Development Bank and Oxford University Press.

—— and Wong, Christine P. W. (1997). 'Equalization issues' in Christine P. W. Wong (ed.), *Financing Local Government in the Peoples' Republic of China*, Hong Kong: Asian Development Bank and Oxford University Press.

White, Gordon (1993). *Riding the Tiger: The Politics of Economic Reform in Post-Mao China*, London: Macmillan.

—— Howell, Jude, and Shang Xiaoyuan (1996). *In Search of Civil Society. Market Reform and Social Change in Contemporary China*, Oxford: Clarendon Press.

World Bank (1995). *Sri Lanka Poverty Assessment*, Report 13431-CE, South Asia Region, Washington, DC.: World Bank.

Zimbabwe, Central Statistical Office (1994). *Income, Consumption and Expenditure Survey Report, 1990/91*, Harare: Central Statistical Office.

Index of Subjects

Index of Names

Index of Provinces